*Contesting the Irani*

Most observers of Iran viewed the Green Uprisings of 2009 as a "failed revolution," with many Iranians and those in neighboring Arab countries agreeing. In *Contesting the Iranian Revolution*, however, Pouya Alimagham re-examines this evaluation, deconstructing the conventional win–lose binary interpretations in a way that underscores the subtle but important victories on the ground, and reveals how Iran's modern history imbues those triumphs with consequential meaning.

Focusing on the men and women who made this dynamic history, and who exist at the center of these contentious politics, this "history from below" brings to the fore the post-Islamist discursive assault on the government's symbols of legitimation. From powerful symbols rooted in Shi'ite Islam, Palestinian liberation, and the Iranian Revolution, Alimagham harnesses the wider history of Iran and the Middle East to highlight how activists contested the Islamic Republic's legitimacy to its very core.

POUYA ALIMAGHAM is a lecturer and historian of the Middle East at the Massachusetts Institute of Technology. He received his PhD in history from the University of Michigan. His thesis, on which this book is based, was awarded the Mehrdad Mashayekhi Dissertation Award by the Association for Iranian Studies in 2016.

# Contesting the Iranian Revolution

## The Green Uprisings

POUYA ALIMAGHAM
*Massachusetts Institute of Technology*

CAMBRIDGE
UNIVERSITY PRESS

# CAMBRIDGE
## UNIVERSITY PRESS

University Printing House, Cambridge CB2 8BS, United Kingdom

One Liberty Plaza, 20th Floor, New York, NY 10006, USA

477 Williamstown Road, Port Melbourne, VIC 3207, Australia

314–321, 3rd Floor, Plot 3, Splendor Forum, Jasola District Centre, New Delhi – 110025, India

79 Anson Road, #06–04/06, Singapore 079906

Cambridge University Press is part of the University of Cambridge.

It furthers the University's mission by disseminating knowledge in the pursuit of education, learning, and research at the highest international levels of excellence.

www.cambridge.org
Information on this title: www.cambridge.org/9781108475440
DOI: 10.1017/9781108567060

First published 2020

Printed in the United Kingdom by TJ International Ltd. Padstow Cornwall

*A catalogue record for this publication is available from the British Library.*

*Library of Congress Cataloging-in-Publication Data*
Names: Alimagham, Pouya, author.
Title: Contesting the Iranian revolution : the green uprisings / Pouya Alimagham.
Description: Cambridge, United Kingdom ; New York, NY : Cambridge University Press, 2020. | Includes bibliographical references and index.
Identifiers: LCCN 2019038198 (print) | LCCN 2019038199 (ebook) | ISBN 9781108475440 (hardback) | ISBN 9781108466899 (paperback) | ISBN 9781108567060 (epub)
Subjects: LCSH: Revolutions–Iran–History. | Protest movements–Iran–History–21st century. | Iran–History–Election protests, 2009. | Iran–Politics and government–1997- | Iran–Politics and government–1979-1997.
Classification: LCC DS318.9 .A447 2020 (print) | LCC DS318.9 (ebook) | DDC 955.06/1–dc23
LC record available at https://lccn.loc.gov/2019038198
LC ebook record available at https://lccn.loc.gov/2019038199

ISBN 978-1-108-47544-0 Hardback
ISBN 978-1-108-46689-9 Paperback

*For my mother and father, Sonia and Shahram Alimagham,*
*For their love, support, and inspiration.*
*For my brother, Nima Alimagham,*
*For being a true older brother.*

# Contents

# Figures

# *Preface*

I applied to the PhD program at the University of Michigan in the fall of 2008. What I had envisioned for my graduate research was completely supplanted by the events of the summer of 2009 in Iran. I matriculated in the fall while watching the post-election turmoil unfold in the country of my birth. By the spring of 2010 when the crisis had largely subsided, I took a course with Geoff Eley, for whom I wrote a seminar paper on crowd action in the Green Uprising – the kernel of what would become my PhD dissertation and later this book.

When I began writing the seminar paper, I used "the Islamic Republic," "the Islamic government," and "the Islamic state" interchangeably. By the summer of 2014, after I had completed my graduate coursework, teaching requirements, and preliminary exams, and was researching and writing my dissertation, I had to go back and remove "Islamic state" from my chapters. By then, the so-called Islamic State group had spread its tentacles over parts of Syria and Iraq, and referring to the Iranian government as "the Islamic state" would have been confusing. The Middle East, indeed, changes quickly – for better or worse – making the job of a graduate history student or a historian all the more interesting and difficult at the same time.

While writing this manuscript and keeping it updated, I have often contemplated how this history will unfold in the years ahead. Of course, it is not the job of the historian to make predictions, but I have striven to write this book in a manner that is open-ended in terms of the history that I have chronicled. In other words, this is not merely a book about what happened in 2009 and how the preceding decades inform that history, but also how the Green Uprising will inform subsequent history.

At the same time, if I am completely honest, I seriously considered not publishing this manuscript at all, and leaving it confined to the dissertation catalog at the University of Michigan. I worried that people or groups would take this research and deploy it in the service of their narrow political agendas. In the end, I decided against burying it because of the connection that I felt to the historical agents present in it. The women and men of this period deserve to have the truth of what happened heard. I do not mean to aggrandize the importance of my scholarship. It may very well be that few read this book – in today's world fewer and fewer books are being read. In any case, I hope to control its uses and potential abuses by outlining my intentions clearly for the reader.

Under no circumstances should this book be used to legitimize confrontation of any kind with Iran. I emphatically believe that the future of Iran should be determined solely by Iranians in Iran – those who know best the reality that they face. More importantly, the fact that Iran's future affects them first and foremost also gives weight to the primacy of their views and wants. They retain their agency, and have erupted in revolt time and again. The Green Movement is part of a long, robust, and organic history of Iranians seeking more humane and representative governance. To be clear, Iran's future is not the business of any other person, group, or government. Foreign heads of state, especially those who speak of freedom for Iranians while either denying it to others or enabling and protecting authoritarian regimes, do more harm than good in their "support" of the Iranian people. Their interference empowers the Iranian government to cast cracking down on dissent as part of an effort to stave off imperialism. Added to this are Iranians in the expatriate community, from which I come, some of whom fail to listen to their counterparts inside the country, instead telling them what they should want, need, or do.

What's more, outside interference has frequently undermined those who seek democratic governance in Iran, with the decisions or actions of another country retarding Iran's organic political evolution. No more obvious example exists than the US-led overthrow of Iran's democratically elected government in 1953. Another example can be found in October 1979, when President Carter decided to allow the Shah into the United States for medical treatment. That decision ultimately led to the militant seizure of the US embassy in Tehran – a crisis that the Islamists exploited to outmaneuver their opponents and pass their constitution. The subsequent Iraqi invasion gave the state the necessary political cover to consolidate power by castigating its challengers as traitors for criticizing the government at a time of war. Two decades later, with his "axis of evil" State of the Union Address, President George W. Bush inadvertently assisted the conservative backlash in Iran against a moderate president, Muhammad Khatami. Most recently, President Donald Trump has violated international law, subverting the Joint Comprehensive Plan of Action (JCPOA, known as "the Iran nuclear deal") by pulling the United States out of the agreement. In doing so, Trump undermined the centrist presidency of Hassan Rouhani by legitimizing the long-standing attacks of his conservative enemies. Before signing the agreement, they had accused Rouhani of naiveté for thinking that the United States would ever honor its agreements with Iran, and doubted whether America could ever reconcile itself to the outcome of the Iranian Revolution. Trump's withdrawal from the JCPOA has certainly given credibility to the conservative push against Rouhani.

I firmly believe that sanctions, military strikes, "regime change," and especially war will set Iran's struggle for democracy back decades – just as the US-led overthrow of Muhammad Mossadeq did in 1953. Above all, such policies would exact a human toll that should be avoided at all costs. Iranians and the people of the region have been through enough. In other words, while this manuscript is a testament to the injustice that so many Iranians have faced at the hands of their own governments, it should not be taken as a license for hawkish foreign policies toward the Persian Gulf country.

On a late Thursday afternoon in spring 2006, my father, Shahram, and I went to the martyrs' section of Behesht-i Zahra Cemetery in Tehran. What we did not know was that every Thursday before the Islamic day of rest, many families gather beside the graves of loved ones who died in the revolution or war. They had watermelon slices, dates, and candy to give to passers-by like us on the promise that we would pray for the soul of their departed.

My father and I approached several families to talk with them and express our condolences. I was unable to speak, but my father uttered my every sentiment without me telling him what to say. After visiting the fourth or fifth family, I took a deep breath and stayed back to talk with a *chador*-clad mother whose son had died in the Iran–Iraq War. She told me something that has stayed with me to this very day, and throughout the writing of this manuscript: "I hope my son didn't die in vain, and this generation fixes Iran's problems." If Iranian history teaches us anything, it is that every generation is up to the task.

I hope that this manuscript attests to the ability of Iranians to rise to the challenge, and I hope we stay out of their way and let them continue with the mantle that generations of fighters have passed onto them.

# Acknowledgments

This book has its roots in a 2010 seminar paper I prepared for a course with Geoff Eley as a graduate student at the University of Michigan, Ann Arbor. It evolved into a dissertation through coursework and other instructive moments with Kathryn Babayan, Valerie Kivelson, and my dissertation committee members, Geoff Eley, Fatma Göçek, Penny Von Eschen, and Juan Cole – my PhD adviser and dissertation chair. Thus, I am enormously indebted to the University of Michigan's Rackham Graduate School, the Department of History, and these patient professors and mentors who have made valuable contributions to the lens through which I have analyzed the Green Uprisings. Throughout my tenure as a graduate student, I gratefully received the generous support of Mina Houtan and The Houtan Scholarship Foundation.

I also thank the Association for Iranian Studies and the Mehrdad Mashayekhi Best Dissertation Award Committee, comprising Ali Akbar Mahdi, Ali Mirsepassi, Afshin Matin-Asgar, and Thomas Ricks, for presenting me with the award. The recognition helped me overcome my reluctance to make the dissertation available publicly in the form of a book. In a related vein, I would like to thank Fataneh Mashayekhi for instituting the award in honor of her late husband. Her award generously gave an early career historian like myself an opportunity to be recognized, which prompted Cambridge University Press's interest in my dissertation. I would like to acknowledge Maria Marsh, my editor at Cambridge University Press, for her belief in the project, and unlimited support at critical junctures. Furthermore, I am appreciative of the anonymous reviewers whose constructive feedback helped me improve the book. I also thank my colleagues, especially Jeffrey Ravel, at the MIT History Department for their moral support and advice throughout the publishing process. Charlotte Minsky at MIT also provided valuable editing and indexing support.

Lastly, nothing could be possible without my family. My older brother, Nima, taught me to think critically. My mother, Sonia, my very first teacher and Persian language instructor, was my fellow traveler sharing in my dream of pursuing a career of profound personal interest to me. She understood my passion and often enabled my focus. My father, Shahram, is the reason why I am interested in history, the Middle East, and fellow world citizens in the first place. I hope my father knows that his strength, passion, knowledge, and brilliance inspired me to tackle this endeavor all the way to its bittersweet end. I consider myself fortunate if I have a fraction of his aptitude and dedication to others. Having said that, whatever shortcomings are present in this study are without question my own.

# Note on Transliteration

I have taken the liberty of using a slightly modified version of the transliteration system as outlined by the *International Journal of Middle East Studies* (*IJMES*). A couple of points warrant specific mention. To avoid confusion between the third Shiʿite Imam – Husayn – and Mir Hussein Mousavi, the main opposition candidate in 2009, I have spelled their names accordingly. Furthermore, I have used words or names as they commonly appear in English, such as Mossadeq, Shiʿite/Shiʿites, and Yasser Arafat, as opposed to Mossadegh, Shiʿi/Shiʿa, or Yasir Arafat – as noted in *IJMES*. Unlike many authors who increasingly choose not to use diacritical marks, I have deliberately included all such marks. Activist slogans are an integral part of this study, yet their rhythmic efficacy is, despite my best efforts, partially lost in translation. Like so many languages around the world, Persian has a rich poetic tradition, brought to bear in the streets of Iran through the expression of creative and potent slogans. Thus, I have translated all the relevant slogans and have accompanied each with an in-text transliteration that includes all the diacritical marks in an attempt to respect their ingenuity.

# 1 | *Situating the 2009 Green Uprising*

## 1.1 Introduction

Iran is one of a number of countries that give real-world application to the Orwellian mantra that "history is written by the victors."[1] Indeed, the militant clerics who consolidated power at the expense of all the other revolutionary factions have worked tirelessly to present their version of the Iranian Revolution's history as the *only* version, best encapsulated by the state's preferred revolutionary slogan, "Independence, Freedom, Islamic Republic" (*esteqlāl, āzādī, jomhūrī-ye eslāmī*). For years, the Iranian government has presented this one-sided history to the benefit of its ruling class and self-affirming ideology.

Just as the events of 1978–1979 are far more complex and disputed than the state would like to admit, the historic uprising of 2009 is equally contentious. Years after the revolt, the Iranian government continued to refer to the Green Movement as "the sedition" – a conspiracy orchestrated from abroad and without organic roots within the country.[2] Inspired by studies that have contested the official

---

[1] The famous quote is tellingly attributed to Winston Churchill, the British premier who ordered his secret service to work hand in hand with the American CIA to orchestrate the overthrow of the Iranian government on August 19, 1953.

[2] "Fetneh-ye 88 toṭ'eh-ye doshman ʿalayh-i īrān būd." Fars News Agency, August 10, 2014. www.farsnews.com/newstext.php?nn=13931007001669. Also see "Fīrūzābādī: yowm allāh-i nohom-i dey maḥṣūl-i ensejām-i ʿomūmī-ye mardom shod." ISNA, January 1, 2014. http://goo.gl/Ymi2h3. There is no doubt that the US government, especially during the second Bush administration, was spending millions of dollars to "promote democracy" in Iran. There is significant doubt, however, about the destination of the allocated US$75 million, an amount that was increased in later years. While the Iranian government suspected that the money was used to finance dissidents and groups to launch a "velvet revolution," the bulk of the funds, according to one seasoned observer, was used for Persian language programming such as Radio Farda and Voice of America. What is certain is that the news of the fund's establishment undermined "the kind of organizations and activists it was designed to help, with U.S. aid becoming a top issue in a broader crackdown on leading democracy advocates over the past year,

1

narrative of the Iranian Revolution, this work aspires to do the same with the official narrative of the uprising in 2009.

Iran's protracted post-election uprising, the Green Movement, erupted more than two years before the protest movement in Tunisia ignited the firestorm of revolution that became known as the Arab Spring ("Arab Uprisings"[3] in Arabic). Iran's revolt was hailed as the largest and most formidable challenge to the Iranian state since the seismic events of 1978–1979 that shaped the way regional leaders, military officers, foreign heads of state, journalists, analysts and commentators, and, most significantly, various peoples view Iran and the Middle East. The Iranian Revolution of thirty years before, perhaps more than any other revolution of the twentieth century, created a "shock-wave" with ramifications that were "felt round the world"[4] and which continue to reverberate throughout the country and the region.

In 2011, observers and politicians viewed Egypt, an Arab country that has not had formal relations with Iran since the Iranian Revolution, through the prism of the very revolution that precipitated the severance of ties between the two. As popular forces engulfed Egypt in revolt against Hosni Mubarak, the country's "Arab president for life,"[5] American and Israeli leaders invoked the specter of Egypt becoming the "next Iran." Israeli Premier Benyamin Netanyahu stated, "Our real fear is of a situation that could develop ... and which has already developed in several countries, including Iran itself: repressive regimes of radical Islam."[6] In an open letter to President Obama,

---

according to a wide range of Iranian activists and human rights groups." See Robin Wright, "Iran on guard over U.S. funds," *The Washington Post*, April 28, 2007. www.washingtonpost.com/wp-dyn/content/article/2007/04/27/AR2007042701668.html.

[3] "Arab Spring" is a misnomer because it incorrectly implies that Arabs were apathetic and complacent until 2011. Arabs have busied themselves with violent and nonviolent uprisings throughout the modern period in the Middle East and North Africa. The Palestinian uprisings (1936–1939, 1987–1993, and 2000–2005) are just three examples of the nonviolent and violent historical occurrences that predate the "Arab Spring."

[4] This phrase is a headline to a news piece in *The Observer*. See "Shock-wave felt round the world," *The Observer*, January 7, 1979, p. 9.

[5] To quote the title of Roger Owen's *The Rise and Fall of Arab Presidents for Life* (Cambridge, MA: Harvard University Press, 2012).

[6] Ian Black, "Egypt set for mass protest as army rules out force," *The Guardian*, January 31, 2011. Accessed March 25, 2011. www.guardian.co.uk/world/2011/jan/31/egyptian-army-pledges-no-force.

American Senator Mark Kirk called for direct US intervention in the affairs of Egypt to support the "secular nationalists" and take action to "defeat" the Muslim Brotherhood so the organization did not "follow Iran's revolution, turning Egypt into a state-sponsor of terror."[7] In the aftermath of Mubarak's ousting, the ruling Supreme Council of the Armed Forces (SCAF) declared that "Egypt will not be governed by another Khomeini."[8] Even Ayatollah ʿAli Khamenei, Iran's Supreme Leader, referenced Iran's 1978–1979 revolution, claiming that it served as an exemplar for action for fellow Muslims in the era of the Arab Uprisings:

Today's events in North Africa, Egypt, Tunisia, and several others, have a different meaning for the Iranian nation. They have a special meaning. These events are part of the Islamic Awakening, which can be said is itself a result of the victory of the great Islamic Revolution of the Iranian nation.[9]

Some similarities such as strikes were key to both the Iranian Revolution and the Arab revolts in Tunisia and Egypt. Despite the fact that no strikes occurred during the heyday of the Green Movement, the Arab Spring had more in common with the Iranian activists of 2009 in terms of their goals, youth demographic, and use of modern technologies, than with the Khomeini-led revolution and its outcome, but such commonalities either made for politically inconvenient comparisons at best or Orientalist generalizations at worst.

According to Kirk, Netanyahu, the SCAF, and Khamenei, it was of no consequence that the Iranian Revolution and the uprising in Egypt were separated by more than three decades with an abundance of differences. Such a generalization and simplification minimizes the

---

[7] Mark Kirk, "Press release of Senator Kirk: Senator Kirk statement on Muslim Brotherhood." Personal Website. February 2, 2011. Accessed March 25, 2011. http://kirk.senate.gov/record.cfm?id=330818. It is also important to note that Senator Kirk's obsession with the Iranian government has led him to advocate policies that not only target the Iranian government but also harm the civilian population. Eli Clifton and Ali Gharib, "Pro-sanction group targets legal humanitarian trade with Iran," *The Nation*, November 13, 2014. Accessed May 22, 2015. www.thenation.com/blog/190601/pro-sanctions-group-targets-legal-humanitarian-trade-iran.

[8] "Army says no to 'Khomeini rule' in Egypt," ahramonline, April 4, 2011. Accessed April 4, 2011. http://english.ahram.org.eg/News/9321.aspx.

[9] ʿAli Khamenei, "Khoṭbehhāye namāz jomʿeh-ye tehrān + tarjomehye khoṭbeh-ye ʿarabī." leader.ir, February 5, 2011. http://farsi.khamenei.ir/speech-content?id=10955.

social, demographic, political, cultural, geographical, and historical factors that distinguish these two countries and their historical trajectories. The leaps of history overlooked many significant differences: economic factors, the fundamental differences between Iranian Shiʿism and Egyptian Sunnism, the role of ideology, the subtle but important distinctions in these countries' Islamist movements, and the degree of autonomy of each countries' religious institutions vis-à-vis the state. Furthermore, the Cold War context crucial to Iran in 1979 and the contemporary political nuances relevant to Egypt, and the geographical realities between Iran bordering the Soviet Union in 1978 and Egypt bordering Israel and a Hamas-ruled Gaza Strip in 2011 are all disregarded to draw problematic parallels.[10] Moreover, such a narrow perspective ignores the crucial role of the sizable Christian minority in Egypt that makes it all the more difficult for Egypt to become the "next Iran."[11]

Similarly, the Green Movement of 2009 could not avoid being seen through the prism of the Iranian Revolution. The actual connection between the two, however, is much more profound. Whereas in the context of the 2011 uprising in Egypt, foreign leaders either drew upon their limited knowledge of the Iranian Revolution in anxiety or invoked that history in the service of their political agendas, journalists inside Iran referenced the Iranian Revolution when reporting nearly every momentous occasion in the uprising in order to underscore its historical gravity. For instance, Al Jazeera's opening line in its report of the second day of the uprising referred to it as "the biggest unrest since the 1979 revolution,"[12] while Reuters called the protests "The largest and most widespread demonstrations since the 1979 Islamic revolution. . ."[13] For outsiders the revolt did indeed invoke the Iranian

---

[10] For a more detailed treatment, see Pouya Alimagham, "The Iranian legacy in the 2011 Egyptian Revolution: Military endurance and U.S. foreign policy priorities," *UCLA Historical Journal*, 24(1) (2013).

[11] The fact that Copts constitute 10 percent, or nearly ten million Egyptians, means that it is far more difficult to establish an Islamic government in Egypt than in Iran, which did not have such a large religious minority in 1979.

[12] "Poll results prompt Iran protests," Al Jazeera, June 14, 2009. Accessed August 7, 2010. http://english.aljazeera.net/news/middleeast/2009/06/2009613172130303995.html.

[13] Parisa Hafezi, "Thousands mourn Iranians killed in protests," Reuters. June 19, 2009. http://in.mobile.reuters.com/article/worldNews/idINIndia-40437520090618.

Revolution because it brought millions of Iranians to the streets in defiance of their government.

The street marches were one of the most awe-inspiring and memorable aspects of the Iranian Revolution. Millions of women and men marched, often under the threat of state violence, to register their revolutionary protest against the monarch's absolutism. Charles Kurzman, author of *The Unthinkable Revolution in Iran*, notes that "It is almost unheard of for a revolution to involve as much as 1 percent of a country's population. The French Revolution of 1789, the Russian Revolution of 1917, perhaps the Romanian Revolution of 1989 – these may have passed the 1 percent mark."[14] Yet, on December 10 and 11, 1978, between six and nine million Iranians (some have estimated the number as high as seventeen million[15]), between a third and half of the population, took part in demonstrations in what Kurzman believes could have been "the largest protest event in history."[16] So vaunted and historically consequential were these street demonstrations that post-revolutionary[17] Iranian leaders advised Palestinians "to deploy the multi-million tactic to destroy the Israeli army and Israel itself."[18] The long span of three decades did not dissuade journalists from invoking the events of 1979 when the 2009 post-election uprising likewise prompted millions of Iranians to once again flood the streets against their government. As before, they voted with their feet, and under the threat of state violence, against a government that they believed did not respect the ballot box.

The uprising in 2009, however, shares a deeper history with 1978–1979 that transcends the time and space of the momentous street demonstrations. The repertoires of action that were cemented in the official narrative of the revolution informed the actions of Green Movement activists in 2009, giving their reprogrammed methods historically infused importance and meaning. Since much of the Green

---

[14] Charles Kurzman, *The Unthinkable Revolution in Iran* (Cambridge, MA: Harvard University Press, 2004), p. 121.

[15] Hamid Dabashi, *Iran, the Green Movement and the USA* (London and New York: Z Books, 2010), p. 207.

[16] Kurzman, *The Unthinkable Revolution in Iran*, p. 122.

[17] By "post-revolutionary," I mean the period immediately after February 11, 1979, the date of the revolution's victory, and not a period in which Iran has begun to move past the goals and ideals of the revolution.

[18] Faleh A. Jaberi, *The Shi'ite Movement in Iraq* (London: Saqi Books, 2003), p. 250.

Movement's symbolism, slogans, and strategies were rooted in the Iranian Revolution, it is prudent to first outline some of the major works on the Iranian Revolution because that history and scholarship inform the framework by which the Green Movement will be approached and analyzed in this book.

## 1.2 The Iranian Revolution and Its Historiography Matter

Scholars of Iran have harnessed a range of theories about revolution as a historical phenomenon to explain the events of 1978–1979 that shocked academics, political leaders, and even Iranians themselves. Historians, sociologists, and political scientists have debated theoretical explanations of the Iranian Revolution at length, not necessarily disputing the facts or events, but contesting each other's final analyses.

Nikki Keddie's *Roots of Revolution*, one of the first books on the Iranian Revolution, situates the event in the context of the West's century-long economic and cultural penetration and political domination of the country. The revolution, Keddie argues, is part of a longer historical trend of Iranian resistance to the country's economic, political, and cultural subjugation. Starting with the Tobacco Revolt of 1890–1892, moving through the Constitutional Revolution of 1905–1911 and Muhammad Mossadeq's oil nationalization movement of the early 1950s, and culminating in the Iranian Revolution of 1979, Keddie shows how Western imperialism provoked a nativist political, cultural, and ideological backlash not only against foreign domination but also against its local agent, Muhammad Reza Shah Pahlavi (r. 1941–1979).

Ervand Abrahamian's magnum opus, *Iran Between Two Revolutions*, approaches the history of modern Iran via class formation and structural factors, while also placing special emphasis on the history of Iran's communist party, the Tudeh Party. Employing a class analysis, Abrahamian outlines Iran's twentieth-century history to argue that the transition from tribalism into social classes without the necessary political modernization served as the main impetus for the revolution. Accordingly, as the Pahlavi dynasty (1925–1979) modernized and expanded the bureaucracy, army, and economy, Iran experienced further class formation and an expansion of the modern middle class without the requisite political modernization, which sowed the seeds of the revolution: "In short, the revolution took place neither because of overdevelopment nor because of underdevelopment but because of uneven development."[19]

In contrast, Misagh Parsa's *Social Origins of the Iranian Revolution* argues that structure and class action are important, but they alone cannot account for the revolution. What is also needed, Parsa argues, are resources, solidarity structures, and organizations, all of which the modern middle class lacked at the time of the revolution. Parsa affirms Keddie and Abrahamian's understanding of Iran's structure by the late 1970s, when

> State development policies clearly served particular rather than general societal interests, as claimed by the government. These policies gave rise to widening economic inequality and burgeoning inflation. In industry, agriculture, and commerce, the government's development strategies consistently favored the upper class over the working classes, urban over rural, and large, modern enterprises over small, traditional ones.[20]

Employing Charles Tilly's resource-mobilization theory of collective action, Parsa goes on to argue that the merchant (*bazaari*) class was especially hurt by the state's policies, and was equipped with the requisite solidarity structures and financial power but not the springboard from which to launch a revolution. Intense state repression meant that political activity in the bazaar was impossible, but they found a resourceful ally in the militant faction of the clergy that was able to harness the power of the nationwide mosque network in order to mobilize the population for revolution.

Parsa's monumental study of the Iranian Revolution is not without its shortcomings. Parsa bases his argument on the premise that the mosque was autonomous and safe enough to avoid state repression and was free to organize the revolution; and that the regime had decimated all other opposition groups, leaving the clergy purposefully unscathed to use religion to counter the growing tide of Marxism.[21]

---

[19] Ervand Abrahamian, *Iran Between Two Revolutions* (Princeton: Princeton University Press, 1982), p. 427.

[20] Misagh Parsa, *Social Origins of the Iranian Revolution* (New Brunswick and London: Rutgers University Press, 1989), p. 63.

[21] Iran under the Shah was not unique in this regard. Many states in the region, such as Egypt and Pakistan, were harnessing Islam for self-legitimation and to combat leftism. Even the Reagan administration backed Islamic ideology in the form of the *jihad* in Afghanistan to counter the Soviets and their Afghan Marxist allies.

The clerical class was thus relatively free and able to launch and lead the revolution. The Shah himself admitted that "for some time my government had been providing our clergy with substantial support."[22] After Ayatollah Khomeini's uprising in 1963, however, the mosque may not have been as safe a place for political activity as commonly understood. Khomeini himself was imprisoned and eventually exiled, and all of the revolution's key clerical leaders, including Khomeini's successor, Khamenei, ʿAli Akbar Hashemi Rafsanjani, Mahmoud Taleqani, and Hussein ʿAli Montazeri – the one-time designated heir to Khomeini – spent years in prison for their political activities. One cleric, Hussein Ghaffari, was tortured to death in 1974.[23] State surveillance of the clergy was so severe that another

[22] Mohammad Reza Pahlavi, *Answer to History: By Mohammad Reza Pahlavi The Shah of Iran* (New York: Stein and Day Publishers, 1980), p. 155.

[23] Batul Ghaffari, the daughter of Ayatollah Hussein Ghaffari and sister of Hadi Ghaffari, details in her memoirs the condition of her father's body after his death, as well as how religious activist women like herself were imprisoned and tortured for their beliefs. Her memoirs also shed light on the horrific torture that women and men from all political leanings endured, from the pulling of nails, whipping, beatings, and cigarette burning to helpless children being dragged into prison and assaulted in front of parents to induce their confessions. She also goes beyond the details of torture to enumerate the horrible conditions of prison life, from brief ice-cold showers, sleeping on cockroach-infested floors, and crowded cells in which more than a dozen would be crammed into a small space, to pebbles in low-quality food, a total lack of privacy during bathroom breaks, and more. "Gozīdeh-ye khaṭerat-i batūl ghaffarī: shekanjehgarhā ān qadr mā rā mīzadand keh khodeshān az ḥāl mīraftand," Fars News, February 16, 1994. Accessed June 30, 2018. www.farsnews.com/amp/8711250479. Incidentally, her brother, Hadi – one of the future leaders of the Iranian Hizbullah – was an acquaintance of my father's. As part of his mandatory military service, my father, Shahram Alimagham, served as a second lieutenant in the Shah's Literacy Corps in the early 1970s. While in Ardebil to monitor junior officers, he shared a room with Ghaffari, who was also fulfilling his service obligations. My father remembers that he had a strict work ethic despite the lack of oversight. Whereas many officers tried to evade their responsibilities, Ghaffari even rode a horse to remote villages when the winter weather prevented travel by car. While my father indirectly signaled that he opposed the Shah's regime, Ghaffari was reluctant to talk about politics, except to inform him that his father was imprisoned by the Shah. Alimagham notes that Ghaffari always observed his prayers, found fault with him for never doing so, and was very ambitious – constantly and successfully petitioning the authorities for resources to which he felt entitled as an officer. Shahram Alimagham, personal interview, June 26, 2018.

cleric was even imprisoned for two years for corresponding with Khomeini.[24] Parsa appears to contradict himself when he notes that several thousand clergymen were informants on the payroll of SAVAK, the Shah's secret police.[25] One reviewer of Parsa's work went so far as to call his assumption that "the mosque was the only organization that had maintained relative autonomy from the state" a "fantasy."[26]

Hamid Dabashi, Mansoor Moaddel, and Hamid Algar emphasize to varying degrees the role of ideology in the making of the revolution. Mansoor Moaddel's *Class, Politics, and the Iranian Revolution* is one of the more comprehensive works to consider the role of ideology in the revolution. His criticism of Parsa's analysis effectively sets the stage for his own contribution to the debate:

It is one thing to argue that the bazaaris were antagonized by the state's policies and therefore supported the Islamic alternative to the Shah's rule. It is quite another to explain the emergence of coordinated actions by members of diverse classes in the revolution and their fascinating harmony in demanding the overthrow of the monarchy and the establishment of Islamic government.[27]

Moaddel does not discount the role of structure and class. Rather, he employs a class analysis that is intertwined with the discourse of Islamic ideology to explain the revolution:

A . . . major problem in these theories involves their excessive emphasis on the notion that people act piece by piece according to their interests or values. But action is necessarily integrated into larger assemblages called strategies of action, and ideology plays an independent causal role because it shapes 'the capacity from which such strategies of action are constructed.'[28]

He goes on to say: "Revolutionary ideology tends to transcend all the class, ethnic, and even sex differences among the participants (those 'locked' within its discursive field), as if they have formed an undifferentiated mass tied together within the imageries and symbolic systems

---

[24] "The Shah's divided land," *Time*, September 18, 1978, p. 35.

[25] Parsa, *Social Origins of the Iranian Revolution*, p. 197.

[26] Hamid Dabashi, Review of *Social Origins of the Iranian Revolution*, by Misagh Parsa. *Contemporary Sociology*, 20(2) (March 1991), pp. 211–212.

[27] Mansoor Moaddel, *Class, Politics, and Ideology in the Iranian Revolution* (New York and Oxford: Columbia University Press, 1993), p. 14.

[28] Ibid., p. 16.

generated by the ideology itself."[29] Indeed, there was class conflict before 1978, but no Islamic revolution occurred. The revolution happened in 1979 because class conflict was now expressed in the oppositional discourse of Islamic ideology that negated the Shah's ideology:

> The revolutionary crisis began when the social discontent was expressed in terms of Shi'i revolutionary discourse. Dual sovereignty emerged because the state and the opposition were constituted by and through two mutually negating ideological universes. The themes of Shi'i revolutionary discourse (that Iran's problems were related to the West's cultural domination and the un-Islamic nature of the institution of monarchy, and that there was a religious solution to these problems) contradicted in essence the monarchy-centered nationalist discourse.[30]

Thus, according to Moaddel, "ideology is not simply another factor that adds an increment to the causes of the revolution. *Ideology is the constitutive feature of revolution.* Ideology makes revolution a phenomenon distinct from the routine contention for power or class conflict."[31]

Charles Kurzman, who like Parsa is a sociologist, contributed to the discussion of the causes of the Iranian Revolution with his *The Unthinkable Revolution in Iran*. He methodologically considers each theory to argue that they are only partially complete. For instance, in terms of the economic factors serving as the catalyst for the revolution, he reasons:

> Revolutions occur when economic problems worsen, especially after a period of relative prosperity. In Iran, the oil boom of the mid-1970s gave way to a troubling recession in 1977. But this recession was no more severe than previous ones, and the groups that suffered the most were not the most revolutionary.[32]

The organizational theory, which Parsa championed in *Social Origins*, is also problematized:

> Revolutions occur when oppositional groups are able to mobilize sufficient resources to contest the regime's hold on the population. In Iran, the Islamists mobilized the nationwide 'mosque network' against the regime. But the

[29] Ibid., p. 19.   [30] Ibid., p. 268.   [31] Ibid., p. 2.
[32] Kurzman, *The Unthinkable Revolution in Iran*, p. 6.

mosque network was not a preexisting resource for the Islamists and had to be constructed and commandeered during the course of the mobilization.[33]

Rather, Kurzman argues that there is too much confusion in a revolution to try to explain it with complex theories. In reality, it is a real-time decision on the ground in which "fence-sitters" decide at a critical juncture that revolution is viable and that an alternative to the regime is possible – an epiphany that subsequently prompts their participation. According to Kurzman, until those fence-sitters – the bulk of the people who ultimately made the revolution – crossed that mental threshold, only the die-hard revolutionaries were on the streets fighting for revolutionary change.

His explanation, or what he calls the "anti-explanation ... runs counter to the project of retroactive prediction... Instead of seeking recurrent patterns in social life, anti-explanation explores the unforeseen moments when patterns are twisted or broken off."[34] In the winter of 1978, Iranians joined the revolution in their millions, crossing that unpredictable mental threshold because they realized that a revolutionary alternative *was* viable, that their presence made it even more feasible, and that the millions sharing the streets with them meant it was safer to participate. It became a self-sustaining cycle that ultimately brought down one of the developing world's most well-armed and powerful dictatorships. As with previous treatments of the Iranian Revolution, however, Kurzman's work is not without its flaws. He analyzes each theory of the revolution separately without considering the possibility that a combination could explain the root causes of the revolution.

The most fascinating aspect of these contributions is how they are in conversation with one another. Each author considers the works of their predecessors and offers an invaluable theoretical assessment of the same historical event. They may not agree with one another, but they all complement each other's work in a fashion that benefits the reader who considers all the arguments together. These warrant careful consideration, not only because they inform the framework through which the Green Movement is analyzed, especially with regard to Moaddel's focus on ideology, Kurzman's anti-explanation, and Parsa's emphasis on resources, solidarity structures, and organizational

---

[33] Ibid., p. 6.     [34] Ibid., p. 138.

capacities, but also because the Iranian Revolution itself is crucial to the historical weight and background of the 2009 movement.

While Senator Kirk, Prime Minister Netanyahu, and Ayatollah Khamenei mistakenly and unjustifiably employed the prism of the Iranian Revolution to analyze Egypt in 2011, and journalists referenced 1979 to highlight the historic nature of the 2009 demonstrations, a new generation of Iranians on the street and on the internet were doing something entirely different with regard to their past: they were contesting the ownership and the very meaning of the Iranian Revolution and its symbols in order to condemn its outcome – the Islamic Republic.

In 2009, 60 percent of Iran's citizens were under the age of thirty,[35] a youth bulge rooted in the Islamic Republic's early years. Islamist leaders believed that family planning was an imperialist plot designed to reduce the populations of Muslim countries and the wider developing world, rendering them more susceptible to foreign subjugation.[36] Many believed that a large population was a sign of strength and power for the country,[37] an outlook that grew in strategic importance during the long conflict with Iraq when future soldiers were needed to prosecute the war. Morally, the leadership argued that early marriage was a key to eradicating moral corruption and consequent social ills.[38] Thus, the state facilitated a baby boom by pursuing a series of pronatalist policies during its first decade in power.[39]

---

[35] This "youth bulge" is not unique to Iran as nearly the same percentage of the Arab world is under the age of thirty. See James Gelvin, *The Arab Uprisings: What Everyone Needs to Know* (Oxford: Oxford University Press, 2012).

[36] Homa Hoodfar and Samad Assadpour, "The politics of population policy in the Islamic Republic of Iran," *Studies in Family Planning*, 31(1) (2000), p. 20.

[37] Ibid., p. 21. Ahmadinejad, backed by Khamenei, announced a return to Khomeini-era reproductive priorities by encouraging and incentivizing families to reproduce, and removing the policies and resources that helped maintain population growth via family planning and access to free contraceptives. Such polices, in part, sparked the One Million Signatures Campaign to End Discriminatory Law.

[38] Ibid., p. 21.

[39] Some of those policies included no longer requiring "a minimum age of marriage (originally sixteen for girls and eighteen for boys)," lowering "the legal age of adulthood to nine for girls and fourteen for boys…" and legalizing polygynous and temporary marriages. Ibid., pp. 21–22. Of state-sanctioned incentives to encourage the baby boom, Caroline Berson notes: "Population growth became part of the national agenda, with incentives to reward families for each additional child. Everything from TVs to cars to food was distributed on a per

When the war ended in 1988, the government quickly realized that the population's rapid growth was a major burden on the state's limited resources and ailing economy – an economy that would one day have to provide jobs for these baby boomers. As a result, it compromised the ideology prioritizing a high birth rate in favor of pragmatism,[40] implementing one of the most advanced contraceptive and family planning systems in the world.[41] While the state was able to curb the post-revolutionary baby boom, reducing the country's growth rate from a high of 3.4 percent in 1986 to 1.5 percent in 1996[42] – described by one author as "the most stunning reversal of population growth in human history"[43] – it still had to contend with the millions

capita basis through a rationing system, making it advantageous to have many children." Caroline Berson, "The Iranian baby boom: Why the Islamic republic has such a youthful population," Slate, June 12, 2009. Accessed February 28, 2014.

[40] Pragmatism superseding ideology began well before the end of the war. One obvious example occurred when the revolutionary government circumvented its own militant opposition to Zionism and imperialism in order to purchase American arms and spare parts at inflated prices through Israel in the mid-1980s during the Iran–Iraq War (more on this later). A less obvious example can be found in the 1982 uprising in Hama, Syria. Revolutionaries in Iran sought to emancipate Muslims everywhere, and supported Palestinians, Lebanese, and Afghans throughout the 1980s. In Syria, however, they sided with the secular Ba'athist regime when it launched a merciless crackdown in Hama against the Muslim Brotherhood-led uprising. The Iranians calculated that they could not afford to antagonize their sole regional wartime ally which had been instrumental in blocking Iraq from exporting its oil through Syrian pipelines.

[41] While parents retained the right to choose how many children they wanted, the government push to reduce birthrates was comprehensive. The program included encouraging couples to have no more than two children (often by emphasizing the equality of girls to boys), and providing free urban (as well as rural) access to a variety of contraceptives: the pill, condoms, IUDs, and even vasectomies and tubal ligation. Making contraceptives available was not enough, however. More importantly, the program also embarked upon a nationwide awareness campaign to teach the population about the importance of family planning. The Ministry of Education incorporated population issues into its social science programming, the clergy utilized its leadership among low-income, underserved communities to inform citizens of such services, and an extensive outreach effort was undertaken to reach the urban poor. Hoodfar and Assadpour, "The politics of population policy," pp. 26–30.

[42] Ibid., p. 32.

[43] Alan Weisman, "What started the biggest population boom in history? How Iran's explosive expansion warns us about our overpopulated future – and shows us how to fix it," *Medium*, February 5, 2014. https://medium.com/matter/what-started-the-biggest-population-boom-in-history-1909ce55ada2.

of wartime births that eventually came to constitute a burgeoning youth population.

This generation had experienced no state authority except that of the Islamic government, which began its consolidation the very moment the revolution made its final push towards the total destruction of the monarchy during the Ten Days of Dawn.[44] The clerical domination of the reins of power was completed by 1982 when the main armed opposition to the Islamic government, the Mujahedin-i Khalq (MEK), was decimated with the death of its field commander, Musa Khiabani.[45]

From the beginning, the clerics labored to ensure that the government was Islamic not just in name but also in form. They achieved this by Islamizing not only the state's institutions, including the constitution and system of governance, the armed forces, and judiciary, but also the education system, arts and culture, and even the physical and aesthetic landscape of the country. Statues and murals, some of which cover entire sides of buildings, visualized in aggrandizing form the leadership, symbols, and martyrs of both the revolution and the Iran–Iraq War.[46] The state aimed to create a population that was both pious in faith and obedient and Islamist in political persuasion.

The result was the emergence of a generation that corresponded with the thirty-year history of the Islamic Republic. These young people were raised fully cognizant of the state's ideology, history, and symbolism, all of which glorified a radical reading of Islam and a politically selective history of the Iranian Revolution.[47] The state, born of the

---

[44] The Ten Days of Dawn (*dah-i fajr*) were the climactic days in the revolution in which Khomeini returned to Iran on February 1 after his long exile and the final stages of the struggle that culminated in a two-day insurrection that precipitated the state's total collapse on February 11, 1979.

[45] The MEK responded to the domestic dismantling of its organization by regrouping in France and Iraq under Saddam Hussein, the latter of which provided the MEK with a military base. For more about the Mujahedin, see Ervand Abrahamian's fascinating *The Iranian Mojahedin* (New Haven: Yale University Press, 1989).

[46] The Islamic government refers to the Iran–Iraq War as the "Imposed War," and its war effort as the "Sacred Defense."

[47] Many factions participated in the Iranian Revolution. Describing the revolution as an Iranian one affords the appropriate space to include all those factions, including the Tudeh Party, the various radical Marxist factions, of which the Fada'iyan was the most important, the MEK, the Mossadeqist National Front, Mehdi Bazargan's Liberation Front, and the militant clergy who rallied behind the leadership of Khomeini. The revolutionary government refers to the Iranian

revolution, rooted its legitimacy in the religious and revolutionary authority of its undisputed leader, Ayatollah Ruhollah Khomeini, 1400 years of Islamic history intertwined with a militant interpretation, and the historic mobilization of 1978–1979 that had shocked the world by bringing one of the developing world's most powerful (and seemingly stable) dictatorships to a definitive end at the hands of a protracted popular uprising. So important is this revolutionary history to the ideological foundation of the Islamic Republic that the founder's successor, Ayatollah ʿAli Khamenei, is hailed as "the Leader of the Revolution." Although he certainly was not the leader of the revolution, this title emphasizes the continuity of the revolution, with Khomeini's legitimacy bestowed on Khamenei – a cleric dwarfed by the religious and political stature of his towering predecessor as well as by many of his peers in the wider Shiʿite world.[48] If Khomeini's charisma and revolutionary credentials legitimated the Islamic system before his death, then the system institutionalized and "routinized" that charisma and history in order to legitimize his successors with such titles as "the Leader of the Revolution." The most obvious visual example of this legitimating continuity is in the ubiquitous display of Khamenei's image beside that of his exalted predecessor (Figure 1.1).[49]

Revolution as Islamic in order to marginalize the contribution of all those non-Khomeinist factions that were vital to the revolution.

[48] Khamenei himself acknowledged his political and religious standing relative to his towering predecessor: "Imam Khomeini was so great that among the great men and world leaders in history, one could hardly imagine a man with such characteristics, except among *prophets* and the *infallibles*. Neither I as a humble theology student with all shortcomings and defects, nor any other man in the Islamic Republic can reach the summit of that distinguished and *exceptional personality*." Ahmad Ashraf, "Theocracy and charisma: New men of power in Iran," *International Journal of Politics, Culture, and Society*, 4(1) (1990), p. 142.

[49] Christia Fotini (photographer). July 2006. "We will continue on the path of the Imam and the martyrs of the revolution," part of *Tehran Propaganda Mural Collection* (Cambridge, MA: H.C. Fung Library, Harvard University). Retrieved from http://id.lib.harvard.edu/images/olvgroup11882/urn-3:FHCL:1268189/ catalog. Hamid Dabashi and Peter Chelkowski have covered a wide array of meaning-laden visuals from before and after the revolution. See Peter Chelkowski and Hamid Dabashi, *Staging a Revolution: The Art of Persuasion in the Islamic Republic of Iran* (New York: New York University Press, 1999).

**Figure 1.1** "We will continue on the path of the Imam and the martyrs of the Revolution".
Photo credit: Fotini Christia

Such history and symbols afford the revolutionary state a claim to authority in Iran and beyond.[50]

Khamenei's pledge serves as the caption of this six-story-high Tehran mural: "We will continue on the path of the Imam [Khomeini] and the martyrs of the Revolution." To emphasize that very point, Khamenei's image is located below that of his predecessor, the charismatic leader who founded the Islamic Republic and bequeathed it to his successor to "continue."

By instilling this history and its associated symbols in a new generation of Iranian youth, the revolutionary government cemented its

---

[50] It can certainly be argued that these historical symbols were and continue to be employed not only to afford the state the legitimacy to rule Iran, but also to empower the government with the authority to serve as the vanguard of the wider Muslim world.

legitimacy and ensured its political durability. Although this ideology, history, and symbolism were designed to authenticate a state born of resistance and revolution, they also equipped the population, especially the young, with the discourse and symbolism to resist that same state.

## 1.3  Contesting the Iranian Revolution of 1979 in 2009 and Post-Islamism

In 2009, Green Movement activists contested the ownership of the state-sanctioned history and symbolism by appropriating and subverting them for their own anti-state purposes. They contested the very meaning of those ideological symbols by reprogramming and leveling them with devastating ferocity at the state whose very legitimacy was rooted in those symbols – a strategy one activist referred to as "political jiu-jitsu":

Among the martial arts, jiu-jitsu is a method of fighting in which one fighter neutralizes the opponent by turning the opponent's attack against himself while expending the least amount of energy... Green activists can use these legitimated symbols in order to de-legitimize the state.[51]

In other words, if the Iranian state justified its authority through the history of the Iranian Revolution, then Green Movement activists contested the meaning and ownership of that revolution in order to legitimate their own uprising against its outcome – the Islamic Republic and "the Leader of the Revolution."

Thus, while the Green Movement may have failed to cancel the election results or bring down the state, it succeeded in discursively undermining the state's ideological foundations. If it is possible to transcend the arbitrary win–lose binary that inevitably marginalizes

---

[51] Jalal Salehpour, "Cheh ghazzeh cheh īrān," *Rahesabz.* September 17, 2009. Accessed March 13, 2015. www.rahesabz.net/story/1653/. To frame the uprising as part of a foreign conspiracy, the Iranian government and others have credited political scientist Gene Sharp with these innovative tactics, but the strategies are wholly consistent with Iranian history. For instance, `Ashura, the annual commemoration of Husayn's martyrdom, had become an occasion for protest in Iran throughout the twentieth century. See Farah Stockman, "Revolution of the mind: Under siege at home, Iran's dissidents draw comfort and ideas from some visionary thinkers based here," boston.com. December 20, 2009. Accessed November 10, 2018. http://archive.boston.com/news/local/massachusetts/articles/2009/12/20/iran_dissidents_draw_ideas_from_us_visionaries/?page=1.

other historically consequential victories of the Green Movement,[52] then it is possible to understand phenomena of 2009 that may very well have ramifications beyond Iran and into the wider realm of Islamic political thought in what Asef Bayat calls the "post-Islamist turn."

In Bayat's formulation,

> ...post-Islamism represents both a *condition* and a *project*, which may be embodied in a master (or multidimensional) movement. In the first place, it refers to political and social conditions where, following a phase of experimentation, the appeal, energy, and sources of legitimacy of Islamism are exhausted, even among its once-ardent supporters.[53]

Simply put, there is a difference between a theory as imagined on paper, and the complications of its real-world implementation. Through the process of establishing a functional system, avid Islamists, including even the architects of the system, gain awareness of the project's contradictions as "they attempt to normalize and institutionalize their rule... trial and error makes the system susceptible to questions and criticisms."[54] Eventually, Islamists responded to their own first-hand experience of the system's shortcomings as well as to popular pressure from below – which in 2009 was exemplified in the Green Uprising – by allowing pragmatism to supersede ideological principles. Bayat notes that the discarding of foundational principles

---

[52] A sample of Western media news outlets, including NBC News, Fox News, *The Guardian*, and *Der Spiegel*, all refer to the Green Uprising as a "failed" revolution because it was unable to cancel Ahmadinejad's election "win" or to topple the system that confirmed his victory. See Robert Windrem, "Who to follow on Twitter? Iranian President Hassan Rohani," NBC News, November 2, 2015. Accessed May 26, 2018. www.nbcnews.com/news/world/who-follow-twitter-iranian-president-hassan-rouhani-flna4B11205274. Perry Chiaramonte, "Hell on Earth: Inside Iran's brutal Evin prison," Fox News, January 28, 2013. Accessed May 26, 2018. www.foxnews.com/world/2013/01/28/inside-evin-look-at-world-most-notorious-political-prison.html. Geoffrey Macnab, "Iran's green revolution in animation," *The Guardian*, January 20, 2011. Accessed May 26, 2018. www.theguardian.com/film/2011/jan/20/iran-animation-the-green-wave. "Germany grants asylum to 50 Iranian dissidents," *Der Spiegel*, January 26, 2010. Accessed May 26, 2018. www.spiegel.de/international/world/long-wait-ends-germany-grants-asylum-to-50-iranian-dissidents-a-708537.html.

[53] Asef Bayat, *Making Islam Democratic: Social Movements and the Post-Islamist Turn* (Stanford: Stanford University Press, 2007), p. 10–11.

[54] Ibid., p. 11.

constitutes a "qualitative shift," which is best illustrated in the belief that Islam is too multi-faceted, complex, and grand to be confined to the mundane reality and trappings of a state bureaucracy, and that to do so risks denigrating and discrediting the faith through the mistakes committed in its name. Moreover, Bayat argues,

…Post-Islamism is neither anti-Islamic nor un-Islamic nor secular, it endeavors to fuse religiosity and rights, faith and freedom, Islam and liberty. It is an attempt to turn the underlying principles of Islamism on its head by emphasizing rights instead of duties, plurality in place of singular authoritative voice, historicity rather than fixed scripture, and the future instead of the past. It strives to marry Islam with individual choice and freedom, with democracy and modernity (something post-Islamists stress), to achieve what some scholars have termed an 'alternative modernity.' Post-Islamism is expressed in acknowledging secular exigencies, in freedom from rigidity, in breaking down the monopoly of religious truth. In short, whereas Islamism is defined by the fusion of religion and responsibility, post-Islamism emphasizes religiosity and rights.[55]

The Green Uprising is a manifestation of this post-Islamist shift both from above, with Ayatollah Montazeri's political evolution from key regime architect to foremost dissident who intensified his criticism of the system during the revolt, and from below, as represented by the actions of millions of Iranians in 2009.

The Green Movement's robust challenge to the Islamic government in the aftermath of the 2009 presidential election repudiated the state by co-opting and subverting its ideology in order to attack it. Large segments of the population, together with "scores of old Islamist revolutionaries" who "renounced their earlier ideas and warned of the dangers of a religious state to both religion and the state,"[56] brought the conflict with the regime's ideology into the open on Iran's streets and in virtual spaces. They challenged the state's "rigidity," and claimed their "civil rights,"[57] a defiance that does not necessarily contradict religion. On the contrary, the movement harnessed the

---

[55] Ibid.     [56] Ibid., p. 11–12.

[57] In harmony with Bayat's conception of "rights," Dabashi refrains from referring to the Green Movement as "revolutionary" in favor of calling it a "civil rights movement." See Hamid Dabashi, "Expert: Protesters want civil rights, not revolution." Interview by John Roberts, CNN, June 22, 2009.
http://am.blogs.cnn.com/2009/06/22/expert-protestors-want-civil-rights-not-revolution.

power of both religion and the government's religio-political symbols in order to emphasize "rights" and attack the state's "monopoly" on Islamic truth with which the government legitimized itself.

Thus, Iran's Green Movement may have failed to impel the government to cancel the election results, but it forced the regime's hand by exposing it as a state that rules through coercive power instead of the ballot box. The uprising also succeeded in developing a subversive counter-narrative to potent Islamic and revolutionary symbols by shattering the regime's hegemony over self-legitimating religious discourse. If, for example, Imam Husayn's seventh-century martyrdom was a vaunted symbol in the state's ideological repertoire, then activists in 2009 appropriated that legacy to sanction and sanctify their protest as a day of action in which the righteous weak stood in revolutionary defiance of the illegitimate state "usurper of power." If spearheading Palestine's (and with it Jerusalem's) liberation was a source of the Islamic Republic's political, religious, and ideological legitimacy, then Palestine too became a symbol of protest that dissidents appropriated in 2009 in order to attack the state's "occupation" of power in Iran. Thus, the Green Movement's effectiveness came not only from its popular marches in the street, but also from the discourse that it employed against the government.

### 1.4 The Ideological Universes of 1979 and 2009

During the era of Reza Shah (r. 1925–1941), the founder of the two-monarch Pahlavi dynasty, the prevailing socio-political paradigm of society, the opposition, and the state shared the same ideological milieu: secular nationalism.[58] During the reign of the last Pahlavi monarch, however, the ideology of the opposition began to change. As a result of the pervasive influence of such ideologues as Ahmad Fardid,[59] Jalal Al Ahmad, ʿAli Shariʿati, Ayatollah Taleqani, Ayatollah Mottahari, Ayatollah Khomeini and others, the Shah's critics started to analyze and critique him through the prism of Islam. Consequently, the

---

[58] Moaddel, *Class, Politics, and Ideology in the Iranian Revolution*, p. 144.
[59] For a fascinating and critical read on Ahmad Fardid, the back story to his notion of "Westoxification" (*gharbzadegi*), and its harmful consequences for Iranian political thought, see Ali Mirsepassi's *Transnationalism in Iranian Political Thought: The Life and Times of Ahmad Fardid* (Cambridge, Cambridge University Press, 2017).

movement in 1978–1979 differed from its predecessors in that its ideology effectively canceled the ideological universe of the state, precipitating a revolutionary predicament in which the triumph of one inevitably meant the total destruction of the other:

> A revolutionary situation is shaped by revolutionary discourse. It is not simply a condition of dual sovereignty. It is a dual sovereignty constituted by and through two mutually negating ideological universes – the state's ideology and the ideology of the opposition. Revolutionary discourse contradicts the discourse of the state and advances an alternative way of viewing – and seeking solutions to – the problem of social life through direct, unmediated revolutionary action of the masses.[60]

In 2009, the Green Movement did not necessarily set out an ideology that "negated" the state's worldview as the revolutionary movement had done in 1979. Rather, it accomplished something entirely different but equally forceful: contesting the ownership and meaning of the "sacred" symbols of the Iranian Revolution as championed by its offspring, the Islamic Republic. By appropriating and reprogramming those symbols and history, they sanctioned their nonviolent assault on the Islamic Republic's ideology and the symbols of its legitimation.

It is important to note that the Green Movement's use of Islamic symbols to contest the legitimacy of an Islamic government is not without precedent. According to Hamid Dabashi:

> From the Umayyads (661–750) to the ʿAbbasids (750–1258) down to all other major and minor Islamic empires and dynasties, there has never been an Islamic form of government that has not been radically challenged and opposed in precisely Islamic terms. As soon as a dynasty has come to power in Islamic terms of legitimacy, a revolutionary movement has arisen to challenge it in precisely Islamic terms.[61]

The Green Movement is the latest manifestation of this historical trend. Certainly, the dynamism of the Green Movement cannot be simply categorized as "Islamic," but it undoubtedly arose to challenge the Islamic Republic "in precisely Islamic terms." By strategically co-opting the core Islamic symbols of the state, the 2009 uprising fired an ideological blow against the state more powerful than any weapon,

---

[60] Moaddel, *Class, Politics, and Ideology in the Iranian Revolution*, pp. 18–19.
[61] Hamid Dabashi, *Iran: A People Interrupted* (New York and London: The New Press, 2007), p. 218.

which is precisely why the government dealt more harshly with the protesters arrested on ʿAshura than on any other day of action. The state accused captured demonstrators of "waging war on God"[62] and "desecrating"[63] the anniversary of Husayn's seventh-century martyrdom simply because they used his sacrality to castigate the Islamic government ruling under the sacred canopy of his legacy.

In the year 680 CE in the desert city of Karbala, Husayn, a quintessential figure in Shiʿism, died a martyr's death that has reverberated throughout Islamic history and beyond. Surrounded and outnumbered, Husayn and his small band of followers refused to pledge allegiance (baiʿah) to those they believed usurped the Caliphate and subverted the message of Husayn's grandfather, the Prophet Muhammad. This death created a legacy in which Shiʿism's moral authority is based on its posture of resistance. Once it achieves power, it ceases to be the Shiʿism of Husayn's martyrdom – one of defiance against power and oppression – and instead assumes the mantle of those who murdered Husayn. In Dabashi's view, it is "morally triumphant when it is politically defiant, and that it morally fails when it politically succeeds."[64] Simply put, Shiʿism thrives on failure and fails upon success. This explains why Shiʿism has a long history of revolt, from the time of Husayn and those who after his martyrdom sought to avenge his death, to subsequent Shiʿite uprisings such as the Nuqtavi, the Hurrifiyya, and the relatively recent Babi revolts, all of which were rooted in Shiʿite millenarianism.[65] Dabashi affirms that in order for Shiʿism to remain morally potent, it "must always be in a posture of resistance."[66] Thus, while the Islamic government in Iran is doctrinally

---

[62] "Ezheī az eʿdām-i 3 nafar az dastgīrshodegān-i ʿāshūrā khabar dād," Rahesabz, January 1, 2009. www.rahesabz.net/story/6865/.

[63] "Rāhpaymāī-ye mardom sarāsar-i keshvar ʿalayh-i bīḥormatī beh ʿāshūrā," Khabar Online, December 30, 2009. www.khabaronline.ir/detail/33396/.

[64] Hamid Dabashi, *Shiʿism: A Religion of Protest* (Cambridge and London: The Belknap Press of Harvard University Press, 2011), p. xvi.

[65] That is not to say that Shiʿism has not experienced moments of political quietism or has not been used to empower the state. ʿAli Shariʿati has written and talked extensively about the difference between Safavid Shiʿism (Black Shiʿism), which is clerically supported and designed to maintain an unjust status quo, while ʿAlavi Shiʿism (Red Shiʿism) is revolutionary and breeds resistance to tyranny. See Shariʿati's *Tashīʿeh ʿalavī va tashīʿeh ṣafavī*. For a more thorough reading on Shariʿati's life and impact, see Ali Rahnema, *An Islamic Utopian: A Political Biography of Ali Shariʿati* (New York: I.B. Tauris, 2000).

[66] Dabashi, *Shiʿism*, p. 313.

rooted in Shiʿism, it paradoxically and unwittingly assumes the mantle of those who murdered the Prophet's grandson, the cornerstone of Shiʿism's martyrology.[67] Conversely, the Islamic Republic has produced a resistance to it in the form of the Green Movement that is not necessarily "Islamic" but has utilized the emotive power of Shiʿism and the ideological universe of the Islamic government in order to legitimize its defiance while delegitimizing the authority of the state.

It is important to note that the Green Movement shares other important characteristics with its predecessors. Modern Iran's political movements, from the Tobacco Revolt (1890–1892) through to the Constitutional Revolution (1905–1911), Mossadeq's nationalist movement (1951–1953), the Iranian Revolution (1978–1979), and the Green Uprising (2009), underscore an unrelenting popular struggle to create a political system in which nobody, especially the country's leadership, is above the rule of law. Iranians of all political backgrounds have fought and sacrificed for generations to foster a system in which the head of state – Nasir al-Din Shah in the case of the Tobacco Revolt – does not freely sell monopoly rights to an important crop to foreign interests, or "the Leader of the Revolution" does not validate an election fraught with irregularities. For decades they have struggled for a government that is independent of foreign powers, is not rife with corruption, and does not arrest and torture political dissidents to induce confessions to be shamefully broadcast to national audiences, as occurred under both the last Pahlavi Shah and the Islamic Republic.[68]

## 1.5 Modern Sources for a Modern Movement: Research and Protest in the Digital Age

Green Movement activists negated the state's ideology, not by producing an alternative to the ideological universe of the state as the revolutionaries of 1978–1979 had done, but by taking ownership of

---

[67] For more on the topic of martyrdom in Islam, see David Cook, *Martyrdom in Islam* (Cambridge and New York: Cambridge University Press, 2007).
[68] See Ervand Abrahamian, *Tortured Confessions: Prisons and Public Recantations in Modern Iran* (Berkeley: University of California Press, 1999). For a personal account of forced confessions, see Maziar Bahari, *Then They Came for Me: A Family's Story of Love, Captivity, and Survival* (New York: Random House, 2011).

the symbols of the state, Islam, and the Iranian Revolution in order to subvert the Islamic government. By 2009, Iran's youth had fully entered the digital age, which ensures that these activists left a digital footprint to substantiate for posterity their strategies, actions, and intentions.

Thus, a constant feature of these chapters is the role of technology, the internet, and social media, and how they empowered activists both to document the history of the uprising as they were making it, and to register their protest digitally. Citizen journalists uploaded thousands of videos that constitute a video archive, providing the Persian-language researcher with a digital window onto events and a way of assessing the uprising's common themes, repertoires of action, activists' demands, slogans, and strategies, as well as the state's conduct. If the Iranian Revolution was the "world's first televised revolution,"[69] then the Green Uprising was the first socially broadcasted revolt in which citizens were their own camerawomen, cameramen, and reporters, and social media and YouTube were the channels through which their raw, grainy footage reached national and international audiences. In other words, they televised their own "pixelated revolution."[70]

YouTube account holder Mehdi Saharkhiz became a main source of video of events in Iran. He first began uploading videos that he received in a mass email.[71] The amateur videos became widely circulated when mainstream news channels like CNN "picked them up and broadcasted them"[72] to people around the world. Activists who heard about his online presence began sending videos directly to him, which became especially important with the state blocking access to YouTube and social media websites after the start of the uprising. Thus, Saharkhiz, who posted the videos with English and Persian titles, served as a

---

[69] Ali Ansari, *Confronting Iran: The Failure of American Foreign Policy and the Next Great Conflict in the Middle East* (New York: Basic Books, 2006), p. 83. Bani Sadr called it "the first revolution in the world whereby the leadership enjoyed such unprecedented coverage." See Abolhassan Banisadr, interview recorded by Zia Sedghi, May 21, 22, 1984, Paris, France. Iranian Oral History Collection, Harvard University, Transcript 5 (seq. 101). Accessed April 22, 2015.

[70] To borrow artist Rahib Mroué's phrase "pixelated revolution" in reference to the Arab Spring uprisings quoted in Kathrin Peters, "Images of protest: On the 'woman in the blue bra' and relational testimony," in Martin Butler, Paul Mecheril, and Lea Brenningmeyer (eds.), *Subjects, Representations, Contexts* (Bielefeld: Transcript Verlag, 2017), p. 140.

[71] Mehdi Saharkhiz, personal interview, May 19, 2013.     [72] Ibid.

conduit for hundreds of time-stamped videos that activists risked their lives to record and transmit through file-sharing websites such as Dropbox and Media Fire.[73] He spent hours organizing, translating, and uploading the files because he knew that the uprising was "very historical" and he wanted it "to be recorded in history because it wasn't something that happened very often."[74]

An estimated 200 foreign media journalists[75] covering the election were either "invited" to leave the country when the post-election uprising erupted, or left after burdensome restrictions prevented them from doing their job effectively.[76] Saharkhiz and the countless citizen journalists filming events, however, wanted the government to know that although foreign journalists were no longer on the ground to record the state's brutality, watchful eyes nevertheless ensured that the "regime's brutality was recorded and broadcasted to the world," in the hope that the visual documentation of bloodshed would render the state "less likely to harm people."[77] Recording government repression makes it far more difficult for the state to commit wholesale violence or to deny doing so. As Saharkhiz put it: "We're able to identify a police car that runs over a protester and have proof of this, not from one angle, not from two angles, but three different angles. That makes even governments change the way they behave because there is proof of every wrong move."[78] Thus, as a consequence of the expulsion of foreign journalists, activists' raw footage from the events make for an invaluable data trove.

Many risked everything to participate, document, and share with the world the details of their historic uprising (Figure 1.2).[79] Unfortunately, since some of these videos contained incriminating evidence of personal involvement in anti-state activity, many Iran-based users

---

[73] Ibid.   [74] Ibid.

[75] Director Ramin Asgar, Dubai, to Central Intelligence Agency et al., June 13, 2009, Wikileaks, https://search.wikileaks.org/plusd/cables/09RPODUBAI247_a.html.

[76] Kay McGowan, Dubai, to Central Intelligence Agency et al., July 29, 2009, Wikileaks, https://search.wikileaks.org/plusd/cables/09RPODUBAI306_a.html.

[77] Mehdi Saharkhiz, personal interview.

[78] Mehdi Saharkhiz, "My YouTube story: Mehdi Saharkhiz," online video clip, YouTube, May 12, 2010. Accessed October 2, 2014. http://youtu.be/AbKqXt8F8fo.

[79] Pouya Alimagham, "YouTube deleted files screenshot." 2018. JPEG file.

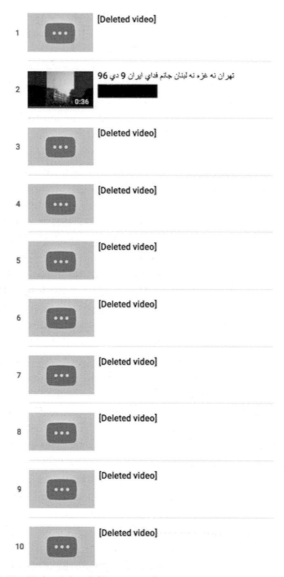

**Figure 1.2** YouTube deleted files screenshot.
The videos of the Iranian protests in late 2017 and 2018 (see Chapter 6) have met a similar fate. Of the sample of ten videos saved onto my playlist, all but one have been removed. The videos dating back to the Green Uprising of nearly a decade before are even harder to locate on YouTube.
Photo credit: Pouya Alimagham

removed their uploaded videos, and some must have been forced to delete them.

For the purposes of this research, all the footage cited has been downloaded, catalogued, and archived as the long-term availability of these videos becomes increasingly limited. Where a file is cited that was available on YouTube but has since been taken down, the original along with its full file information is stored in the author's archive and will not be re-uploaded in order not to jeopardize the safety of those who captured the footage.

Other digital sources empower this study. In 2013, Ervand Abrahamian, the eminent historian of modern Iran, noted: "the State Department has failed to observe its own declassification rule and has found various excuses for delaying the release of documents on Iran..." and "it is easier for a camel to pass through the eye of a needle than for a historian to gain access to the CIA and MI6 files on the coup."[80] The Anglo-American coup culminated on August 19, 1953, yet seasoned historians such as Abrahamian have long struggled to access state files on a fateful event that transpired more than half a century ago. It has been even more difficult to obtain diplomatic and intelligence files pertaining to the more recent 1978–1979 revolution. Yet, the massive and historic leaks orchestrated by such people of conscience as Chelsea Manning and Edward Snowden provide rare access to diplomatic files on the 2009 uprising that may not otherwise have been accessible for another fifty or more years. It is important to note that this study does not overly rely on these cables; the politically sensitive material chronicled in the diplomatic documents has been thoroughly corroborated. For instance, one cable relevant to Chapter 5 noted the abuse of activists detained at Kahrizak, a report confirmed through the Iranian government's semi-official Mehr News Agency. Contested information is also cross-referenced. Chapter 3, for example, quotes Tehran's mayor in 2009, Muhammad Baqir Qalibaf, as stating in an online publication that three million people partici-pated in the historic June 15 march. The page was subsequently taken down; doubtless the government did not want officials publicly admit-ting such numbers. The estimate, however, was not only echoed in US

---

[80] Abrahamian invokes chapter 7 (verse 40) of the Quran to highlight the impossibility of gaining access to such files. See Ervand Abrahamian, *The Coup: 1953, the CIA, and the Roots of Modern U.S.-Iranian Relations* (New York and London: The New Press, 2013), pp. 6, 149.

diplomatic cables, but activist footage taken on a pedestrian overpass clearly records a monumental turnout. It is fitting that the study of one of the twenty-first century's first and most dynamic uprisings has been able to harness such recent sources as both diplomatic cables[81] and modern media such as YouTube, social media, and the internet in general to document personal testimonies, analyze acts of protest, and consider the informative writings of those on the ground in Iran who struggled on behalf of the Green Movement.

## 1.6 Outline of the Book

The post-1979 government was fiercely independent, yet did not speak with a single voice. The plurality of worldviews, therefore, is important to this study as it outlines how a faction within the power structure ultimately transitioned to become key reformist figures around which the Green Movement coalesced. As such, Chapter 2 chronicles Iran's political history between the 1978–1979 revolution and the eve of the presidential election of 2009.

Since crowd action was such a spectacular and memorable part of the movement's history, Chapter 3 utilizes digital sources to explain how the movement crystallized under the cover of the presidential campaign, and transformed into a protest movement in its contentious aftermath. Activists contested the state's control of the streets as an integral part of the wider campaign of co-opting the state's ideology through the appropriation of already legitimated celebrations, holidays, and anniversaries. Street marches became a potent nonviolent weapon for the Green Movement, which systematically and strategically upended religio-political holidays to register its protest against the government. One such day of action is the subject of Chapter 4. On Quds Day (Jerusalem Day), the last Friday of the holy month of Ramadan, Muslims across the Islamic world protest in solidarity with the Palestinians and against Israel's occupation, especially its seizure of East Jerusalem (Quds), the site of Islam's third holiest mosque and

---

[81] The United States embassy in Iran has been defunct since the hostage crisis of 1979–1981, with American embassies in neighboring countries serving the visa and travel needs of Iranians from Iran. Specifically, the US embassy in Dubai has also served as a major center for intelligence and data gathering on Iran.

original *qibla*.[82] Quds Day is especially important to Iran, as it was the revolutionary Islamic government that established this day of solidarity, which subsequently spread to other Muslim countries.

In 2009, in protests unprecedented in the thirty-year history of the Quds Day holiday, Green activists subverted the state's Palestine-centered symbolism in a variety of ways: denouncing Palestine in order to contradict the Islamic Republic,[83] or appropriating it so as to equate the state with the Israeli occupation. In the latter instance, they situated their resistance against the regime with that of the Palestinian struggle against the Israeli occupation.

The wider historical context of Palestine as a symbol and political cause for Iran and Iranians helps to illuminate the potency of the 2009 Quds Day protests and to explain what Palestine meant to the revolutionary generation of 1978–1979, and how the revolutionary government institutionalized Palestinian liberation as a core ideological tenet for an entire generation of Iranians raised under its authority.

Chapter 5 addresses Ayatollah Montazeri's life and his death in the tumultuous month of December 2009, which became another occasion for protest. His passing and the anti-government mourning processions provide an opportunity to examine Montazeri as a case study in post-Islamism. The customary seventh day of mourning for his death coincided with *Tasu'a* and *'Ashura*, the two days in which Shi'ite Muslims all over the world commemorate the martyrdom of Husayn and his valiant half-brother, 'Abbas. *'Ashura* has special significance for the Islamic Republic not only because it governs theoretically according to the will of the Hidden Imam, the twelfth direct descendant of the Prophet Muhammad, but also because the historic mobilization on *'Ashura* in 1978 helped bring the Iranian Revolution to its crescendo.

---

[82] Following the Jewish tradition, Jerusalem was the first *Qibla* (the direction in which Muslims the world over pray) during the early years of Muhammad's prophethood. After several years of revelation, however, he designated the Ka'ba in Mecca to serve as the *Qibla*, the first and only change in the direction of Muslim prayer.

[83] The tactic of negating the symbolic value of Palestine was so dominant and enduring that it was recycled in protests in late 2017 and early 2018. Masoud Dalvand, "Tehrān na ghazzeh na lobnān, jānam fadā'-ye īrān 9 day 96." Online video clip, YouTube, December 30, 2017. Accessed May 22, 2018. https://youtu.be/HLAG0I6YJO4.

In 1978, revolutionary Iranians in the most populous Shiʿite Muslim country harnessed ʿAshuraʾs defiant message to organize the largest anti-government march in the entire history of the Iranian Revolution. The enormity of the march helped persuade the Shah to finally abdicate and leave the country a month later. The Islamic government came to power through such a massive ʿAshura protest, and has since employed rhetoric imbued with Husayn's legacy to affirm its Islamic credentials and authority.

On December 27, 2009, however, Green activists appropriated already legitimated mourning ceremonies, deploying Husayn's legacy to equate the state with the murderers of the third Imam. Just as protesters likened the state to the Israeli occupation and themselves to the oppressed Palestinians on Quds Day, demonstrators on ʿAshura similarly cast themselves as righteous rebels akin to Husayn, and the state in the same vein as Yazid – the infamous caliph who ordered the massacre at Karbala in 680 CE. Once again they were co-opting and subverting the state's Islamic discourse, leveling it to devastating effect against the government.

Both ʿAshura and Montazeri's death are the subject of a single chapter because they occurred within days of each other and are conceptually linked. The seventh day of mourning for Montazeri's death coincided with Tasuʿa and ʿAshura, and Husayn's anniversary and Montazeri's passing work in tandem with each other in terms of post-Islamism. As with Chapter 4, foregrounding is necessary. ʿAshuraʾs history and its meaning as a cataclysmic event in Islamic history, as well as its role in mobilizing protests across the Middle East in the 1970s, are crucial to understanding the blistering anti-state message of ʿAshura, 2009.

The final chapter explains how and why the state was able to impose a temporary but meaningless "defeat" on the movement on February 11, 2010, the anniversary of the Iranian Revolution's triumph (22 Bahman). The legacy of the Green Movement is examined, together with its impact on the 2013 presidential election in which the centrist Hassan Rouhani succeeded the disputed winner of the 2009 election, Mahmoud Ahmadinejad, the potential role it played in the leadership's decision to compromise over its nuclear program in 2015, and its connection to protests in late 2017 and early 2018. The conclusion will not end by predicting the final outcome of the historic events of 2009 because it is increasingly difficult, as well as amateurish, to predict the future of Iranian history and other complex histories.

Before the study proceeds, it is important to posit a disclaimer. The Green Movement belongs to those who fought for it, risked their lives, livelihoods, and futures, and ultimately paid a heavy price for it. The question of who is allowed to speak for such a multi-faceted movement is a delicate matter. This work does not pretend to be the impossible voice of those millions of people who came out onto the streets of Iran to repudiate a domineering state. Rather, it consists of a diversity of materials, such as illuminating opinion pieces by activists, social media posts, footage from the events in question, interviews, memoirs, diplomatic cables, and Persian and English news articles from 2009. The contemporary material is intertwined with wider Iranian history, encompassing testimonies recorded in the 1980s through Harvard University's Iranian Oral History Project,[84] memoirs of veteran leaders of the 1979 revolution, diplomatic cables and news articles from the 1970s, and secondary sources. This analysis of this wide-ranging material transcends the oppressive win–lose binary, deconstructing the limiting simplicity of viewing the Green Uprising through the narrow lens of 2009, and enabling a more non-linear and in-depth discussion of the protest movement.

As for objectivity and neutrality, it is fitting and prudent to quote the fearless Sara Roy, author of *Failing Peace: Gaza and the Palestinian-Israeli Conflict*: "Neutrality is often a mask for siding with the status quo and objectivity – pure objectivity – does not exist and claiming it is dishonest."[85] In the mid-1980s, after the Iranian Revolution and during the Iran–Iraq War, my father obtained political asylum in the United States for his family of four. The revolution and war formed a big part of our family history, despite our distance from Iran. My

---

[84] Note that of 134 people interviewed for the Iranian Oral History Project (IOHP), only eleven were women, four of whom were involved by virtue of their husbands. For example, Fatemeh Pakravan's husband, General Hassan Pakravan, was the head of SAVAK (1962–1965), and was instrumental in preventing Khomeini's execution in 1963, only to himself be executed by the post-revolutionary state in 1979. The IOHP presumably interviewed her only because her husband was deceased by the time of the oral history project. Given that the IOHP disproportionately interviewed men, their insights feature more prominently in this study whenever the IOHP is sourced.

[85] Sara Roy, *Failing Peace: Gaza and the Palestinian-Israeli Conflict* (London and Ann Arbor: Pluto Press, 2007), p. xvi.

interest in Iran and the wider region took an academic turn at the University of California where I had the opportunity to learn beyond my family narrative. Yet, far from deluding myself with any notion of neutrality or objectivity when approaching the Green Movement, I have consciously deployed emotive language in an attempt to capture the intensity of the next chapter in Iran's long history of resistance. In other words, passion is part of this history, and I have sought to tell it with that in mind.

Having said that, I trust that the reader, who will likewise be invested in this work with emotion as they undertake the journey of reading it, will judge this study based on the facts and evidence.

# 2 | From the Theory of Islamic Republicanism to Practice, 1979–2009

## 2.1 War on Two Fronts

The first decade in the history of the Islamic Republic (1979–1989) was the most tumultuous. The disparate factions that united under the banner of Khomeini's broad revolutionary coalition had little in common beyond their anti-Shah fervor. After the Shah fled the country on January 16, 1979, the coalition gradually splintered into mutually hostile camps, the most violent clash of which pitted the Mujahedin-i Khalq (MEK) against the Khomeini-led clerical consolidation of power. From June 1981 until the early summer of 1982, Iran was engaged in a low-intensity civil war that claimed the lives of the prime minister, Muhammad Javad Bahonar, the president, Muhammad-Ali Rajai, the head of the judiciary and leader of the Islamic Republican Party, Ayatollah Beheshti, scores of other high-ranking leaders, and thousands of leftists caught in the state's campaign of revenge, of which the MEK bore the brunt with the loss of an estimated 30,000 lives.[1] A mailbomb almost claimed the life of Khamenei himself and disabled his right arm.

Fearful of the United States restoring the Shah to power, as it had done in 1953 with the US-led "Anglo-American coup"[2] against Muhammad Mossadeq, revolutionary student followers of Khomeini

---

[1] Anoushiravan Ehteshami, *After Khomeini: The Second Republic* (London and New York: Routledge, 1995), p. 22.

[2] The coup is often described simply as the "Anglo-American coup," which is a misnomer because it suggests that the British spearheaded the overthrow. While they certainly encouraged it, it was the American CIA that planned, provided the resources for, and executed Operation Ajax. See Mark J. Gasiorowski, "The CIA looks back at the 1953 coup in Iran," *Middle East Report*, 216 (Autumn, 2000), p. 4. For a more detailed account of the US role, see Gasiorowski's earlier work on the coup in which he notes, *inter alia*, that even British assets such as the Rashidian brothers, who were integral to the coup, had been "turned over to the CIA by MI6 when the British left Tehran in November 1952," and that Zahedi, the coup's "nominal leader, hid in a CIA safehouse until the coup was virtually

seized the US embassy – the same institution through which the Central Intelligence Agency (CIA) had staged the overthrow twenty-six years earlier. The November 4 capture of the diplomatic mission occurred against the backdrop of the Shah's arrival in the United States for cancer treatment on October 22. Iranian revolutionaries worried that the Shah's admission to New York for medical reasons was a ruse designed to conceal the first stage in a counter-revolutionary coup orchestrated by the United States through its embassy in Tehran. Consequently, militant students sacked the embassy and held its staff hostage to ward off any such conspiracy. Khomeini did not order the attack, but endorsed it *ex post facto* to affirm his anti-imperialist credentials – a popular move given the country's long history of falling victim to foreign intervention. Khomeini exploited these anti-imperialist sentiments and international crises – including the subsequent Iraqi invasion – to consolidate power. During the vote on the draft constitution, for instance, which was held while Iran was deep in the throes of the hostage crisis, Khomeini outmaneuvered opposition by factions including his provisional prime minister, Mehdi Bazargan,[3] by arguing that voting against the Islamic constitution during the stand-off with the US was akin to siding with imperialism.[4]

The hostage crisis left the country isolated, and the post-revolutionary purges depleted its military strength, rendering the country vulnerable to foreign aggression. Saddam Hussein seized the opportunity to order the invasion of Iran, a ruinous eight-year undertaking that was to become the longest conventional war of the twentieth century. During the first two years of the war, Iran was burdened with internal as well as external conflicts – dealing with infighting while also trying to retrieve Iraqi-occupied territory. Once the Khomeinists had largely defeated their most determined challengers in the form of the

---

completed." Gasiorowski, "The 1953 coup d'état in Iran," *International Journal of Middle East Studies*, 19(3) (August 1987), pp. 272, 277.

[3] According to Abrahamian, Bazargan and his Liberation Movement aspired to a constitution that was modeled on Charles de Gaulle's Fifth Republic; a republic that was "Islamic in name but democratic in content." The final product bears the stamp of the competing visions of Bazargan and Khomeini, which produced a constitution that has dual sovereignty split between "divine rights and the rights of man; between theocracy and democracy…" Ervand Abrahamian, *A History of Modern Iran* (Cambridge and New York: Cambridge University Press, 2008), p. 163.

[4] Ibid., p. 168.

MEK, the state was able to devote all of its attention and resources to liberating the border regions.

The war became a focal point of tension among the Khomeini-led Islamists. The radical internationalist faction that wanted Iran to prioritize spearheading Islamic resistance and revolution throughout the Muslim world included, among others, Mir Hussein Mousavi, Khomeini's prime minister throughout the 1980s; Ayatollah Hussein ʿAli Montazeri, the one-time designated successor to Khomeini; Montazeri's famously zealous son, Muhammad; Ayatollah Mohtashamipour, the Iranian ambassador to Syria from 1982 to 1986 who along with Montazeri served as a key architect in exporting Iran's ideology to Lebanon; and Behzad Nabavi, a founder of the Mujahedin of the Islamic Revolution Organization (MIR). For those in the left-leaning Islamist faction, social justice at home, the total emancipation of Palestine, and other international liberation struggles warranted the Islamic Revolution's unbridled commitment. In other words, Iran was a springboard for a wider Islamic Revolution that would free the world's Muslims from Western imperial servitude. By contrast, the conservative faction held that the Iraq war was paramount, and had little stomach for opening up other fronts that would divert resources and manpower from the central battlefield.

Montazeri had much in common with the Islamic left in terms of his global outlook. During his four stints in prison in pre-revolutionary Iran, he held many discussions with leftists, expanding his knowledge beyond his seminary studies and increasing his understanding of international causes. His son, Muhammad, also played an important role in developing his father's worldview. Throughout the 1970s, Muhammad had traveled from Afghanistan and Pakistan across the Middle East to Europe, creating a transnational network of activists along the way.[5] Like so many in the Iranian guerrilla movement of the 1970s, he saw Palestine as a vanguard liberation struggle, and received training in asymmetrical warfare from Palestinians in Lebanon.[6] After the revolution, when the elder Montazeri was placed in charge of the newly created Liberation Movements Unit (LMU) within the Islamic Revolutionary Guards Corps (IRGC), Muhammad worked with his

[5] Sussan Siavoshi, *Montazeri: The Life and Thought of Iran's Revolutionary Ayatollah* (Cambridge: Cambridge University Press, 2017), p. 125.
[6] Ibid.

father on real-world applications of these ideals. While the IRGC was formed to safeguard the revolution by protecting its leadership – an urgent necessity given that the Anglo-American overthrow of 1953 succeeded by using a faction within the military to topple Mossadeq – the LMU was established to assist Islamic resistance movements from Afghanistan to Palestine.

1982 was a pivotal year. The power struggle in Iran largely came to an end with the Khomeinists prevailing over the liberals and the radical left, and the Revolutionary Guards fought alongside the Iranian army in Operation Bayt al-Moqaddas[7] to liberate Khorramshahr after a brutal two-year siege. Less than two weeks later, on June 6, 1982, Israel invaded Lebanon to eject the entrenched forces of the Palestine Liberation Organization. The invasion gave the radical faction within the Islamist camp in Iran the opportunity to implement their vision of Islamic resistance and revolution abroad, and co-founded what would become one of the most effective unconventional fighting forces in the world – Hizbullah.

Emboldened by military successes at the battlefront, Khomeini – despite his hesitancy[8] – heeded the advice of those who, like ʿAli Akbar Hashemi Rafsanjani, advocated a counter-invasion of Iraq, and pushed forward with the express purpose of overthrowing Saddam and liberating the Shiʿite shrine cities. The war dragged on for another six years, during which the pendulum occasionally swung in Iran's favor, such as when it occupied the strategic Faw Peninsula in February 1986. The occupation of Faw ended in 1988 only after Iraq launched extensive chemical attacks on Iranian forces.[9] The war ultimately concluded after a host of Arab and Western countries[10] poured

---

[7] According to Afshon Ostovar, prior to Bani's Sadr's fall, he "attempted to cultivate a closer relationship with the military" since he did not have his own constituency. Thus, as commander-in-chief, Bani Sadr empowered the military – at the expense of the IRGC – to lead the war effort. His ousting in the spring of 1981 enabled the IRGC to have more of a say in the conduct of war planning. This development combined with the near completion of the post-revolutionary power struggle in 1982 to allow the state and the IRGC to focus on the battlefront. Afshon Ostovar, *Vanguard of the Imam: Religion, Politics, and Iran's Revolutionary Guards* (New York: Oxford University Press, 2016), pp. 70–79.

[8] Ibid., p. 80.       [9] Ibid., p. 97.

[10] Western support of Iraq was limited not only to quantity of arms but also to their quality: "Although France's military sales to Iraq were about a third of what the USSR provided Saddam – approximately $4.5 billion 1982 and

hardware, manpower, and billions of dollars into the Iraqi war machine, eventually convincing Iran that toppling Saddam was a lost cause. Kuwait, Saudi Arabia, and even the United States became directly involved in the conflict at one point in what became known as the Tankers War. The Reagan administration also provided funding, logistical support, and crucial diplomatic cover at the United Nations (UN) throughout much of the war. Long before the US-led invasion of Iraq in the spring of 2003 over allegations of the existence of weapons of mass destruction (WMD),[11] Saddam's regime had used chemical weapons on Iranian troops and civilians. At the time, the USA protected Iraq diplomatically when Iran protested at the UN.[12] When on July 3, 1988 the USS *Vincennes*, a guided missile cruiser, accidently shot down an Iranian passenger plane, Iran Air Flight 655, Iranian leaders interpreted the tragedy as a signal from the United States that it would never let Iran win the now long-running conflict with Iraq.[13]

In contrast to Iraq, Iran was largely without allies during the war. Syria, and to a much lesser extent Libya, were the only Arab governments that did not support Iraq. The former's support for Iran was vital to the strategy of enveloping Iraq from east and west. Syria's support meant that Baghdad was prevented from exporting its oil via pipelines that ran through Syria, rendering Iraq dependent on shipping lanes that were vulnerable to Iranian attacks in the Persian Gulf. Against the backdrop of the war and of Syria's role as a conduit in Iran's efforts to establish and sustain Hizbullah, Iran welcomed all the

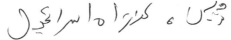

1986 – they included some of Iraq's most sophisticated weaponry, including the Mirage F-1 and Super Étendard combat fighter aircraft, Super Frelon helicopters, and Exocet AM39 air-to-surface missles." Ibid., p. 82.

[11] Saddam's regime had been effectively disarmed of WMD by 1998.

[12] The United States provided Iraq with satellite intelligence of Iranian troop movements, knowing Iraq would use chemical weapons to ward off an Iranian attack. See Shane Harris and Matthew M. Aid, "Exclusive: CIA files prove America helped Saddam as he gassed Iran," *Foreign Policy*, August 26, 2013. Accessed June 28, 2018. https://foreignpolicy.com/2013/08/26/exclusive-cia-files-prove-america-helped-saddam-as-he-gassed-iran/. For the US role in scuttling Iran's attempts at the UN to hold Iraq accountable for such use of banned chemical weapons, see Juan Cole, "US protected Iraq at UN from Iranian charges of chemical weapons use," *Informed Comment*, August 28, 2013. Accessed June 28, 2018. www.juancole.com/2013/08/protected-charges-chemical.html.

[13] Ostovar, *Vanguard of the Imam*, p. 99.

revolutions that took place in the Arab Uprisings era except the one in the Levantine country.

## 2.2 The Learning Curve: Revolutionary Statecraft and Education

The war ended nearly two months after the downing of Iran Air Flight 655. Less than a year later, on June 3, 1989, Khomeini died – only the second twentieth-century Iranian leader to pass away in the country and not in exile or while under house arrest.[14] The end of the war did not result in the demobilization of the IRGC. The military force, originally founded to protect the leadership of the revolution, was deemed too ideologically and organizationally important to be disbanded, even though the war was over and the state no longer faced any serious domestic challengers. Instead, the mandate of the revolutionary state's bastion of devotees was expanded during Rafsanjani's presidency (1989–1997) – with the blessing of Khomeini's successor, ʿAli Khamenei – to encompass social, cultural, and economic spheres in order to shore up the regime's support base. At the same time, Rafsanjani worked with the conservative power structure to sideline the radical, left-leaning faction. For example, when screening candidates for the parliamentary elections of 1992, the Guardian Council prevented candidates such as Nabavi and Mohtashamipour from standing for office.[15] With these left-leaning Islamists removed from power, Rafsanjani's government of technocrats was free to institute an era of privatization of state-owned industries and structural adjustment for the purposes of economic reform and post-war reconstruction.[16]

---

[14] The only other leader to die in Iran while not under house arrest was Mozzafar ad-Din Shah, who passed away quietly in Tehran in 1907. His successors, Muhammad Ali Shah and Ahmad Shah, died in exile in Sanremo, Italy in 1925 and Paris, France in 1930, respectively. Reza Shah passed away in 1944 in exile in Johannesburg, South Africa. Muhammad Mossadeq died while under house arrest in Ahmadabad in 1967. Muhammad Reza Shah died in exile in Cairo, Egypt in 1980.

[15] Mohtashamipour, who served as Interior Minister in the late 1980s, was left out of Rafsanjani's cabinet after the latter assumed the presidency in 1989. That his absence persisted despite 130 members of parliament signing a letter urging the president to reinstate him attests to the ascendancy of the conservatives and the marginalization of the radicals. Ehteshami, *After Khomeini*, pp. 59–60.

[16] Ehteshami and Zweiri note that such reforms were so comprehensive that they garnered the approval of the International Monetary Fund (IMF). Anoushiravan

The continuity of the revolution under Rafsanjani and Khamenei's dual leadership prioritized fostering Iran's Islamic system, with a pragmatic approach to foreign policy.[17] The objective was to reform the economy, partly by improving the country's international relations to attract foreign finance.[18] However, support for Hizbullah, the state's most important foreign policy success, continued. Radicals such as Mohtashamipour, Nabavi, and Montazeri, the latter of whom was eventually placed under house arrest, became marginal actors in Iran's political life throughout the 1990s.[19] Mousavi and his wife, Zahra

Ehteshami and Mahjoob Zweiri, *Iran and the Rise of Its Neoconservatives: The Politics of Tehran's Silent Revolution* (London and New York: I.B. Tauris, 2007), p. 4. Siavoshi notes that Montazeri was vehemently opposed to foreign borrowing, believing that independence was "at the core" of the revolution, "and foreign borrowing, in his view, was its antithesis." Siavoshi, *Montazeri*, p. 163.

[17] So pragmatic was this faction that its figurehead, Rafsanjani, was the key figure facilitating the purchase of American arms and spare parts through Israel during the Iran–Iraq War. These purchases were part of a complex web that included overpriced, illegal weapons sales to Iran to persuade its government to use its clout over pro-Iran groups in Lebanon during the civil war to release US hostages. The profits of such inflated sales were then, in violation of the congressional Boland Amendment, sent to counter-revolutionary right-wing death squads ("the Contras") in Nicaragua. The entire scandal became known as the "Iran–Contra Affair" and almost brought down Reagan's presidency. Iranian revolutionaries who had long derided the United States as "The Great Satan" were as embarrassed as the Reagan administration, which had promised never to "negotiate with terrorists." The American-backed ally on the other side of the war, Saddam Hussein, predictably felt betrayed by his American counterparts. Many believe that the US involvement in the subsequent Tankers War phase of the Iran–Iraq War aimed to placate its ally in Baghdad. For more on how the Iranian government compromised on its ideology in favor of pragmatism, see Adam Tarock, *Iran's Foreign Policy Since 1990: Pragmatism Supersedes Islamic Ideology* (Hauppauge: Nova Science Publishers, 1999).

[18] Ehteshami, *After Khomeini*, p. 42.
[19] The radical faction was at odds with the conservatives over economic, social, and foreign policies, the latter formally precipitating the clash that led to it being ousted from the corridors of power. The radicals wanted to assist Islamic liberation movements worldwide, prioritized combating imperialism and Zionism, and were emphatically opposed to buying US weapons via Israel during the Iraq war. The office of Mehdi Hashemi, the brother of Montazeri's son-in-law, Hadi, leaked the secret arms dealings that Rafsanjani headed. The strategy backfired, however, as Khomeini sided with Rafsanjani, and Hashemi was arrested and executed. The scandal, Hashemi's execution and that of others after the MEK's Operation Merced, prompted Montazeri's break with the regime and the sidelining of the radical faction. Ostovar, *Vanguard of the Imam*, pp. 118–120.

Rahnavard, however, remained politically active indirectly, eventually serving as presidential advisors to Rafsanjani's successor, Muhammad Khatami (r. 1997–2005), a junior cleric and parliamentarian whom Mousavi had appointed[20] Minister of Culture and Islamic Guidance in 1982.[21]

From the onset, the revolutionary state sought to improve the lot of the underprivileged by distributing confiscated agro-business lands and allocating a quarter of its annual budget to subsidize basic foodstuffs as well as fuel.[22] Furthermore, under the banner that education was an "Islamic right," the government set about transforming the country's educational system and improving literacy levels from a massive 63.5 percent illiteracy rate for the total population aged fifteen and above (51.8 percent for men and 75.6 percent for women).[23] The state's goal was to achieve social justice by improving schooling, closing the educational gap that separated the rich from the poor.[24] The focus on improving literacy in the Persian language[25] was highly successful. In the revolution's first decade, for instance, there was a 50 percent increase in enrollment of girls in primary schools.[26] By 2008, there

---

[20] Khatami returned the favor when he appointed Mousavi head of the Iranian Academy of the Arts in 1999.

[21] It is important to note that censorship during the Pahlavi period was strict, but those reading texts for subversive material were merely low-level bureaucrats. Censorship under the Islamic government, however, reached new levels. The people reading books for nonconformist or subversive meanings were ideologically committed employees who took their jobs much more seriously than their predecessors. On his appointment as Minister of Culture and Islamic Guidance, Khatami tried to relax the stringent vetting of books, complaining of a suffocating, backward climate. When the conservative press attacked him, he quietly resigned his post to serve as the director of the National Library.

[22] Abrahamian, *A History of Modern Iran*, p. 180.

[23] Golnar Mehran, "Social implications of literacy in Iran," *Comparative Education Review*, 36(2) (May 1992), p. 194–195. Mehran notes that there was also an urban–rural divide with 44 percent of the urban population and 83 percent of the rural population unable to read.

[24] Golnar Mehran, "The paradox of tradition and modernity in female education in the Islamic Republic of Iran," *Comparative Education Review*, 47(3) (2003), p. 278.

[25] In order to foster a more cohesive national community, the literacy campaign focused on Persian and Quranic Arabic to the exclusion of Iran's diverse linguistic heritage.

[26] Ali Akbar Mahdi, "The Iranian women's movement: A century long struggle," *The Muslim World*, 94 (October 2004), p. 427–448, p. 441.

had been a dramatic rise in literacy rates for women, which reached 96 percent.[27]

While many women from secular middle- and upper-class backgrounds, as well as women from non-Muslim religious communities, found the new Islamic educational order restrictive, others saw it as an opening. Among the government's Islamization measures were single-sex grade-school classrooms taught by members of the same sex,[28] and mandatory veiling for girls as early as age six, which were viewed positively by more traditional women – especially those from the lower social strata.[29] Whereas many conservative families had previously objected to education for their daughters, regarding schools and universities as godless dens of vice, they now heeded the state's encouragement to send them to school, believing that the Islamization of the educational system and the observance of "appropriate behavior" rendered such opposition moot.[30] The government's goal was to "create the ideal female citizen who is socialized, politicized, and Islamized and can serve traditional needs of a religious society as well as the modern demands of the country."[31] The aim was to produce exemplary wives and mothers for the home – women who were at the same time publicly engaged in Iran's economic, social, and political life.[32]

As part of its Islamization of education, the regime established a committee, which included ʿAbdulkarim Soroush, to launch a Cultural Revolution. In 1980 it closed down the university system for three years to purge students and faculty members with non-conformist, especially Marxist, ideological leanings. At the same time, the state embarked upon expanding primary and secondary education. On re-opening the universities, the government initially deemed some fields

---

[27] Alex Shams, "Revolutionary religiosity and women's access to higher education in the Islamic Republic of Iran," *Journal of Middle East Women's Studies*, 12(1) (March 2016), p. 129.

[28] Universities were not segregated by gender. In addition, as a result of a shortage of classrooms in rural areas as well as a lack of female teachers, rural schools were often mixed and taught by male instructors. Mehran, "The paradox of tradition and modernity," p. 277.

[29] Mahdi, "The Iranian women's movement," p. 436–437.

[30] Mehran, "Social implications of literacy in Iran," p. 200.

[31] Mehran, "The paradox of tradition and modernity," p. 270.

[32] Ibid., p. 274–275.

of study "feminine" and "masculine," and closed them to the opposite gender.[33] Men were precluded from studying fields "inappropriate" for males, such as gynecology, nursing, family health, dental hygiene, and fashion design; women were prohibited from studying rigorous and physically demanding subjects as agriculture, veterinary medicine, animal husbandry, natural resources, and mining and petroleum engineering.[34] All such restrictions were removed by the mid-1990s after the successful lobbying of the Women's Cultural and Social Council[35] – a further testament to women's persistent drive against exclusion – though many of these gains were drastically rolled back in 2012.[36]

In 1982, a private higher education institution, Islamic Azad University, was founded. With branches opening across the country it eventually became Iran's largest university. Improved adult literacy and the expansion of the education system was designed to create the "New Muslim Person" among the youth and foster the Islamization of the adult population.[37] These improvements in literacy and access to education led to an overall increase in college-educated Iranians, with women forming the majority of university students in the first decade of the twenty-first century.[38] By 2009, women constituted almost half (43 percent) of all of master's-level students and 33 percent of doctoral students.[39]

---

[33] Mehran, "Doing and undoing gender: Female higher education in the Islamic Republic of Iran," *International Review of Education*, 55(5/6) (November 2009), p. 552.

[34] Ibid., p. 552–553.     [35] Ibid., p. 553.

[36] In 2012, universities across the country prohibited women from studying a range of fields, though each university had a different list of majors open exclusively to men. The University of Tehran, for instance, only disallowed women from majoring in mining engineering, natural resource engineering, and forestry. By contrast, the Petroleum University of Technology prohibited women from majoring in business management, industrial management, safety engineering, electrical engineering, mechanical engineering, and petroleum engineering. "Ḥazf-i paẕīresh-i dokhtarān az 77 reshteh-ye 36 dāneshgāh/ mohandesī rekorddār-i ḥazf." Mehr News Agency, August 6, 2012. Accessed July 15, 2018. https://goo.gl/nVfiPa.

[37] Mehran, "Social implications of literacy in Iran," p. 196.

[38] Khadijeh Aryan, "The boom in women's education," in Tara Povey and Elaheh Rostami-Povey (eds.), *Women, Power and Politics in 21st Century Iran* (New York: Routledge, 2016), p. 35. In contrast, women constituted less than a third (31 percent) of university students on the eve of the revolution. Mehran, "Doing and undoing gender," p. 549.

[39] Shams, "Revolutionary religiosity and women's access to higher education," p. 129.

Unintended consequences followed these reforms, however, as education produced an empowered, more globally connected citizenry with higher expectations in terms of quality of life, rights, and good governance, as well as a better understanding of the root causes of the injustices they faced at home.

## 2.3 Reformism and Deadlock

In 1997, Muhammad Khatami won a landslide presidential victory after campaigning on the promise of reforms that emphasized the polity's republican aspects over its rigid Islamist ones – political inclusion, civil and individual liberties instead of political exclusion, duties, obligations, and social restrictions. A Qom-trained disciple of Khomeini with a degree in Western philosophy from the University of Isfahan, Khatami sought to foster a more representative and accountable government that was less intrusive and patriarchal. Women were a force throughout post-revolutionary Iran,[40] but became especially consequential when they helped bring Khatami to power after he talked about ending "male supremacy" in Iran.[41] His ascendancy also marked the rise of the youth movement, members of which came of age under the Islamic Republic and voted for the first time.

The Second of Khordad Movement – the name of which is rooted in the Iranian calendar marking Khatami's election win – was aided intellectually by such thinkers as Ayatollah Montazeri, Mohsen Kadivar, who studied under Montazeri, Muhammad Mojtahed Shabestari, and Soroush, all of whom wrote influential works pertinent to Iran's experiment with Islamic government. Soroush, for example, argued that pluralism is inherent to Islam through the "diversity of interpretation of religious experiences" rooted in the "diversity of

---

[40] At the same time, the potential for women's activism in the early post-revolutionary period was hindered not just by the Islamists, but also by the left. The Organization of Iranian People's Fada'i Guerrillas (OIPFG), for instance, de-prioritized "…raising issues affecting women's personal lives, relations between the sexes, or any discussion of Islamic Sharia in this respect" in favor of "'more important' political goals and the long-term interests of the anti-imperialist struggle…" Haideh Moghissi, *Populism and Feminism in Iran: Women's Struggle in a Male-Defined Revolutionary Movement* (New York: St. Martin's Press, 1994), p. 122.

[41] Ahmad Siddiqi, "Khatami and the search for reform in Iran," *Stanford Journal of International Relations*, 6(1) (2005).

understanding religious texts" rendering religion incompatible with a religious state based on dogmatism.[42] Rather, he harnessed this Islamic pluralism to posit that Islam is compatible with democracy ("religious democracy").[43] In other words, the Reform Movement did not begin with Khatami, but had its roots in such thinkers and in the civil society that had transcended the Islamism of the state without repudiating religion.

Khatami, along with many of those who had been sidelined or grew disillusioned and stepped down from positions of power, exemplified the trend by which many of the early leaders of the Islamic Republic had transitioned to becoming reformists after witnessing – or, in the case of Montazeri, falling victim to – so many of the system's excesses. Time, age, and the regime's mistakes had tempered the zeal of many revolutionaries, such as Nabavi, Montazeri, Karroubi, Mousavi, and Soroush.

Conversely, Khatami's victory shocked the conservative establishment, which had thrown its whole weight behind its candidate, 'Ali Akbar Nateq-Nouri, the Speaker of parliament. The conservatives came to view the Reform Movement as a threat to the vitality of the revolution, and maneuvered to obstruct its efforts. They were well-positioned for the task as the powerful unelected organs of the state – such as the Guardian Council, the judiciary, intelligence and interior ministries, and the IRGC and its own intelligence agency – remained in their hands and proved effective at stonewalling the new president.

The ensuing showdown highlighted the contradiction inherent to Iran's unique political system. The Islamic Republic bases its legitimacy in both divine and popular sovereignty – God's will via Islamic law, and the people by way of the ballot box. Conservative unelected institutions such as the twelve-member Guardian Council[44] and the Guardianship of the Jurist (*vilāyat-i faqīh*), the country's highest political authority, exemplify the former and have veto power over the latter, which is manifest in the parliament and president. The Guardian Council specifically ensures that candidates standing for office believe

---

[42] Mohammed Hashas, "Abdolkarim Soroush: The neo-Mu'tazilite that buries classical Islamic political theology in defence of religious democracy and pluralism," *Studia Islamic*, 1(1) (2014), p. 160.

[43] Ali Mirsepassi, *Democracy in Modern Iran: Islam, Culture, and Political Change* (New York and London: New York University Press, 2010), p. 87–90.

[44] Juan Cole likens the Guardian Council to the US Supreme Court.

sufficiently in the system, and that parliament's legislation accords with Islamic law. During the 1980s, however, it became apparent that the rivalries within the power structure were politicizing the Guardian Council's veto power. Thus, in 1988 Khomeini called for the creation of a thirteen-member Expediency Council – a body that mediated between the two by assessing the value of legislation in terms of the greater good to society. The Expediency Council was later expanded to twenty and enshrined in the revised constitution of 1989.

On April 23, the eve of his death, Khomeini ordered the creation of a twenty-two-member assembly tasked with changing the constitution in preparation for a post-war, post-Khomeini era by formalizing and clarifying the division of power to foster stability within the Islamic system.[45] Clarification was needed because Khomeini's authority often extended beyond his constitutionally delineated powers. The 1989 document abolished the premiership in favor of an executive president, augmented the powers of the Guardian Jurist,[46] and, most importantly, no longer required that the next cleric to hold the office be a Source of Emulation (*marja'-i taqlīd*). This change paved the way for Iran's president, 'Ali Khamenei – a junior cleric – to be promoted to the rank of Ayatollah overnight, becoming Khomeini's successor and the next "Leader of the Revolution."[47] In sum, the amended constitution was the product of ten years of trial and error.

The duality of the system is the product of the diverse political coalition that brought about the revolutionary overthrow of the monarchy in 1978–1979, but was ultimately designed to maintain clerical control over the polity. Khatami extolled Khomeini, believed in the revolution, and lauded the constitution, but did not think that it was a timeless, immutable document. The conservatives, however, insisted on preserving their privileged position – even though their challenger

---

[45] Ehteshami, *After Khomeini*, p. 37.

[46] For instance, the revised constitution abolished the Judicial High Council, which was the highest judicial authority, in favor of a Guardian Jurist-appointed judicial chief, who had the authority to appoint all senior judges. Ibid., p. 40.

[47] Incidentally, just as Khomeini used the hostage crisis to pass the original Islamist constitution, he appointed a twenty-member assembly to revise the constitution during the crisis over his February 14 *fatwa* calling for the death of writer Salman Rushdie. Khomeini ordered the assassination of Rushdie, a British citizen, over his fourth novel, *The Satanic Verses*, which many Muslims deemed offensive to Islam, the Quran, and the Prophet.

was a cleric – and struck back with a string of closures of reformist newspaper[48] after Khatami's allies swept to victory in the Islamic Republic's first ever local elections in February 1999. Even though he had stressed the importance of improving civil liberties, especially freedom of expression,[49] Khatami was unable to prevent a restrictive press law being passed in July 1999 – an early sign of his institutional weakness. Having secured a parliamentary majority in the 2000 elections, his allies proposed legislation to revoke the restrictions of the 1999 press law, but Khamenei, in an unusual intervention, thwarted it even though the Guardian Council would probably have vetoed it anyway. Reformists may have held the democratically elected reins of power, but domineering, unelected clerical bodies undermined them at every critical juncture.

Under the weight of the conservative establishment, Khatami and the Reform Movement buckled politically. When student protests erupted in July 1999 after the closure of a reformist newspaper, *Salam*, the IRGC blamed Khatami and threatened to act if he did not resolve the situation.[50] Instead of coming out forcefully in support of his constituents, however, Khatami played a balancing act between the two sides, disappointing his student supporters by his "apparent unwillingness to come to their aid and by his public endorsement of the very establishment against which they were rebelling"[51] – a telling sign of his feeble institutional grounding.

The reformists tried to level the power imbalance, tabling two bills in parliament in 2003 that aimed to curtail the power of conservative bodies by removing the Guardian Council's authority to vet parliamentary candidates and "enabling the president to challenge the judiciary."[52] Unsurprisingly, the Guardian Council vetoed both bills, and Khatami's subsequent threats of resigning in protest came to naught.

---

[48] By the end of 2002, the judicial authorities had ordered the closure of around 100 reformist newspapers. Ehteshami, *After Khomeini*, p. 11.

[49] The new press law included "compelling journalists to reveal their sources, barring opposition journalists and editors from 'any form of press activities,' and strengthening conservative influence over media." Siddiqi, "Khatami and the search for reform in Iran."

[50] Ostovar, *Vanguard of the Imam*, p. 157–158.

[51] Ehteshami, *After Khomeini*, p. 26.          [52] Ibid., p. 14.

According to Ali Mirsepassi, the Reform Movement suffered from institutional weaknesses as well as lacking a concrete vision for Iran:

They have presented vague ideas and agendas around notions of civil society and political development and dialogue between civilizations that have been useful to a point, distinguishing them from the xenophobia and fanaticism of the conservatives, but still hardly significant enough to jump-start a genuine opening. Their slogan, 'Iran for All Iranians,' which vaguely implies readmitting 'purged' or exiled political players into the political process, could be replaced with the more straightforward slogan, 'Freedom for All Political Parties.' [53]

Nonetheless, one of Khatami's most important successes, in Abrahamian's estimation, is that he changed the tone of public discourse from "revolution," "jihad," "imperialism," "the downtrodden," and "Westoxification," to popularizing such terms as "democracy," "pluralism," "equality," "civil society," "human rights," "political participation," "dialogue," and "citizenship."[54] Furthermore, the fact that Khatami was re-elected in 2001 – the fourth consecutive reformist election victory – further affirmed how large segments of the population yearned for systematic change, an important development in and of itself.

Internationally, Khatami deployed a softer rhetoric vis-à-vis the United States and sought better relations with its neighbors – though his conservative enemies viewed his overtures as weakness that invited imperialist aggression. He was the first international leader to condemn the attacks of September 11, which surprised many in the US, but was wholly consistent with the conciliatory demeanor of his administration. Beyond the rhetoric, Iran coordinated with the United States to oust their mutual enemy, the Taliban in Afghanistan. After the toppling of the Taliban by the US-led coalition, President George W. Bush undermined Khatami with his State of the Union address placing Iran within a so-called axis of evil with its archfoe, Saddam Hussein, and North Korea. This rhetoric, however disconnected from reality, emboldened Khatami's conservative enemies within Iran to further mobilize against a president they deemed naïve.

---

[53] Mirsepassi, *Democracy in Modern Iran*, p. 100.
[54] Abrahamian, *A History of Modern Iran*, p. 186–188.

## 2.4 The Conservatives Strike Back

Khatami's failure to curtail the powers of the system's unelected bodies eventually came at a cost. Many women and young people – his core supporters – became disillusioned with the idea that political change in Iran could be achieved through the ballot box. The record 80 percent turnout at the 1997 presidential election gave way to a gradual decline (67 percent in 2001 and 63 percent in 2005).[55] The downward trend in voter participation, combined with the Guardian Council's disqualification of thousands of reformists – even eighty-three incumbents,[56] including Khatami's brother, Nabavi, and Mohtashamipour – precipitated a string of conservative election victories. First, they won the local elections in February 2003, after which Tehran's city council appointed Mahmoud Ahmadinejad mayor of Tehran, then they regained control of parliament in February 2004. The momentum of these two victories prompted them to set their sights on the most prized elected office – the executive. The Guardian Council disqualified more than a thousand candidates in favor of six men, four of whom were former IRGC commanders, including Ahmadinejad, an Islamist revolutionary populist and a blacksmith's son, who secured a second-round victory on June 24, 2005.[57] After eight years of reformist control, Iran's "neoconservatives" were ascendant.[58]

Of the main political periods in modern Iran's history, the Qajar dynasty (1796–1925) can be characterized as "traditional patrimonialism," the constitutional period is best described as "democratic parliamentarianism," the Pahlavi era amounted to a "modernizing autocracy," and Islamic Republicanism embodies "revolutionary ideology."[59] Ahmadinejad's emergence, however, symbolizes the suspension of "democratic pluralism of the reform movement,"[60]

---

[55] Ibid., p. 186. While fewer people voted in 2001, Khatami nonetheless secured a larger percentage of the votes (78 percent) than he had in 1997 (70 percent). For a detailed breakdown of Iran's presidential elections until 2013, see Arman Aramesh's "Rekordhāyeh 38 sāl-i entekhābāt riāsat jomhūrī dar īrān." BBC Persian. May 9, 2017. Accessed July 7, 2018. www.bbc.com/persian/iran-features-39779188.

[56] Siddiqi, "Khatami and the search for reform in Iran."

[57] The other three were Ali Larijani, Muhammad Baqer Qalibaf, and Mohsen Rezaei.

[58] See Ehteshami and Zweiri, *Iran and the Rise of Its Neoconservatives.*

[59] Forough Jahanbakhsh quoted ibid., p. 1.          [60] Ibid.

although the Green Movement gave it renewed vitality. The first non-cleric to hold the presidency since Rajai in 1981, Ahmadinejad represented a new generation of Islamists, many of whom had cut their political teeth during the formative years of the Iran–Iraq War. For them, the paramount objective was to preserve the revolution's Islamic values as well as national security in a post-9/11 era that saw the world's sole superpower – the one-time patron of the Shah, and backer of Saddam's Iraq during the war – encircle Iran.

Ahmadinejad believed that revitalizing the Islamic principles of the early years of the revolution meant fighting corruption, tightening social controls, especially for women,[61] and tending to the economic needs of the downtrodden masses, all of which supplanted his predecessor's goal of reforming the political system. In fact, this new clique felt that

their hard-fought-for revolutionary aims had been undermined by Khatami's reforms. They felt a real sense of isolation and alienation in what they regarded to be 'their' Islamic Republic. The reform movement – in their eyes – focused on political change, forgetting the role of these social groups in establishing the Islamic state and in protecting its ruling regime. They felt that they had been betrayed, and that the regime had been 'kidnapped' by liberals, intellectuals, and unreligious people.[62]

In other words, Ahmadinejad's first term focused on social and economic justice rather than political rights, and sought to marginalize the leaders and intellectuals of reformism. As with the Cultural Revolution of the early 1980s, the universities were targeted as part of the campaign to revive "Islamic values." Ahmadinejad's administration either fired or induced the resignation of many liberal university heads, including Rahnavard, chancellor of the all-women's Alzahra University. Civil society did not fare any better.[63] Moreover, the pressing regional security climate prompted a militarization of the state, with

---

[61] For example, unlike in the Khatami era, the Ahmadinejad administration enforced stricter dress codes that targeted tight-fitting and colorful women's clothes as well as pushed-back head coverings. Men with non-conforming hairstyles were also fined.

[62] Ibid., p. 71.

[63] For how civil society and the women's movement during the Ahmadinejad period created alternative spaces for movement making, see Mahboubeh Abbasgholizadeh, "'To do something we are unable to do in Iran': Cyberspace, the public sphere, and the Iranian women's movement," *Signs*, 39(4) (2014), p. 831–840.

IRGC veterans, many ill-suited to political responsibilities, filling almost half of cabinet appointments.[64]

Internationally, Ahmadinejad embodied Iran's conservative backlash against a right-wing prime minister in Israel, Ariel Sharon, and a right-wing president in the United States, George W. Bush, who was on the warpath after invading a second country neighboring Iran as part of America's Global War on Terror. Surprisingly, Iran found its most powerful international adversary removing its two next-door anti-Iranian, anti-Shi'ite archenemies which had effectively quarantined its regional ambitions. At the same time, Iran now had to contend with sharing two borders and the Persian Gulf with US forces under a commander-in-chief buoyed by what were initially two quick and easy military victories.

Ahmadinejad also sparked international controversy with repeated statements and interviews with Western media in which he questioned first the Holocaust, then the legitimacy of Israel, arguing that if the Shoah had indeed occurred, the Palestinians should not have been punished for it, and that Israel should have been established in Europe and not the Middle East as a refuge for persecuted European Jews. Many Iranians both at home and abroad were appalled by this rhetoric and the consequent renewed stigmatization of their nation.

Finally, Ahmadinejad openly and defiantly defended Iran's nuclear program. In sum, the first four years of his presidency were marked by polarization at home and abroad, the tightening of international sanctions over the country's nuclear program, and anemic economic growth, although certain reforms, such as changing the privatization law, benefitted the poor.[65]

---

[64] Ehteshami and Zweiri (*Iran and the Rise of Its Neoconservatives*, p. 69) identify at least ten of Ahmadinejad's cabinet members as IRGC veterans or affliates: Manouchehr Mottaki, Mostafa Muhammad-Najjar, Muhammad Hossein Saffar Harandi, Gholam-Hossein Mohseni-Eje'i, Mostafa Pour Muhammadi, Masoud Mirkazemi, Muhammad Reza Eskandari, Muhammad Rahmati, Alireza Tahmasbi, and Parviz Fattah.

[65] Economist Nader Habibi notes that Ahmadinejad inherited the Rafsanjani-era privatization program but believed that it benefitted the elite at the expense of the poor. Thus, he garnered the backing of the Supreme Leader and revised the privatization law to make it more equitable. The new law "set aside 40 percent of the shares of privatized firms for distribution among low-income households at highly discounted prices. These shares were labeled 'justice shares.' As many as two thousand public enterprises were targeted for privatization under this plan, their value estimated at between 100 and 140 billion dollars... In the first phase of this process, justice shares were distributed to 4.6 million eligible voters; the value of these shares were assessed at $2.3 billion." Nader Habibi, "The economic legacy of Mahmoud Ahmadinejad," *Middle East Brief*, 74 (June 2013), p. 3. www.brandeis.edu/crown/publications/meb/MEB74.pdf.

## 2.5 The Green Movement

The voter apathy in 2005 that was partially responsible for Ahmadinejad's election had a powerful impact on future voters. After four years with Ahmadinejad at the helm, many concluded that while the electoral process in Iran was highly controlled, with the conservative Guardian Council continuing to screen presidential candidates, the election result nonetheless had a material impact on voters' lives. Many young people, galvanized by Mir Hussein Mousavi's candidacy, ignored calls for a boycott in 2009.[66] Their popular campaign in favor of the reformist candidates, Mousavi and Karroubi, and the uprisings after the June 12 vote constitute the Green Movement.

---

[66] With 85 percent of the electorate participating (assuming that these numbers are accurate) the 2009 election produced the largest voter turnout for a presidential election in the history of the Islamic Republic.

# 3 | On the Streets and Beyond

Crowd Action and the Symbolic
Appropriation of the Past

## 3.1 Introduction: The Significance of the Crowd as a Social Concept

Until the 1960s, study of the political crowd was largely considered unworthy of scholarly attention. Gustav Le Bon, the nineteenth-century "arch-conservative" social psychologist, describes the crowd as composing "criminal elements, riffraff, vagrants, or social misfits."[1] According to George Rudé, a pioneer in the study of crowd action, "social historians of the eighteenth century in England have tended to adopt this view: though avoiding the more prejudicial of these labels, they have been inclined to see the urban 'mob' in terms of the 'slum population' of large cities or the poorest of the poor."[2] It is no surprise, therefore, that there was such a dearth of material pertaining to the study of the crowd. Historian Ervand Abrahamian notes that this disregard is "especially true of the Middle East."[3] To date, only a handful of academics have written about the historical role of the crowd in the region.

A number of influential scholars eventually challenged and undermined Le Bon's assessment that the crowd was undeserving of academic consideration. British Marxist historians such as E. P. Thompson, George Rudé, Christopher Hill, Eric Hobsbawm, and Raphael Samuel, along with Marc Bloch and Georges Lefebvre, the latter of whom coined the phrase "history from below," and sociologist Charles Tilly, all contributed to the study of history that circumvents the typical focus on men of power and nation-states in favor of a

---

[1] Ervand Abrahamian, *The Coup: 1953, the CIA, and the Roots of Modern U.S.-Iranian Relations* (New York and London: The New Press, 2013), p. 205.

[2] George Rudé, *The Crowd in History: A Study of Popular Disturbances in France and England 1730–1848* (New York and London: John Wiley & Sons, Inc., 1964), p. 198.

[3] Ervand Abrahamian, "The crowd in Iranian politics, 1905–53," *Past & Present*, 41 (December 1968), Oxford University Press, p. 184.

"bottom-up" approach emphasizing the role of people and collective action in the making of history. Hobsbawm specifically credits Bloch and Lefebvre with establishing a new way of looking at history: "...it was the French tradition of historiography as a whole, steeped in the history not of the French ruling class but of the French *people*, which established most of the themes and even the methods of grassroots history..."[4] Ervand Abrahamian, the Iranian heir to that tradition, was one of the first historians to study Iranian "history from below."[5]

Le Bon was not alone in his disdain for the crowd: "local conservatives have frequently denounced it as 'social scum' in the pay of the foreign hand..."[6] On June 14, 2009, two days after the disputed Iranian presidential election, the incumbent and declared winner, Mahmoud Ahmadinejad, unwittingly affirmed Le Bon's notion by referring to protesters alleging fraud as "riffraff" or "street trash" (*khas o khāshāk*).[7] Other hardliners accused protesters of being "Israeli mercenaries,"[8] and opposition leaders of constituting a "fifth column"[9] in the service of the foreign "enemy," all of which was "part of a plan by the US and Britain to destabilize Iran."[10]

A comprehensive study of the crowd not only problematizes such sweeping and slanderous attacks but also provides an opportunity to supplant the typical historical lens focusing on "great men" in favor of "history from below." The Green Movement was a popular uprising that at certain junctures surprised its own leaders: Mousavi, Rahnavard, Karroubi, and Khatami. Thus, to view the movement

---

[4] Eric Hobsbawm, *On History* (New York: The New Press, 1997), p. 203.

[5] Ervand Abrahamian, "The crowd in the Persian Revolution," *Iranian Studies*, 2 (4) (Autumn 1969), pp. 128–150. Years later, the likes of Stephan MacFarland and Stephanie Cronin followed Abrahamian's lead. See Stephen L. MacFarland, "Anatomy of an Iranian political crowd: The Tehran bread riot of December 1942," *International Journal of Middle East Studies*, 17(1) (February 1985), pp. 51–65; Stephanie Cronin, "Popular protest, disorder, and riot in Iran: The Tehran crowd and the rise of Riza Khan, 1921–1925," *International Review of Social History*, 50(2) (2005), p. 167–201.

[6] Abrahamian, "The crowd in Iranian Politics, 1905–53," p. 184.

[7] "Daftar-i aḥmadinezhād, khas o khāshāk khāndan-i montaqedān tavasoṭ-i vey rā tashīḥ kard." Khabar Online. June 18, 2009. http://goo.gl/ZArwtC.

[8] "Farātar az khaṭā." *Kayhan*. September 13, 2009. http://kayhanarch.kayhan.ir/880622/2.HTM#other200.

[9] "Kayhān mūsavī rā sotūn-i panjom-i doshman khānd." Rahesabz. July 4, 2010. www.rahesabz.net/story/18751/.

[10] "Iranian protesters 'not agents'." BBC News. August 27, 2009. August 4, 2010. http://news.bbc.co.uk/2/hi/middle_east/8223606.stm.

"from below" rightly situates the crowd as the central agent of contestation in this electrifying history.

With the leadership of the uprising de-centered in favor of the
political crowd – the women and men who constituted the uprising's
historical agents – it becomes apparent that the crowd was not only
highly disciplined and sophisticated, contrary to Ahmadinejad's claims
of hooliganism, but also served a deeper purpose than revoking the
election results or refuting the incumbent's insults. Studying the
actions, slogans, and strategies of the crowd in 2009, both before
and after the June 12 election, provides the reader with the opportunity
to witness a development unprecedented in Iran's modern history. The
Green Movement's challenge to the Iranian government in 2009 was a
total attack on the state's Islamist ideology, a historical occurrence in
which a large segment of the Iranian population, including veteran
leaders of the Islamic system, entered what Asef Bayat refers to as the
"post-Islamist turn."[11]

Authorities tend to categorize anti-state political crowds as "street
trash" in the "pay of foreigners" in order to justify its violent suppression and ignore its legitimate grievances. This generalization aptly
describes the post-election Iranian street scene in 2009, when the state
continued to legitimize its acts of repression. The crowd as a subject of
historical study disallows such white-washing; history may be written
by the victors, but that history is contested, as is the victory.[12]

Study of the crowd and the context in which it operates has historically been difficult because participants in crowd action have seldom left
any archival material.[13] However, in the digital age and with the rise of
the citizen journalist equipped with digital cameras and cellular phones
with built-in cameras, crowd participants are able to record history as
it unfolds and broadcast it to the world through YouTube, social
networking sites, and the wider internet.

The Persian language researcher can thus shed light on the multi-
faceted role of the crowd in the election campaign that overnight
turned into a mass movement shaking the foundations of the Islamic
Republic of Iran to the core. It is clear from a survey of their slogans,

---

[11] Asef Bayat, *Making Islam Democratic: Social Movements and the Post-Islamist
Turn* (Stanford: Stanford University Press, 2007), p. 10–11.
[12] The deconstruction of the false win–lose binary will be continuously revisited
throughout this study.
[13] Cronin, "Popular protest, disorder, and riot in Iran," p. 169.

attire, actions, and strategies that the crowd was anything but "rif-fraff" or "street trash." On the contrary, its sophistication empowered participants to use Islamic history as well as the state's own Islamist ideology and symbolism to subvert the ideological universe of that very state.

This chapter documents the emergence of the crowd and its ingenu-ity in conducting protests in an increasingly repressive environment by leveraging Iran's own revolutionary history. Specific focuses of study include the events and slogans of the week before and after the presi-dential election; the anniversary of the assassination of Ayatollah Muhammad Beheshti, a principal architect of the political system; Ayatollah ʿAli Akbar Hashemi Rafsanjani's Friday sermon; the anni-versary of embassy takeover; and Student Day. All these events repudi-ate allegations of banditry on the part of the crowd while demonstrating the efficacy of its ideological subversion of the state. Chapters 4 and 5 separately examine Jerusalem Day; the death of Ayatollah Hussein ʿAli Montazeri; and *Tasuʿa* and *ʿAshura*, the anni-versary of the seventh-century death of Imam Husayn and his half-brother.

The political climate in which the crowd came to dominate the streets is an opportune starting point. It is important to consider the election context and the security climate which explain when and why the crowd emerged, and how it eventually evolved in response to the intense and suffocating pressure of the re-instated political atmosphere.

## 3.2 Situating the Phenomenon of the Iranian Crowd

Charles Tilly argued that "to the extent that relations between govern-ments and their subjects remain intermittent, mediated, coercive, and particular, incentives to join in collective, public claim making by means of social movement . . . displays remains minimal, indeed mostly negative."[14] The lack of democratic freedoms and legal protection from the state's monopoly on violence generally precludes crowd action and social movement activity:

Repression is a key factor affecting opportunities for action. In general reduced repression increased the likelihood of insurgency, while an upsurge

---

[14] Charles Tilly and Lesley J. Wood, *Social Movements 1768–2008* (Boulder: Paradigm Publishers, 2009), p. 137.

in repression reduces the likelihood of protest by raising the cost of mobilization and collective action. Under repressive situations, victims of social processes find themselves incapable of overcoming their adversaries, not because they cannot conceive of alternative possibilities, but because they are unable to maintain their resources, networks, and solidarity structures in the face of repression.[15]

At the same time, Tilly emphasizes the importance of "opportunity" in facilitating social movement activity. Opportunity ranges from a period in which the state's repression is voluntarily or involuntarily suspended, to the moment when a political cover such as infighting at the top or the death of an opposition leader affords the opposition the breathing room to emerge in order to publicly register its protest.

Iran has experienced a number of intervals in which the population has enjoyed a respite from the state's repressive capacity and seized the opportunity to mobilize politically. 1941 marked the resuscitation of the country's political life when the Allies occupied Iran during the Second World War and deposed Iran's strongman, Reza Shah.[16] Mossadeq's premiership (r. 1951–1953) was especially noteworthy for its commitment to constitutional laws, exploited by the British and American intelligence agencies seeking the overthrow of Iran's democratically elected government.[17] Iran's burgeoning political life

---

[15] Misagh Parsa, *Social Origins of the Iranian Revolution* (New Brunswick and London: Rutgers University Press, 1989), p. 24.

[16] It was in this period that the first freely elected parliamentary elections were conducted, marking Mossadeq's return to politics after his internal exile. See Abrahamian, *The Coup*, p. 35. This was also the time when Taleqani returned to Tehran after the state-imposed internal exile was no longer enforceable, and continued his ideological work and dissident activities. Iranian communists took the opportunity of Reza Shah's downfall to establish the Tudeh Party. See Hamid Dabashi, *The Theology of Discontent: The Ideological Foundation of the Islamic Revolution in Iran* (New Brunswick: Transaction Publishers, 2008), p. 222.

[17] According to Taleqani's chief aide, Mohammad Shanehchi, who was politically active at the time, Iran enjoyed "absolute freedom" during Mossadeq's brief leadership in which newspapers and radio stations were free and unimpeded. Specifically, two newspapers, *Ettela'at* and *Kayhan*, both of which were in the hands of Mossadeq's enemies (the latter was funded by the court and run by the conservative Massoudi family) and were among the mostly widely read papers of the time, were unhindered in their relentless criticism of the prime minister. See Mohammad Shanehchi, interview recorded by Habib Ladjevardi, March 4, 1983, Paris, France. Iranian Oral History Collection, Harvard University, Transcript 1 (seq. 22). Accessed April 30, 2015. Also see Abrahamian in *The Coup*, p. 58. On the Anglo-American exploitation of Mossadeq's commitment

and short-lived experiment with democracy came to an abrupt end with the Anglo-American coup of 1953.[18] Historically, Mossadeq's overthrow marked the conclusion of what one political scientist called "the slow, halting progress that Iran had been making since the early 1900s toward a more representative form of government and toward freedom from foreign interference."[19] The Iranian Revolution once again created the space for a vibrant political life to emerge in the period between the collapse of the monarchy and the militant clergy's consolidation of power. Unlike its counterpart in the middle of the century, the 1979 Spring of Freedom lasted only a few months. The next opening was even shorter, spanning only a few weeks in 2009, but its brevity does not detract from the historic mobilization of millions of Iranians.

Before the start of the 2009 election season, Iran had experienced years of social and political restrictions, which were tightened under Ahmadinejad's presidency. The security forces and paramilitaries ensured that student gatherings and demonstrations were a costly undertaking. Access to internet sites such as Facebook and Twitter

to constitutional laws in order to overthrow him, see Abrahamian's entire work but specifically the third chapter in *The Coup*, pp. 149–204.

[18] The importance and fateful consequences of the coup, especially for Iran, has inspired an ever-growing literature on the subject. Foremost among them is Abrahamian's *The Coup*, which dispels the established narrative that the "British negotiated in good faith, the United States made serious attempts to act as an honest broker, and Mossadeq failed to reach a compromise because of his intransigence – traced invariably to his presumed 'psychological makeup' and Shi'i 'martyrdom complex.'" (Ibid., p. 2). Abrahamian also questions "the conventional wisdom that places the coup squarely and solidly within the context of the Cold War – within the conflict between East and West..." Rather, he situates "the coup firmly inside the conflict between imperialism and nationalism, between First and Third Worlds..." (Ibid., pp. 3–4). For another important work on the subject, see Stephen Kinzer, *All the Shah's Men: American Coup and the Roots of Middle East Terror* (Hoboken: John Wiley & Sons, Inc., 2003). It is also important to consider that the coup was not only disastrous for Iran but for the wider developing world. The obvious American role in the overthrow alerted right-wing forces in other countries that they had a potential ally in the United States for their own anti-democratic plans. Thus, it should come as no surprise that the CIA and right-wing forces in Guatemala, for instance, began drawing up their coup plans almost immediately after the "success" of Mossadeq's ousting. Zachary Karabell, *Architects of Intervention: The United States, the Third World, and the Cold War, 1946–1962* (Baton Rouge: Louisiana State University Press, 1999), pp. 62–91.

[19] Mark J. Gasiorowski, "The 1953 coup d'etat in Iran," *International Journal of Middle East Studies* 19(3) (August 1987), p. 278.

was blocked and critical journalism often resulted in arrests and newspaper closures. How, then, with political rights and civil liberties severely curtailed, did the crowd come to rule the streets of Iran in June 2009?

## 3.3 The Crowd before the Election

Antonio Gramsci, one of the most important Marxist thinkers of the twentieth century, understood that a popular uprising must be preceded by preparation: "Every revolution has been preceded by an intense labour of criticism, by diffusion of culture and the spread of ideas..."[20] Iran's Reform Movement, which became a powerful political force from the late 1990s onwards, was not revolutionary, but called into question much of the Iranian government's dogma. Reformist president Muhammad Khatami (r. 1997–2005) tried to emphasize the republican aspects of the system by strengthening the power of the elected government bodies, the parliament and the presidency, and the individual rights of citizens. He argued that for nearly two decades of the Islamic Republic, Iran had experienced more of the "Islamic" at the expense of the "Republic," and he aimed to curtail the veto power of unelected clerical bodies. It is important to note that Khatami did not start the Reform Movement, which was born of pressures from below. Iranians had long been organizing student associations and women's groups to demand a relaxation of social controls, greater gender equality, freedom of assembly, speech, and thought, and an end to arbitrary arrest and torture.

Large segments of the population refused to abide by the government's ideological rigidity with miniscule acts of defiance. Alcohol consumption and mingling of the sexes, for example, are banned, but some Iranian youth[21] attended underground social gatherings and consumed alcohol, often at great personal risk. Similarly, many women who did not wish to wear the *hijab*, the state-mandated headscarf, did so but on their own terms. Wearing lightly colored scarves, sometimes even slightly transparent ones, pushed back as far as legally

[20] Thomas J. Butko, "Revelation or revolution: A Gramscian approach to the rise of political Islam," *British Journal of Middle Eastern Studies*, 31(1) (May 2004), p. 57.
[21] I cautiously say "some Iranian youth" so as to not generalize all of Iran's young people as one monolith that partakes in the same social habits.

permissible, represented for many a subversive repudiation of the Islamic government's social and ideological controls. According to Asef Bayat,

Iran's postrevolutionary young had turned into 'youth,' a collective social agent. Their movement did not embody a coherent organization, ideology, and leadership (unlike the student movement), but rather 'collective sentiments' in asserting youthful, albeit fragmented, identities. Theirs was a movement whose principal expression lay in the politics of presence, tied closely to everyday collective being, cultural struggle, and normative subversion. This mass of fragmented individuals and subgroups shared common attributes and expressed common anxieties in demanding individual liberty and in asserting their collective identities.[22]

The actions of these young people gave meaning not only to what they *did*, but also to how they *were*: "The youth movement's identity is based not so much on collective *doing* as on their collective *being*; and they make their claims less through collective protest than *collective presence*." In other words, they challenged the state simply by wearing certain clothes, sporting distinct hairstyles, or wearing lipstick. Tellingly, one woman is quoted as saying: "Lipstick is not just lipstick in Iran. It transmits a political message. It is a weapon."[23] Seemingly mundane behavior constitutes an indirect marker of protest: what Bayat later called "life as politics."[24] ʿAli Akbar Nateq-Nouri, a conservative stalwart and former Speaker of the parliament, contrasted the political attire of the revolution with the subversive style of today:

During the monarchy, if a youth wanted to resist the government, he would raise the flag of Islam and change his appearance accordingly... Boys would don shirts that had a cleric's collar and beard, and girls would go to public places such as universities with a complete veil or *chador*. And now, when a youth wants to behave in a way to show opposition to the government ... they show their protest by changing their appearance and with bad veiling.[25]

---

[22] Bayat, *Making Islam Democratic*, p. 65.

[23] Ali Akbar Mahdi, "The Iranian women's movement: A century long struggle," *The Muslim World*, 94 (October 2004), p. 443.

[24] Asef Bayat, *Life as Politics: How Ordinary People Change the Middle East* (Stanford: Stanford University Press, 2010).

[25] "Qalʿ o qamʿ-i dokhtarān va pesarān eshtebāh ast." Tabnak. June 2, 2014. http://goo.gl/lh45qU.

On the eve of the Shah's final departure from Iran in the face of the revolutionary uprising, *Time* noted, "One striking feature of the anti-Shah demonstrations has been the presence of masses of Iranian women. In Tehran they marched by the thousands, encased from head to foot in black, shapeless chadors ... as a form of political involvement and protest against the Shah's autocratic rule."[26] If the *hijab* and facial hair signified one's revolutionary predisposition in 1978–1979, then "bad *hijab*" and changing one's appearance highlighted dissent for many in 2009. Iranian youth "wore their politics on their sleeves" in both 1979 and 2009, but in 2009 they inverted the meaning of the revolution's stylistic protest symbols.

Women and the youth's collective presence during the presidential campaigns showed signs of what Gramsci called the "war of movement," in which some campaigners, even before Mousavi, Karroubi, and their supporters alleged fraud, used the election as a cover to protest the state proactively and directly, as opposed to passively with their appearance. After the June 12 vote, when millions accused the state of rigging the election, the campaign developed into a full-scale "frontal attack" on the government, with passive dissent replaced by open confrontation on the streets and in cyberspace. This attack did not necessarily offer a new ideology in place of the Islamic government's, but rather repudiated the state's ideology as a whole.

Gramsci argued that the elite or ruling "hegemon" controlling the state imposes a set of self-affirming ideas or ideology on the population, eliciting the requisite consent in order to perpetuate its rule: "...each individual is fundamentally influenced by the ideas of the ruling 'Hegemon'... this influence is felt unconsciously through the hegemon's projection of 'common sense'" in a set of ideas that are

...used to acquire the 'consent' of the masses to its rule – [and] are nothing more than the narrow and selfish interests of the elites superimposed on the general interests of the people. As a result, the masses accept the morality,

[26] "Back to the chador," *Time*, December 25, 1978, p. 37. *Time* also included an important interview by an activist who supported the revolution but refused to don the *hijab* "even as a symbol of protest, insisting that Iranian women will never go back to the old ways." See "A case of warring perceptions: Some voices, pro- and anti-Shah, in Iran's internal debate," *Time*, December 25, 1978, p. 38.

the customs, and the institutionalised rules of behaviour disseminated throughout society as absolute truths that cannot or should not be questioned.[27]

Put differently, by accepting the state's "common-sense" worldview, citizens are acquiescing to the power dynamic of the ruler and the ruled. Gramsci further argued that citizens become revolutionaries when they refute the state's "universal truths" and free their minds to find their true revolutionary consciousness. In 2009, however, protesters did not reject the state's "universal truths." Rather, they freed their minds from the belief that those universal truths were fixed or belonged exclusively to the state. In doing so, they appropriated and subverted them, giving them new meaning that rendered them powerful nonviolent symbols and occasions of protest against that very state.

In its 2009 Iran report, Freedom House[28] acknowledged that "supporters of all candidates seemed to enjoy a relatively relaxed and politically vibrant atmosphere"[29] in the period leading up to the vote. This seemingly relaxed political environment was intentional: the government wanted Iranians to participate, fearing disinterest or voter apathy would lead them to reject the process in what would have amounted to a vote of no confidence in the system that organized the election, jeopardizing the legitimacy of the Islamic system as a whole (Figure 3.1).[30] The opposite, the government believed, was also true: Iranians' participation in an important state-sanctioned political event

---

[27] Butko, "Revelation or revolution," p. 43.

[28] Freedom House is not an unbiased source as it produces some very political reports. For instance, see its phrasing of how it explained its downgrading of America's democracy ranking: "The United States retreated from its traditional role as both a champion and an exemplar of democracy amid an accelerating decline in American political rights and civil liberties." Certainly, many in the developing world, especially the Middle East, would take issue with the United States being referred to as a "champion … of democracy." See Freedom House, "Freedom in the world 2018: Democracy in crisis" (2018). Its analysis of the pre-election climate in Iran is nevertheless accurate. https://freedomhouse.org/sites/default/files/FH_FITW_Report_2018_Final_SinglePage.pdf.

[29] Freedom House, "Freedom in the world – Iran." August 4, 2010. www.freedomhouse.org/template.cfm?page=363&year=2010&country=7842.

[30] Pouya Alimagham, "The 13th anniversary of the Islamic Republic of Iran's establishment." 2018. JPEG file.

**Figure 3.1** Casting a ballot: "The 13th anniversary of the Islamic Republic of Iran's establishment".
The Islamic government has vested much of its legitimacy in the electoral process, however flawed and controlled. It even printed stamps of Khomeini casting a ballot to harness his authority posthumously in order to encourage voter participation.
Photo credit: Pouya Alimagham

would acknowledge and affirm the state's legitimacy and authority by default.[31] Thus, the government encouraged a relatively free climate in which Iranians could develop an interest in the election by reading, exchanging views, and organizing and campaigning for their candidates. To that end, the government unblocked Facebook and other

---

[31] Predictably, Khamenei said that such a massive turnout of "Forty million people" proved that the people "believe in the system." See "Khoṭbeh-ye namāz jomʿeh-ye tehrān." Khamenei.ir, September 11, 2009. http://farsi.khamenei.ir/speech-content?id=8033.

social networking sites.[32] Increased connectivity enabled candidates to relay their political platforms to a tech-savvy young population. It was the first Iranian presidential election in which candidates had harnessed the power of YouTube, Facebook, and Twitter to reach a wider audience.[33] The Mousavi campaign went so far as to send text messages to citizens' mobile phones to garner support.[34] One partisan credits the former prime minister's election team's use of Facebook's organizing capacity with a "successful campaign," noting that the "campaign managers organized supporters, planned gatherings and garnered support through Facebook pages dedicated to the Reformist candidate."[35] Many Mousavi supporters also developed a Facebook presence, inviting their peers to "become green,"[36] the color of the campaign. Most importantly, the use of these technologies enabled candidates to level the playing field with the state's preferred candidate, Ahmadinejad, who had greater access to state resources, especially radio and television air time.[37]

Just as with previous movements in modern Iranian history, technology played an important role in 2009 in facilitating communication and coordination. In the Tobacco Revolt of 1890–1892 and the Constitutional Revolution of 1905–1911, revolutionaries used the telegraph to organize and communicate across large swathes of territory. In the 1950s, nationalists used the next-generation communication technology, the telephone, to spearhead the national movement against the British Empire's control over Iran's natural resources. During the Iranian Revolution of 1978–1979, revolutionaries smuggled cassette-

[32] Babak Rahimi, "The sacred in fragments: Shi'i Iran since the 1979 Revolution," in *From Theocracy to the Green Movement*, edited by Negin Nabavi (New York: Palgrave Macmillan, 2012), p. 69.
[33] "Gozāresh-i abc az noāvarīhāye tablīghāt-i entekhābāti-i mūsavī." Aftab News, May 19, 2009. http://goo.gl/VZkUiv.
[34] Ibid.
[35] Octavia Nasr, "Tear gas and Twitter: Iranians take their protests online." CNN, June 15, 2009.
      www.cnn.com/2009/WORLD/meast/06/14/iran.protests.twitter/index.html.
[36] "Jonbesh-i 'sabz' dar īrān dar āstāneh-ye entekhābāt-i riāsat jomhūrī." DW, February 6, 2009. http://goo.gl/cl8Oh8.
[37] "Gozāresh-i abc az noāvarīhāye tablīghāt-i entekhābāti-i mūsavī." Aftab News, May 19, 2009. http://goo.gl/VZkUiv.

tape recordings[38] of Khomeini's fiery anti-Shah speeches[39] into Iran, where the likes of Ayatollah Beheshti transmitted "them by telephone to mosques and villages all over the country."[40] The immediate audience of such speeches would then relay Khomeini's messages to their friends and neighbors, ensuring that even those who did not frequent the mosques or have access to the tapes received his political messages.[41] In 2009, cell phones equipped with the capacity to make phone calls, send messages, and capture pictures and footage, as well as access the internet – encompassing the blogosphere, social media websites such as Facebook and Twitter, and video-sharing sites such as YouTube – were instrumental in relaying messages to a larger audience. Although the internet was especially useful for organizing the presidential campaigns prior to the uprising, its subsequent role should not be overstated. While Western media hailed Iran's uprising as a "Twitter Revolution"[42] (one former aide to President Bush even bizarrely argued that Twitter should be awarded the Nobel Peace Prize for its role in facilitating the uprising[43]), the reality on the ground was a bit more complicated, as will be discussed further.

[38] By the time of the revolution, these cassette tapes came to constitute a small but thriving business venture. Khomeini's speeches were in such demand that the merchants selling the tapes were making more than a six-fold profit per sale. See "The Ayatullah's hit parade," *Time*, February 12, 1979, p. 37.

[39] In one such tape, Khomeini stated that "if the religious leaders had been in power, they would not have allowed the Iranian nation to become the captive of the Americans and the British... They [the religious leaders] would have punched the government in the mouth." (Ibid.). "Punching the government in the mouth" is an especially important phrase that will be addressed in detail further below.

[40] David Butler et al., "The Mullah's men," *Newsweek*, February 12, 1979, p. 47. Veteran activist and Taleqani's chief aide, Mohammad Shanehchi, noted that when Khomeini was in Paris his speeches were transmitted to all corners of Iran in a matter of hours through the use of tape recordings that were relayed to Tehran from Paris via telephone and were transcribed, copied, and disseminated all over the country, including remote rural areas. See Mohammad Shanehchi, interview recorded by Habib Ladjevardi, March 4, 1983, Paris, France. Iranian Oral History Collection, Harvard University, Transcript 4 (seq. 93). Accessed May 2, 2015.

[41] "A case of warring perceptions: Some voices, pro- and anti-Shah, in Iran's internal debate." *Time*, December 25, 1978, p. 38.

[42] "Editorial: Iran's Twitter revolution." *The Washington Times*, June 16, 2009. www.washingtontimes.com/news/2009/jun/16/irans-twitter-revolution/.

[43] Mark Pfeifle, "A Nobel Peace Prize for Twitter?." *The Christian Science Monitor*, July 6, 2009. www.csmonitor.com/Commentary/Opinion/2009/0706/p09s02-coop.html.

The relaxation of political restrictions and censorship signaled the temporary suspension of the repressive climate. Sensing the change in the environment occasioned by the presidential election, they seized the opportunity to organize and came onto the streets under the guise of supporting their candidate's campaign. Unlike in the United States, where the election season is unusually long (and expensive), there are only four to five weeks of active campaigning in Iran.

Interest in the contest gradually grew in the weeks preceding the election, peaking with the occurrence of televised one-on-one presidential debates, the first in modern Iran.[44] Iran had experienced televised presidential debates in the past, but this was the first time the candidates had faced each other one on one, enabling more focused and adversarial debates that sparked the population's interest. The second of six television debates was especially electrifying for both camps. Mousavi faced a combative Ahmadinejad, who accused his chief rivals, Mousavi, Karroubi, and Rezai, of being part of a plot financed by Rafsanjani to unseat him. The premise of the accusation was that each candidate appealed to a certain faction in Ahmadinejad's base: Rezai, the former commander of the Islamic Revolutionary Guards Corps (IRGC), was thought to be able to siphon off votes from the military establishment that had played an important role in Ahmadinejad's 2005 election victory;[45] Karroubi, a seasoned cleric and politician, could erode his support amongst the clerical and religious classes; and Mousavi and his wife, Zahra Rahnavard, could appeal to the leftists, secularists, and female voters.[46] According to the incumbent, Rafsanjani was seeking revenge after losing to him in the 2005 presidential race, and epitomized the corruption that plagued the government both past and present. In other words, the president of the Islamic Republic presented himself as an "anti-establishment candidate"[47] locked in an existential battle with those corrupt individuals

---

[44] Jason Rezaian, telephone interview, July 26, 2010.

[45] Anoushiravan Ehteshami and Mahjoob Zweiri, *Iran and the Rise of Its Neoconservatives: The Politics of Tehran's Silent Revolution* (London and New York: I.B. Tauris, 2007), p. 63.

[46] Director Ramin Asgard, Dubai, to Central Intelligence Agency et al., June 3, 2009, Wikileaks, https://search.wikileaks.org/plusd/cables/09RPODUBAI232_a.html.

[47] Director Ramin Asgard, Dubai, to Central Intelligence Agency et al., June 4, 2009, Wikileaks, https://search.wikileaks.org/plusd/cables/09RPODUBAI233_a.html.

undermining the revolution from within. Mousavi, in turn, condemned
Ahmadinejad's foreign as well as economic policies, critiques of which
appealed to middle- and lower-class voters, the latter of whom were
not unanimous in their support of the president. Mousavi also challenged Ahmadinejad's pro-Palestinian credentials, criticizing his focus
on the Holocaust as harmful to Iran's national interest,[48] and accusing
him of setting Iran on the path to "dictatorship."[49]

The most distasteful part of the debate transpired when Ahmadinejad accused Mousavi's wife of obtaining her academic credentials
through dubious means.[50] The personal attack was designed to discredit Rahnavard, an academic, artist, and political force in her own
right who had been generating interest among women voters in Mousavi's candidacy by actively campaigning for her husband, which was
unprecedented in Iran. So groundbreaking was her presence in his
campaign that it garnered national as well as international attention,
with CNN even referring to her as "Iran's Michelle Obama,"[51] a
reference Rahnavard declined in favor of invoking as her inspiration
Fatima al-Zahra, the Prophet Muhammad's daughter.[52]

[48] Ahmadinejad basked in giving combative interviews to foreign media in which
he would question the Holocaust, and then argue that if it was a fact, the
Palestinians should not have been punished for a crime that took place in
Europe. Mousavi's denunciation of Ahmadinejad's Holocaust rhetoric indirectly
challenged the latter's pro-Palestinian credentials.

[49] Ibid.

[50] "Matn-i kāmel-i monāżereh-ye mūsavī va aḥmadīnezhād." Aftab News, June 4,
2009. http://aftabnews.ir/fa/news/90164. Ahmadinejad completed his doctorate
at the Iran University of Science and Technology while he was governor of
Ardebil. His PhD supervisor was Hamid Behbahani, whom Ahmadinejad, when
president, appointed Minister of Roads and Transportation. Amir Mianji, an
Iran University of Science and Technology alumnus, suggests some potential
impropriety. Amir Mianji, "Nāmeh-ye sargoshādeh-ye ham daneshgāhī-ye
aḥmadīnezhād darbāreh-ye madrak-i doktorā-ye ū." Khabar Online, June 10,
2009. Accessed July 30, 2018. www.khabaronline.ir/detail/10501/Politics/
parties.

[51] Reza Sayah, "Thousands gather to hear, cheer Iran's Michelle Obama." CNN,
May 24, 2009. Accessed June 20, 2018. http://edition.cnn.com/2009/WORLD/
meast/05/24/iran.wife/index.html. The Iranian press even covered the reference.
"Moqāyeseh-ye zahrā rahnavard va mīshel obāmā dar CNN." Aftab News,
May 24, 2009. Accessed June 20, 2018. https://goo.gl/xBqpqi.

[52] "Forṣat-i 24 sāʿateh-ye zahrā rahnavard beh aḥmadīnezhād." Tabnak, June 7,
2009. Accessed June 20, 2018. https://goo.gl/mdqWxx. The legend of Fatima
has been used at various times to expound differing conceptions of womanhood.
In the fifteenth century, Mullah Husayn Waiz Kashifi interpreted Fatima's life
through the context of the question of succession after the Prophet

Ahmadinejad's direct attacks on Rahnavard in the debate only attested to how important she had become to the contest, and for many women she was the closest thing to a female candidate in an election that encompassed four main candidates – all male. Iranian women did not gravitate towards Mousavi merely because his wife was beside him on the campaign trail, but as a result of her enthusiastic campaign speeches in which she issued wider political and economic demands that connected with them. In a rally on June 9, for instance, she condemned the state for not only failing to support women, but allowing men to have multiple wives "in the name of supporting families," eliciting rhythmic chants from the crowd of "Rahnavard, Rahnavard, the equality of woman and man!" (*rahnavard, rahnavard, tasāvī-ye zan o mard!*).[53] At the same rally she called for the release of political prisoners and the right to free speech, and railed against the police patrols and the country's overall security climate, growing class disparities, skyrocketing rents, the influx of imports ruining local industries, youth unemployment, and the availability of cheap, illegal drugs.[54]

The impact of the television debate cannot be understated. Accusations of fraud, corruption, and embezzlement were broadcast to a shocked national audience. According to one respondent, all the issues people had been talking about at home were now being debated on live television, and the historical importance of the occasion resonated with

---

Muhammad's death: "...the prophet's desired successor is none other than his beloved daughter's husband, whom the prophet selects with forethought and divine guidance." In other words, her virtue, piety, and sacrality affirmed Ali's claim to the leadership of the Muslim community because the Prophet had blessed Ali with his daughter's hand in marriage. In contrast, Shari'ati viewed her life through the moral and ideological exigencies of pre-revolutionary Iran, positing a modern, Islamic alternative of womanhood: industrious rather than an indolent consumer, dignified and culturally proud rather than a Europeanized sex object, and educated and politically active rather than superstitious and quietist. See Firoozeh Kashani-Sabet, "Who is Fatima? Gender, culture, and representation in Islam," *Journal of Middle East Women's Studies*, 1(2) (2005) 1–24.

[53] "Hoshdār-i zahra rahnavard beh vezārat-i keshvar darbāreh-ye ehtemāl-i hargūneh taqalob dar entekhābāt." Aftab News, June 9, 2009. Accessed May 28, 2018. http://aftabnews.ir/vdcjtxeh.uqeyxzsffu.html.

[54] Ibid.

viewers, creating a sort of "political chemistry."[55] One activist believed that it was during the television debate that people realized "who is on the side of the people and who is not, who sides with the government and who sides with the people."[56] Apathy gave way to the conviction that although all the candidates were screened by the Guardian Council, the powerful conservative body of twelve unelected clerics and laymen, there was a real difference between the candidates, especially between incumbent Mahmoud Ahmadinejad and Mir Hussein Mousavi, the former prime minister-turned-reformist with the charismatic wife who often eclipsed him. One source went so far as to say that the television debate between Mousavi and Ahmadinejad undermined the state's control over the election, with green appearing "everywhere" overnight.[57] After the first televised debate, excitement translated into a Mardi Gras-like atmosphere in Tehran in which the four main candidates' bases, especially that of Ahmadinejad and Mousavi, came out in force. With election fever in full swing, crowds emerged onto the streets with slogans, placards, pictures, and displays of unity. Participants marched throughout the streets every day until the day before the election, when a mandatory 24-hour lull was customarily enforced.

Young people constituted the bulk of the street crowds and 50 percent of the electorate.[58] Iran in 2009 had a population of roughly seventy million people with a median age of twenty-seven.[59] The youth are the overwhelming majority of a population living under a system of limited political rights and severely curtailed civil liberties. With much of the constitution inspired by a dogmatic interpretation of Islam, youth are prohibited from mingling with the opposite sex (to the degree enforceable) and are limited in their ability to voice political

---

[55] Chargé d'Affaires Richard LeBaron, London, to Secretary of State Hillary Clinton, June 18, 2009, Wikileaks, https://search.wikileaks.org/plusd/cables/09LONDON1442_a.html.

[56] S. V., personal interview. April 14, 2014.

[57] Chargé d'Affaires Richard LeBaron, London, to Secretary of State Hillary Clinton, June 18, 2009, Wikileaks, https://search.wikileaks.org/plusd/cables/09LONDON1442_a.html. "Everywhere" in this instance is a generalization most relevant to urban centers as Ahmadinejad enjoyed considerable support in rural areas.

[58] "Guide: How Iran is ruled." BBC, June 9, 2009. http://news.bbc.co.uk/2/hi/middle_east/8051750.stm.

[59] Central Intelligence Agency. "Iran." cia.gov. Central Intelligence Agency website, 2009. Accessed November 16, 2018.

criticisms. Needless to say, dancing on the streets, playing loud music in cars, and shouting overtly political slogans, *inter alia*, are forbidden. The election facilitated an environment in which regular prohibitions were either suspended or ignored, prompting the crowd to circumvent a number of the state's social and political taboos.

This normally forbidden "Mardi Gras effect" gripped the streets every day and did not dissipate with nightfall. One witness to the election carnival attested:

> As afternoon fades into evening, the streets grow increasingly crowded and restless. Tehran's notorious rush hour traffic morphs into a supercharged campaign carnival that marches non-stop until around 2:00 a.m. The throngs of pedestrian campaigners absorb ever greater numbers, and inch further and further on to the streets, choking the flow of traffic. Drivers honk their horns when they see likeminded campaigners. Crowds boo at cars boasting a rival's poster. By late evening, electioneering dissolves into frenzy... A car suddenly stops mid-traffic, its stereo blasting party music. Its passengers, almost certainly Mousavi supporters, disembark and break into frenetic dancing, joined by gleeful onlookers.[60]

Thousands clogged the streets and walked alongside cars stuck in bumper-to-bumper traffic. People clapped their hands over their heads repeating Mousavi's name: "Hands in the air, Mousavi! Hands in the air, Mousavi!" (*dastā bālā, mūsavī! dastā bālā, mūsavī!*) like football fans at a match.[61] Similar scenes were replicated elsewhere in the capital, such as when a massive pro-Mousavi rally concluded with large numbers of people roaming "the city in cars and on foot, honking horns, and chanting slogans" that equated Mousavi with freedom: "Mousavi, liberty!" (*mūsavī, āzādī!*).[62]

On June 8, 2009, four days before the election, young women and men formed a 20-kilometer human chain spanning from Tajrish Square to Tehran's railway station through a main thoroughfare, Vali Asr Street. Edited footage from segments of the chain showed that

---

[60] ʿAlireza Doostdar, "Cheeseburgers and sharks: Iran's election campaign is in full swing." The Dawn Blog, June 11, 2009. Accessed August 3, 2010. http://blog.dawn.com/2009/06/11/cheeseburgers-and-sharks-iran%E2%80%99s-election-campaigns-in-full-swing/.

[61] AFP. "Youth rallies for Mir Hossein Mousavi." Online video clip, YouTube, June 10, 2009. Accessed July 3, 2010. https://youtu.be/G-Pl7Gtliog.

[62] Ambassador Anne E. Derse, Baku, to Secretary of State Hillary Clinton, June 12, 2009, Wikileaks, https://search.wikileaks.org/plusd/cables/09BAKU474_a.html.

nearly half of the participants were women. It is not surprising that so many women were active in both pre-election campaigning and the post-election uprising: the marginalized often become the incubators of change.

Women have long played a decisive role in modern Iran's political movements, from Qurrat al-'Ayn's leadership in the Babi movement in the mid-nineteenth century to the Constitutional Revolution of the early twentieth century, when they donated their jewelry – typically their only real assets – to help create a national bank and prevent imperial powers from using Iran's foreign debts as a pretext for invasion.[63] Some women even gave their lives, taking up arms, fighting, and dying for the cause of constitutionalism.[64] They rose up as guerrillas[65] in the 1970s, and marched in their millions in the Iranian Revolution of 1978–1979. After the revolution when many of their civil rights stalled or were undermined, women did not wait until 2009 to mobilize,[66] but continued their activism, launching websites and magazines devoted to women's issues, pushing back in the courts as lawyers after being barred from the bench,[67] and spearheading

---

[63] Janet Afary, *The Iranian Constitutional Revolution, 1906–1911: Grassroots Democracy, Social Democracy, and the Origins of Feminism* (New York: Columbia University Press, 1996), p. 179.

[64] Ibid., p. 194–195.

[65] Sometimes female guerrillas even outnumbered their male counterparts. In one militant cell in which all four Fada'iyan fighters died in a shootout, three were women. Margaret P. Grafeld, Iran Tehran, to Secretary of State, April 4, 1977, Wikileaks, https://search.wikileaks.org/plusd/cables/1977TEHRAN02873_c.html. Of the Fada'iyan's 341 known dead, 39 were women. Despite such sacrifices, the Organization of Iranian People's Fada'i Guerrillas remained a patriarchal organization with only one woman, Ashraf Deghani, serving on the Central Committee. Haideh Moghissi, *Populism and Feminism in Iran: Women's Struggle in a Male-Defined Revolutionary Movement* (New York: St. Martin's Press, 1994), p. 115–117.

[66] In the unique post-revolutionary circumstances, women were also able to progress in some areas. While women were precluded from accessing certain jobs and fields of study, and had limited family rights, family planning and a social welfare state created many educational and employment opportunities. See Catherine Sameh, "From Tehran to Los Angeles to Tehran: Transnational solidarity politics in the One Million Signatures Campaign to end discriminatory law," *Women's Studies Quarterly*, 42(3/4) (Fall/Winter 2014), p. 168.

[67] On the eve of the revolution, 316 women served as judges. Guity Nashat, "Women in the Islamic Republic of Iran," *Iranian Studies*, 13(1–4) (1980), p. 168.

campaigns such as One Million Signatures[68] and Stop Stoning Forever in 2006 to promote gender equality in the civil and penal codes.[69] Women founded non-governmental organizations (NGOs), as they had done with *anjomans* in the early twentieth century fighting for constitutionalism and women's advancement, to continue to advocate for women's rights,[70] such as when they successfully organized opposition to a 2007 bill that would have lessened restrictions on polygamy.[71] The trusted horizontal networks of women that developed from these activities were able to activate for the next political struggle, the presidential election of 2009.

Young women and men lined the street to bid Ahmadinejad farewell with a resounding pro-Mousavi slogan: "Ahmadi bye bye" (*aḥmadī bāī bāī*).[72] These campaigners used the occasion of the election not

---

[68] The One Million Signatures Campaign "involves a massive petition that demands reforms such as the abolition of polygamy, equal rights for women as witnesses in courts of law and in divorce, the joint custody of children, and increasing the minimum legal age of responsibility to eighteen (currently it is fifteen for boys and nine for girls, subjecting them to harsh punishments included in the criminal law, or Qisas)." Haideh Moghissi, "Islamic cultural nationalism and gender politics in Iran," *Third World Quarterly*, 29(3) (2008), p. 552.

[69] Golbarg Bashi, "Feminist waves in the Iranian Green tsunami," in Nader Hashemi and Danny Postel (eds.), *The People Reloaded: The Movement and the Struggle for Iran's Future* (New York: Melville House Publishing, 2010), p. 37. Stoning is not inherently a women's issue as men are also sentenced to the punishment, but prostitution and adultery (often the "chastity crimes" that prompt the sentence) disproportionately affect women. See Laura Secor, "The war of words: A woman's battle to end stoning and juvenile execution in Iran," *The New Yorker*, January 4, 2016. Accessed June 18, 2018. www.newyorker.com/magazine/2016/01/04/war-of-words-annals-of-activism-laura-secor. According to Abbasgholizadeh, "the typical female victim of stoning generally has a low literacy level, has no right to divorce her husband, and has not married him on her own volition. In cases where a woman has been charged with adultery, she often has no financial independence and has been forced to engage in a relationship with a man other than her husband in the midst of a crisis that has arisen from these pressures. The other man often plays the role of savior in her life." Mahboubeh Abbasgholizadeh, "'To do something we are unable to do in Iran': Cyberspace, the public sphere, and the Iranian women's movement," *Signs*, 39(4) (2014), p. 835–836.

[70] Afary, *The Iranian Constitutional Revolution*, p. 177–208.

[71] The bill would have removed the provision that required the husband to obtain the permission of his first wife to take an additional wife. Abbasgholizadeh, "'To do something we are unable to do in Iran'," pp. 836–837.

[72] Al Jazeera English. "Presidential candidates court Iran youth." Online video clip, YouTube, June 10, 2009. Accessed July 4, 2010. https://youtu.be/381DirqYxoE.

**Figure 3.2** "Assistance from God leads to victory"
This stamp issued in 1982 commemorates the Iranian war effort. The inscription on the flag reads: "Assistance from God leads to imminent victory," an expanded version of which was a slogan aired by Mousavi's supporters to condemn the government before the election turmoil.

only to support their candidate, but also to voice their protest against the government as a whole, holding hands as part of the human chain and chanting: "Assistance from God leads to imminent victory, death to this deceptive government"[73] (*naṣron min allāh fatḥon qarīb, marg bar īn dowlat-i mardom farīb*[74]). Perhaps the most fascinating aspect of this and other slogans was that it was popularized during the Iranian Revolution and Iran–Iraq War (Figure 3.2).[75] These campaigners were employing Iran's revolutionary past to condemn the revolutionary

---

[73] Goodzila82. "20-km human chain in Tehran – June 8th." Online video clip, YouTube, June 8, 2009. Accessed August 3, 2010. www.youtube.com/watch?v=PP-iji4VTQQ.

[74] This is a verse from the Quran (Sūrat aṣ-Ṣaff 61:13). Translations for the verse vary; visit alim.org for four common translations. I have translated it in a manner that works in the Persian context of the protest.

[75] Pouya Alimagham, "Assistance from God leads to victory." 2018. JPEG file.

government even before the post-election crisis gripped Iran. The election climate indeed provided an opportunity to voice subversive political sentiments, such as when 6,000 supporters chanted in unison "Death to the Taliban – in Kabul and Tehran"[76] at a pro-Mousavi election rally in which they explicitly attacked clerical rule in Iran. Such slogans underscored the anti-government sentiment even before partisans believed their victory was stolen from them. Mashalah Shamsolvaezin, a political commentator and former director of several reformist newspapers, observed: "What's happening now is more than what should happen before an election... This is an expression of protest and dissatisfaction by people. They are venting their frustration and feeling very powerful."[77]

The massive pro-Mousavi rallies and street marches imbued campaigners with a sense of confidence that their candidate was going to be Iran's next president unless he and his supporters were robbed of their electoral destiny. Recognizing such a possibility, they declared, "If there's no fraud, Mousavi will win"[78] (*agar taqalob nasheh, mūsavī avval mīsheh*).[79] The fear of a rigged election was so real that it prompted hundreds of University of Tehran students to demonstrate in front of the Ministry of the Interior, warning, "If there's fraud, Iran will revolt" (*agar taqalob besheh, īrān qīyāmat mīsheh*).[80]

The crowd's immense presence on the streets, and their overtly political slogans, became an enormous cause for concern among the authorities. Brigadier General Yadollah Javani, the deputy commander of political affairs for the powerful IRGC, accused Mousavi supporters on the streets of being part of a "velvet revolution," and promised that

---

[76] "Hāshīeh hāyeh sokhanrānī-ye mūsavī dar sālon-i 6000 nafarī-ye mashhad." *Aftab News*, April 24, 2009. http://goo.gl/eK581u.

[77] Robert Worth, "Huge campaign rallies snarl Tehran." *The New York Times*, June 8, 2009. Accessed April 23, 2014. www.nytimes.com/2009/06/09/world/middleeast/09iran.html.

[78] It is important to note that as in many cultures, the poetic tradition is an integral part of Iranian culture. Many, if not all, the slogans uttered before and after the election have a powerful rhythmic flow that does not effectively translate into English.

[79] Goodzila82, "20-km human chain in Tehran – June 8th."

[80] Sullivansilver, "Tajamoʿ-i dāneshjūyān-i dāneshgāh-i tehrān dar moqābel-i vezārat-i keshvar." Online video clip, YouTube, June 7, 2009. Accessed August 3, 2010. www.youtube.com/watch?v=46P9VHgnpeg.

"any kind of velvet revolution will not be successful in Iran."[81] That
the crowd combined its massive street presence with the appropriation
of a potent Islamic symbol caused the regime even more consternation.
For the first time in contemporary Iran, a candidate adopted a color to
symbolize their campaign. The Mousavi camp selected green to highlight that he was a *sayyid*, a descendant of the Prophet Muhammad,[82]
giving Mousavi and his campaign an aura of religious legitimacy in the
eyes of the conservative establishment. Green is associated with Islam
because it is believed to have been Muhammad's favorite color. Additionally, the Quranic chapter "The Human" describes heaven as a
place where people wear "garments" of "fine green silk."[83] For these
reasons and others, Islamic groups, states, and empires have historically employed green in their flags to convey an Islamic character and
legitimacy to their authority.[84] Iran's pre- and post-revolutionary flags
likewise incorporate green.

The fact that green afforded Mousavi's candidacy and campaign an
Islamic veneer posed a significant challenge to the state. The former
premier, who was the longest-serving prime minister during Khomeini's guardianship (*velāyat*), was part of the early leadership of the
Islamic Republic when it was forging its political and ideological
foundations, causing many to refer to him as the "Imam's prime
minister."[85] Now, campaigners had donned the color and were campaigning for a Mousavi who was promising reform. Moreover, others
garbed in Islamic green were using the cover of the campaign to

[81] Shervin Omidvar, "Sepāh mūsavī rā tahdīd kard: enqelāb-i makhmalī rā dar
noṭfe khafeh mīkonīm." Rooz Online, June 9, 2009. Accessed December 20,
2014. www.roozonline.com/persian/news/newsitem/archive/2009/june/09/
article/-16589c36c9.html.

[82] "Battle of colors in Iran's presidential campaign." PressTV, May 28, 2009.
Accessed June 29, 2010. www.presstv.ir/detail.aspx?id=96233&sectionid=
351020101.

[83] Taqi-ud-Din Al-Hilali, Muhammad, Muhammad Muhsin Khan, *Interpretation
of the Meaning of the Noble Qur'an in the English Language* (Riyadh: Dar us-
Salam Publishers, 1996), 29: 21.

[84] For example, the flags for both the Palestinian Islamic group Hamas and Saudi
Arabia, a self-avowed Islamic state, are green with Islamic writing on them. The
flag of the Fatimid Caliphate that ruled Egypt from the tenth to the twelfth
centuries was solid green.

[85] "Faryād-i āzādi-ye nakhost vazīr-i emām dar dāneshgāh-i amīr kabīr." Kaleme,
April 14, 2014. www.kaleme.com/1393/01/25/klm-180544/. Khomeini favored
Mousavi so much that he intervened twice to prevent his resignation in the
1980s. Ehteshami, *After Khomeini*, p. 24.

denounce the entire Islamic system, using slogans that either invoked the anti-government revolutionary fervor of the Iranian Revolution, or mentioned the theocracy in the same breath as the Taliban, a movement that the Iranian government opposed ideologically and militarily.[86]

The Mousavi campaign's strategy of adopting Islamic green as its color, however, roused the suspicion of the authorities not merely because of the specific choice but because a color was adopted in the first place. Weeks before the election, the conservative media accused "Mousavi's supporters of following in the footsteps of those who staged color revolutions in some former Soviet republics."[87] Regime authorities grew more nervous as Iran's youth controlled the streets in the run-up to the election, wearing a single unifying color. In other words, the more Mousavi supporters openly wore green, the more they could identify each other, see their self-affirming strength in numbers, and inspire others to join the momentum. The more people enlisted, the more threatening they became in the eyes of the state. Consequently, three days prior to the election, the Islamic Revolutionary Guards took the extraordinary step of warning that the adoption of a color for the "first time in the elections signaled that a velvet revolution was underway for the tenth presidential elections" and promised that it will be "nipped in the bud."[88]

The 20-kilometer human chain, which was "cause for excitement" among spectators who were increasingly interested in the campaign, was peppered in green.[89] Prohibited from holding each other's hands, young men and women lined the streets holding a green rope, which served as a chain linking the campaigners. Participants clenched the rope wearing green headscarves, headbands, armbands, wristbands, visors, shirts, and ties. Several even wore green capes.[90] Merchants took advantage of the occasion, selling all sorts of green goods, from Mardi Gras-style beads to pom poms, and some painted their faces

---

[86] The Islamic Republic sustained the resistance to the Taliban by providing critical financial and military assistance to the armed opposition in the late 1990s when the Taliban controlled 90 percent of Afghanistan.

[87] "Battle of colors in Iran's presidential campaign."

[88] Shervin Omidvar, "Sepāh mūsavi rā tahdīd kard: enqelāb-i makhmalī rā dar noqte khafeh mikonīm." Rooz Online, June 9, 2009. Accessed December 20, 2014.

[89] ʿAlireza Doostdar, email interview. August 2, 2010.

[90] Goodzila82, "20 km human chain in Tehran – June 8th."

"resembling the Incredible Hulk."[91] In more conventional political fashion, demonstrators raised green campaign posters depicting Mousavi alongside former president Muhammad Khatami, a reformist cleric who publicly backed Mousavi's candidacy and was widely popular among young people. So widespread was the use of green to show solidarity with the Mousavi campaign that Iran's national football team jumped into the fray of the post-election turmoil by coming onto the field in South Korea wearing green wristbands.[92]

The campaign's decision to adopt green as Mousavi's color was designed to bestow an aura of Islamic legitimacy on their candidate. In the aftermath of the election when the political crisis brought Iran to a standstill, campaigners turned into determined protesters who voiced their political demands wearing the Islamic color green, amplifying the meaning of these political acts. When activists invoked the Iranian Revolution by shouting specific slogans at the government that had come to power through that same revolution, those slogans were imbued with greater intensity and posed a more serious ideological challenge *because* demonstrators uttered them while wearing the quintessential Islamic color. Activists were transforming green from merely invoking Islam and affirming Mousavi's "religious credentials" into an Islamic color that became a marker of protest and a central nonviolent weapon in the movement's arsenal which they deployed to attack the Islamic regime at both discursive and ideological levels. The government's own Islamic symbols, including green and revolution-era slogans, were now being used by the opposition to contest the product of the Iranian Revolution: the Islamic Republic.

Before this dramatic transition, however, there was a mandatory lull in campaigning the day before the election. The crowd, spirited and hopeful, went home to rest before the fateful June 12 vote. In hindsight, this was the proverbial "calm before the storm," though a storm was not entirely unexpected. On the eve of the election, classified

---

[91] Jason Rezaian, telephone interview.
[92] "Mardom-i īrān moḥtāj-i honarnamāī-ye ʿarabhā barāye baghā-ye ākharīn omīd + film." Tabnak, June 17, 2009. Accessed August 7, 2010. www.tabnak.ir/fa/pages/?cid=52190. Post-election demonstrators returned the gesture by carrying placards that read "Iran's champions" emblazoned "over a photograph of the players wearing 'Mousavi green.'" See Timothy Richardson, Dubai, to Central Intelligence Agency et al., July 1, 2009, Wikileaks, https://search.wikileaks.org/plusd/cables/09RPODUBAI269_a.html.

American documents accurately describe the possible outcomes that lay ahead:

> Similar to the campaign period itself, which has been punctuated by personal attacks and the massive mobilization of voters across Iran's fractured society, the outcome of the election is likely to be polarizing. Either of the probable outcomes - a Mousavi win in the first or second round, or the re-election of Ahmadinejad tainted by the perception of fraud - will, at a minimum, spark a struggle over verification of the results. There are signs that both camps are setting the scene to contest the results, with Ahmadinejad supporters also alleging malfeasance by his opponents' camps and laying down unrealistically high bench marks of the number of votes Ahmadinejad should [win] in a fair contest. Social unrest is also possible given the conviction among large swaths of society now that Ahmadinejad can not [sic] win fairly; conversely, Ahmadinejad has portrayed himself as a champion of disenfranchised Iranians and a potential martyr at the hands of a corrupt establishment. His supporters are not likely to take defeat well.[93]

## 3.4 The Tenth Presidential Election and Its Aftermath

The Interior Ministry reported that nearly forty million Iranians, or 85 percent of the electorate, voted in the election, with incumbent Mahmoud Ahmadinejad sweeping to victory by more than ten million votes over his closest rival, Mir Hussein Mousavi.[94] The size of Ahmadinejad's majority caused widespread outrage, as many believed there had been gross irregularities. The final result was especially suspicious given that the youth voted in droves, and precedent indicated that the more young people participated in an election, the higher the probability of a reformist victory.[95] The speed with which the election results were announced also shocked many. Although votes were cast by paper ballot, the Interior Ministry "released results from a first batch of five million votes just an hour and a half after polling stations closed.

---

[93] Director Ramin Asgard, Dubai, to Central Intelligence Agency et al., June 11, 2009, Wikileaks, https://search.wikileaks.org/plusd/cables/09RPODUBAI245_a.html.

[94] "Natayej-i nahāyī-i dahomīn doreh entekhābāt-i rīāsat jomhūrī." Ministry of the Interior, March 24, 2009. Accessed August 7, 2010. http://moi.ir/Portal/Home/ShowPage.aspx?Object=News&CategoryID=832a711b-95fe-4505-8aa3-38f5e17309c9&LayoutID=dd8faff4-f71b-4c65-9aef-a1b6d0160be3&ID=5e30ab89-e376-434b-813f-8c22255158e1.

[95] Al Jazeera English. "Presidential candidates court Iran youth."

Over the next four hours, it released vote totals almost hourly in huge chunks of about five million votes – plowing through more than half of all ballots cast."[96] Semi-official news agencies even "began indicating he had won before polls closed and before counting was to have begun."[97] The most damning accusation came from Mousavi, who alleged that the number of votes for nearly 170 electoral precincts exceeded the number of voters.[98]

There continues to be considerable debate as to whether, and to what extent, fraud occurred. What really transpired is actually unimportant. The perception of the truth is far more consequential. Millions of Iranians believed that widespread fraud had taken place, prompting a popular nonviolent uprising in the days and months after the election.

The regime's fear of a velvet or color revolution seems to have become a self-fulfilling prophecy. The morning after the election results were announced, the political crowd, enraged at what they perceived to be a rigged election, took to the streets.[99] With the ballot a closed avenue, crowd action in the streets became a vital alternative for political expression in Iran. The nature of the street as an inclusive physical space is crucial to understanding why it became an important site for contestation:

When people are deprived of or do not trust electoral power to change things, they tend to resort to their own institutional power to exert pressure on adversaries to meet their demands – like workers or university students going on strike. But for those (such as the unemployed, housewives, and

---

[96] "Speed of Iran vote count called suspicious." Associated Press, June 15, 2009. Accessed August 7, 2010.
    www.msnbc.msn.com/id/31375293/.

[97] Director Ramin Asgard, Dubai, to Central Intelligence Agency et al., June 15, 2009, Wikileaks, https://search.wikileaks.org/plusd/cables/09RPODUBAI249_a.html.

[98] "Bayānīeh shomāreh-ye panj-i mīr hussein mūsavī kheṭāb be mardom: nagozārīd dorūghgūyān va moteqalebān parcham-i defāʿ az nezām-i islāmī rā az shomā berobāyand." Gooya News, June 20, 2009. http://news.gooya.com/politics/archives/2009/06/089606.php.

[99] "Eʿterāżāt-i mardomī dar saṭh-i shahr-i tehrān." Aftab News, June 13, 2009. http://aftabnews.ir/vdcbazb9.rhbg5piuur.html.
    "Poll results prompt Iran protests." Al Jazeera, June 14, 2009. Accessed August 7, 2010. http://english.aljazeera.net/news/middleeast/2009/06/2009613172130303995.html.

broadly the 'informal people') who lack such institutional power or settings, streets become a crucial arena to express discontent.[100]

The crowd flooded the streets again, this time shouting, "We told you that if fraud occurs, Iran will revolt!" (*goftīm taqalob besheh, īrān qīyāmat mīsheh!*), and pelted the riot police from afar with stones.[101] The Associated Press agency reported that

Thousands of protesters – mostly young men – roamed Tehran looking for a fight with police and setting trash bins and tires ablaze. Pillars of black smoke rose among the mustard-colored apartment blocks and office buildings in central Tehran. In one side road, an empty bus was engulfed in flames.[102]

Protests were also reported elsewhere, including the shrine city of Mashhad.[103]

At the start of the revolt, the government re-instated its usual blocking mechanisms for YouTube, Facebook, and Twitter. It also put counter-measures in place against those who were able to circumvent the filtering of these websites, such as slowing down internet speeds.[104] Activists unable to access YouTube adapted by learning how to reduce video file sizes so they could be emailed to supporters abroad, many of whom would then upload them onto the video-sharing website on their behalf.[105] From there, videos would be linked, copied, and shared across social media platforms, eventually finding

---

[100] Asef Bayat, *Revolution without Revolutionaries: Making Sense of the Arab Spring* (Stanford: Stanford University Press, 2017), p. 104.

[101] Amirpix, "Clash between election protestors and police in Tehran." Online video clip, YouTube, June 14, 2009. Accessed August 7, 2010. https://youtu.be/Lp0KRMF78IY.

[102] Brian Murphy, "Election battles turn into street fights in Iran." Associated Press, June 14, 2009. Accessed August 7, 2010. www.thejakartapost.com/news/2009/06/14/election-battles-turn-street-fights-iran.html.

[103] "Taẓāhorat-i khīābānī dar chand shahr-īrān dar eʿterāż beh natāyej-i entekhābāt." Radio Farda, June 23, 2009. www.radiofarda.com/content/f4_riots_Iran_election_result/1753532.html.

[104] Matthew Weaver, "Iran's 'Twitter revolution' was exaggerated, says editor." *The Guardian*, June 9, 2010. www.theguardian.com/world/2010/jun/09/iran-twitter-revolution-protests.

[105] Mehdi Saharkhiz, "The role of social media in the Iranian people's struggle." Interview by Behnood Mokri, Voice of America, Washington DC, February 28, 2011.

their way onto global news channels. These tools served as a conduit to convey to the world the reality on the ground in Iran.

Mehdi Saharkhiz, a main source of videos from Iran that included footage of politically sensitive events, noted that "Social media was more about sending information out of the country than about organizing. It allowed people to transmit information from Iran to the world in a remarkably quick fashion. The internet was too slow for coordination."[106] Basic word of mouth, however, was instrumental in the coordination of the uprising.[107] One activist who was arrested during the first week of the uprising and held in Iran's notorious Evin Prison observed that word of mouth was far more important for organizing events than social media. He attested that he even saw an activist holding a sign giving information about the next day's protest time and location while standing in the middle of an ongoing demonstration.[108] Iran's cab drivers,[109] who have developed a keen ability to profile passengers based on their attire, style, and speech,[110] played a pivotal role in spreading information about forthcoming demonstrations to would-be activists and sympathizers.[111] Many dissidents were able to sidestep government filters and access Mousavi's Facebook page,[112] which also provided useful information about times and

---

[106] Mehdi Saharkhiz, personal interview, May 19, 2013.
[107] Kay McGowan, Dubai, to Central Intelligence Agency et al., June 18, 2009, Wikileaks, https://search.wikileaks.org/plusd/cables/09RPODUBAI255_a.html.
[108] B.S., personal interview, June 30, 2012.
[109] Too often Western journalists travel to north Tehran and converse with only cab drivers and the English-speaking elites of the city, and then generalize the entire country based on their narrow and selective window onto Iran. Whilst cab drivers could not offer a view of all Iran's complexities, they did play a role in relaying information about such upcoming events. Khomeini recognized their role when he blamed them for spreading false rumors against the Islamic government in the 1980s. "Matn-i kāmel-i vaṣīat nāmeh-ye emām khomeinī (rah)." ʿAsr-i Iran, October 6, 2009. Accessed September 27, 2018. goo.gl/3nkNpE.
[110] Anonymous, personal interview, June 25, 2011.
[111] Chargé d'Affaires Don Lu, Baku, to Central Intelligence Agency et al., July 21, 2009, Wikileaks, https://search.wikileaks.org/plusd/cables/09BAKU575_a.html.
[112] Ibid. Mohammad Sadeghi, who at the time was 27 and residing in Germany, launched Mousavi's Facebook page in January before the election. The growth in the number of the page's followers prompted Mousavi's campaign to contact Sadeghi, facilitating coordination in the run-up to the election. Afterwards, with government repression and the arrest of many of Mousavi's staff

places of protests.[113] Social media's role in coordinating protests should not be overstated; Twitter's part in the so-called Twitter Revolution was especially exaggerated.[114]

Activists recorded short, pixelated videos that provided a window onto what was unfolding on the ground. One such video shows protesters walking peacefully, only to be disrupted by policemen on motorcycles cutting through the march, causing demonstrators to rush aside. Most of the motorcycles carried two policemen, the pillion rider striking at protesters with his baton. Once satisfied that they had adequately disrupted the march, the police would rush back the same way they came. The crowd, angered and provoked by the seemingly unjustified assault, attacked the rear motorcyclist knocking him to the ground. As he tried to run away, the crowd descended upon him with one person yelling "hit him" as the crowd-turned-mob exacted revenge. Bruised, exhausted, and shell shocked, he was carried to safety by demonstrators while others called for him to "come out" as they torched his motorcycle.[115] This scene was not an isolated incident and was replicated several times.[116] The impulsive desire to fight back when provoked was repeated throughout the history of the protest movement but most, if not all, of these incidents have one significant feature in common: whenever the crowd descended upon one of its attackers, activist women played an important role in saving the

members, coordination ceased but the page continued to serve as a hub for many activists inside and outside Iran coordinating days of action and tactics. Graphic designers-turned-digital activists also submitted their work to illustrate their defiance.

[113] Mousavi's Facebook page provided times and locations for protests across the country on June 15, when the Green Movement produced the largest protests in the history of the uprising. See Mir Hossein Mousavi Facebook page, "E'teṣāb, rāhpaymāī va tajamoʿ-i fardā, farmān-i allāh akbar-i emshab." Facebook, June 14, 2009. Accessed January 22, 2014. http://goo.gl/kHZwzk.

[114] Matthew Weaver, "Iran's 'Twitter revolution' was exaggerated, says editor." *The Guardian*, June 9, 2010. www.theguardian.com/world/2010/jun/09/iran-twitter-revolution-protests. Also see Liat Clark, "Study: Twitter was not the driver behind 2009 Iranian protests." Wired, June 4, 2013. Accessed May 4, 2015. www.wired.co.uk/news/archive/2013-06/04/iran-twitter-use.

[115] Mousavi1388, "Riot police caught by crowd – Protests in Tehran after election." Online video clip, YouTube, June 14, 2009. Accessed August 7, 2010. https://youtu.be/dSECAvBTanQ.

[116] Amirpix, "Clash between election protestors and police in Tehran." Online video clip, YouTube, June 14, 2009. Accessed August 7, 2010. https://youtu.be/CCwrqBpbqjA.

paramilitary's life. Women repeatedly either beseeched their country-men to stop their assault or thrust themselves into the melee to shield the attacker-turned-attacked.[117] Iranian women using their bodies to protect their countrymen is not unprecedented. In 1905 during the Constitutional Revolution, for instance, women formed a human barrier to prevent counter-revolutionary forces from attacking the clergy who had taken refuge (*bast*) inside the Shah ʿAbdul ʿAzim shrine in Tehran.[118]

The intensity of popular anger over the election results should not be understated. Iranian journalist Saeed Kamali Dehghan interviewed Morineh Tahmasebi, a 57-year-old mother, whose insight reflects a widely held sentiment:

I lost one of my sons in the Iran–Iraq war, he was killed for defending his country and now my mouth is completely shut. [The election results are] not what my son and my family wanted – it doesn't have anything to do with Islam. These riot police are worse than any criminals in the world. Now I feel ashamed to say that there was a time when I defended the Islamic Republic. It's not what we wanted. It's worse than a dictatorship. I regret that I lost my son for this regime now.[119]

Such resentment helps explain why the first day after the election was marred by rioting, provoked or otherwise.

In his seminal book, *The Crowd in History*, George Rudé writes, "...the intrusion of the unexpected might create a panic or otherwise divert the crowd from its original purpose: in such cases, the charge of fickleness would appear to have some substance. But, in general, such 'mobility' of behavior was not typical of the riotous crowd."[120] Although subsequent days saw more clashes, often provoked by the riot police, the crowd showed extraordinary restraint even as its size increased dramatically. The few incidents of violence

---

[117] This was especially evident in the clashes during the chaos of ʿAshura on December 27, 2009. See Steve W., "Tehrān – 6 dey 1388 – ʿāshūrā – dastgīrī-ye 3 basījī." Online video clip, YouTube, December 27, 2009. Accessed June 9, 2018. https://youtu.be/IEi-YprarhA.

[118] Afary, *The Iranian Constitutional Revolution*, p. 178.

[119] Saeed Kamali Dehghan, "Iran disputed elections: The aftermath." *The Guardian* News Blog, June 15, 2009. Accessed August 7, 2010. www.guardian.co.uk/news/blog/2009/jun/15/iranian-elections.

[120] Rudé, *The Crowd in History*, p. 253.

should not detract from the crowd's generally disciplined approach to street protest.

For example, on June 16, four days after the election, hundreds of thousands marched on Vali Asr Street in protest at the election results in a manner that rebuked the regime's characterization that they were thugs, hooligans, or riffraff. Making the symbolic peace (and victory) gestures with hands raised above their heads, they marched in near complete silence and with remarkable self-control.[121] Angry with the state media for depicting them as hooligans, they marched in front of Iran's Radio and Television Station carrying signs that stated: "Lies are forbidden."[122] Their silence not only showcased the crowd's discipline but also protested biased reporting and the lack of media coverage, which in the days after the election focused on Ahmadinejad's victory rallies and street interviews with his supporters. One frustrated activist explained in her own words the reasoning behind the silent protests:

...You flip through the channels of Iranian TV and see Ahmadinejad supporters, you see Ahmadinejad making light of this situation and other officials calling the pro-Mousavi protesters 'sore losers' or 'no good looters who want to cause havoc in society.' Since their voices are not heard, the protesters have been protesting in silence. They say silence speaks louder than words and this is a prime example of that (both the silence of the protesters and the silence of the government on this issue).[123]

On Thursday, June 18, 2009, Mousavi called for a funeral procession to be held in Tehran to mourn those who had died in the post-election violence. Responding to his call, hundreds of thousands[124] of opposition mourners gathered at Imam Khomeini Square in Tehran holding gruesome photographs of those killed and signs that pledged, "Our martyred brothers, we will take back your votes," and asked, "Why did you kill our brothers?"[125] Clad in black, the traditional

---

[121] Thenima1, "Iran silent protest ... Valiasr Street ... 16 June 2009." Online video clip, YouTube, June 16, 2009. Accessed April 25, 2014. www.youtube.com/watch?v=GVBZQCsqdjo.

[122] Ibid.     [123] Anonymous, email interview, June 20, 2009.

[124] "Sūgvari-ye jamʿ-i anboh-i moʿtarezān dar tehrān." BBC Persian, June 18, 2009. Accessed August 7, 2010. www.bbc.co.uk/persian/iran/2009/06/090618_ba-ir88-funeral-demo.shtml.

[125] Parisa Hafezi, "Thousands mourn Iranians killed in protests." Reuters, June 18, 2009. Accessed August 7, 2010. www.reuters.com/article/idUSTRE55F54520090618.

color of mourning, and green – the campaign color that had been
transformed into a color of protest – the crowd sang nationalist and
anti-state revolutionary songs.[126] As we shall see in Chapter 5, revolutionary slogans and mourning ceremonies became powerful occasions
for protest.

Perhaps no single day in post-election Iran was as memorable as
June 15, 2009. According to Tehran's mayor, Muhammad Baqer
Qalibaf, nearly three million people marched on Freedom Square in
the largest protest event since the revolution of thirty years before.[127]
Sociologist Charles Kurzman, author of *The Unthinkable Revolution
in Iran*, argues that the larger the protests, the greater sense of "safety
through numbers" is felt by the participants.[128] On their way to
Freedom Square the protesters gave voice to this notion when they
chanted, "Don't be afraid, don't be afraid, we are all together"
(*natarsīn, natarsīn, mā hameh bā ham hastīm*).[129]

One participant's initial reaction to the massive march captures the
sentiment behind the momentous occasion:

I had heard that people were converging on Freedom Square so my friends
and I drove there but nobody was around. We assumed that they hadn't
arrived yet so we decided to go find a parking spot that had easy access to a
freeway in case paramilitaries attacked and we'd have to escape quickly.
Finding a parking spot and getting back to the square took nearly 30
minutes. But when we got there, we began to feel the ground tremble from
under our feet. I climbed a pedestrian bridge and got very emotional at what
I saw. The march was so immense that I could not see the end of the

[126] Iranriggedelect, "Massive mourning rally." Online video clip, YouTube, June
    18, 2009. Accessed August 7, 2010. https://youtu.be/M091xSOCNL8.
[127] The link to the source has since been deleted but the attempted erasure
    demonstrates that not even governments can exert total control over the
    medium of cyberspace. An Iranian activist uploaded footage of the day of
    protest onto YouTube. It is apparent that several million people did participate
    in the historic march. See Saeidkermanshah, "Protest continued – Protestors are
    going to Freedom (Azadi) Square." Online video clip, YouTube, June 15, 2009.
    Accessed August 7, 2010. https://youtu.be/9_hr7G4At84. Classified American
    cables echoed the estimates as ranging from one to three million. Alan Eyre,
    Dubai, to Central Intelligence Agency et al., February 24, 2010, Wikileaks,
    https://search.wikileaks.org/plusd/cables/10RPODUBAI47_a.html.
[128] Charles Kurzman, *The Unthinkable Revolution in Iran* (Cambridge, MA:
    Harvard University Press, 2004), p. 123.
[129] MrDemocrature, "15th June 2009. Millions protest in Iran against election
    fraud in Iran." Online video clip, YouTube, June 16, 2009. Accessed April 24,
    2014. www.youtube.com/watch?v=FjQLC4w1XMY.

approaching crowd. Tears filled my eyes because I was proud of my country-men's unity – it was a beautiful thing.[130]

The view from a pedestrian overpass directly over the awe-inspiring crowd confirmed the size and magnitude of the march onto Freedom Square, with protesters filling the main street leading to the square literally as far as the eye could see.[131] The sheer vastness of the crowd made it impossible to see where the protest began and where it ended, leaving one journalist, Maziar Bahari, who was imprisoned shortly after, to attest "that the horizon had become green."[132] Two years before Egypt's Tahrir (Liberation) Square captured the world's attention as the epicenter of the Arab Uprisings, millions of Iranians converged on Azadi (Freedom) Square in Tehran.

Freedom Square had been a focal point for crowd action during the Iranian Revolution of 1978–1979, and is the site of annual state-sponsored mass marches marking the victory of the revolution. Before the revolution, however, it was known as Shahyad Tower (Shah's Memorial Tower), the symbol of Iran's millennia-old tradition of monarchy and the last Pahlavi monarch's White Revolution.[133] On December 10, 1978, the largest protest event in the history of the revolutionary movement culminated in the royalist square where millions rejected the Shah's ideological universe by demanding the abolition of the monarchy. One Iranian who witnessed the revolutionary gatherings at Azadi Square in 1978 returned as a journalist in 2009 and noted that the scene reminded him "of the demonstrations against the shah."[134] He interviewed a 54-year-old man who participated in both historic marches and who likewise saw many parallels:

[130] Anonymous, Payman, personal interview, August 6, 2010.
[131] Saeidkermanshah, "Protest continued – Protestors are going to Freedom (Azadi) Square."
[132] Maziar Bahari, *Then They Came for Me: A Family's Story of Love, Captivity, and Survival* (New York: Random House, 2011), p. 77. Tabnak is one of the few remaining news sites inside Iran that has not taken down the pictures from the massive protest. See "Taṣāvīr: tajamo'-i ārām-i mo'tarezīn." Tabnak. June 16, 2009. www.tabnak.ir/fa/pages/?cid=52048.
[133] Nicholas Gage, "Protesters march for 2D Day in Iran; Violence is limited." *The New York Times*, December 12, 1978. The White Revolution was a series of reforms, of which land reform was the cornerstone, that the Shah implemented in 1963 in order to avert a "red" communist revolution. It was later renamed "The Shah and People's Revolution."
[134] Bahari, *Then They Came for Me*, p. 75–76.

"We walk along this route because it has taken us a long time to reach freedom since the revolution... I see many similarities between what happened then and now."[135]

Three decades after the seismic events of 1978–1979, nearly three million women and men appropriated the same politically significant square to condemn the election results. In 2009, however, the square did not exalt the monarchy, but attested to the glory of the Iranian Revolution through its "memory of struggle."[136] It is all the more subversive that such a symbolically loaded space, with its history of contention, became the site where the Green Movement brought the largest upheaval in post-1979 Iran to a crescendo, using a repertoire of revolution-era slogans.

### 3.5 *"Allahu Akbar"*

Belying allegations of hooliganism, the crowd demonstrated its ingenuity by invoking history in order to give weight and meaning to its contemporary demands. Slogans, places of political significance like Azadi Square, important dates in Iran's political calendar, and powerful methods of expressing opposition, all of which had historical precedents in Iran's revolutionary past, were co-opted and re-programmed to convey opposition to the Islamic regime.

One such method was the riveting and highly symbolic night-time rooftop chants of *"Allahu akbar"* (God is great), which had been a common way for people to show their opposition to the monarchy and their support for the revolutionary movement in 1978–1979.[137] *"Allahu akbar,"* the cornerstone of the Islamic faith that affirms that there is no greater being than the Almighty, became a way for revolutionaries in 1978 to voice their opposition to the Shah's US-backed dictatorship. Revolutionaries kept hope and the momentum of the revolution alive during the darkest days of the Shah's military crackdown when the streets were unsafe for protest activity by going up to their rooftops and repeatedly declaring two authoritative words: *"Allahu akbar."* One contemporary observer noted that the tactic

[135] Ibid.

[136] For the utility of the spatial flexibility of squares and the "memory of struggle" imbued in such symbolic sites, see Bayat, *Revolution without Revolutionaries*, p. 126–128.

[137] Kurzman, *The Unthinkable Revolution in Iran*, p. 119.

was "an ingenious way to harness the momentum of the marches, to literally raise the volume of fury and discontent..."[138] In one episode on December 2, 1979, for example, when the Shah had backtracked on political reforms and installed an emergency military government that imposed a strict 9 p.m. curfew, protesters in Tehran emerged from evening prayers at exactly 9 p.m. to challenge the curfew. From the rooftops of working-class neighborhoods, thousands cheered the demonstrators on by repeatedly shouting their battle cry: "God is great."[139] Wearing white burial shrouds signifying their readiness to die for the revolution, the protesters met their fate when the crackle of machine-gun fire punctuated their chants.[140]

For three decades, the Islamic Republic had used the emotive power of this history by which it had established its authority, and called upon the people to go onto their rooftops every February 11 (the anniversary of the revolution's triumph) and chant *"Allahu akbar."*[141] In 2009, a new generation of activists invoked this instruction in a manner that contradicted the government's aims.

Green activists revamped this tactic of "powerful passive resistance"[142] to express opposition to the Islamic government that had come to power riding a wave of innovative protest activity thirty years earlier. In the words of one participant, *"Allahu akbar"* was "the symbol of the [Iranian] revolution."[143] If shouting *"Allahu akbar"* in 1978 professed revolutionary support for Khomeini, then in 2009 it proclaimed opposition to the system Khomeini founded: the Islamic Republic.

The first night after the election results were announced, after a day of clashes with security personnel, protesters across Iran took to their rooftops to chant *"Allahu akbar"* under the cover of darkness. One Iran correspondent claimed, "All of Tehran is shouting 'Allahu akbar' from rooftops."[144] The chants were so loud and numerous that it prompted one observer to refer to the phenomenon as the "wailing

---

[138] Shirin Ebadi, *Iran Awakening: A Memoir of Revolution and Hope* (New York: Random House, 2006), pp. 36–37.

[139] Youssef M. Ibrahim, "Teheran is decked with symbols of death." *The New York Times*, December 2, 1979, p. 3.

[140] Ibid.     [141] Ebadi, *Iran Awakening*, p. 37.

[142] Jason Rezaian, telephone interview.

[143] S.V., personal interview, April 14, 2014.

[144] Saeed Kamali Dehghan, "Iran disputed Elections: The aftermath."

of wolves."[145] To ensure that the chants echoed across the country, Mousavi's Facebook page relayed the information nationwide to users who were able to circumvent the government's filtering of Facebook. Those users who accessed Mousavi's page on June 14, 2009, were advised to begin the "*Allahu akbar*" chants at 9 p.m. and continue until 11 p.m. "tonight and every night."[146]

The chants of "*Allahu akbar*," often intermingled with "Death to the dictator," served several important functions. First and foremost, it was a way for the crowd to leverage the power of the revolutionary past in order to express outrage at the present political situation. One veteran observer who participated in the Iranian Revolution noted, "The shouting from the rooftops already has some regime leaders thinking of 1978–79 rather than 1999."[147] These chants indicated to the authorities that the 2009 uprising constituted a more formidable challenge than the short-lived, week-long student protests a decade before. Furthermore, it was a way for the movement to legitimate itself and dispel accusations of serving a foreign plot in pursuit of a velvet revolution, a point affirmed by Mousavi: "A generation had been accused of having fallen out of religion. But it rose with the chants of Allahu akbar... How unjust are those whose minor self-interests prompt them to declare this Islamic miracle a foreign plot and 'velvet revolution.'"[148]

Citizens also used the night-time chants to remind their compatriots that they were not alone in the struggle: "It's the way we reassure ourselves that we are still here and we are still together," says Nushin, a young housewife who had never participated in oppositional activity

[145] Martin Fletcher, "'Wailing of wolves' in Iran as cries of Allahu akbar ring from roofs." *The Times*, June 25, 2009. Accessed August 9, 2010. www.thetimes.co.uk/article/wailing-of-wolves-in-iran-as-cries-of-allahu-akbar-ring-from-roofs-djddkh20tnk.
[146] Mir Hossein Mousavi Facebook page, "E'teṣāb, rāhpaymāī va tajamo'-i fardā, farmān-i allāh akbar-i emshab." Facebook, June 14, 2009. Accessed January 22, 2014. http://goo.gl/kHZwzk.
[147] Deputy Principal Officer Sandra Oudkirk, Istanbul, to Secretary of State Hillary Clinton, June 17, 2009, Wikileaks, https://search.wikileaks.org/plusd/cables/09ISTANBUL220_a.html.
[148] "Bayānīeh-ye shomāreh-ye panj-i mīr hussein mūsavī khaṭāb be mardom: nagoẓārīd dorūghgūyān va moteqalebān parcham-i defā'az nezām-i islāmī rā az shomā berobāyand." Gooya News, June 20, 2009. http://news.gooya.com/politics/archives/2009/06/089606.php.

prior to the 2009 protests.[149] She noted, "Even my little daughter joins me, and I can see how she feels that she is part of something bigger."[150] This sentiment was echoed by a woman who recorded such anonymous resistance to the backdrop of her defiant words: "They can take away our SMS, our internet, and our cell phones but we can show them with our cries of '*Allahu akbar*' that we can still gather amongst ourselves."[151] This sense of solidarity was an especially pressing message a week after the election when the state implemented a widespread crackdown, stifling the street protests. Indeed, it enabled activists and sympathizers to continue to protest after security forces had "cleared" the streets.[152] The chants' effect on unity even persuaded those unconvinced that fraud had taken place to participate, as it was a way of showing sympathy with protesters in the face of government repression.[153]

Alongside the theme of unity, the act was a robust discursive challenge in which even the state's hegemony over God was contested. The same Tehran resident who recorded the chants as they pierced the night, referenced the regime's derogatory remarks about the crowd to make her divine appeal:

Once again cries of '*Allahu akbar*' are rising – one of the simplest and effective ways to call people to come together... People are calling God with all their heart. Maybe their voices will shake the Kingdom of God. Defenseless people who have been called thugs and vagrants, defenseless people who have been called 'dirt and dust,' defenseless people who have expressed themselves with silent and peaceful protest, now at night from the Kingdom of God ask for help.[154]

---

[149] Martin Fletcher, "'Wailing of wolves' in Iran as cries of Allahu akbar ring from roofs."

[150] Ibid.

[151] Oldouz84, "ALLAHO AKBAR ARSHE ELAHI RA BE LARZE DAR KHAHAD AVARD 26 KHORDAD." Online video clip, YouTube, June 16, 2009. Accessed August 9, 2010. https://youtu.be/ztE-z0ooXd4.

[152] Chargé d'Affaires Doug Silliman, Ankara, to Secretary of State Hillary Clinton, August 13, 2009, Wikileaks, https://search.wikileaks.org/plusd/cables/09ANKARA1185_a.html.

[153] Alireza Doostdar, email interview.

[154] Mightierthan, "Poem for the rooftops of Iran: Defenseless people." Online video clip, YouTube, June 16, 2009. Accessed August 9, 2010. www.youtube.com/watch?v=p6bbEMxo2Xo.

It is important to note that the overtly religious nature of the chant should not distract from its oppositional significance; the chants are a popular means through which Iranians from all religious backgrounds participated. The Tehran citizen journalist attested:

Many of us don't even believe in God, but each night we come and on God we call for the others, for those who died, for me, for you, for Iran. The voices are coming from far away. They [the chants] leave you shaken. They give you hope, but they also show helplessness. They show that there are still people searching for justice and show how defenseless they are – that the only thing left for them to do is cry '*Allahu akbar*.'[155]

Shouting "*Allahu akbar*" also served as a warning. Nushin, cognizant of Iran's revolutionary past, noted, "This is what people did before the revolution and I hope it warns the regime about what could happen if it doesn't change its way."[156] Above all, it was a potent declaration of anti-state conviction best encapsulated by one Facebook user who reminded his compatriots to begin shouting "*Allahu akbar*" at a certain hour in order to "backhand this bastard cleric [Khamenei] in the mouth."[157]

   Although the political language is crude, there is something historically forceful and resonant about hitting somebody "in the mouth" in the context of modern Iran. Khomeini gave his first official address to the nation on his triumphant return to Iran on February 1, 1979, memorably proclaiming that he would "hit" the last vestiges of the Shah's government[158] "in the mouth."[159] For an entire generation of

[155] Mightierthan, "Poem for the rooftops: Let us not forget." Online video clip, YouTube, June 21, 2009. Accessed August 9, 2010. www.youtube.com/watch?v=QocvegFNuzc.

[156] Martin Fletcher, "'Wailing of wolves' in Iran as cries of Allahu akbar ring from roofs."

[157] Mani Sabz, "Emshab alaho akbar saat 22 faramosh nashe baraye to dahani zadan be in akhound harom zade.V." Facebook comment, December 30, 2009.

[158] By "last vestiges of the Shah's government," I mean the armed forces, especially the Imperial Guard, and the recently appointed premiership of Shahpour Bakhtiar, an opposition leader who broke with his National Front to take the reins of power in order to prevent the total collapse of the system. He subsequently fled the country and was assassinated in France twelve years later by agents of the Islamic Republic.

[159] Ruhollah Khomeini, "Ghayreqānūnī būdan-i majles va dowlat-i mansūb-i shāh va mafāsed-i rezhīm." February 1, 1979. Tehran. Vol. 6, p. 16. http://farsi.rouhollah.ir/library/sahifeh?volume=6&tid=7.

Iranians who had been reeling under the heavy boot of the Shah's military apparatus and dreaded intelligence agency, SAVAK, and were on the verge of their revolution's final push towards total victory,[160] these words from the aged leader of the unfolding revolution were full of redemptive revolutionary zeal. After more than three and a half decades of the Shah's rule and more than a year of revolutionary struggle on the streets of Iran, the simple but powerful words uttered by this frail 76-year-old man gave potent affirmation to the millions who were on the cusp of bringing the hated and once-feared government to a definitive end. In 2009, in a twist of political fate, the electrifying and historically charged night-time chants of *"Allahu akbar"* represented self-affirmation for Iranian citizens, likewise symbolically striking Khomeini's successor "in the mouth."

The appropriation of such protest activity with a revolutionary precedent was a powerful way of casting doubt on the legitimacy of the election and of the regime as a whole. The quintessential Islamic slogan *"Allahu akbar"* on par with "There is no god but God," predates the emergence of the Islamic Republic by nearly a millennium and a half, and came to be an integral part of the state's set of "universal truths" in the modern era. After the election, however, it was not negated (as Gramsci outlined) as a necessary precondition for obtaining "true consciousness," but was co-opted and redirected as a nonviolent assault on the state's ideological monopoly and hegemony over the sacred. "God" no longer belonged strictly to the state, but was also on the rooftops of those who invoked His emotive power against the Islamic government.

The rooftop chants were not the only form of protest appropriated from Iran's revolutionary past. The government's stifling and systematic response to the post-election demonstrations prompted a new approach to crowd action that was both ingenious and historically significant.

---

[160] The Shah fled Iran on January 16, 1979. Khomeini returned to Iran after fourteen years of exile on February 1, 1979. Ten days later, the revolution achieved victory after a two-day armed insurrection spearheaded by guerrilla groups, mass defections in the armed forces, a revolutionary seizure of Iran's police station, army barracks, and state radio and television stations, and the announcement of the military's neutrality.

## 3.6 Subverting Iran's Political Calendar

On the first Friday after the election, the country's highest authority, Ayatollah ʿAli Khamenei, delivered Iran's most important sermon at the University of Tehran. Typically, the Office of the Supreme Leader chooses Friday prayer leaders across the country on a rotating basis to relay the state's message nationwide. Khamenei rarely leads the Friday prayer, but when he does it is because an important occasion necessitates his presence.[161] On this occasion the nation, as well as many abroad, tuned in with anticipation to hear his response to the unfolding crisis.

During the sermon, he affirmed the legitimacy and fairness of the vote, demanded an end to the demonstrations, accused the United States and Israel of a conspiracy to stage a velvet revolution akin to the one that transpired in Georgia in 2003, and warned that if the demonstrations continued, the government would not be held responsible for the inevitable bloodshed.[162] Though clashes had occurred throughout the week before and dozens had been killed, Khamenei's Friday sermon – hailed as historic by the state and denounced by activists as the Sermon of Blood[163] – amounted to a declaration of a full-scale war against the protesters in which compromise was impossible and a total end to the street protests was the state's only objective. From that moment onwards, a comprehensive crackdown was fully implemented.

The effective and systematic security operation to bring the protests to an end was overwhelming, according to one eye-witness:

They [security personnel] have blocked off the roads and have not been allowing anyone to approach the meeting point for the protest. Friends who tried to go, returned scared and alarmed, they warned that we should stay home and not even think about leaving. Everyone is calling their friends and family to tell them about the number of police who have lined the streets leading up to Enghelab and Azadi (Freedom) Square. Anyone who has seen the police are advising others to not come close to the area. I have heard

---

[161] Bahari, *Then They Came for Me*, p. 87.
[162] ʿAli Khamenei, "Khoṭbehhāyeh namāz jomʿeh-ye tehrān." leader.ir, June 19, 2009. http://farsi.khamenei.ir/speech-content?id=7190.
[163] See, for example, "Sokhanān-i rahbarī-ye enqelāb dar namāz jomʿeh-ye tārīkhī-ye tehrān." Alef, June 19, 2009. http://alef.ir/vdcawany.49n0u15kk4.html?47820.

reports from friends working in different parts of town that the police are out on the streets in large numbers (Vanak Square, Villa Street, and many other main areas leading up to Enghelab Ave). The fully geared Special Forces police and the helmet-wearing plain clothed Basijis (militiamen) are staged all over Tehran's major squares and their presence has been stern and threatening.[164]

Another observer noted that there were various groups of security personnel, each serving a different function. One unit, for example, aimed to disperse gatherings and make arrests by using stun grenades that demobilized demonstrators in order "to bind their hands and put them into black vans," and gathered intelligence by taking photographs and filming activists.[165] Another group served as a deterrent by lining up in rows to prevent entry into main squares such as Revolution Square.[166]

Khamenei's speech and subsequent crackdown, however, did not address or assuage the crowd's grievances. In fact, his endorsement of Ahmadinejad and the election results, and his decision to unleash the security forces as a solution to the crisis, meant that he was now party to the conflict on the side of the incumbent and against the demonstrators. Widespread resentment persisted and the demonstrators now had a new target in Khamenei and the Islamic system that he personified and over which he uncompromisingly presided. With their demands unfulfilled, the protesters continued with their action, voicing their grievances while evolving and adapting to the new security situation.

With security personnel flooding the streets in even greater numbers than before, the crowd needed a new kind of political cover to come out into the open and protest the regime. Charles Tilly argued:

When connected dissidents face authoritarian regimes, they commonly have three choices: bide their time in silence, engage in forbidden and clandestine acts of destruction, or overload the narrow range of tolerated occasions for assembly and expression. In the third case, criticism of regimes often occurs in the course of public holidays and ceremonies – Mardi Gras, inaugurations,

---

[164] Anonymous, email interview, June 20, 2009.
[165] Kay McGowan, Dubai, to Central Intelligence Agency et al., June 23, 2009, Wikileaks, https://search.wikileaks.org/plusd/cables/09RPODUBAI258_ a.html.
[166] Ibid.

funerals, royal weddings, and the like – when authorities tolerate larger and more public assemblies than usual.[167]

Iran's political and cultural calendar provided a plethora of opportunities for the government to tolerate "larger and more public assemblies than usual," with unexpected consequences. Under the security crackdown, the crowd improvised by using specific state-sanctioned political holidays as an opportune cover for continued action.

From its beginnings, the Islamic government incorporated politically significant days, especially ones important to the Iranian Revolution, into its calendar as a way to have the masses walk in step with the regime. Official days on which the regime mobilizes shows of support include: Jerusalem Day,[168] which falls on the last Friday of the holy month of Ramadan; the anniversary of the seizure of the US embassy on November 4; the anniversary of the assassination of Ayatollah Mohammad Beheshti and other top leaders on June 28 (*haft-i tīr*); Student Day on December 7; and the Ten Days of Dawn leading up to the triumph of the revolution on February 11. The government had also sought to blur the line between state and religion by integrating Islamic holidays into its political calendar, the most significant of which is *'Ashura*. Under the cover of these politically important days, the crowd emerged onto the streets to denounce the election results and the regime. One continuous uprising became several Green Uprisings spread out over a period of seven months from mid-June to late December.

### 3.6.1 Ayatollah Beheshti's Anniversary

Opposition leader Mir Hussein Mousavi explained the strategy of appropriating Iran's religio-political calendar for crowd action:

The most important issue is that the vast 'Green' social movement that has been formed across the country ... should use all these religious celebrations

---

[167] Charles Tilly, *The Politics of Collective Violence* (Cambridge: Cambridge University Press, 2003), p. 73.

[168] Although Iran uses the solar calendar, the Islamic calendar relies on the lunar calendar. Thus, lunar-based religious holidays fall on different dates on the solar calendar each year. In 2009, Jerusalem Day occurred on September 18, 2009.

by relying on their creativity... Every day, we can have an agenda for illuminating and for pursuing the long-term goals of our extensive 'Green' movement.[169]

The crowd, however, had already begun refining its strategy, or perhaps its actions informed Mousavi of the strategy (Figure 3.3).[170] Before Mousavi's speech, a large crowd gathered in front of the Qoba Mosque to mark the 28th anniversary of the June 28, 1981 bombing[171] that killed many top leaders of the Islamic Republic, of whom Ayatollah Mohammad Beheshti was the most significant. A founder of the Islamic Republic, Beheshti was one of the most powerful men in post-revolutionary Iran. As leader of the Islamic Republic Party, he facilitated the militant clergy's consolidation of power during the post-revolutionary power struggle that eventually led to the decimation of virtually all the other factions that had united to make the revolution. He led the campaign to Islamize Iran's judiciary, one of the most important power centers in the Islamic system, and was instrumental not only in the writing of the Islamic constitution but also in its interpretation and implementation.

The authorities commemorate Beheshti's "martyrdom" annually with ceremonies that are open to the public.[172] Thus, in 2009, the day provided the crowd with a legitimate opportunity to assemble in a climate where crowd action was otherwise forcefully prohibited.

[169] Mir Hussein Mousavi, "Matn-i kāmel-i sokhanān-i mīr ḥussein-i musavī dar jam'-i farhangīān va tashakol hāyeh mo'alemān-i īrān." Ghalam News, July 27, 2009. Accessed August 16, 2010.
      www.facebook.com/note.php?note_id=112950157605.
[170] Mir Hossein Mousavi Facebook page, "Like clockwork - Co-opting political holidays." November 26, 2009, Facebook post. www.facebook.com/mousavi/photos/a.172726419453.118347.45061919453/186592639453/?type=3& theater.
[171] There is still considerable debate about who carried out the bombing. The government blamed the Mujahedin-i Khalq, which at the time was waging an armed struggle in which suicide attacks, mail bombs, and hit-and-run tactics were commonly deployed against the post-revolutionary clerical consolidation of power. Many, however, argue that regime insiders orchestrated the mass assassination as part of an internal power struggle, and credit Rafsanjani with the bombing as part of a campaign to eliminate his rivals, namely Beheshti. He is believed to have been expected at the meeting that was bombed but was absent or was present but left early.
[172] Tara Mahtafar, "Beheshti's ghost." Tehran Bureau, June 28, 2009. Accessed August 10, 2010. www.pbs.org/wgbh/pages/frontline/tehranbureau/2009/06/beheshtis-ghost.html.

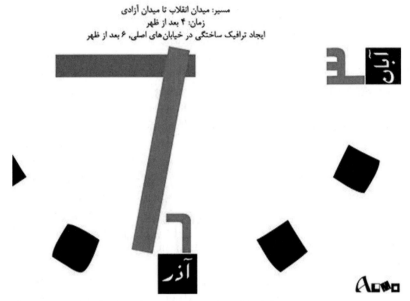

**Figure 3.3** Like clockwork: co-opting political holidays
Mousavi's Facebook page posted (on November 26, 2009) what is presumably an activist-made image, visualizing the strategy of co-opting state-sanctioned political holidays in order to stage anti-regime marches and rallies. The goal was to underscore the continuity of the movement by demonstrating on Student Day (December 7) as noted at the bottom with the clock's long hand, which in the color of the movement points to the next Green day of action. The day of action highlighted at the right is the anniversary of the embassy seizure, or National Struggle Against Global Arrogance Day. The caption above plans two protest actions: a march from Revolution Square to Freedom Square starting at 4 p.m.; and a protester-induced traffic jam to block the main roads at 6 p.m.

For the first time in the history of the commemoration, attendees came to voice their opposition to the state that Beheshti had helped establish. After a speech by Beheshti's son ʿAlireza, a top Mousavi advisor, Green Movement activists broke into chants of "Greetings to Beheshti, salutations to Mousavi" (*dorūd bar beheshtī, salām bar mūsavī*).[173] By placing Mousavi's name alongside Beheshti's, the

---

[173] FreeIran4life, "Front of Ghoba mosque in Tehran." Online video clip, YouTube, June 28, 2009. Accessed August 10, 2010. www.youtube.com/watch?v=7njmARTzzKU.

crowd subverted a day typically reserved for mourning one of the founding figures of the system in order to denounce that very system. The fact that Beheshti was one of Khomeini's most trusted lieutenants and an architect of the state they were protesting did not prevent the crowd from appropriating his legacy to present their case for Mousavi. Furthermore, the government, for all its organizational and military capacity, seemed unprepared to deal with the ingenuity of these Green Movement activists who legally seized the opportunity of Beheshti's commemoration to register their protest. Had the government prevented the crowd from congregating at the Qoba Mosque, it would have effectively prevented people from "observing" the "martyrdom" of one of the regime's most revered personalities. The crowd transformed the anniversary into a rally reminiscent of the pre-election atmosphere, as campaigners-turned-protesters raised their hands above their heads clapping and chanting in unison: "O'Husayn, Mir Hussein."[174]

The mosque was filled to capacity, and a huge crowd gathered outside. When rumor spread that Mousavi had arrived, "People, hands raised in the 'V' sign, as far as the eye could see in both directions down the street, [began] chanting pro-Mousavi slogans. The chorus spread like lightening, and indoors erupted as well with fervid chanting."[175] When they heard that mosque officials had barred him from entering the mosque compound, the 4,000-strong crowd inside went onto the streets chanting, "Long live Karoubi, long live Mousavi."[176] Marchers on Shariati Street leading up to the mosque shouted "*Allahu akbar*," "Death to the dictator," and "The Iranian will die before accepting subjugation" (*īrānī mīmīrad, zellat nemīpazīrad*).[177] This last slogan, popularized during the Iranian Revolution of 1978–1979, once again demonstrates the crowd's

---

[174] Khajesharif, "Yā ḥussein, mīr ḥussain – tajamoʿ-i eʿterāzāmīż-i mardom – masjīd-i qobā." Online video clip, YouTube, June 28, 2009. Accessed August 10, 2010. https://youtu.be/oney1QF03iM.

[175] Tara Mahtafar, "Beheshti's ghost."

[176] TheElection88, "Karoobi among the people in Ghoba street." Online video clip, YouTube, June 28, 2009. Accessed August 10, 2010. https://youtu.be/TZupydS90jY.

[177] SamaniAli, "Tehran. Shariaty St. 28 June 2009." Online video clip, YouTube, June 28, 2009. Accessed August 11, 2010. https://youtu.be/B2vjeXJk6Jc.

ability to leverage history to its advantage. George Rudé notes that slogans serve particular functions, such as "to unify the crowd itself and to direct its energies toward precise targets and objectives."[178] The slogans help explain the crowd's motives and the significance of the occasion "as [the slogans] may help to throw further light on the event itself and tell us something of the social and political aims of those that took part in it."[179] By denouncing the system on the day of the "martyrdom" of one of its founders, the crowd contested the ownership of Beheshti's anniversary and the slogans of the revolution, subverting a state whose ideological legitimacy rested partially on that glorified history.

The co-opting of Beheshti's anniversary was a key moment in the unfolding of the protest movement. The government's inability to prevent activists from gathering under this political umbrella proved the utility of appropriating political dates and historically evocative slogans and turning them against the regime – tactics that were replicated in a more organized and systematic manner as the uprising continued sporadically in the coming months. By reprogramming and re-directing these profoundly symbolic, often poetic, and rhythmic declarations, the crowd drew a parallel between 1978–1979 and 2009, showing that dictatorship endures in Iran and so does resistance to it.

### 3.6.2 *Ayatollah Rafsanjani's Friday Sermon*

Sociologists such as Tilly stress the importance of "opportunity" in fostering the moment for collective action. The run-up to the presidential election prompted the temporary suspension of state repression, giving activists and campaigners the space and opportunity to mobilize. A week after the election, Khamenei ordered a full-scale crackdown in an attempt to end street protests, prompting the opposition to evolve and adapt to the reinstituted and more stifling security climate. Divisions at the top with some political leaders openly backing the opposition provided the protesters with additional breathing room. Parsa, referencing both Tilly and Walter Korpi, opines that

---

[178] Rudé, *The Crowd in History*, p. 245.     [179] Ibid., p. 11.

Another key variable affecting mobilization and collective action, especially by groups with few resources, is the structure of opportunities, or balance of power, among contenders. In general, as the balance of power changes in favor of aggrieved groups over their adversaries, it increases the likelihood that such groups will instigate conflicts. On the basis of this principle, the likelihood of insurgency by aggrieved but weakly organized groups increases under the following conditions: when weakly organized groups anticipate a favorable response from government authorities or are able to form alliances with more powerful groups, such as a segment of the dominant class. Such situations arise especially when a reformist government comes to power, promising social change, or when the dominance class is divided. Under such conditions, weak aggrieved groups will benefit from the resources and support of others to mobilize for action.[180]

Ayatollah 'Ali Akbar Hashemi Rafsanjani, the billionaire "consummate insider"[181] and former president who in 2009 was the chairman of two powerful government institutions, the Expediency Council[182] and the Assembly of Experts,[183] has long been one of the most politically and financially formidable figures in post-revolutionary Iran, and openly championed the opposition in defiance of his one-time ally, Khamenei, and Ahmadinejad. His support and that of many others within the government meant that the government was not

[180] Parsa, *Social Origins of the Iranian Revolution*, p. 23–24.

[181] Director Alan Eyre, Dubai, to Central Intelligence Agency et al., December 10, 2009, Wikileaks, https://search.wikileaks.org/plusd/cables/09RPODUBAI532_a.html.

[182] The main purpose of the Expediency Discernment Council of the System (Expediency Council for short) is to arbitrate between parliament and the Guardian Council. The fate of legislation passed by parliament but vetoed by the Guardian Council is decided by the Expediency Council. Parliament-approved legislation that contradicts Islamic law may still be ratified by the Expediency Council if that legislation is deemed to serve the greater good. The governing principle is *maṣlaḥat*, or the interest of the community. Some scholars of Islam have opined that the incorporation of such a principle has resulted in Iran's Shi'ite system becoming "Sunnified" in this regard. Others have argued that *maṣlaḥat* has, in fact, long been a part of Shi'ite theology.

[183] The Assembly of Experts is a council of Islamic theologians who are vested with the power to appoint, and, in theory, to dismiss the Supreme Leader. The council, for instance, was instrumental in ensuring a smooth transition after Khomeini's death by appointing Khamenei as his successor in 1989.

speaking with one voice, enabling the movement to re-emerge on July 17.

On that day Rafsanjani, a staunch Mousavi supporter and bitter Ahmadinejad rival, was permitted to give a Friday sermon in the country's most important and politically sensitive Friday prayer venue, the congregation hall at the University of Tehran – the location of Khamenei's charged sermon a month earlier. This occasion gave Green activists, with telling historical awareness, the opportunity to gather again as they had for Beheshti's anniversary, and protest the election results and the state. Alternative media sources advised activists to avoid wearing green armbands until they were inside (presumably to ensure admission into the hall) and to chant "the opposite" of the state-sanctioned slogans.[184]

The nationwide mosque network had been instrumental in mobilizing the population for the revolution in 1978–1979, as it was with the Arab Uprisings of 2011. The mosque has a natural organizing capacity, especially on Fridays when Muslims, pious or not,[185] congregate for Friday prayers. Parsa argues that the mosque provided the militant clergy, their religious followers, and political allies with the "autonomous organizations and resources, communication networks, and favorable opportunities"[186] to carry out the revolution in 1978–1979 – a point affirmed by one contemporaneous dissident lawyer who contrasted his disadvantaged organizational capacity with that of the clergy:

We have not been allowed to form political parties. We have no newspapers of our own. But the religious leaders have a built-in communications system. They easily reach the masses through their weekly sermons in the mosques and their network of mullahs throughout the nation.[187]

Parsa prophetically noted that the Islamist consolidation of power after the revolution and the subsequent state takeover of the mosques

---

[184] Chargé d'Affaires Don Lu, Baku, to Central Intelligence Agency et al., July 21, 2009, Wikileaks, https://search.wikileaks.org/plusd/cables/09BAKU575_a.html.

[185] One does not have to be "pious" to attend Friday prayers, and some do so merely out of habit or to find solace.

[186] Parsa, *Social Origins of the Iranian Revolution*, p. 22–23.

[187] "The Shah's divided land." *Time*, September 18, 1978.

effectively meant that the nationwide mosque network could not serve as a springboard for dissident activity as it had during the Iranian Revolution.[188] Since the establishment of the Islamic Republic, the Office of the Supreme Leader has been responsible for appointing all the Friday prayer leaders of the country's mosques, ensuring the political obedience of the clerics and precluding mosques from becoming centers of dissent. A month after the election in 2009, however, both divisions in the upper echelons of power and the organizational capacity of the mosque were being exploited to once again facilitate protest activity.

In addition to the presence of expected pro-regime attendees, countless opposition activists amassed under the cover of Rafsanjani's Friday sermon to renew their denunciations of the election and the system that ratified them. Numerous sources attest to the vastness of the crowd. One young participant, for example, observed that it was the largest Friday prayer gathering he had seen in his life,[189] while state media acknowledged the presence of hundreds of thousands[190] – and the opposition claimed that one million people attended.[191]

Inside, Rafsanjani invoked his own revolutionary credentials and his proximity to Khomeini to authenticate his criticism:

What you are hearing now is from a person who has been with the revolution moment by moment from the very beginning of the struggle, which our leader Imam [Khomeini] started. We are talking about sixty years ago until today. I know what the Imam wanted and am familiar with the basis of the Imam's thoughts.[192]

He proceeded to discuss the election results diplomatically but in a way that nevertheless favored the opposition:

---

[188] Parsa, *Social Origins of the Iranian Revolution*, p. 314.
[189] S.V., personal interview.
[190] Timothy Richardson, Dubai, to Central Intelligence Agency et al., July 20, 2009, Wikileaks, https://search.wikileaks.org/plusd/cables/09RPODUBAI293_a.html.
[191] Borzou Daragahi and Ramin Mostaghim, "Tehran's streets erupt after a key cleric speaks." *The Los Angeles Times*, July 18, 2009. http://articles.latimes.com/2009/jul/18/world/fg-iran-prayer18.
[192] Shabakeh-ye khabarī-ye tebān-i īrān. "Fīlm-i kāmel-i namāz jomʿeh-ye 26 tīr 1388." Online video clip, YouTube, July 17, 2009. Accessed August 20, 2014. www.youtube.com/watch?v=N1OlYlESRDU.

Doubt [about the election results] came down on our nation like a plague. Of course, there are two separate currents. There is a group of people who have no doubts... But there is also another group whose numbers are not few and include a great section of our erudite and knowledgeable people, who say: 'We doubt.' We should take measures to remove this doubt.[193]

The seasoned politician balanced his opposition towards his rivals without undermining the system and his political standing within it, urging unity, the release of political prisoners, and a relaxation of the opposition's media, all while beseeching attendees "to not contaminate the position and the sanctuary of Friday prayers by inappropriate comments and slogans," to which the crowd responded with cries of "Freedom! Freedom!"[194]

The crowd outside denounced Ahmadinejad's victory by shouting "Liar, shame on you, resign" (*dorūghgū, ḥayā kon, mamlekato rahā kon*) and "O'Husayn, Mir Hussein."[195] As they passed the university's main gate, the crowd walked passed riot police standing guard behind an iron gate, prompting marchers to ask: "Brother soldier, why kill your brother?" (*barādar arteshī, cherā barādar koshī?*),[196] a slogan from the Iranian Revolution that had been particularly effective in sapping the morale of conscripts. Protesters in 1978–1979 famously marched passed soldiers posing this very same question as they pleaded with their fellow countrymen to avoid fratricide, causing many to defect to the revolutionary movement.[197] Another historically meaningful chant aired was, "The canon, the tank, the *basiji*, no longer have an effect" (*tūp, tānk, basījī, dīgar aṣar nadārad*).[198] The *basij*, the regime's hardline paramilitary force that is used to violently

---

[193] Ibid.

[194] "Rafsanjani: Iran in crisis." Al Jazeera English, June 17, 2009. Accessed August 11, 2010. http://english.aljazeera.net/news/middleeast/2009/07/200971793040418381.html.

[195] Irsngreen1, "Namāz jome'h-ye tehrān dāneshgāh-i tehrān." Online video clip, YouTube, July 17, 2009. Accessed August 11, 2010. www.youtube.com/watch?v=FRQQydgYBLU.

[196] Ibid.

[197] Nikki R. Keddie, *Roots of Revolution: An Interpretive History of Modern Iran* (New Haven and London: Yale University Press, 1981), p. 255.

[198] Irsngreen, "Namāz jome'h-ye tehrān dāneshgāh-i tehrān." Online video clip, YouTube, July 18, 2009. Accessed January 11, 2014. http://youtu.be/IkgW44w9tuI.

disperse crowds, normally acts as the country's morality police and reserve force.[199] "The canon, the tank, the machine gun, no longer have an effect" (*tūp, tānk, mosalsal, dīgar aṣar nadārad)*, the original slogan from the Iranian Revolution, was appropriated and re-configured against the *basij* and the regime that used it against the crowd.

The reprogramming of slogans demonstrates how the aims, mean-ing, and symbolism of the Iranian Revolution were being contested. The state rests part of its legitimacy on the revolution that brought it to power, and it has drilled the population, especially the youth raised under its authority, in the images, symbols, slogans, and history of that revolution. During Rafsanjani's Friday sermon, activists co-opted these revolutionary slogans that had been designed to express opposition to the Shah's repression in 1978, infusing them with new meaning and purpose against the Islamic government's repression in 2009. The Green Movement was determined to appropriate not just slogans important to the government, but even the same public spaces that were used to mobilize the population for the Iranian Revolution that brought it to power.

The government recognized that the opposition was using the "opportunity" of political and religious events to gather and give continuity to the movement and its demands, and responded in kind. Khatami was scheduled to be the prayer leader for the Night of Power (*shab-i qadr* in Persian, *laylat al-qadr* in Arabic), which is both the night Muslims believe the first Quranic verses were revealed to the Prophet Muhammad and the occasion of his son-in-law's martyrdom, which in 2009 fell on September 8. The annual event typically takes place at Khomeini's shrine, a site of national and transnational import-ance. This space, with its political and religious associations, is man-aged by his grandson, Hassan Khomeini, a supporter of the opposition. Having heard that the opposition was planning to "turn out in force as a show of strength,"[200] the government pressured

---

[199] On the post-war mandate of the *basij*, see Afshon Ostovar, "Guardians of the Islamic Revolution: Ideology, Politics, and the Development of Military Power in Iran (1979–2009)." PhD Thesis, University of Michigan, 2009, p. 140–142.

[200] Director Alan Eyre, Dubai, to Central Intelligence Agency et al., September 8, 2009, Wikileaks, https://search.wikileaks.org/plusd/cables/09RPODUBAI373_a.html.

Hassan Khomeini to prevent Khatami from speaking in the hope that it could control the event, which for the past two decades had been broadcast to the nation. Khomeini refused to prevent Khatami from speaking, and instead canceled the event,[201] infuriating and embarrassing the government. Not only were the authorities snubbed, but they were also prevented from presenting an image of normality returning to the country.

To ensure that there was no doubt about the meaning of his decision to cancel the event, Hassan Khomeini who sparked controversy after being absent from Ahmadinejad's inauguration, visited Mousavi's advisor, 'Alireza Beheshti, who had been recently released from detention.[202] Responding to the rebuke, state media, along with allies in the conservative press, attacked Khomeini: "The least that was expected was for you to not cancel the religious gathering at the holy shrine of the Imam for the sake of somebody like Khatami."[203]

Although the government emerged bruised from the Night of Power incident, days later it prevented the opposition from co-opting another state-sanctioned event, the annual commemoration of Ayatollah Taleqani's death.

Iranian Marxists often referred to Taleqani, a black-turbaned cleric, as the "red-turbaned cleric" (*ākhūnd-i 'amāmeh qermez*) to emphasize his populist worldview.[204] The Mujahedin-i Khalq, for instance, a group that during the revolutionary period blended Islamic

---

[201] "Marāsem-i shab-i aḥyā-ye ḥaram-i khomeinī laghv shod." Tabnak, September 4, 2009. www.tabnak.ir/fa/pages/?cid=62560.

[202] Arash Motamed, "Ḥamalāt-i jadīd-i kayhān va īrnā beh ḥassan khomeinī." Rooz Online, September 14, 2009. www.roozonline.com/persian/news/newsitem/archive/2009/september/14/article/-053a405c12.html.

[203] Ibid.

[204] Taleqani's fusion of Islamic discourse with Marxist terminology certainly helped garner popular standing. Montazeri, who spent time with Taleqani in the Shah's prisons, observed in his memoirs that Taleqani was exceptional in his warm relations with revolutionaries of various worldviews in prison. See Hussein 'Ali Montazeri, *Khāṭerāt* (Los Angeles: Ketab Corp, 2001), p. 381–382. Taleqani's son, Mojtaba, was a Mujahid who subsequently converted to Marxism. Rafiqdoost discusses Mojtaba's problems with the regime after the revolution in some detail. See Mohsen Rafiqdoost, *Barāye tārīkh mīgūyam: khāṭerāt-i moḥsen-i rafīqdūst (1978–1989)* (Tehran: Andisheh Press, 2013), p. 83. Abrahamian documents Mojtaba's letter to his father in which he outlines his conversion in spectacular fashion. See Ervand Abrahamian, *The Iranian Mojahedin* (New Haven: Yale University Press), p. 157–162.

monotheism with Marxist economic theory,[205] continues to refer to the revolutionary as "Father Taleqani."[206]

Taleqani, a principled and committed dissident and "symbol of revolutionary purity"[207] who "commanded the streets of the capital,"[208] was critical of the post-revolutionary clerical consolidation

[205] I refer to the MEK's ideology in the past tense intentionally. The closer the group has grown to Western and Israeli intelligence agencies and American neo-conservatives, the further it has moved away from the radical ideology of its founders, many of whom died for their beliefs in an armed struggle against the monarchy. See Seymour Hersh, "Our men in Iran?" *The New Yorker*, April 5, 2012. www.newyorker.com/news/news-desk/our-men-in-iran. The term "Marxist-Islamists," was a propaganda label deployed by the Shah to attack and discredit the MEK as a group that was "eclectic" in its naïve and deviant blending of Islam and Marxism. See Mohammad Shanehchi, interview recorded by Habib Ladjevardi, March 4, 1983, Paris, France. Iranian Oral History Collection, Harvard University, Transcript 2 (seq. 48). Accessed April 30, 2015. Massoud Rajavi, the MEK's leader (along with his wife), who argued that they are not only Muslims, but believers in the "true Islam," was required by Khomeini to profess his faith after the revolution. Despite this insult, Rajavi wrote a letter affirming his belief via the *shahada*, which was subsequently published on the front page of various Iranian dailies as "The Mujahedin professes their faith." Rajavi says that he accepted the insult to deprive Khomeini of the chance to accuse the MEK of unbelief. See Massoud Rajavi, interview recorded by Zia Sedghi, May 29, 1984, Paris, France. Iranian Oral History Collection, Harvard University, Transcript 1 (seq. 20). Accessed April 23, 2015.

[206] Maryam Rajavi, "On 4 March, 100th anniversary of Father Taleghani's birth, true spirit of Iran's anti-monarchical revolution, we honor his memory #iranelection." March 4, 2010, 8:45 a.m. Tweet. Massoud Rajavi likewise referred to him as "Father Taleqani," as well as the MEK's "spiritual father." See Massoud Rajavi, interview recorded by Zia Sedghi, May 29, 1984, Paris, France. Iranian Oral History Collection, Harvard University, Transcript 1 (seq. 20–21). Accessed April 23, 2015.

[207] Director Alan Eyre, Dubai, to Central Intelligence Agency et al., September 8, 2009, Wikileaks, https://search.wikileaks.org/plusd/cables/09RPODUBAI373_a.html.

[208] David Butler, et al., "The Mullah's men," *Newsweek*, February 12, 1979. Taleqani was so popular that he garnered the most votes in the country's first election for the Assembly of Experts, the council tasked with drafting a new constitution. See Ervand Abrahamian, *The Iranian Mojahedin* (New Haven: Yale University Press, 1989), p. 54–55. His chief aide noted that Taleqani was especially close to university students, intellectuals, scholars and professors, with all of whom he was in constant contact through his Hedayat Mosque. It was such relationships, according to the aide, that set Taleqani apart from other clerics in terms of thought, awareness, and understanding. Consequently, unlike other clerics, he never viewed the Marxists and secularists as his enemies. See Mohammad Shanehchi, interview recorded by Habib Ladjevardi, March 4, 1983, Paris, France. Iranian Oral History Collection, Harvard University, Transcript 2 (seq. 35, 48). Accessed April 30, 2015.

of power, opposed the imposition of the *hijab,* which he believed was intended to encourage women to stay at home,[209] and specifically objected to the establishment of the *vilāyat-i faqīh.*[210] He was the first post-revolutionary Friday prayer leader of Tehran,[211] but died less than a year after the revolution, probably due to the enduring effects of the torture that he suffered during fifteen years of imprisonment under the monarchy.[212] To this day, he continues to epitomize an Islamic revolutionary ideal that transcends the rigidity of clerical rule in Iran. Consequently, the Islamic government in 2009 feared that the annual commemoration of his life and legacy would result in another opportunity for anti-regime protests, and for the first time in thirty years required Taleqani's family to obtain permission to hold the gathering. Their request was promptly and predictably denied.[213]

The government was willing to insult its previous president, Khatami, and a revolutionary icon, Taleqani, because of the overriding necessity to prevent the protest movement from enduring through such opportune annual events. The state's problem, however, was that it had programmed too many of these events into Iran's political calendar over the decades, and not all could be canceled.

[209] Tahereh Talegani, "Pedaram mokhālef-i ḥejāb-i ejbārī būd." Rahesabz, September 13, 2013. www.rahesabz.net/story/75520/#taheretaleghani.

[210] Montazeri, "Khāṭerāt: bakhshī az khāṭerāt-i faqīh va marjʿa ʿalīqadr haẓrat-I āyatollāh al'oẓmā montaẓerī," p. 455–458. Taleqani's untimely death after the election, however, removed a major obstacle to enshrining the *vilāyat-i faqīh* in the Islamic constitution. Some believe that hardliners killed him to facilitate their consolidation of power. Shanehchi details the suspicious circumstances of Taleqani's heart attack. See Mohammad Shanehchi, interview recorded by Habib Ladjevardi, March 4, 1983, Paris, France. Iranian Oral History Collection, Harvard University, Transcript 2–3 (seq. 53–62). Accessed April 30, 2015.

[211] Many Shiʿite clergymen believed that Friday prayers complete with *khutbah* (*khotbeh* in Persian, "sermon" in English) were forbidden during the period of unjust authority in the Age of the Occultation. The infallible Imams had not granted permission to hold Friday prayers, so the ones held before the revolution, according to some clerics, were invalid. Montazeri convinced Khomeini that since the revolution had toppled the unjust monarch and facilitated the emergence of an Islamic government, full Friday prayers could be reinstated as permission from the Imams was implied. Montazeri, "Khāṭerāt: bakhshī az khāṭerāt-i faqīh va marjʿa ʿalīqadr haẓrat-i āyatollāh al'oẓmā montaẓerī," p. 441–443. See also Michael Fischer, *Iran: From Religious Dispute to Revolution* (Cambridge, MA: Harvard University Press, 1980), p. 217.

[212] "Iran grief-stricken over Taleghani's death." *The Jerusalem Post,* September 11, 1979.

[213] "Posht-i pardeh-ye laghv-i bozorgdāsht-i āyatollāh ṭāleqānī dar ḥosseinī ershād va eʿlām-i maḥal-i jadīd-i bargozārī-ye marāsem." Rahesabz, September 8, 2009. www.rahesabz.net/story/1273/.

### 3.6.3 Dens of Spies: The Anniversary of the US Embassy Takeover

The shows of support organized by the Iranian government on its many political holidays are intended to underscore its popular and revolutionary roots. Mass marches are especially important because they invoke the legacy of the popular movement which overthrew the monarchy in 1978–1979, affirming the government's own revolutionary history and legitimacy. On November 4, 2009, however, the security climate was relaxed to encourage government supporters to participate in mass rallies marking the anniversary of the US embassy seizure. Green Movement activists exploited this opportunity to pour onto the streets to use the state's symbolism against itself.

The historical backdrop to this annual political event underscores its importance. In 1953, in concert with the British and a faction of the Iranian army, the US Central Intelligence Agency (CIA) spearheaded the overthrow of the democratically elected government of Prime Minister Muhammad Mossadeq. The American embassy in Tehran served as the base of operations for Operation Ajax.[214] Twenty-six years later, on October 22, 1979, and less than a year after the revolution prompted him to go into exile, the Shah was admitted into the United States for cancer treatment, causing concern among revolutionaries that the US wanted to repeat history in Iran by overthrowing the new revolutionary order and re-installing the ousted monarch. Revolutionary forces were especially alarmed after the publication of pictures showing a meeting in Algiers between moderate Prime Minister Mehdi Bazargan and Foreign Minister Ibrahim Yazdi with President Jimmy Carter's National Security Advisor, Zbigniew Brzezinski.[215] Fearing a covert American plan for yet another coup in Iran, 400 radical students breached the walls of the US embassy on November 4, 1979. After initially releasing some of the staff, they held fifty-two American personnel for 444 days.

---

[214] Principal Deputy Assistant Secretary Patrick Moon, Kathmandu, to Secretary of State Hillary Clinton, June 18, 2009, Wikileaks, https://search.wikileaks.org/plusd/cables/09KATHMANDU520_a.html.
[215] Keddie, *Roots of Revolution*, p. 262.

While Khomeini did not order the attack, its popularity prompted him to endorse the capture of what he came to call "the nest of spies,"[216] a label that has become part of the official lexicon of the state.[217] The militant students initially planned to use the hostages to pressure the Carter administration into extraditing the Shah so he could stand trial in Iran.[218] When these demands were rejected, Khomeini refused to order the release of the hostages. The moderates, who had wanted the embassy personnel freed and hoped for a new more balanced relationship with the United States, realized that they did not hold any real power in post-revolutionary Iran and resigned their positions. This was hailed by Khomeini as the "Second Islamic Revolution,"[219] and cemented the anti-imperialist outlook of the revolution. If the first revolution was against the Shah, then the second was decidedly against the United States.

That Khomeini refused to release the hostages even after the Shah left the US points to how the embassy personnel had become pawns in the post-revolutionary power struggle over the drafting of the new constitution. He harnessed the popularity of the embassy seizure not only to solidify the anti-imperialism of the revolution, but also to outmaneuver those who opposed the ratification of his Islamic constitution.

It is important to note that the seizure of the US embassy was a pivotal moment in the history of modern Iran (Figure 3.4).[220] For

---

[216] It is also often translated as "den of spies."

[217] "13 ābān-i emsāl porkhorūsh tar az hamīsheh sīlī-ye mellat, ashk-i āmrīkā rā darāvard." *Kayhan*, November 4, 2009. http://kayhanarch.kayhan.ir/880814/3.htm#other306.

[218] "Iran may try American hostages as 'spies' unless shah returned." *The Jerusalem Post*, November 19, 1979. It is important to note Richard Falk's argument: that the Shah was not extraditable because "the evidence against him is connected with his repressive rule, but extradition is not available against someone accused of 'political crimes.'" At the same time, Falk railed against an international legal system that confers such protection on the powerful, asking: "...Why should 'asylum' be available to a cruel tyrant associated with the massive commission of state crimes, including torture, arbitrary execution, and economic plunder?" Richard Falk, "The Iran hostage crisis: Easy answers and hard questions," *The American Journal of International Law*, 74(2) (April 1980), p. 412.

[219] Ervand Abrahamian, *A History of Modern Iran* (Cambridge and New York: Cambridge University Press, 2008), p. 168.

[220] Pouya Alimagham, "A new beginning: The seizure of the U.S. Embassy." 2018. JPEG file.

**Figure 3.4** A new beginning: the seizure of the US embassy.
Photo credit: Pouya Alimagham.

many Iranians, it signified a break with a past in which first the British and Russians, then the Americans had undermined and subjugated the country to safeguard their imperial interests. Whereas before, foreign powers had intervened in Iran, Iranians were now invading the diplomatic soil of the world's eminent superpower. The takeover not only marked a rupture in relations between Iran and the United States, but also constituted a purifying act of defiance that redeemed the country from a long humiliation – so much so that one American writer equated the event with the Boston Tea Party.[221] The students'

---

[221] Mark Bowden, *The Guests of the Ayatollah. The Iran Hostage Crisis: The First Battle in America's War with Militant Islam* (New York: Grove Press, 2006), p. 562. The comparison is problematic, especially since the Boston Tea Party did not include hostage taking. The parallel is apt, however, in terms of a

spokeswoman, Ma'soumeh Ebtekar, affirmed how the seizure marked a new beginning:

The Islamic Revolution of Iran represents a new achievement in the ongoing struggle between the people and the oppressive superpowers... Iran's revolution has undermined the political, economic, and strategic hegemony of America in the region... We Muslim students, followers of Ayatollah Khomeini, have occupied the espionage embassy of America in protest against the ploys of the imperialists and the Zionists. We announce our protest to the world; a protest against America for granting asylum and employing the criminal shah ... for creating a malignant atmosphere of biased and monopolized propaganda, and for supporting and recruiting counterrevolutionary agents against the Islamic Revolution of Iran... And finally, for its undermining and destructive role in the face of the struggle of the peoples for freedom from the chains of imperialism.[222]

Since 1979, the anniversary of the embassy seizure has been a state-sanctioned event highlighting the ongoing struggle with the United States and imperialism. The day, officially known as National Struggle Against Global Arrogance Day,[223] underscores the state's revolutionary anti-imperialist credentials,[224] while also emphasizing the country's "will to remain independent."[225] November 4, 2009, however, proved to be a unique day in the history of its commemoration.

Aware that the opposition might seek to co-opt and reprogram the event, the government was nevertheless unable to cancel it since it was a national holiday and a fixture in the state's political calendar.

weaker country committing a defiant act to mark a revolutionary rupture with a colonial power.
[222] David Farber, *Taken Hostage: The Iran Hostage Crisis and America's First Encounter with Radical Islam* (Princeton: Princeton University Press, 2005), p. 136.
[223] "13 ābān-i emsāl porkhorūsh tar az hamīshe sīlī-ye mellat, ashk-i āmrīkā rā darāvard." *Kayhan*, November 4, 2009. http://kayhanarch.kayhan.ir/880814/3.htm#other306.
[224] The day is most important for marking the anniversary of the embassy seizure, but it is historic for other reasons as well; it coincides with the anniversary of when the Shah exiled Khomeini to Turkey in 1964, and when the Shah's forces killed several protesters at the University of Tehran during the revolutionary upheaval in 1978.
[225] Director Alan Eyre, Dubai, to Central Intelligence Agency et al., November 2, 2009, Wikileaks, https://search.wikileaks.org/plusd/cables/09RPODUBAI469_a.html.

The Mousavi campaign used social media to inform those supporters who were able to circumvent government filters of the necessity of coming out in their millions.[226] With official media either not covering Green protests or presenting such demonstrations in a negative light, the campaign urged voters-turned-protesters to spread the news of the forthcoming event: "you are the media."[227]

While thousands came out in solidarity with the regime and against the United States and imperialism, a large crowd congregated at Haft-i Tir Square to continue protesting both the election results and the government that ratified them. This was the first major anti-regime gathering in nearly two months,[228] despite the Revolutionary Guards warning that the "Iranian nation will not allow any group to impose itself and use diversionary and false slogans on 13 Aban [November 4]."[229]

With green ribbons tied to their wrists and clenched in their hands, protesters once again appropriated slogans from the revolution, changing words to create new slogans: "The canon, the tank, Kahrizak[230] [detention center], no longer have an effect" (*tūp, tānk,*

---

[226] Mir Hossein Mousavi Facebook page, "13 ābān." Facebook, October 14, 2009. Accessed January 22, 2014. www.facebook.com/photo.php?pid=2494413&id=45061919453.

[227] Ibid.

[228] The last major demonstration until November 4 occurred during the Quds Day rallies on September 18. See Chapter 4.

[229] Director Alan Eyre, Dubai, to Central Intelligence Agency et al., November 2, 2009, Wikileaks, https://search.wikileaks.org/plusd/cables/09RPODUBAI469_a.html.

[230] Kahrizak is a detention facility that gained notoriety when three activists arrested for protesting the election results died under torture. The government denied that their deaths resulted from physical abuse and blamed their deaths on meningitis. It was only with the death of Mohsen Rouhalamini, the son of a prominent conservative official who headed the Ministry of Health's Pasteur Institute and served as an adviser to the other conservative presidential candidate, Mohsen Rezaei, that allegations of prisoner abuse became undeniable. Khamenei ordered the closure of the facility in July 2009. Karroubi, however, refused to allow the government to put the issue to rest quietly, and penned a strongly worded letter to speaker of parliament, Ali Larijani, claiming that he had documented proof of both torture and rape. An official investigation ruled out rape but acknowledged the deaths were the result of prisoner abuse, blaming Tehran's Prosecutor General Saeed Mortazavi, who effectively became the "fall guy" for the government. By this time, Kaleme noted that a fourth prisoner, Ramin Aqazadeh, had also died at Kahrizak. The prisoner abuse discredited the government but also created a sense of fear for many activists who dreaded such a fate. See Timothy

*kahrīzak, dīgar aṣar nadārad).*[231] Another slogan attacked the head of
the Guardian Council: "Damn you Jannati, you are the nation's
enemy" *(jannatī-ye la'natī, to doshman-i mellatī).*[232] The original
slogan had attacked the Shah for being brought to power by a foreign
government: "Shah you American, you are God's enemy" *(ey shāh-i
emrīkāyī, to doshman-i khodāyī).*

Instead of the typical slogans critical of the US, the crowd usurped
Khomeini's 1979 rhetoric to condemn one of the few countries that
congratulated Ahmadinejad on his victory and was perceived to be
protecting the regime[233]: "The Russian embassy is 'a nest of spies'"
*(lāneh-ye jāsūsīyeh, sefārat-i rūsīyeh).*[234]

More directly, the marchers brazenly shouted, "Khamenei is a murderer, his mandate is null and void" *(khāmeneī qāteleh, velāyatash
bāṭeleh),*[235] and committed illegal acts that would have been unthinkable before the post-election turmoil. In one such incident, the crowds
chanted "O'Husayn, Mir Hussein," as a protester climbed onto a
billboard of Khamenei and tore it down to loud cheers and raised
hands.[236]

Richardson, Dubai, to Central Intelligence Agency et al., July 27, 2009,
Wikileaks, https://search.wikileaks.org/plusd/cables/09RPODUBAI301_
a.html; "Eʿlām āmādegī-ye karūbī barāye erāʾeh-ye mostanadāt nāmehash beh
masʾūlan-i neẓām." Aftab News, August 18, 2009. Accessed May 13, 2015.
https://goo.gl/iE14n0. "'Rāmīn āqāzādeh' chahāromīn qorbānī-ye kahrīzak
moʿarefī shod." Kaleme, January 23, 2010. Accessed May 13, 2015.
www.kaleme.com/1388/11/03/klm-9298/; Alan Eyre, Dubai, to Central
Intelligence Agency et al., January 12, 2010, Wikileaks, https://search
.wikileaks.org/plusd/cables/10RPODUBAI11_a.html.

[231] UNITY4IRAN, "Iran Tehran 4 November 2009. Shariati St Seyed Khandan
protest P37." Online video clip, YouTube, November 4, 2009. Accessed
August 11, 2010. https://youtu.be/WGqGiXi0Ct8.

[232] Ibid.

[233] Chargé d'Affaires Doug Silliman, Ankara, to Secretary of State Hillary Clinton,
January 8, 2010, Wikileaks, https://search.wikileaks.org/plusd/cables/
09ANKARA1185_a.html.

[234] 1388sabz, "Shoʿārhāye mardomī ʿalayh-i istebdād dar sālrūz 13 ābān." Online
video clip, YouTube, November 4, 2009. Accessed August 11, 2010.
https://youtu.be/8vuAuz6J520.

[235] UNITY4IRAN, "Iran Tehran 4 November 2009. Shariati St Seyed Khandan
protest P37."

[236] Freedom Messenger, "Pāreh kardan-i plākārd-i bozorg-i khāmeneī." Online
video clip, YouTube, November 4, 2009. Accessed August 11, 2010.
https://youtu.be/nVjqewNANCY.

They even took aim at the physicality of Khamenei, who had lost the use of his right arm in a mail-bomb attack during the post-revolutionary power struggle when many of the Islamic Republic's early leaders were assassinated.[237] His disabled right arm is a potent reminder of his revolutionary credentials derived from his proximity to Ayatollah Khomeini, time as a dissident in the Shah's prisons, and a near-death assassination attempt that caused him permanent injury. So important are such political bona fides that he invoked his ailment in the closing remarks of his first post-election sermon to a sobbing audience when he said in a cracking voice: "I have only my humble life. My body is handicapped. I have a good name that you have bestowed upon me, and I am ready to sacrifice all I have for the sake of Islam and the revolution. . ."[238] It is precisely this nobility in physical suffering that protesters on the National Struggle Against Global Arrogance Day mocked, ridiculing his injury to discredit the very physical and revolutionary credentials that affirmed his political legitimacy: "Our leader is a jack ass, crippled in one arm" (*rahbar-i mā olāgheh, ye dastesham cholāqeh*).[239]

Although Khamenei was theoretically above the factionalized politics of the state, his political standing became intertwined with Ahmadinejad's the moment he endorsed his election "victory." In the first week after the election, slogans were directed against both the results and Ahmadinejad himself, but after his Friday sermon, Khamenei, Khomeini's successor as "the Leader of the Revolution," also became the target of the Green Movement's fury, and by the anniversary of the embassy seizure, he had supplanted Ahmadinejad to bear the brunt of activists' slogans, anger, and subversive zeal.

It was noticeable that the state was increasingly willing to forcibly repress the crowds. Unlike the September 18 Quds Day protesters, crowds on November 4 experienced a number of violent reprisals by a government increasingly frustrated with a movement that refused to

[237] See, for example, chapter 9 in Abrahamian's *The Iranian Mojahedin* (New Haven: Yale University Press, 1989), p. 206–23.
[238] ʿAli Khamenei, "Khoṭbehhāyeh namāz jomʿeh-ye tehrān." leader.ir, June 19, 2009. http://farsi.khamenei.ir/speech-content?id=7190.
[239] GREENPOWER0, "Rahbar-i mā olāgheh, ye dastesham cholāqeh/13 ābān." Online video clip, YouTube, November 25, 2009. Accessed May 15, 2015. https://youtu.be/X1huhn49Zcc.

accept the election results as a *fait accompli* nearly five months after the vote.[240] Security forces, working with Revolutionary Guards, police, and *basij* units, deployed tear gas, clubbed protesters with batons, and even shot into the air in a bid to prevent large crowds from congregating.[241] Zeynab, a 22-year-old student, attested: "We started our protest very peacefully but riot police attacked us with batons and teargas on our way in Vali-e-Asr Street. I saw people who were bleeding badly from the head."[242] Another participant stated: "They chased us down a dead end. We were all crushed together and the riot police shot something like five teargas canisters into the alley."[243] Even Karroubi, who attended the opposition rallies, was tear-gassed and slightly burned by a canister.[244]

Protests were reported in Rasht, Isfahan, Zahedan, Kermanshah, Mashhad, Shiraz, Tabriz, which saw its first large protests in months, and, of course, Tehran, the focal point of the street movement against the state.[245] While the number of demonstrators to brave the regime's threats cannot be verified, estimates range from tens of thousands to as much as a million.[246] One of the day's most noteworthy successes was that it showed both the state and many Green sympathizers (or "fence-sitters") that given the opportunity, protesters would take to the streets to renew their demands even after long gaps; the last day of mass protest, Quds Day, had taken place seven weeks before.

---

[240] Director Alan Eyre, Dubai, to Central Intelligence Agency et al., November 4, 2009, Wikileaks, https://search.wikileaks.org/plusd/cables/09RPODUBAI474_a.html.

[241] Director Alan Eyre. Dubai, to Central Intelligence Agency et al., November 5, 2009, Wikileaks, https://search.wikileaks.org/plusd/cables/09RPODUBAI479_a.html.

[242] Ian Black and Saeed Kamali Dehghan, "Iran protesters hijack 30th anniversary of US embassy seizure," *The Guardian*, November 4, 2009. Accessed August 11, 2010. www.guardian.co.uk/world/2009/nov/04/iran-protests-embassy-30th-anniversary.

[243] Ibid.

[244] "Ḥamleh-ye nīrūhā-ye ḥokūmatī beh mehdī karrūbī va zakhmī shodan-i moḥāfeẓānash." Radio Farda, November 4, 2009. www.radiofarda.mobi/a/F8_13_ABAN_RALLY_KAROUBI_UNDER_ATTACK/1869011.html.

[245] Director Alan Eyre, Dubai, to Central Intelligence Agency et al., November 5, 2009, Wikileaks, https://search.wikileaks.org/plusd/cables/09RPODUBAI479_a.html.

[246] Ibid.

Iran's political calendar provided many opportunities for crowd action but they often fell many weeks apart. The month of December, however, afforded ample openings for the political crowd. The first, Student Day, was on December 7 and it provided a natural day of spirited defiance since it was born of radical protest. The second was the passing of a major regime critic and one of the most senior religious leaders in Iran and the wider Shi'ite Muslim world: Ayatollah Montazeri. The climax of crowd action in December took place on *Tasu'a* and *'Ashura*, the anniversary of the death of Imam Husayn and his valiant half-brother, which in 2009 fatefully fell on December 26 and 27, coinciding with the seven-day mourning period for Montazeri's passing.

## 3.6.4 The Return of National Student Day

Iran has a long and rich history of student activism that even transcends the country's national borders.[247] Vanguard student activism inspired, affirmed, and echoed the voices of the wider population. As with mosques in the pre-revolutionary period, high schools and especially universities provided a natural venue for organization, leadership, and collective action:

Schoolteachers were a social group that played a brief but significant role in the conflicts of the early 1960s. The unique position of teachers gives them the potential to influence political processes through their contact with students, who are often very active politically in developing societies. Student networks have linkages with other elements of society and can be activated during times of conflict. These networks are often critical in forming coalitions and escalating conflicts.[248]

Universities were hotbeds of subversive ideas where students formed trusted social networks and political organizations in order to one day mobilize for revolutionary upheaval. For many, it was newly established friendships and exchanges of ideas with fellow radical students

---

[247] When I was a student leader at UC Berkeley, veteran community activists would often speak with respect and admiration for radical Iranian students who had studied in Berkeley during the revolutionary 1970s. One went so far as to opine that those Iranians were the "most radical" of Berkeley's activists.

[248] Misagh Parsa, "Mosque of last resort: State reform and social conflict in the early 1960s," in John Foran (ed.), *A Century of Revolution: Social Movements in Iran* (Minneapolis: University of Minnesota Press, 1994), p. 145.

that gained them clandestine access to banned literature. For example, one Marxist Feda'i activist, 'Alireza Mahfoozi, was able to further develop his militant ideas through his tenure as a university student where such information was more readily accessible.[249]

A biographer of the Shah notes that university activism was so powerful that the teachers' strike of 1961 "left an indelible mark on the Shah's political psyche, as well as on the Kennedy administration's perception of the internal situation in Iran."[250] In exile after revolution, the Shah expressed his bitter disdain of student activism, which he in large part blamed for the tumult that led to his fall:

Today I have come to realize that the events of 1978–79 are attributable in part to the fact that I moved too rapidly in opening the doors of the universities, without imposing a more severe preliminary selection. The entrance exams were too easy… Some of our students were not prepared to face so many novelties. They lacked the spiritual maturity to confront the apparent ease of their new lives. Sometimes they slid into laziness but most often took to confrontation and disputation. They had received so much without any effort that appeared natural to them to claim ever more. Like spoiled children, these students caused so many confrontations that Iranian universities finally sank into anarchy.[251]

The efficacy and potency of student activism had reached a crescendo by the time of the revolution, when university students and faculty mobilized to form the National Organization of Universities (NOU) in 1978. So instrumental was their role in the revolution that they helped sustain the oil strike that brought the Shah's oil-dependent state to its knees[252] by urging university employees, through the NOU, to donate a day's salary to striking oil workers.[253] Even the estimated 100,000 Iranians studying abroad formed a "vocal vanguard against the Shah in almost every major city in the [Western] world, airing their opposition with slogans in the London subway or demonstrations in Los Angeles, Washington or New York City."[254] Most memorably, on

[249] 'Alireza Mahfoozi, interview recorded by Zia Sedghi, April 7, 1984, Paris, France. Iranian Oral History Collection, Harvard University, Transcript 1 (seq. 5). Accessed April 25, 2015.
[250] Abbas Milani, *The Shah* (New York: Palgrave Macmillan, 2012), p. 251.
[251] Mohammad Reza Pahlavi, *Answer to History: By Mohammad Reza Pahlavi The Shah of Iran* (New York: Stein and Day Publishers, 1980), p. 116.
[252] Ibid., p. 167.    [253] Parsa, *A Century of Revolution*, p. 155.
[254] "The Shah's divided land," *Time*, September 18, 1978.

November 15, 1977, when the Shah and the Shahbanou (Empress) Farah were welcomed by President Carter and the First Lady in front of the White House, a large group of Iranian students chanted "Death to the Shah!" and clashed with a smaller group of his supporters, many of whom were there at the behest of the Iranian embassy.[255] The police fired tear gas into the melee, and the morning breeze carried the fumes towards the Carters and the royal couple, all of whom had to publicly acknowledge the clashes by wiping gas-induced tears from their faces in front of the international press.[256]

It was in Iran's high schools and universities, however, that the regime met some of the most persistent, impassioned, and determined anti-Shah resistance. After 1979, the Islamic government was keenly aware of the critical role Iran's universities had played in fomenting the revolution, and sought to neutralize that historic stronghold of anti-state radicalism. Furthermore, the universities were considered insufficiently Islamic, thus constituting a potential center for opposition to the Islamist takeover. As Khomeini put it: "We are not afraid of economic sanctions or military intervention. What we are afraid of is Western universities and the training of our youth in the interest of West or East."[257] The newly established Cultural Revolution Council, despite the opposition of Iran's first president, Abolhassan Bani Sadr, sought to eliminate subversive centers of power by ordering the closure of the nation's universities in what effectively amounted to a systematic purge of leftist students and faculty.[258] So disruptive was this purge to

---

[255] Linda Charlton, "Clashes and tear gas mar Shah's welcome in capital," *The New York Times*, November 16, 1977.

[256] Farber, *Taken Hostage*, p. 181.

[257] Bayat, *Revolution without Revolutionaries*, p. 53. Khomeini was so concerned about the prospects of Iran's educational institutions once again becoming bastions of secular politics that he focused on the issue more than any other in his last will and testament, warning future generations of the threat to the nation's independence posed by such un-Islamic Eastern or Western ideas. "Matn-i kāmel-i vaṣīat nāmeh-ye emām khomeinī (rah)," ʿAsr-i Iran, October 6, 2009. Accessed September 27, 2018. goo.gl/3nkNpE.

[258] In his memoirs, Bani Sadr contends that the real aim of the closure of the universities was not to "Islamize" Iran's educational system, as the Cultural Revolution Council explicitly stated, but to eliminate the organizational capacity of leftist students and guerrilla groups and deprive Bani Sadr of a vital support base in order to eventually unseat him. See Abolhassan Bani Sadr, *Dar sar-i tajrobeh: khāṭerāt-i abolḥassan-i banī ṣadr, avvalīn raʾīs jomhūr-i īrān* (Frankfurt: Islamic Revolution Publishing, 2013), p. 272–281. Ali Mirsepassi notes that the Cultural Revolution also intended to redefine "all knowledge,

the organizational capacity of the student movement that when
workers' unions were subsequently attacked during the clerical consolidation of power, the students were unable to muster effective resistance because they had been demobilized after the universities were shut
down.[259] Three years later when the universities reopened, Khomeini
ruled that only those students without affiliations to foreign ideologies
would be permitted to enter.[260] Needless to say, many futures were
ruined.

After the purge, a two-pronged approach by the Islamic government
ensured that Iran's universities would not revert to their historical
legacy of revolutionary activity. First, it cracked down on the student
movement by jailing or expelling non-conformist students, closing
their newspapers, and generally curtailing their speech. Second, it
granted admission to students from particular backgrounds: religious,
underprivileged and working class; or connected to the state through
family, as children of veterans or martyrs of the revolution and war, or
through membership of official organizations like the *basij*. This guaranteed that a growing segment of the student population could be
relied upon to counter left-leaning dissident students. Whenever anti-
government student protests erupted, these loyalists were marshaled to
counter and challenge the dissenters.[261]

The political and social utility of the university for the Iranian
government is most tellingly demonstrated by its establishment of
the country's foremost Friday prayer hall at the University of Tehran.
That the Islamic government created a sacred space for Iran's most
important Friday prayers at the University of Tehran, of all places,

both new and old, from the perspective of religion" in order to "inaugurate a
just and virtuous community and polity." Ali Mirsepassi, *Democracy in
Modern Iran: Islam, Culture, and Political Change* (New York and London:
New York University Press, 2010), p. 85–86. Such an inauguration amounted
to a Third Islamic Revolution. Abrahamian, *A History of Modern Iran*, p. 177.
[259] Parsa, *Social Origins of the Iranian Revolution*, p. 297.
[260] Ibid., p. 267. The government often conducted a thorough background check
to ensure that students seeking admission were not "contaminated" by foreign
ideologies. Such a check might include sending an official to the student's home
to ask them questions, see if they had any subversive books in their possession,
consult with neighbors, and/or require the student to have a cleric or official
attest in writing to their worldview.
[261] Hooman Majd, *The Ayatollah Begs to Differ: The Paradox of Modern Iran*
(New York: First Anchor Books (Random House), 2009), p. 115.

attests to the clerical desire to ensure that Islamic forces have an undisputed presence in Iran's most politically influential university. Every Friday, thousands of the regime's most hardline supporters congregate at the University of Tehran, an institution with a potent pre-revolutionary legacy of radical activism. Despite all its counter-measures, however, the state has not been entirely successful in reducing university-wide, anti-government opposition. The uprising in 1999 and protests in 2003 are reminders that student activism endured in the face of the government's best efforts. It is therefore unsurprising that universities were one of the early centers of the uprising against the election results, and one of the first targets of the regime's subsequent crackdown. At least twelve students were killed on June 14, 2009, when government paramilitaries forcibly sought to quell a "wave of campus rebellions" in Tabriz, Isfahan, Hamedan, Babol, Kermanshah, Amirkabir University, the University of Tehran, and the University of Shiraz, both of which stood above their counterparts in producing "martyrs."[262]

By December 2009, with the streets overrun by security personnel and the mosques under government control, the universities filled the void and kept the flame of the protest movement burning. Student Day (December 7, 2009) saw the largest and most coordinated nationwide student protests since the closure of Iran's universities in 1980.

---

[262] Robert Tait and Saeed Kamali Dehghan, "Iran: Twelve students reported killed in crackdown after violent clashes." *The Guardian*, June 15, 2009. Accessed May 12, 2015. www.theguardian.com/world/2009/jun/15/iran-students-protest-election-results. The BBC counted seven fatalities. See "Daftar taḥkīm-i vahdat: haft dāneshjū koshteh shodehand," June 17, 2009. Accessed May 12, 2015. www.bbc.co.uk/persian/iran/2009/06/090616_si_ir88_tahkim_students .shtml. Iranian-Canadian *Newsweek* journalist, Maziar Bahari, who was in Iran to cover the election and was arrested, detained, and became the focus of an international campaign to secure his release, had this to say about the attack on the University of Tehran: "After the police and Basij units entered the dormitory, security closed the gates so that no one could get out. Every student from the dorm – whether he had taken part in the demonstrations or not – was dragged out of his room. Outside the dorm, the anti-riot police piled them together and beat them with clubs. Many were kicked until they became unconscious. In some cases, the anti-riot police sodomized the students with clubs. At least several were killed." Maziar Bahari, *Then They Came for Me*, p. 66.

Iran's first modern institute for higher learning, the University of Tehran, was founded in 1934, and, like other Iranian universities, it has served as a "hotbed of political activism and protest since inception."[263] Its reputation for radicalism is distinguished from its peers after British and American intelligence agencies overthrew Premier Muhammad Mossadeq in 1953. Three months later, Vice President Richard Nixon came to Iran to show the Eisenhower administration's full support for the coup government,[264] a visit that kindled the Shah's enduring friendship with one of the most controversial American presidents in US history.[265] Nixon's endorsement of the Shah's regime outraged an already aggrieved populace, with the University of Tehran the main bastion of university agitation. Protests on December 6 and 7 led to the deaths of three students at the University of Tehran's Faculty of Engineering (FOE).[266] It was Iran's equivalent of the Kent State Massacre that occurred in the United States sixteen years later. Since that turbulent year, December 7 (*shūnzdah-i āzar* in colloquial Persian) has been unofficially marked as Student Day and commemorated

---

[263] Muhammad Sahimi, "16 Azar: Iran's Student Day." Tehran Bureau, December 6, 2009. Accessed August 12, 2010. www.pbs.org/wgbh/pages/frontline/tehranbureau/2009/12/16-azar-irans-student-day.html.

[264] Director Alan Eyre, Dubai, to Central Intelligence Agency et al., December 7, 2009, Wikileaks, https://search.wikileaks.org/plusd/cables/09RPODUBAI521_a.html.

[265] Pahlavi, *Answer to History*, p. 16–17.

[266] Unlike in the United States, engineering students in Iran have a history of radicalism. In my discussions with many engineering graduates from the 1970s, I have been able to glean two common explanations as to why such students were (and continue to be) especially militant. First, many engineering students were imbued with a sense of political purpose in that they felt an obligation to acquire the skills necessary to help develop the country. It was natural for these students to transition from a politicized field to political agitation once they entered the university. A second more Marxist explanation is that many students from lower socio-economic backgrounds saw a degree in engineering as a way of moving up the social ladder. Radical ideologies organically appealed to these students who felt that such worldviews spoke to their own situation or the plight of their families that they left behind to attend college. That engineering is so math-intensive certainly helped many of these students understand Marx's *Das Kapital*. As is often the case, the truth probably lies somewhere in between the two theories.

"as a symbol of the struggle of Iranian students against dictatorship."[267]

Throughout much of the twentieth century (from the consolidation of Reza Shah's rule in 1921 onwards), a strong central government in Iran stifled political activity.[268] One student activist at the University of Tabriz, however, attested to the important role of the university in this climate:

> You realize that outside of the universities, there was practically no political movement. That is, the strangulation and surveillance which had been introduced, which the regime had introduced in all official spheres, was very heavy... The only place it couldn't completely control was the university, since the university was principally a place of gatherings...[269]

In keeping with the legacy of 1953, each Student Day was marked by demonstrations that raged across Iran's campuses, where schools' organizational capacity and the proximity of students to one another provided a unique environment for coordination. One student who studied at the FOE in the 1970s affirmed the endurance of student activism:

> In the 1970s, when I was a student in the FOE, we always commemorated 16 Azar [December 7]. My freshman year in 1972–1973 also coincided with the tenth anniversary of the Shah's so-called White Revolution of February 1973. The year before, 16 Azar was particularly powerful and marked by large demonstrations at the University of Tehran. The demonstrations in 1974 were so large that the engineering faculty was shut down for the entire 1974–1975 year. In 1975, two of my classmates, Mohammad Ali Bagheri and Hamid Aryan, who had started their studies at the FOE in the same year that I had, were killed by the Shah's security forces. In fact, many of my contemporaries in the FOE were jailed or killed, either by the Shah's regime or the Islamic Republic after the 1979 Revolution.[270]

After the revolution, the Islamic government officially recognized Student Day in an attempt to control its message, seeking to circumvent its legacy of fiery anti-government activity in favor of a more subdued and apolitical occasion when officials would visit campuses to stress the

---

[267] Sahimi, "16 Azar: Iran's Student Day."

[268] The period 1941–1953 and the short-lived "Iranian Spring" after the revolution are obvious exceptions.

[269] Kurzman, *The Unthinkable Revolution in Iran*, p. 103.       [270] Ibid.

importance of higher education to the future of the country.[271] In 2009, however, radical students sought to leverage the true legacy of the day to denounce the regime.

Aware of the potential for anti-state protests, the authorities took measures to prevent or control the day's demonstrations. Guards were posted at university entrances to prevent non-students from augmenting the anticipated student crowds.[272] Several streets were closed and security personnel on motorbikes patrolled Tehran's universities and neighboring areas.[273] In contrast to the pre-election climate when restrictions on communication channels including the internet were relaxed to encourage voter interest and participation, the mobile phone and text messaging networks were brought down on Student Day and the internet was "sluggish and heavily filtered" to prevent activist coordination and the transmission of non-state-sanctioned news and information abroad.[274] The government may have avoided closing down the internet altogether in favor of a "sluggish" connection, believing that would-be participants deprived of internet access were more available to attend the rallies. Reduced speeds, on the other hand, would cause those same people to remain in front of their computers in the hope that pages would eventually load. At the same time, the slowdown would inhibit real-time coordination.

In the run-up to the event, pro-Ahmadinejad media announced that they planned to air the confession of Abdollah Momeni, a prominent student leader imprisoned since June 21, two days after Khamenei's June 19 sermon. Momeni's wife argued that the government's aim was to instill fear among students ahead of their quintessential day of protest.[275]

---

[271] Director Alan Eyre, Dubai, to Central Intelligence Agency et al., December 7, 2009, Wikileaks, https://search.wikileaks.org/plusd/cables/09RPODUBAI521_a.html.

[272] "Gozāresh-i taḥavolāt-i rūz 16 āẕar dar tehrān va barkhī shahrhā." Tabnak, December 7, 2009. www.tabnak.ir/fa/pages/?cid=76033.

[273] Ibid.

[274] Director Alan Eyre, Dubai, to Central Intelligence Agency et al., December 7, 2009, Wikileaks, https://search.wikileaks.org/plusd/cables/09RPODUBAI521_a.html.

[275] "Takẕīb-i edeʿāye pakhsh-i eʿterāfāt-i ʿabdollāh moʾmenī." Rahesabz, December 3, 2009. www.rahesabz.net/story/4844/.

Since their last day of mass action, November 4,[276] students around the country had been planning to transform Student Day into a "Green Student Day"[277] and renew their protest.[278] Likewise, Mousavi anticipated mass action when he attested to the historical importance of the day and what it meant for post-election Iran:

University Student Day is ahead of us. In our modern history the student movement has always been the flagbearer and has acted as the reason and purpose for the people's movement. During the bitter days following the coup, and in some of the darkest times in the history of our nation when all hope seemed lost, what happened in the 16th of Azar of 1332 (December 7, 1953) was a clear sign that the spirit of the people and their historical demands were still alive. After half a century, those 'three drops of blood' and 'three godly Azar' that created a basis for Student Day are still a vivid and enlightening reminder in the memory of the people because they signified the existence of a greater reality in the lives of the people. In the years and generations that followed, these signs were, and continue to be maintained through the student movements.[279]

Most of the demonstrations shared similar attributes. They all happened on school premises and virtually all the participants were students, both women and men. Many of the protests included the singing of a particularly significant political song, "My grade-school friend" (*yār-i dabestānī-ye man*), which had first been heard in a revolution-era political film, *From Cry to Terror*.[280] The rousing lyrics encapsulated Iran's long struggle for freedom:

---

[276] Mir Hossein Mousavi Facebook page, "16 āzar." Facebook, November 8, 2009. Accessed January 29, 2009. http://goo.gl/dlLHcO.

[277] Mir Hossein Mousavi Facebook page, "16 āzar: rūz dāneshjū-ye sabz." Facebook, November 26, 2009. Accessed January 29, 2009. http://goo.gl/Pi45VM.

[278] Director Alan Eyre, Dubai, to Central Intelligence Agency et al., December 7, 2009, Wikileaks, https://search.wikileaks.org/plusd/cables/09RPODUBAI521_a.html.

[279] Mir Hussein Mousavi, "Bayānī-ye shomāreh-ye 16 mohandes mūsavī beh monāsebat-i 16 āzar." Kalame, December 6, 2009. Accessed August 15, 2010. www.kaleme.org/1388/09/15/klm-4896.

[280] Saya Ovaisy, "My grade-school friend," Tehran Bureau, November 17, 2009. Accessed August 12, 2010. www.pbs.org/wgbh/pages/frontline/tehranbureau/2009/11/my-grade-school-friend.html.

*My schoolmate*
*You're with me and going along with me*
*The alphabet stick is above our heads*
*You're my spite and my woe*
*Our names have been carved*
*On the body of this blackboard*
*The stick of injustice and tyranny*
*Still remains on our body*

*This uncivilized plain of ours*
*Is covered with weeds*
*Good, if good*
*Bad, if bad*
*Dead is the hearts of its people*
*My hand and yours*
*Should tear up these curtains*
*Who can, except you and I*
*Cure our pain?*

*My schoolmate*
*You're with me and going along with me*
*The alphabet stick is above our heads*
*You're my spite and my woe*
*Our names have been carved*
*On the body of this blackboard*
*The stick of injustice and tyranny*
*Still remains on our body.*[281]

"My grade-school friend" first became prevalent during Khatami's presidency, reaching unprecedented levels of popularity during the post-election turmoil when it became the anthem of resistance.[282] Although activists publicly sang the song on many occasions throughout the 2009 protests, on Student Day it became the unofficial fight song of all universities, with crowds of students conveying their contempt for the government in a unified melodic voice.

Dressed in green and with faces covered to conceal their identities, students at the University of Tehran sang, marched and clapped in

---

[281] "An Iranian revolutionary song: My schoolmate (Yar-e Dabestani-e Man)." Payvand News, June 15, 2009. Accessed August 15, 2010. http://payvand.com/news/09/jun/1152.html.
[282] Ibid.

rhythm with the anthem.[283] At the Tehran branch of Islamic Azad University, students walked in a large circle on the campus courtyard singing the *alma mater* and clapping.[284] At Shahid Beheshti University in Tehran, they filled an auditorium and clapped and sang along to a slideshow that featured the song. The slideshow ended in defiance of Iran's theocratic system by displaying Iran's Islamic flag without the "Allah" emblem in the center, causing the audience to cheer.[285]

The Islamic government had changed Iran's historic flag[286] shortly after the revolution, replacing the lion and sun motif with that of an "Allah" shaped like a tulip – the symbol of martyrdom in Shiʿism. "Allah" on the revolutionary flag has another layer of meaning: when deconstructed "Allah" spells "There is no god but God" (Figure 3.5).[287] Green Movement students singing the resistance anthem subverted the Iranian flag by removing the Islamic Republic's iconic motif from it, thus refuting not God but the legitimacy and the ideological foundation of the state.

Students at a university in Qazvin chanted: "Rape, criminality, death to [Khamenei's] authority" (*tajāvoz, jenāyat, marg bar īn velāyat*),[288] marching behind a banner declaring "The university is alive" (*dāneshgāh zendeh ast*), a profound declaration of the universities' vitality considering the state's systematic attempts at control and the suppression of free thought. One university student who was expelled

---

[283] GREENPOWER0, "Tehran uni protest 7dec/sorūd-i yār-i dabestānī dāneshgāh-i tehrān16āẕar." Online video clip, YouTube, December 7, 2009. Accessed August 12, 2010. https://youtu.be/Myn_Cm6bgZI.

[284] Mowjcamp, "16 Azar, Azad University Tehran Shomal." Online video clip, YouTube, December 7, 2009. Accessed August 12, 2010. http://youtu.be/ZdIVmrKEZGI.

[285] Farhad50626, "Taẓāhorāt-i dāneshjūyān-i dāneshgāh-i shahīd beheshtī dar rūz-i 16 āẕar." Online video clip, YouTube, December 7, 2009. Accessed August 12, 2010. https://youtu.be/_IuUoFzD7bw.

[286] Many Iranians mistakenly believe that Iran's Lion and Sun flag belongs to the Pahlavi dynasty. The flag in fact predates the dynasty, and Muhammad Reza Shah Pahlavi affirmed in his autobiography that the Lion and Sun flag "does not date from our dynasty, under whose folds [sic] millions of Iranians have sacrificed themselves during many centuries…" Pahlavi, *Answer to History*, p. 190. Should there be a crown situated above the lion, however, then that flag is the marker of the Pahlavi dynasty.

[287] "Ṭarḥ-i ārm-i jomhūrī-ye eslāmī taṣvīb shod." *Kayhan*, May 11, 1980.

[288] IranFree88, "Dāneshgāh-i qazvīn 16 āẕar." Online video clip, YouTube, December 7, 2009. Accessed August 13, 2010. https://youtu.be/2kUOh1fzWWI.

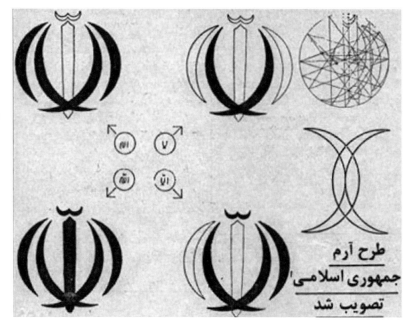

**Figure 3.5** The emblem of the Islamic Republic's flag
Soon after the victory of the Iranian Revolution, the government published
illustrations of the layers of meaning inherent in the new flag's emblem.

for her Green Movement activism expanded on the meaning of "The
university is alive," affirming: "It means that if they [the authorities]
can stifle thoughts and ideas everywhere, the university will remain
defiant in safeguarding those thoughts and ideas."[289]
    Students at the Najafabad branch of Islamic Azad University
gathered to voice their support for Mousavi, and declared that "Torture, rape, no longer have an effect" (*shekanjeh, tajāvoz, digar asar
nadārad*).[290] Young partisans at Bu'ali Sina University in Hamedan
reassured one another by chanting "Don't be afraid, don't be afraid,
we are all together" (*natarsīn, natarsīn, mā hāmeh bā hām hastīm*) and

[289] G.T., personal interview, October 22, 2013.
[290] GREENPOWER0, "Taẓāhorāt-i dāneshjūyān-i dāneshgāh-i najafābād 16
    aẕār." Online video clip, YouTube, December 7, 2009. Accessed August 12,
    2010. https://youtu.be/7Kr1BPVWlnI.

wished "Death upon the *basiji*" (*marg bar basījī*).[291] At Amirkabir University of Technology, students shouting "*Allahu akbar*" tore down the gate that separated them from the crowd outside, and chanted for the outsiders to "come in" (*bīyā tū*).[292] Students at Iran University of Science and Technology threatened: "We are women and men of war, fight us so we fight!" (*mā zan o mard-i jangīm, bejang tā bejangīm!*).[293] To leave no doubt as to the target of their fury on Student Day, the students even took aim at the founder of the Islamic Republic, Ayatollah Khomeini, who suffered the indignity of having his picture torn up,[294] a highly inflammatory and illegal act that signified the total rejection of Iran's Islamic system.

At a university in Mashhad, opposition students confronted student supporters of the regime, each trying to drown out the other with chants, with the Green activists eventually prevailing. This scene was replicated at Sharif University, where students shouting "Death to the tyrant, whether the Shah or the [Supreme] Leader" (*marg bar setamgar, cheh shāh bāshe, cheh rahbar*) were temporarily interrupted by Islamist students, only to be inundated by boisterous chants of "Death to the *basiji*" (*marg bar basījī*).[295]

By naming "the Leader" in the same breath as the Shah, the students invoked the history of the Iranian Revolution, when the overwhelming majority of the population had been united in fervent opposition to the Shah. The Islamic authorities, who came to power on a popular wave of anti-Shah resentment, were now being equated with a reviled and

---

[291] Freedom Messenger, "Dāneshgāh-i būʿali-i hamadān 16 azar." Online video clip, YouTube, December 14, 2009. Accessed April 24, 2014. https://www.youtube.com/watch?v=4R4PCwFiQAc.

[292] Ghovaza, "VIDE0524." Online video clip, YouTube, December 7, 2009. Accessed August 12, 2010. https://youtu.be/qG5xM8YTRng.

[293] IranFree88, "Dāneshgāh-i ʿelm o sanʿat 16 azar." Online video clip, YouTube, December 7, 2010. Accessed August 12, 2010. https://youtu.be/u54Hva9a_eI.

[294] "Desecration of Imam Khomeini portrait sparks protests." PressTV, December 12, 2009. Accessed August 14, 2010. www.presstv.ir/detail.aspx?id=113544&sectionid=351020101. There is considerable controversy surrounding this "desecration," with some activists arguing that the regime staged the whole episode so as to incriminate the opposition and provoke regime supporters to rally against such sacrilege. Having said that, I do believe that strands within the Green Movement were capable of making such a provocative statement as publicly tearing an image of Khomeini.

[295] Khajesharif, "Marg bar setamgar, cheh shāh bāsheh, cheh rahbar / dāneshgāh-i sharīf 16 azar." Online video clip, YouTube, December 7, 2009. Accessed August 12, 2010. https://youtu.be/zVfGynPs07Q.

popularly overthrown monarch. Furthermore, slogans that simultaneously condemned the Shah also belied the state's allegations that the
opposition was composed of counter-revolutionaries trying to restore
the monarchy – a common feature of expatriate Iranian politics manifest in revisionist royalist programming beamed into the country by
satellite.[296]

The severity of these political chants is in contrast with the quintessential slogan of the movement's early days: "Where is my vote?" The
protracted crackdown either marginalized moderate voices or facilitated their transition to more radical political expressions. While the
original slogan demanded an equitable solution to the election crisis
through either a recount or a re-run of the election, more radical
slogans that predominated later on in the uprising took aim at the
entire system and its personification, Ayatollah Khamenei.

In an impassioned speech at Amirkabir University on December 7,
Majid Tavakoli, a student activist who had emerged as a leader and
had previously been arrested,[297] spoke of the importance of Student
Day, promising: "We will no longer accept tyranny."[298] The student
crowd punctuated his speech with chants of "Death to the dictator"
and "The student will die before accepting humiliation and
suffering."[299] Two days later, Fars News Agency (associated with
Iran's *comitatus,* the IRGC[300]) reported Tavakoli's arrest, branding

[296] Narges Bajoghli wrote an insightful piece on how such programming has
impacted the worldview of some Iranian protesters in late 2017, early 2018. See
Narges Bajoghli, "A London television station has convinced Iran the Shah was
great," *Foreign Policy,* January 12, 2018. http://foreignpolicy.com/2018/01/12/
a-london-television-station-has-convinced-iran-the-shah-was-great/.
[297] Tavakoli was arrested in 2007 and again in February 2009 (before the
election), serving fifteen months in prison and 115 days in solitary confinement,
respectively.
[298] Mehdi Saharkhiz, "Majid Tavakoli's speech December 7th 09 16." Online
video clip, YouTube, December 7, 2009. Accessed August 13, 2010.
https://youtu.be/Lin9PWr55RU.
[299] Ibid.
[300] Ostovar, the foremost scholar on the IRGC, prefers referring to the *comitatus*
rather than the Praetorians – the latter being commonly used in English –
because praetorianism is "used to describe regimes with militaries that overstep
their traditional role, regularly intervene in politics, and come to dominate all
civilian institutions of the state" thereby undervaluing "the importance of the
supreme leader's authority to the organization." In contrast, *comitatus* was a
simple form of political organization in Central Eurasia in which the "political
structure composed of a lord and his personal guard corps. The members of this

him a "coward" for allegedly wearing a woman's *hijab* to avoid detection, and even publishing photos of him wearing the headscarf.[301] Eyewitnesses belied these claims, and activists accused the government of seeking to humiliate Tavakoli.[302]

The *hijab* has been called by one sociologist the "emblem of the Islamic Republic."[303] Immediately after the revolution in 1979, the state made head covering mandatory for all women, regardless of piety, religion, or even nationality.[304] Like many around the world, the Iranian government has long viewed the female body as a battlefield which must be regulated and controlled for the sake of the "moral order" and a stable and healthy functioning of society.[305] In the words

guard swore absolute loyalty to their leader. They served him with complete submission, and in extreme instances committed suicide and were buried with the leader after he died. In order to sustain their loyalty, the lord rewarded the guards with riches and lavish gifts... What makes the *comitatus* a useful conceptual model for the IRGC is the inextricable place of the leader within its structure." Whereas praetorianism can supplant civilian authority, the leader in Iran's Islamic system is the IRGC's "life force." Afshon Ostovar, *Vanguard of the Imam: Religion, Politics, and Iran's Revolutionary Guards* (New York: Oxford University Press, 2016), pp. 11–12.

[301] "Dastgīrī-ye majīd tavakolī bā lebās-i zanān lakke nangī bar dāman efrāṭīyūn bāqī goẕāsht." Fars News Agency, December 9, 2009. Accessed August 13, 2010. www.farsnews.net/newstext.php?nn=8809171609. His image was published alongside a similar picture of then President Bani Sadr, who allegedly wore the *hijab* to avoid detection as he fled the country after being ousted in 1981.

[302] Robert Mackey, "Iran's state media mocks arrested student leader pictured in women's clothing," *The New York Times* Blog, December 9, 2009. Accessed August 13, 2010. http://thelede.blogs.nytimes.com/2009/12/09/irans-state-media-mocks-arrested-student-leader-pictured-in-womens-clothing/.

[303] Haideh Moghissi, "Islamic cultural nationalism and gender politics in Iran," *Third World Quarterly*, 29(3) (2008), p. 546.

[304] The issue of attire is part of a wider discussion of Iran's struggle to balance modernity with maintaining its sense of identity. Reza Shah constituted one extreme when he banned the *hijab* outright. The Islamic government falls on the opposite but equally extreme end by mandating the Islamic headdress.

[305] See, for example, Laura Briggs' *Reproducing Empire: Race, Sex, and U.S. Imperialism in Puerto* Rico (Berkeley and Los Angeles: University of California Press, 2002) in which she uncovers the consequences of colonialism that transcend economics and politics. Briggs factors in race and gender to underscore how American colonial administrators in Puerto Rico sought to control seemingly "deviant" working-class women's sexuality through "scientific methods," including hygiene and birth control (even sterilization), preserving the racial purity and health of white men who partook in sexual activity with Puerto Rican women, the supposed incubator of venereal disease.

of one anthropologist, "women's bodies are also spaces of contestation over which battles over authenticity, cultural dominance and political control are fought."[306] The *hijab*, it is argued, prevents permissiveness and instead "encourages youth to marry to fulfill their sexual needs," strengthening the institution of the family.[307] It is further argued that the presence of covered women in schools and workplaces is less distracting to men, enabling increased productivity.[308] Lastly, according to official doctrine, the veil increases women's "value" and respect.[309]

In December 2009, however, Green activists contested the "sanctity" of the *hijab* and expressed solidarity with Tavakoli, with hundreds of men[310] in Iran and abroad, including non-Iranians, posting pictures of themselves wearing the headscarf as part of the "Be a Man" campaign. By turning the *hijab* into a symbol of protest they aimed to nullify the government's shaming of the activist,[311] leveling a significant ideological challenge at the regime.

It is important to note that it is men who often debate and decide issues that invariably affect women first and foremost, such as veiling and spaces that women are permitted to frequent.[312] For example, it was Reza Shah who in 1936 decreed the forcible banning of the headcover – a prohibition that was relaxed by his successor but then reversed after 1979 when Khomeini mandated it for all women. That is not to say that women were passive and devoid of agency with regard to the man-made decisions that affected them. On the contrary, the women-led protests that erupted after Khomeini's directive were,

---

[306] Sherine Hafez, "The revolution shall not pass through women's bodies: Egypt, uprising and gender politics," *The Journal of North African* Studies, 19(2) (2014), p. 175.

[307] Moghissi, *Populism and Feminism in Iran*, p. 64.      [308] Ibid.

[309] Ibid., p. 65.

[310] For a compilation of the photos, see Īstādeh bā mosht's video, "Mā hameh majīd tavakolī hastīm." Online video clip, YouTube, December 10, 2009. Accessed February 2, 2015. http://youtu.be/xNgN1rbXjLc.

[311] "Iranian men don hijabs in protest at student's arrest." BBC News, December 12, 2009. Accessed August 13, 2010. http://news.bbc.co.uk/2/hi/middle_east/8409778.stm.

[312] As of 2018, for example, women are still not allowed to enter stadiums to observe male sporting events.

according to one scholar, "the largest spontaneous demonstrations in the history of the women's movement in Iran..."[313]

When the issue of the *hijab* came to the fore again in 2009 with the publication of the Tavakoli image, the male-dominated state and activist men, not women, were again the topic of the conversation. The headscarf as a tool of authenticity and political control was now weaponized by men, for men. The same state that promoted the *hijab* as a mechanism for good had deployed it as a weapon against Tavakoli, humiliating and symbolically castrating him. Other men, meanwhile, expressed their manhood by courageously donning women's attire to show opposition to that same state. Either way, women were yet again excluded from the discussion.

There was, however, a time when the *hijab* was a means by which women expressed their agency. In 1978, many ideologues argued that the Shah, as a secular head of state beholden to the United States, was a conduit for the tide of decadent Western culture inundating Iran. Discos and cabarets, private casinos, liquor stores, brothels, cinemas showing Western films encouraging lax sexual mores, all considered culturally foreign and alien to the nation's Islamic norms, were legalized or tolerated during the Pahlavi rule. The government even imported new living standards and amenities (including flush as opposed to squat toilets[314]), and dress styles, which symbolized the degree to which the Shah preferred foreign cultural tastes to his own. He even seemed to bask in giving interviews in English and French. These Western standards of lifestyle, consumption and luxury, according to Khomeini, led to a national identity crisis that facilitated the imperial subjugation of the country.[315]

---

[313] Homa Hoodfar and Shadi Sadr, "Islamic politics and women's quest for gender equality in Iran," *Third World Quarterly*, 31(6) (2010), p. 891.

[314] At the time of the revolution, both my parents, Shahram and Sonia Alimagham, worked in the state-run National Iranian Oil Company's (NIOC) computer division. After the revolution, they witnessed first-hand the Islamic authorities' decision to have all the flush toilet bowls, which were perceived as symbols of the West's cultural domination of Iran, ripped out in favor of flush squat toilets, which were considered indigenous to Iran and the region. These disruptive changes only took place in the NIOC-owned buildings (and probably other state-owned structures), not those in which the company were tenants. It is interesting to note that anatomically speaking, squat toilets are more natural and healthier.

[315] "Matn-i kāmel-i vaṣīat nāmeh-ye emām khomeinī (rah)." *Asr-i Iran*, October 6, 2009. Accessed September 27, 2018. goo.gl/3nkNpE.

In other countries, the typical colonialists were identifiable – they came from abroad with their foreign languages, attires, habits, and agendas. They ruled harshly and exploitatively, justifying their patronizing control by belittling native cultures in the name of "civilizing" their subjects with their own cultural norms. While Iran was never *formally* subjected to colonial rule, the Pahlavi Shahs facilitated the same function in terms of undermining Iran's Islamic mores, doing so more effectively because they were indigenous to the land. Speaking the common language, Persian, they presented these Westernizing cultural norms through word (and deed) as "progress" *en route* to the "Great Civilization." They even subscribed to a colonial racial index that placed the US-installed Shah – the so-called Light of the Aryans – at the top of the hierarchy. The condescension and heavy-handed exploitative rule of the colonialists and the Pahlavi dynasty eventually sparked nativist backlashes in Iran and across the Global South. In the build-up to the 1979 revolution, for example, many activist women, including those without a devout worldview, wore the *hijab* as a revolutionary symbol of defiance against the government's subservience to foreign-power governments' seeming betrayal of Iranian culture and the head of state's authority.[316]

In 2009, the *hijab* as a mechanism for contestation came full circle in an unexpected and unprecedented way. In a bizarre twist of fate, Iranian and non-Iranian men, some even with full beards, wore the *hijab* to snub the government, just as pious and secular Iranian women had donned the headscarf to show their opposition towards the Shah in 1978. Once again, Iranian activists (and their international sympathizers) were attacking the state's ideological repertoire by using its own symbols.

These acts of solidarity with Tavakoli, however, did not convince the government to show the imprisoned student leader any leniency. Tavakoli was convicted of a range of Orwellian charges, such as "participation in an illegal gathering with the aim of harming national security," "propaganda against the state," and "insulting" the Leader and the president, and was eventually sentenced to eight and a half years in prison.[317] A year later, the Revolutionary Court banned him

---

[316] The fact that so many women donned the *hijab* to show their support for the revolution made it easier for Khomeini to make the headscarf compulsory.

[317] "Ta'īd-i ḥokm-i hasht sāl o nīm-i zendān-i majīd tavakolī dar dādgāh-i tajdīdenaẓar." Rahesabz, September 18, 2010. www.rahesabz.net/story/23673/.

from pursuing his education while in prison or even after the completion of his sentence.[318]

Tavakoli's arrest, prosecution, and sentencing underscore the increasing severity of the state's repressive measures. With protests continuing on specific political holidays throughout the months after the election, the government augmented its security presence on the streets and stepped up its efforts to hinder access to the internet and SMS as specific days of action approached, making activist coordination more difficult. Dissidents were being jailed with greater frequency and reports of prisoner abuse became widespread, especially at Kahrizak. The death toll on the streets continued to rise, and the regime began executing dissidents in a bid to de-mobilize activists.

Yet, student demonstrations occurred at more than a dozen universities and even several high schools – including an all-girls' school[319] – throughout the country.[320] Although there is no exact tally for the number of students who participated in the Student Day demonstrations, the estimates of "tens of thousands"[321] are likely to be accurate. Both sympathizers and the authorities, who avoided students' wrath by not entering campuses to deliver their perfunctory annual Student Day addresses, were reminded that the movement was alive and well a month after the last day of mass protests on November 4 and six months after the June 12 election.

In Chapter 5, two final events that occurred in December, before the regime succeeded in driving the movement underground, are examined: the death of dissident cleric Grand Ayatollah Hussein ʿAli Montazeri, and ʿ*Ashura*. ʿ*Ashura's* emotive power is derived from a

---

[318] "Ḥokm-i jadīd-i dādgāh-i enqelāb: maḥrūmīyat-i dā'emī-ye majīd tavakolī az edāmeh-ye taḥṣīl," Kalame, September 18, 2011. www.kaleme.com/1390/06/27/klm-73521/?theme=fast.

[319] Freedom Messenger.,"Taẓāhorāt-i dānesh āmūzān-i yek dabīrestān-i dokhtāraneh." Online video clip, YouTube, December 7 2009. Accessed February 2, 2015. http://youtu.be/Ee60WyR3YZg.

[320] Chargé d'Affaires Doug Silliman, Ankara, to Secretary of State Hillary Clinton, December 8, 2009, Wikileaks, https://search.wikileaks.org/plusd/cables/09ANKARA1744_a.html.

[321] Director Alan Eyre, Dubai, to Central Intelligence Agency et al., December 8, 2009, Wikileaks, https://search.wikileaks.org/plusd/cables/09RPODUBAI525_a.html.

long history which must be considered in order to fully appreciate the magnitude of the Green Movement's explosive 'Ashura day protests.

## 3.7 Conclusion

The Islamic government came to power through the marches of millions of women and men intertwined with an Islamic discourse that negated the ideological universe of the Shah. Whereas protests and challenges to power in the past had employed the Pahlavi dynasty's own secular-nationalist discourse, the Islamic Revolution posited a new discourse that was diametrically opposed to the monarchy's ideological worldview.

For three decades after the revolution, the Islamic government drilled an entire generation of youth raised under its authority in Islamist ideology. In 2009, however, aggrieved segments of the population used that ideology and symbolism to castigate the very regime that relied on them for legitimation. These activists used what Gramsci referred to as the ruling elite's "common sense," not necessarily to negate the state's ideological universe as in 1978–1979, but as emotive tools that were appropriated, re-programmed, and subverted in order to challenge the Islamic government using its own language.

The election campaign created the necessary breathing room for voters to mobilize for their candidates. Some even used the temporary lifting of repression to voice their rejection of the state as a whole. The government, hoping the relaxation of the political environment would encourage voter participation in a state-sanctioned political event, grew increasingly concerned with what was more and more looking like a street movement than an election campaign.

After the election, Iranians from all walks of life, especially the young and women of all ages, participated in a week-long uprising as the state struggled to rescind the political opening that it had facilitated for the sake of fostering interest in the election. When Khamenei's Friday sermon affirmed Ahmadinejad's victory, activists adapted to the security crackdown by transitioning from one continuous uprising after the June 12 election into many uprisings spread out along Iran's religio-political calendar. Political occasions and holidays such as Beheshti's anniversary, Rafsanjani's Friday sermon, the anniversary of the embassy seizure, Student Day, and others provided activists with renewed opportunities to register their protest in a climate that was otherwise hostile to any sort of non-state-sanctioned political activity. The government canceled several events to deprive the opposition of the opportunity to mobilize, but some could not be called off as they were staples in the calendar of the Iranian state. The government had even more difficulty shutting down Student Day, the anniversary of which continues to evade government control despite its best efforts – a reality echoed by Majid Tavakoli, who seven months after his arrest wrote a letter from prison to mark the anniversary of student uprising in 1999, defiantly observing: "...the university remains the ruling government's biggest nightmare."[322] If the government could not cancel the event in question, then it did its best to either suppress or control protests. The state's increasingly repressive measures in the run-up to each day of action may have persuaded some to stay at home, and crowds did gradually decrease in size in comparison to the first week of protests after the June 12 election.

Days imbued with a history that dates back to the Iranian Revolution were appropriated, along with slogans and other symbols from the historic era to protest the very state that came to power atop that unprecedented revolution. "*Allahu akbar*," the quintessential Islamic profession on a par with "There is no god but God" with which activists proclaimed their support for the revolution, was likewise appropriated along with the Islamic color green in order to attack the state's legitimacy using its own discourse, symbolism, and "common sense." Even women's headdress was subverted to express solidarity with Majid Tavakoli and to condemn both the state's repressive tactics and the system as a whole.

Belying allegations of hooliganism, the protesters showed increased sophistication by leveraging Iran's revolutionary past for the contentious present. The Green Movement may have failed to cancel the election results, but its tenacity and endurance, ability to absorb the state's repression, and its consequent evolution caused it to transcend the initial demand of canceling Ahmadinejad's election win. Khamenei and his position as the Guardian Jurist, clerical rule as a whole, and the entanglement between religion and state were added to the movement's list of demands, especially as the protest movement continued and

---

[322] Majid Tavakoli, "'My bitter memories' | A letter by Majid Tavakoli on the anniversary of university attacks." Trans. By Negar Irani. Persian2English, July 7, 2010. Accessed May 12, 2015. http://persian2english.com/?p=12549.

hardened in the face of the state's systematic reprisals. Although the Green Uprisings failed to change the composition and nature of the state in the short term, they succeeded in casting a robust discursive challenge to the Islamic Republic unparalleled in its thirty-year history. In doing so, activists did not renounce the faith of the overwhelming majority of Iranians. Rather, they contested the state's hegemony over "God" and Islamic history and the ownership of the Iranian Revolution and its symbols and meanings, and used the state's own discourse and symbolism to transcend the rigidity of the state in what Bayat argues amounts to a "post-Islamist turn."

# 4 | Contesting Palestine
## Generating Revolutionary Meaning

## 4.1 Introduction

For decades, the struggle in Palestine has galvanized millions across the region and beyond. Although Arab leaders and citizens of the Middle East and North Africa have long focused[1] on the issue, it nonetheless transcends Arabism, Islam, and even the region. Perhaps nothing encapsulates this point better than a mural in Northern Ireland in which a Palestine Liberation Organization (PLO) fighter stands next to an Irish Republican Army (IRA) militant, jointly clutching a Russian rocket-propelled grenade (RPG) launcher above a caption that declares the two peoples as fighting "one struggle" for liberation (Figure 4.1).[2] Many around the world have been able to make common cause with the Palestinians despite religious and linguistic differences as well as geographic distances.

---

[1] In the case of Arab leaders, I can add a caveat that such focus typically only amounted to "lip-service."

[2] Liz Curtis, photographer. 1982. "PLO-IRA," part of *Peter Moloney Collection*. Retrieved from https://petermoloneycollection.wordpress.com/1982/02/16/plo-ira/. The mural is on Beechmount Avenue (or "RPG Avenue"), Belfast. Another mural depicts two political prisoners, one Irish and the other Palestinian, reaching through their respective prison bars to grasp one another's hands in solidarity. One user on the social networking and news website, Reddit, where a different photograph of the same mural was posted, noted, "I live here in Belfast, about 20 minutes away from where this picture is taken. There are murals like that all over the place here, each with their own strong political agenda from both sides..." Another user responded to a question about the popularity of the Palestinian issue in Northern Ireland, stating: "Amongst Catholics/Republicans it is pretty popular... We usually just ignore it [the religious dimension of the conflict] in favour of taking an anti-American/British/Israel stance on the whole thing." See "Pro-IRA/Pro-Palestine mural (Belfast, Modern)," Reddit, November 6, 2014. Accessed March 3, 2015. For a fascinating read on the politics of solidarity murals in Northern Ireland, see Bill Rolston, "'The brothers on the walls': International solidarity and Irish political murals," *Journal of Black Studies*, 3(3) (January 2009), pp. 446–470. It is also interesting to note that political memorabilia that underscore the unity of the two struggles are listed for sale on eBay and other online marketplaces.

137

**Figure 4.1** PLO and IRA: one struggle

Countless Iranians both before and after the revolution have likewise identified and sympathized with the struggle in Palestine. In the 1970s, for example, leftist Iranian guerrillas bombed Israeli targets in Iran both in solidarity with the Palestinians and to defy their monarch's proximity to the Israelis. After the revolution, the Islamic Republic situated the emancipation of Palestine at the core of its ideology and foreign policy. In 2009, a generation of Iranian youth raised under the authority and ideology of the Islamic government co-opted this legitimated Palestine-centered discourse and subverted it to condemn that very state.

To provide context for what follows, this chapter begins by deconstructing common perceptions about the Green Movement to clear the way for alternative perspectives as posited by activists themselves. The next section briefly chronicles the history of Palestine in relation to Iran, exploring how Iranians of different political persuasions gave Palestine the exalted political status that is central to appreciating the magnitude of the Green Movement's contestation of Palestine as an ideological symbol in 2009. The chapter's third part outlines how the revolutionary state institutionalized Palestinian liberation as a cornerstone of its Islamist ideology. Only when the ideological importance of

Palestine to Iran under the Islamic Republic is established can the enormity of the anti-government protests on Jerusalem Day be fully understood. The final part of the chapter documents how the Green Movement co-opted Palestine's symbolic value, infused it with new meaning, and deployed it against the very state that legitimated itself through such a potent transnational symbol.

## 4.2 Generating Revolutionary Discourse

The Green Movement did not begin as a protest movement, but rather a street campaign that championed both reformist candidates, Karroubi and Mousavi (and Rahnavard). Although there were rumblings of protest before the presidential election, with partisans using the cover of the campaign to demonstrate against the system of governance,[3] it did not become a bona fide protest movement until after the election results were announced and allegations of election fraud became widespread. It was then that the campaign-turned-movement rallied to protest the government *en masse*.

Much has been made of the character or aims of the protest movement. Some have called it revolutionary while others have referred to it as a civil rights movement akin to the pivotal campaign that challenged the racial status quo in mid-century America.[4] Among intellectuals and academics, this reference has gained the most traction, which is not entirely surprising as the Green Movement has been overwhelmingly nonviolent, and calls from within the movement, echoed by its leadership, have focused on civil rights rather than revolutionary change[5] or armed struggle.[6]

---

[3] See Chapter 3, p. xx. Sensing the political shield provided by the campaign, the pre-election protesters declared "Assistance from God [leads to] imminent victory death to this deceptive government." See Goodzila82, "20-km human chain in Tehran – June 8th," Online video clip, YouTube, June 8, 2009. Accessed September 24, 2013. www.youtube.com/watch?v=PP-iji4VTQQ.

[4] Hamid Dabashi, *Iran, the Green Movement, and the USA* (London and New York: Zed Books, 2010), p. 12.

[5] It would certainly be difficult to argue that the leaders of the movement, or rather the personalities around which the movement often gathered, including Mousavi, Karroubi, Khatami, and Rafsanjani, sought revolutionary change. These leaders are some of the Islamic Republic's senior statesmen and have long worked *for* rather than *against* the foundation of the system of governance.

[6] There was very little about the movement to suggest that an armed insurrection or a civil war was ever on the political horizon. Of course, that did not prevent

Some of the movement's detractors have gone so far as to categorize it as just another Islamist movement that shares in the symbolism and worldview of the ruling Islamic system. On the face of it, this label also has some merit. With the sole exception of Rahnavard, all the main political figures associated with the movement were veteran leaders of the Islamic Republic, including Mousavi, Karroubi, Khatami, and Rafsanjani. Mousavi and Rafsanjani were especially close to Ayatollah Khomeini, the founder of the Islamic Republic. The former is considered the "Imam's prime minister,"[7] as he was Iran's wartime premier throughout much of the 1980s when Khomeini was the final arbiter of power, and the latter was one of Khomeini's closest aides – so close that he is credited with persuading him to end the ruinous eight-year war with Iraq.[8] While it is true that activists on the ground spearheaded and led the movement, often causing Mousavi and others to comment on an event after the fact,[9] he was the candidate behind whom the movement rallied and crystallized in the first place. More to the point, the facts that such "Islamic figures" are associated with the Green Movement and that some of the movement's slogans were, to all apppearances, religious in theme, have prompted many to downplay the movement as part of an internal Islamist power struggle.

Any attempt at categorizing such a multi-faceted movement, however, is a disservice to the plurality of voices and worldviews

some from positing sensationalist analyses. For instance, on the eve of the Iranian government's most vaunted political holiday, the anniversary of the revolution's victory (February 11), Reza Aslan wrote: "as Iran braces for what could be the largest and most violent demonstrations since the election that returned Mahmoud Ahmadinejad to power, the country may be on the brink of civil war." See "Iran on the brink," *The Daily Beast*, February 8, 2010. When that theory failed to materialize, Aslan offered another equally sensationalist prophecy three days later: "If the mullahs and the merchants begin joining forces with the protesters, even as the Revolutionary Guard becomes more entrenched in the political sphere, a civil war may be inescapable." See "Iran's eerily silent streets," *The Daily Beast*, February 11, 2010.

[7] "Faryād-i āzādi-ye nakhost vazīr-i emām dar dāneshgāh-i amīr kabīr," *Kaleme*, April 14, 2014. www.kaleme.com/1393/01/25/klm-180544/.

[8] Ali Reza Eshragi and Yasaman Baji, "Debunking the Rafsanjani myth," Al Jazeera, February 21, 2012. Accessed September 24, 2013. www.aljazeera.com/indepth/opinion/2012/02/2012215164958644116.html.

[9] It was only after anti-government demonstrators adapted their protest activities to the new security climate on Beheshti's anniversary that Mousavi instructed demonstrators to use political holidays to give continuity to the movement and renew their demands.

predominant in the uprising. In Rahnavard's estimation, the revolt created the space for millions of Iranians from other social movements, such as "the women's movement, the labor movement, the students' movement and the teachers' movement, among others" to protest under the "umbrella" of the Green Movement.[10] The uprising was open, inclusive, and horizontal, and it used the emotive universe and discourse common to all Iranians to enable a wide array of aggrieved women and men to mobilize. Activists invoked a shared discourse that included religious symbolism as well as symbols that have come to be associated with religion (including what the state refers to as "Islamic Palestine") to pursue a variety of aims. Their objectives ranged from canceling the election results, protesting the government's repression, and advocating for women's rights, to goals that transcended Ahmadinejad's "victory" to include the complete overthrow of the Islamist system, the cornerstones of which are the Islamic constitution and Khamenei's position as Guardian Jurist (*valī-ye faqīh*).

If it is possible to circumvent these labels and challenge the traditional notion of what it means for a movement to be "revolutionary,"[11] then the conversation changes entirely. In the most basic context of protest movements (and ignoring issues of social relations and the means of production), "revolutionary" usually describes a movement that seeks a change in the system of governance. The military coups that overthrew the monarchies in Egypt in 1952 and Iraq in 1958 were championed as "revolutionary" since they both abolished their monarchies and proclaimed republics.[12] Iran's leaders

---

[10] Zahra Rahnavard, "'If a nation wants to change its destiny…' Zahra Rahnavard on women's rights and the Green Movement," in Nader Hashemi and Danny Postel (eds.), *The People Reloaded: The Movement and the Struggle for Iran's Future* (New York: Melville House Publishing, 2010), p. 265.

[11] The debate regarding what constitutes a revolutionary movement is too cumbersome to outline here. Suffice it to say that a movement can be considered revolutionary in its most basic form if it seeks to replace the governing system with an entirely different polity, i.e., replacing the monarchy with a republic.

[12] Throngs of people came out in support of the coups, flooding the streets, blocking roads and preventing a counter-coup military mobilization, which supports the argument that the coups were "coups-turned-revolutions." This is especially true in Iraq, where a small group of men drew up the coup plans in secret and without the involvement of the people in the initial stages of the "revolution." Subsequent popular participation, however, was integral to the revolutionary change that swept the country. At least 100,000 poured onto the streets of Baghdad to show their support for the coup. Their numbers were vital to safeguarding the coup from counter-revolutionary activity or armed

hailed its 1978–1979 protest movement as "revolutionary," as it laid waste to the entire monarchical order and its ruling political, financial,[13] and military class. Indeed, members of the financial elite that supported the pre-revolutionary order, as well as the military generals who upheld the Pahlavi dynasty,[14] were executed or fled the country.[15] The Islamist government not only purged the military but created parallel armed forces, most notably the Islamic Revolutionary Guards Corps, to protect the revolution's leadership – the defense of which was deemed a dire necessity given the Iranian military's role in the Anglo-American coup against Premier Mossadeq in 1953.[16] The judiciary,

interference by members of the Baghdad Pact, the potential intervention of which expressly concerned many of the coup plotters before the event. Hanna Batutu observes that by crowds "clogging streets and bridges, not only in Baghdad but in many other towns, it hindered possible hostile counteractions." Most of the 3,000 troops who had spearheaded the destruction of the monarchy did not carry any ammunition, but the bodies of the demonstrations literally provided sufficient arms to ensure that the action was not merely a brief moment in history but a coup that had turned into a popular revolution. See Hanna Batutu, *The Old Social Classes and the Revolutionary Movements of Iraq: A Study of Iraq's Old Landed and Commercial Classes, and of Its Communists, Bathists, and Free Officers* (Princeton: Princeton University Press, 1978), p. 805. Interestingly, when Bani Sadr was based in Paris before the revolution and before the Algiers Accord (1975) ended animosities between the Shah and Saddam, personnel from the Iraqi embassy approached Iran's future president and advised him that there was no other way but through the military to bring about change in Iran, and that he should establish contact with the officer corps inside the country. Bani Sadr retorted that just because such a plan worked in Iraq or Egypt, it did not mean that it had universal application, and that "the problem of Iran belongs to Iranians and whatever we do is for us to decide, and that it would be better if you didn't involve yourself in these affairs." See Abolhassan Banisadr, interview recorded by Zia Sedghi, May 21–22, 1984, Paris, France. Iranian Oral History Collection, Harvard University, Transcript 4 (seq. 84). Accessed April 22, 2015.

[13] The financial elite entail "business and industrial figures" who left the country and took with them a "drain of capital . . . into the billions of dollars." See "The Khomeini era begins," *Time*, February 12, 1979, p. 40.

[14] This is a constant theme throughout Abrahamian's *Iran Between Two Revolutions* (Princeton: Princeton University Press, 1982), but he specifically stresses the point in periodic detail from page 135 onwards.

[15] My grandfather, Major General Sohrab Jahangiri, was one such military officer who was put to flight.

[16] As early as ten days before Khomeini's historic return to Iran, Ayatollah Montazeri's son, Muhammad, first argued for the necessity of a "revolutionary guard corps" to "preserve the revolution," by which he doubtless meant the revolution's leadership, and Khomeini in particular, whose return was imminent. See Mohsen Rafiqdoost, *Barāye tārīkh mīgūyam: khāṭerāt-moḥsen-i*

media, education system, even the physical landscape of the country, and most importantly the constitution, were Islamized, producing an entirely new and revolutionary order, although there was no change to the social relations of production.[17] This total transformation stands in stark contrast to the endurance of the vested interests in Egypt in the era of the Arab Uprisings. The lack of deep-seated change in Egypt, it is argued, was a main reason for the counter-revolutionary coup that ousted the democratically elected government of Muhammad Morsi in 2013.[18]

A discussion limited to whether the Green Movement was revolutionary in a Marxist sense will miss out some of its most fascinating and historical aspects. While elements within the movement undoubtedly sought a radical change in Iran's polity, the potency and enduring legacy of the movement lay in the fact that it was innovative in an entirely different way. The Green Movement was revolutionary not for what it wanted but for what it did: it seized the Islamic Republic's symbols with all their emotive power, and reprogrammed and repurposed them against the state which had relied on them for legitimation. To put it in Mansoor Moaddel and Antonio Gramsci's words, the Green Movement's appropriation of the Islamic Republic's ideological symbols harnessed the power of the state's understanding of "common sense,"[19] subverted them, and used them as symbolic weapons to either infuse their protests with a discursive power against

*rafīqdūst (1978–1989)* (Tehran: Andisheh Press, 2013), p. 48. The need to "preserve" the revolution was indeed real, as some Mossad officials at the time felt that Khomeini would not constitute a threat because the Shah's security apparatus would assassinate him. See Yossi Alpher, *Periphery: Israel's Search for Middle East Allies* (Lanham: Rowman & Littlefield, 2015).

[17] Parsa discusses this in detail in *Social Origins*, arguing that little changed socially other than a new, albeit Islamist, elite supplanting the old one.
[18] Egypt in the era of the Arab Uprisings provides an effective case study. The revolutionary change in Egypt was not as comprehensive as in 1979 in Iran, allowing the Mubarak-era vested interests in the military, media, and the economy (the so-called deep state) to stage a comeback in the form of a counter-revolutionary coup in the summer of 2013. For further reading, see Pouya Alimagham, "The Iranian legacy in the 2011 Egyptian Revolution: Military endurance and U.S. foreign policy priorities," *UCLA Historical Journal*, 24(1) (2013), pp. 45–59.
[19] Thomas J. Butko, "Revelation or revolution: A Gramscian approach to the rise of political Islam," *British Journal of Middle Eastern Studies*, 31(1) (May 2004), p. 43.

the government or altogether "negate"[20] the state's ideology. Palestine is one of the most potent symbols in the ideological armory of the Islamic Republic, and it was masterfully co-opted by the Green Movement.

The discussion of Palestine as a symbol of contestation must be viewed in the wider context of protest against the Iranian state. This chapter contends that to fully understand the gravity of the Green Movement's revolution and challenge to the government in 2009, it must not be regarded as a phenomenon restricted to the date and location of its occurrence. The movement that erupted in 2009 drew upon a history of struggle to deliver its post-Islamist attack on the state. Furthermore, the digital age has created opportunities for new and creative ways of protest, and acts of dissent on the streets are part of a larger canvas entailing acts of protest online and social media.

## 4.3 Iran and Palestine: A Brief History

The establishment in 1948 by Zionist leaders of an independent Jewish state of Israel in Mandate Palestine affected the calculus of the entire region, including "non-Arab" Iran,[21] creating a dilemma for the Shah's government. Israel's founding was strategically beneficial since Arab money, manpower, attention, and resources would be directed toward confronting the Jewish state instead of Iran. This was important as Iran saw first Egypt, then Arab Iraq after the 1958 coup, as specific regional threats.[22] During the Yom Kippur War of 1973,[23] for instance, Iraq sought a guarantee from Iran that it would not take advantage of Iraq

---

[20] Mansoor Moaddel, *Class, Politics, and Ideology in the Iranian Revolution* (New York and Oxford: Columbia University Press, 1993), p. 268.

[21] I put "non-Arab" in quotes because such a phrase is not very useful, especially since Iran has a large Arab minority in its southern regions. Incidentally, it is just as problematic to refer to Iraq as an "Arab country" since it has a very sizeable Kurdish population, or Israel as a "Jewish state" when it is not governed by Jewish law and has a rapidly growing Muslim and Christian population.

[22] Three decades later this suspicion was realized when Iraq under Saddam Hussein invaded Iran on September 22, 1980. Many Arab states, with the exception of Syria and Libya, supported Iraq with funds, military hardware, and even manpower. Furthermore, it is widely believed that Saddam invited King Hussein of Jordan to fire the opening shot that officially launched Iraq's invasion of Iran.

[23] Also known as the October War and the Ramadan War.

removing its troops from its border with Iran and committing them to the Syrian battlefront of the war.[24]

While Israel inadvertently helped regional rivals like Iraq divert attention from Iran, the Shah nevertheless had to maintain a balancing act in order to avoid both Arab scorn across the region and popular antipathy at home. When false rumors of Iran's formal recognition of Israel spread to Qom, Iran's center of religious learning, the Shah's government was forced to vehemently deny the rumor to quell the uproar.[25] When Egypt's President Nasser accused Iran of recognizing Israel, the Shah's government so strongly rebuked the allegation that it expelled Egypt's ambassador and severed diplomatic relations with the most populous Arab country in the world.[26] Despite this political grandstanding, however, Iran under the Shah frequently tilted in the direction of close ties with Israel. The Jewish state shared mutually hostile relations with surrounding Arab states, and sought to penetrate the wall of isolation by forming alliances with non-Arab states such as Iran, Turkey, and Ethiopia, as well as forming pacts with religious minorities and non-Arab peoples, such as Lebanese Christians and Kurds, respectively.[27]

This strategy, known as the Periphery Doctrine, meant that the longevity and stability of the Pahlavi regime was an absolute priority for Israel. Consequently, Israel's national intelligence agency, Mossad, in collaboration with the American CIA,[28] helped form and train Iran's own intelligence agency, SAVAK, which was notorious for its

[24] Lowrie, Cairo, to Department of State, November 7, 1973, Wikileaks, https://search.wikileaks.org/plusd/cables/1973STATE219402_b.html.

[25] Hussein ʿAli Montazeri, *Khāṭerāt* (Los Angeles: Ketab Corp, 2001), pp. 146–149.

[26] "Iran cuts Cairo tie in dispute on Israel," Reuters, July 28, 1960.

[27] Trita Parsi, *Treacherous Alliance: The Secret Dealings of Israel, Iran, and the U.S.* (New Haven and London: Yale University Press, 2007), p. 21.

[28] The Shah himself admitted that "...Many SAVAK officials went to the U.S. for training by the CIA." See Mohammad Reza Pahlavi, *Answer to History: By Mohammad Reza Pahlavi The Shah of Iran* (New York: Stein and Day Publishers, 1980), p. 157. It is also worth noting that such training included methods that were "based on German torture techniques from World War II." See Alfred McCoy, *A Question of Torture: CIA Interrogation, From the Cold War to the War on Terror* (New York: Owl Books, 2006), p. 74. Iranian Marxists, who bore the brunt of the SAVAK's repression, justifiably blamed successive American presidents for arming the Shah "...with billions of dollars of U.S. arms..." and providing "...the most extensive secret police network and mechanisms for repression developed by the U.S." See "Shah's U.S. visit: Newest plot against Iranian people," *Resistance* (A Publication of I.S.A.U.S., Member of Confederation of Iranian Students) 4(8) (September 1977).

efficiency in torturing and "disappearing" dissidents.[29] One of the reasons why Iran's 1979 revolution was so anti-Israel was that Israel "helped set up the SAVAK secret police that later terrorized the nation,"[30] a fact recognized by the population reeling under SAVAK's heavy boot. According to R. K. Ramazani,

This close identification of Israel with the Shah's regime and its repressive policies was widely held and largely accounted for anti-Israeli sentiments. Even before the revolutionary forces took power, the Shah's alignment with Tel Aviv was condemned by his last prime minister, Shahpour Bakhtiar.[31]

[29] In 1975, Amnesty International (AI) issued a sharp condemnation of the Shah's regime in its annual report, noting: "The Shah of Iran retains his benevolent image despite the highest rate of death penalties in the world, no valid system of civil courts and a history of torture which is beyond belief." See Martin Ennals, "Amnesty International Annual Report 1974/75." 1975, p. 8. A more detailed account can be found on page 128, where AI offers an unconfirmed range of between 25,000 to 100,000 political prisoners in Iran. One of the worst kinds of modernization that the Shah's regime imported from the West was its torture techniques, which were rooted in science and designed to inflict maximum pain on their victims to prompt dissidents to divulge information. See Ervand Abrahamian, *Tortured Confessions: Prisons and Public Recantations in Modern Iran* (Berkeley: University of California Press, 1999), pp. 106–107. One legendary guerrilla, Ashraf Dehghani, who was captured and tortured before undertaking any armed action, describes in her memoirs her agonizing torture, which included multiple rounds of beatings, the whipping of the soles of her feet, after which she was forced to walk on them, electric shocks, rape, sodomy, the pouring of boiling hot water into her rectum, and much more. See Ashraf Dehghani, *Hemaseyeh moqavemat* (Siahkal.com. 1971), chapter 2. Accessed April 25, 2015. www.siahkal.com/english/part1.htm#Chambers. So serious and effective were these torture techniques that guerrillas often kept cyanide tablets on their bodies in case of their imminent capture at hands of SAVAK agents. As a result of the real fear that even the most committed guerrilla fighter might break under such effective torture and reveal critical information about their organization, many would ingest the tablets if the necessity for "revolutionary suicide" arose. Interestingly, one guerrilla considered his tablet as the only "weapon" he carried. See ʿAlireza Mahfoozi, interview recorded by Zia Sedghi, April 7, 1984, Paris, France. Iranian Oral History Collection, Harvard University, Transcript 1 (seq. 7–8). Accessed April 24, 2015. Dehghani described how "revolutionary suicide" was indeed a weapon when one of her comrades poisoned himself rather than being taken alive, opining: "Comrade Kazem once again proved the regime's impotence and inefficacy through a true revolutionary's glorious self-sacrifice" (Dehghani, *Hemaseyeh moqavemat*, p. 4).

[30] "Iran cuts Israel ties," *The Boston Globe*, February 19, 1979.

[31] R. K. Ramazani, *Revolutionary Iran: Challenge and Response in the Middle East* (Baltimore and London: The Johns Hopkins University Press, 1986), p. 151.

Nearly three weeks before the Shah's final departure from Iran, Ayatollah Khomeini underscored Israel's hand in the Shah's repression: "Israel is the biggest supporter of the Shah and is responsible for setting up SAVAK. For this reason, Israel is a partner in the crimes of the SAVAK and the Shah."[32] This was not, however, the only reason for Iranians' aversion: the issue of Palestine also prompted many clergy, radical student groups, and even state officials to hold Israel in contempt.

For the militant clergy, Palestine was an Islamic issue that affected all Muslims regardless of sect, ethnicity, or nationality. Khomeini, for example, did not recognize ethnic and national divisions amongst Muslims. For him, the suffering of Muslims in Afghanistan, Palestine, or elsewhere was not confined to the national boundaries of those countries, but concerned Muslims all over the "Islamic world"[33]:

We do not regard Islam as being confined to Iran. Islam is Islam everywhere. It is the same Islam in Egypt, Sudan, Iraq, the Hijaz, Syria and other places. We cannot separate our fate from that of other Muslims... We cannot consider the Arabs or the destiny of the Arabs nor that of the other (Muslim) countries as being separate from ours. It is the same Islam everywhere, and all Muslims – us included – are duty bound to protect Islam wherever it is.[34]

In *Kashf al-Asrar* (*The Revealing of Secrets*), published nearly four decades before he led a revolution in the name of Islam, Khomeini argued that "the walls that they have erected throughout the world in the name of countries are the products of man's limited ideas" and that the world is "the homeland of all the masses of people ... under the law of God..."[35] Almost thirty years later in his seminal tract, *Islamic Government*, he argued against the continued existence of such nation-states, blaming the imperial powers for dismembering the Ottoman

---

[32] Ruhollah Khomeini, "Bayān-i dīdgāh-i islām dar mored-i masā'el-i mokhtalef," interview, December 28, 1978, Neauphle-le-Château, Paris. Vol. 5, p. 295. http://farsi.rouhollah.ir/library/sahifeh?volume=5&tid=70.

[33] I use the phrase "Islamic world" rather cautiously because it is not very descriptive, seemingly suggesting Muslims inhabit an entirely separate world.

[34] Ruhollah Khomeini, "Ahamīat-i ḥefẓ-i jomhūrī-ye islāmī – naqsh-i roḥānīat dar ṭūl-i tārīkh – ṭarḥ-i khīānatbār-i sāzesh bā isrā'īl," November 16, 1981. Tehran. Vol. 15, pp. 369–70. http://farsi.rouhollah.ir/library/sahifeh?volume=15&tid=176.

[35] Ruhollah Khomeini, *Kashf alasrār*, 1942, p. 276.

Empire when they "separated various segments of the Islamic nation
from each other and artificially created separate nations ... about 10 to
15 petty states."[36]

After the revolution, factions within the Islamic Republic labored to
make Khomeini's vision for the Islamic world a reality, with a particular focus on the emancipation of Palestine. The internationalist faction
co-founded[37] Hizbullah, an armed socio-political movement established in Lebanon in part to fight Israel in solidarity with what Khomeini referred to as "Islamic Palestine."[38] In 1985, Hizbullah echoed
Khomeini's Islamic internationalism when it published an open letter
declaring its existence:

> We are linked by a strong ideological and political connection – Islam. From
> here, what befalls the Muslims in Afghanistan, Iraq, the Philippines or
> anywhere else verily afflicts the body of our Islamic nation of which we are
> an inseparable part, and we move to confront it on the basis of our main
> legal obligation and in the light of a political view decided by our leader the
> *Wilayat al-Faqih* [Ayatollah Khomeini].[39]

Ayatollah Mottahari, an architect of Iran's Islamic system, whose
assassination in 1979 prompted an official day of national mourning,[40]
effectively positioned Palestine within both an Islamic context and
history:

[36] Ruhollah Khomeini, *Ḥokūmat-i islāmī: vilāyat-i faqīh*. mu'aseseh-ye āmūzeshī-
ye pazhoheshī-ye emām khomeinī, 1970, p. 30. It is important to note that
Khomeini's book was banned in Iran, therefore, many Iranians had not read it
and did not know exactly what Khomeini aspired to achieve beyond his vague
public references to freedom.
[37] I purposely say "co-founded" because Muhammad Montazeri, Jalal al-Din
Farsi, Ayatollah ʿAli Akbar Mohtashamipour, and guardsmen from the Islamic
Revolutionary Guards Corps (with Khomeini's blessing) were instrumental in
Hizbullah's formation but do not deserve all the credit since it was militant
Lebanese Shiʿites who likewise provided crucial leadership and the foot soldiers
for the organization. Roschanack Shaery-Eisenlohr, *Shiʿite Lebanon:
Transnational Religion and the Making of National Identities* (New York:
Columbia University Press, 2008), p. 96.
[38] Ruhollah Khomeini, "Hoshdār be moslemīn-i jahān dar mored-i felestīn va
efshā-ye jenāyathāye rezhīm-i shāh," February 1979. Najaf, Iraq. Vol. 2, p. 322.
http://farsi.rouhollah.ir/library/sahifeh?volume=2&tid=269.
[39] Hala Jaber, *Hezbollah: Born with a Vengeance* (New York: Columbia
University Press, 1997), pp. 54–55.
[40] "Iran mourns killing of top Khomeini aide," *The Jerusalem Post*, May 3, 1979,
p. 4.

What would the Prophet of Islam do if he was still alive today? What issue would occupy the Prophet's thoughts? By God we are responsible regarding this crisis. By God we have responsibility. By God we are being ignorant. By God this very issue would break the heart of the Prophet today. The problem that would fill Husayn ibn ʿAli's heart with sorrow today is this issue.

If Husayn ibn ʿAli was here today, he would say 'if you want to mourn for me today, if you want to lament over me, your slogan today must be "Palestine."' The Shimr[41] of 1300 years ago is dead and gone. Get to know the Shimr of today. Today the walls of this city should tremble to the slogan of Palestine. And what efforts have we Muslims exerted for Palestine? By God it's a shame for us to call ourselves Muslims. It's a shame to call ourselves Shiʿites of ʿAli ibn Abi Talib. The enemy has ravaged our fellow Muslim's land, murdered and imprisoned their men, violated their women and took their jewelry from their ears and hands... Are they not Muslims?[42]

Mottahari situated the issue of Palestine overtly within a distinct Islamic narrative by equating Israel's treatment of the Palestinians with the seventh-century massacre in Karbala. The supporters of Husayn are unable to reverse the course of history by preventing his martyrdom at the Battle of Karbala, but they can enliven his legacy today by coming to the aid of suffering Palestinians. That is, resisting Israel with the goal of Palestine and Quds' total liberation is the proper expression of Shiʿite piety; Husayn, Palestinians,[43] and Iranians are Muslims, intertwining their timeless fates as the global Muslim community, theoretically, constitutes one *ummah*, or "Islamic homeland."[44]

For the militant clergy, however, Palestine was not a Muslim issue simply because Palestinians were predominantly Muslim, but also because Palestine is home to Islam's third holiest site, Jerusalem (*al Quds* in Arabic). Muslims believe the Prophet Muhammad visited Jerusalem in his Night Journey, ascended to heaven from there, met and prayed with the great prophets of the Abrahamic tradition, and

[41] Shimr is infamous for beheading Husayn at the Battle of Karbala in 680 CE.
[42] The text of his famous speech is posted in full online and the actual audio clip can be found on YouTube. See Ruh, "Shahīd morteżā mottaharī va felesṭīn," Doshmantarin, November 15, 2010. Accessed September 24, 2013. http://doshmantarin.blogsky.com/1389/08/24/post-10/. ʿAlireza Bahmanpour, "Ayatullah's historical speech about Palestine," Online video clip, YouTube, June 18, 2010. Accessed September 24, 2013. http://youtu.be/-SxOUMLfX7c.
[43] The Islamist depiction of Palestinians as Muslims is not entirely accurate as around one-fifth to a quarter of Palestinians are Christian.
[44] Khomeini, *Ḥokūmat-i islāmī*, p. 93.

returned. Following the Jewish tradition, it is also Islam's original *qiblah*, the direction in which the first Muslims prayed.

Jerusalem's centrality in the Abrahamic faiths and the Crusades have also prompted an Islamic preoccupation with safeguarding the city. As Rashid Khalidi notes in his seminal *Palestinian Identity*,

[The] idea of Palestine's special importance is, at least in part, rooted in the heightened Islamic concern for Jerusalem and Palestine that followed the traumatic episode of the Crusades. This idea was widespread, and persisted for centuries thereafter. One of the most eminent eighteenth-century religious figures in Jerusalem, Shaykh Muhammad al-Khalili, in a *waqfiyya* document of 1726 establishing an endowment that survives to this day, warned that the transfer of *waqf* property to foreigners in Jerusalem constituted a danger to the future of the city, which must be built up and populated if Jerusalem were to be defended against the covetousness of these external enemies.[45]

The advent of nationalism in the region sparked renewed conflict over the city, and in 1967 Israelis conquered and occupied East Jerusalem, officially annexing it in 1980.[46] This was regarded by the likes of Khomeini as an affront to the honor and territorial integrity of the wider Muslim nation, or "Islamic homeland." He repeatedly argued for the return of Palestine and Jerusalem (Quds) to the "Islamic homeland" as a matter of supreme importance:

I ask of God the Blessed and Exalted that our brother nation of Palestine will overcome its difficulties. We are their brothers. From this movement's inception more than fifteen years ago, I have always, in my writings and speeches, spoken of Palestine and brought attention to the crimes that Israel has perpetrated there. God willing, after we are freed from these fetters then, to the same degree that we stood with you at that time and are now standing with you, I hope that we will confront the problems together like brothers. I beseech God the Blessed and Exalted to exalt Islam and the Muslims and to return Quds to our brothers.[47]

---

[45] Rashid Khalidi, *Palestinian Identity: The Construction of Modern National Consciousness* (New York: Columbia University Press, 1997), p. 30.

[46] This annexation is not recognized by much of the world simply by virtue of the Geneva Conventions, which, in summary, considers territorial conquest and annexation unlawful. See Sharon Korman's *The Right of Conquest: The Acquisition of Territory by Force in International Law and Practice* (Oxford: Oxford University Press, 1996), p. 224.

[47] Ruhollah Khomeini, "Ghalabeh-ye īmān bar qodrathāye shayṭānī," February 17, 1979. Tehran. Vol. 6, p. 179. http://farsi.rouhollah.ir/library/sahifeh?volume=6&tid=72.

Even in the final years of his life, as the revolutionary head of state with the country's media and resources at his disposal, he continued to call for the return of Palestine to the Islamic fold:

Defending the honor of Muslims, defending the lands of Muslims and defending their resources is an imperative and we must ready ourselves for achieving these divine goals. In the present circumstances particularly, where the true sons of Islamic Palestine ... let out the cry of 'oh Muslims' as they sacrifice their lives, we should stand against Israel and the aggressors with all the spiritual and material strength at our disposal...[48]

Khomeini, whose authority was rooted in his religious standing, the loyalty of followers within and beyond Iran's borders, and his position as the leader of the revolution, referred to Palestine as "Islamic Palestine," affirming the priority of the issue for Islamic revolutionaries. Unequivocal with regard to Israel even before the Shah's demise, he pledged that a future revolutionary Iran would never sell oil to Israel, nor recognize the country.[49]

Many strata of Iran's population sympathized with the Palestinian cause. Two guerrilla groups, the Organization of Iranian People's Fada'i Guerrillas (Fada'iyan-i Khalq or OIPFG) and the Mujahedin-i Khalq (MEK), galvanized an entire generation of radical students in the 1970s by launching a guerrilla war against the monarchy. Inspired by the revolutionary model of the Moncada Barracks Attack in 1953 that eventually led to the Cuban Revolution six years later, the Fada'iyan declared war on February 8, 1971, by launching a guerrilla assault on a gendarmerie in the northern town of Siahkal, Gilan.[50] The two groups subsequently competed with each other to become

---

[48] Ruhollah Khomeini, "Etteḥād shūm qodrathā dar moqābel-i islām," February 28, 1988. Tehran. Vol. 20, p. 486. http://farsi.rouhollah.ir/library/sahifeh?volume=20&tid=257.

[49] Ruhollah Khomeini, "Taẓāhorāt-i tāsūʿa va ʿāshūrā sīāsat-i jomhūrī-ye islāmī," December 11, 1978. Paris. Vol. 5, p. 207. http://farsi.rouhollah.ir/library/sahifeh?volume=5&tid=46.

[50] In his guerrilla manifesto, Ahmadzadeh argued: "Didn't the Cuban experience show that a small armed motor [band of guerrillas] can launch the insurrection thereby gradually provoking the masses [the large motor] to join the rebellion?" See Massoud Ahmadzadeh, "Mobārezeh-ye mosalaḥāneh ham estrātezhī, ham tāktīk," Siahkal.org, 1971, p. 30. For a primer on the guerrilla war of the 1970s in general and the Siahkal attack in particular, see Ervand Abrahamian, "The guerrilla movement in Iran, 1963–1977," *MERIP Reports*, 86 (March–April 1980), pp. 3–15.

Iran's revolutionary vanguard, launching one spectacular attack after another.

Although the Cuban model provided a historical precedent, Palestinian revolutionary groups such as George Habash's Popular Front for the Liberation of Palestine (PFLP) and Yasser Arafat's Fatah Organization marked the incredible rise of guerrilla groups in the late 1960s and 1970s, serving as immediate exemplars of action for Iran's radical student organizations and guerrilla movement.[51] These groups, along with their counterparts in Iran, perceived Israel both as a colonial enterprise and as America's imperial outpost in the Middle East.[52] Unlike the militant clergy who viewed Palestine through an Islamic lens, Iran's guerrillas saw the struggle in Palestine through the prism of Third World liberation movements.

The Fada'iyan and the Mujahedin aspired to follow the path of Cuban and Palestinian revolutionary groups by violently overthrowing the Shah's government, which they likewise viewed as a product of Western imperialism. Said Mohsen, a member of the Mujahedin's central cadre, offered the following defense during his military trial:

> The present situation leaves one with no choices but to take up arms against the royalist regime. Why do we advocate armed struggled? We advocated armed struggle because we have examined carefully both the revolutionary experiences of other countries and the last seventy years of Iranian history: particularly the constitutional movement; the crushing of that movement by Reza Khan; the overthrow of Dr Mossadeq in the infamous coup of August 1953; and, of course, the bloody massacres of June 1963. What is more, the revolutionary experiences of Vietnam, Cuba, Algeria and the Palestinians have shown us the new road... We have two choices: victory or martyrdom.[53]

---

[51] The meteoric rise of the guerrillas was precipitated by the monumental Arab defeat in the 1967 Six-Day War. Although guerrilla groups existed before the war, afterwards they were augmented by volunteers who had lost all hope in the ability of Arab armies to fight Israel using conventional means. It was also a time in which Palestinians began to rely more on themselves than their neighbors to alleviate their plight, and took matters into their own hands as never before. The spectacular emergence of groups such as al-Fatah and the PFLP galvanized the radicals of the region, Arab and Iranian alike.

[52] Parsi, *Treacherous Alliance*, p. 82.

[53] Ervand Abrahamian, *The Iranian Mojahedin* (New Haven and London: Yale University Press, 1989), pp. 133–134.

So important was Palestine to this generation of radical activists that their solidarity extended beyond words and into action. Both groups sent activists to Fatah and PFLP guerrilla training camps[54] in Lebanon in the 1970s, with explosive consequences. Some stayed and fought side by side with Palestinian groups against Israel.[55] Others returned home, several with Palestinian wives at their side,[56] to wage the guerrilla war. On their return to Iran, they staged bold attacks against the regime, American installations and personnel. Official American cables noted "twenty-eight confirmed explosions (eleven of which [were] directed against US presence)" in the four months spanning the spring and summer of 1972.[57] Targeting the US presence in Iran was also connected to international conflicts in which the United States fought or supported the fight against popular forces, for example in Vietnam,

[54] In his memoirs, Massoud Rajavi, the Mujahedin leader, confirms that the MKO received military assistance from Arafat's al-Fatah organization. See Massoud Rajavi, interview recorded by Zia Sedghi, May 29, 1984, Paris, France. Iranian Oral History Collection, Harvard University, Transcript 2 (seq. 21). Accessed April 24, 2015. See also Wolfgang Saxon, "Arab leaders call Iran shift historic: Saudis are worried about anarchy and others are cautious, but the P.L.O. appears joyful," *The New York Times*, February 14, 1979, p. A9.

[55] "Facing the New Realities: After the changes in Iran, it's now or never at Camp David," *Time*, March 4, 1979, p. 40. According to Ostovar, many militants, including Montazeri's son Muhammad and Yahya Rahim Safavi, who would later become an IRGC commander, established strong ties with the PLO in Lebanon during the 1970s. Such relations not only resulted in their own training and military involvement in PLO operations, but also facilitated the secret deployment of Iranian guerrillas to Lebanon for training. See Afshon Ostovar, "Guardians of the Islamic Revolution: Ideology, Politics, and the Development of Military Power in Iran (1979–2009)." PhD Thesis, University of Michigan, 2009, p. 93.

[56] According to Taleqani's chief aide, Taleqani's son, Mojtaba, a member of the Mujahedin, sided with the Marxist faction during the schism that produced two groups – one that stayed true to its original Islamic worldview and the other, the Marxist Mujahedin, which eventually became Paykar. Mojtaba, imprisoned in pre-revolutionary Iran for these memberships, fled the country upon his release and went to Lebanon to collaborate with Palestinian factions. While in Lebanon, he married a Palestinian woman who returned with him to Iran and occasionally served as a translator between Ayatollah Taleqani's office and the Palestinian diplomatic corps that established an official presence in Iran after the revolution. See Mohammad Shanehchi, interview recorded by Habib Ladjevardi, March 4, 1983, Paris, France. Iranian Oral History Collection, Harvard University, Transcript 4 (seq. 66–67). Accessed May 2, 2015.

[57] Farland, Tehran, to Secretary of State, August 10, 1972, Wikileaks, https://search.wikileaks.org/plusd/cables/72TEHRAN4789_a.html.

Oman, and Palestine itself.[58] In 1972, guerrillas bombed the Jordanian embassy to protest King Hussein's state visit and avenge Black September, the rout of the PLO in Jordan by King Hussein's army in 1970.[59]

Even senior members of the Shah's government were sympathetic to the plight of the Palestinian people. The Foreign Ministry was especially known for criticizing Iran's proximity to Israel on humanitarian grounds rather than on religious or revolutionary principles. A former Iranian official explained the reluctance with which they were tasked with cooperating with Israel: "Even those technocrats that were helping Israel, in their hearts they were really unhappy that Israel was doing these things to the Palestinians."[60] When the issue of Zionism as a form of racism was put to a vote at the United Nations, "ambivalent feelings of Iranian Foreign Ministry bureaucrats about Israel turned out to be a critical factor influencing Iran's vote."[61] Even though Iran's government was closely aligned with the Jewish state, sympathetic officials in the Foreign Ministry nevertheless expressed their solidarity with the Palestinians by voting in favor of the resolution.

When the Iranian Revolution swept away Israel's ally, pro-Palestinian sentiments came to the fore. On February 11, 1979, the day of the revolution's victory, guerrilla groups and armed volunteers[62] dealt the regime its *coup de grace*[63] by attacking police stations,

---

[58] Abrahamian, *Iranian Mojahedin*, p. 140. The Shah also worked to stamp out such revolutionary movements. Specifically, he sent troops to help the Omani Sultan put down the Dhoffar Rebellion, which was backed by the Soviet Union and the allied People's Democratic Republic of Yemen.

[59] Ibid.    [60] Parsi, *Treacherous Alliance*, p. 63.

[61] Ibid., p. 64. The resolution passed on November 10, 1975 with seventy-two voting for it, thirty-five against, and thirty-two abstentions. A decade and a half later, the United States undermined the resolution in a bid to placate Israel after it was not invited to join the US-led coalition during the Persian Gulf War.

[62] Rafiqdoost, *Barāye tārīkh mīgūyam*, p. 41.

[63] One Fada'i guerrilla specifically credits the Fada'iyan with its role in the *coup de grace* when it mobilized fighters to defend the spontaneous Homafaran mutiny in Doshan Tappeh against the Imperial Guard's siege. The successful defense of Doshan Tappeh set in motion the series of assaults elsewhere that precipitated the culmination of the revolution. See ʿAlireza Mahfoozi, interview recorded by Zia Sedghi, April 7, 1984, Paris, France. Iranian Oral History Collection, Harvard University, Transcript 1 (seq. 20–22). Accessed April 28, 2015. Abrahamian succinctly chronicles the final guerrilla insurrection against the Shah's regime, including a telling quote from Bazargan: "the revolution would

the offices of the secret intelligence service, government buildings, military barracks, television and radio stations, and political prisons, and a "yelling crowd"[64] laid siege to Israel's mission in Tehran.

Although the Shah's government did not have full diplomatic relations with Israel, the mission to all intents and purposes functioned as an embassy, even though the Israeli flag was not raised, and Israeli diplomats did not participate in official ceremonies that necessitated the presence of other diplomats.[65] This was so the Shah could maintain deniability in his relations with Israel, refraining from agitating a population and wider region that was emphatically pro-Palestinian. The revolutionaries, however, aware of the scale of the Shah's alignment with Israel, sacked and torched the mission during the final insurrection.

The attack on the Israeli mission preceded the infamous seizure of the US embassy by almost nine months. No ties with another country were severed as abruptly as with Israel, including the United States, which had brought the Shah to power in the first place.[66]

Even the Shah's last prime minister[67] attempted to appease a mobilized population to ward off the revolution's final push towards the total destruction of the state by terminating relations with Apartheid South Africa, ending oil exports to Israel, and expressing solidarity with the Palestinians: "The government of Iran will continue its ties with its Arab brothers and will support them, particularly the

---

not forget the role played by the guerrillas and the Tudeh Party." This quote dispels later claims that groups like the Mujahedin were inconsequential to the revolution. Ervand Abrahamian, "The guerrilla movement in Iran, 1963–1977," *MERIP Reports*, 86 (March-April, 1980), p. 10. It is also important to note that the insurrection precluded a military coup, which was a likely possibility. See Montazeri, *Khāṭerāt*, p. 782.

[64] "Iran cuts Israel ties," *The Boston Globe*, February 19, 1979.

[65] Parsi, *Treacherous Alliance*, p. 27.

[66] Ramazani, *Revolutionary Iran*, p. 151.

[67] Shapour Bakhtiar was the Shah's last premier but the National Front leader only agreed to the position on the condition that the Shah leave Iran on an "extended vacation." See *Khāṭerāt-i shāpūr bakhtīār: nakhost vazīr-i īrān (1979)*. Iranian Oral History Project (Center for Middle Eastern Studies Harvard University), (Bethesda: IranBooks, Inc., 1996), p. 100. In fact, Bakhtiar was a life-long and committed opponent of the Shah and the Pahlavi dynasty. Not only did Bakhtiar envision a Mossadeqist parliamentary system in which the king would reign and not rule, but Bakhtiar also had a personal incentive for opposing Pahlavi rule: the dynasty's founder, Reza Shah, executed Bakhtiar's father. Ibid., p. 110.

Palestinians in achieving their goals."[68] The revolutionary government
went so far as to blacklist foreign companies that had in the past
indirectly sold Iranian oil to Israel, and sought to ensure that companies would not resell Iranian oil to Israel.[69] Khomeini even took his
own provisional government by surprise when he severed diplomatic
relations with Egypt in protest against the Egyptian-Israeli peace treaty
and in solidarity with the Arab states that opposed it.[70]

That Yasser Arafat, the chairman of the PLO, was the first world
leader, despite not being a head of state,[71] to visit Iran a week after the
triumph of the revolution, should come as no surprise.[72] Although he
came uninvited, he and his thirty-one-member delegation[73] received a
hero's welcome, with crowds marking his arrival with chants of "Palestine will be victorious, Israel will be destroyed" (*felestīn pīrūz ast,*

[68] "Iran to cut off oil to Israel, South Africa," *The Jerusalem Post*, January 12,
1979, p. 1.
[69] "Iran bans firms that sold Israel oil," *The Jerusalem Post*, March 8, 1979, p. 4.
[70] John Kifner, "Khomeini orders Iranian regime to break relations with Egypt,"
*The New York Times*, May 1, 1979, p. A3. Khomeini went on to say that
Sadat's peace treaty with Israel was a "betrayal to Islam, Muslims, and
Arabs..." See Ruhollah Khomeini, "Ṣolḥ-i meṣr va isrāīl (kamp dayvīd)."
March 25, 1979. Qom. Vol. 6, p. 410. http://farsi.rouhollah.ir/library/sahifeh?
volume=6&tid=164.
[71] Bani Sadr was emphatic in his memoirs that under no circumstance would he
receive help from foreign governments. When it came to the Palestinians,
however, he was open to the idea of not only receiving Palestinian support but
also reciprocating that support. Bani Sadr said that he personally was not given
any aid but he would not have been opposed to such a relationship because "In
our opinion his [Arafat's] circumstances were different than that of a
government because we considered them [the Palestinians] as a movement much
like ours..." See Abolhassan Banisadr, interview recorded by Zia Sedghi, May
21–22, 1984, Paris, France. Iranian Oral History Collection, Harvard
University, Transcript 4 (seq. 86). Accessed April 22, 2015.
[72] Just as Iranians were honored to have Arafat be the first world leader to visit the
country to mark the revolution's success, the pro-Palestinian press in Lebanon
likewise touted the fact that Arafat was the first world leader to be received in
revolutionary Iran. Sheryl P. Walter, Lebanon Beirut, to Department of State,
February 19, 1979, Wikileaks, https://search.wikileaks.org/plusd/cables/
1979BEIRUT00977_e.html. Incidentally, that Arafat was the first to visit Iran
after the revolution led credence to the outrageous conspiracy theory popular
among monarchists in the expatriate community that blamed the Palestinians for
the revolution. Anoushiravan Ehteshami, *After Khomeini: The Second Republic*
(London and New York: Routledge, 1995), p. 6.
[73] James Markham, "Arafat in Iran, reports Khomeini pledges aid for victory over
Israel," *The New York Times*, February 19, 1979, p. A6.

*isra'īl nābūd ast*).[74] When asked why he had come to Iran without an invitation, he is believed to have retorted: "One does not need an invitation to go home, therefore, I did not need an invitation,"[75] and reportedly said, "When we flew into Iranian airspace I thought I was visiting Jerusalem."[76] Moreover, the keys to the Israeli mission, which had been partially burned a week before, were given to Arafat who "proclaimed it the office of the PLO in Iran ... and raised the PLO flag to the cheers of 200 onlookers."[77] He "hailed the 'common goals' of the Iranian and Palestinian revolutions...," emphasized the sacred importance of Quds,[78] and repeated Khomeini's mantra, "Today Iran, Tomorrow Palestine."[79]

The optimism of the Palestinian delegation in Iran and the Palestinian movement as a whole about the triumph of the Iranian Revolution cannot be overstated. Beirut, for instance, where the PLO was stationed at the time of Iran's revolution, "echoed with machinegun fire" as they "saluted" the revolution's triumph.[80] Other Palestinian

---

[74] DamnFool2k, "'Arafāt dar īrān – sāl-i 1357." Online video clip, YouTube, September 14, 2013. Accessed February 18, 2015. http://youtu.be/EPXWG_ZDWxY.

[75] "Javāb-i nā ārām-i 'arafāt," *Ghanoon Daily*, November 28, 2012. http://goo.gl/rIQZiM. It is important to note that Arafat's position in the Arab-Israeli conflict was increasingly weakened as Egypt, the largest and most powerful Arab country, was removed from the conflict through the Camp David Accords. Consequently, Arafat descended upon Iran a week after the revolution's triumph in a desperate attempt to find a powerful ally to replace Egypt.

[76] "Arafat and Khomeini denounced Israel as their common enemy," *The Jerusalem Post*, February 19, 1979, p. 1.

[77] "Iranians vow aid as Arafat takes over Israeli legation," *The Jerusalem Post*, February 20, 1979, p. 1.

[78] Ramazani, *Revolutionary Iran*, p. 153.

[79] Markham, "Arafat, in Iran." Khomeini and Arafat's jovial relations were short-lived as the two had completely different visions for Palestine. In Khomeini's Iran, state-sanctioned pro-Palestinian sentiment exalted Quds and an "Islamic Palestine" that was part of the transnational Islamic nation, which was at odds with Arafat's secular nationalist goals. Furthermore, that Arafat took credit for the early release of the women and African American US embassy personnel, the remaining fifty-two of whom endured captivity for 444 days, angered Khomeini. That Arafat failed to broker a ceasefire between warring Iran and Iraq and subsequently sided with Saddam only ensured that Arafat never set foot in Iran again.

[80] "PLO jubilant over Khomeini victory," *The Jerusalem Post*, February 13, 1979. For a more detailed discussion regarding the global impact of the Iranian Revolution, see John Esposito, *The Iranian Revolution: Its Global Impact* (Miami: Florida International University Press, 1990).

factions such as the PFLP, a guerrilla group that trained many Iranian Fada'iyan fighters in the 1970s, declared that "the victory of the Iranian revolution is a victory for the Palestinian people and the Arab masses."[81] The Palestinians were so hopeful for Iran's revolution that they supplied their allies with weapons[82] and training[83] to help revolutionary forces defend and consolidate their gains. The revolution marked Iran's entry into the Arab-Israeli conflict,[84] though in the worldview of Iran's Islamist leaders it was a conflict that pitted Muslims against Zionists and their imperialist backers, the United States.

[81] Ibid. Even before Iran helped to establish Hizbullah, Lebanese Shi'ites were likewise hopeful that Iran's revolution would ameliorate their plight. According to Amal's first leader after Imam Musa al-Sadr's disappearance: "...as Arabs we know that Israel with its intentions ... is against Arabs and Israel's policies have resulted in the occupation of Jerusalem and of Arab lands. The success of the Iranian revolution with its anti-Israeli policy can help us free our Lebanese land in South Lebanon." Shaery-Eisenlohr, *Shi'ite Lebanon*, p. 105.

[82] In his memoirs, Rafiqdoost, one of the founders of the Revolutionary Guards, claims: "Before the war, the first weapons and ammunition that I purchased was from Arafat in Lebanon. I remember they [Arafat's forces] developed their own missile launchers and Kalashnikov bullets... During one trip, I bought 2,000 Kalashnikov rifles, 200,000 Kalashnikov bullets, 500 rocket launchers, and 5000 rockets and took them to Iran." See Rafiqdoost, *Barāye tārīkh mīgūyam*, p. 143.

[83] One aspect of the training aimed to prepare the IRGC in guerrilla warfare in mountainous regions. This was especially important as the Iranian Kurds and the Islamist forces had a falling out in the spring of 1979, and the Kurds are famous for using mountainous terrain to their advantage. Such training not only better equipped the IRGC to fight the Kurds, but to also benefit from such landscape in the future. Sheryl P. Walter, Iran Tehran, to Department of Defense et al., October 16, 1979, Wikileaks, https://search.wikileaks.org/plusd/cables/1979TEHRAN11002_e.html.

[84] One can make the argument that Iran has long been a party to the conflict through its alignment with Israel before the Iranian Revolution. *Time* affirmed this point succinctly after Arafat's visit to Iran: "It was the Shah of Iran who sold oil to the Israelis, who used it to power tanks and planes that were fighting the Palestinians." See "Facing the new realities: After the changes in Iran, it's now or never at Camp David," March 4, 1979, p. 40. Months before *Time* made that point, Khomeini affirmed the sentiment in the fall during the revolutionary uprising when he said: "The Shah gives Islamic Iran's oil to Israel to repress Muslims." See Khomeini's letter to Arafat: "Tashakor az 'elām-i hemāyat – poshtībānī az felesṭīn," September 19, 1978. Najaf. Vol. 3, p. 476. http://farsi.rouhollah.ir/library/sahifeh?volume=3&tid=289. Iran after the revolution, however, became a different kind of party to the conflict by switching sides.

Perhaps the most fascinating aspect of this transnational solidarity is that it defies common perceptions of the Cold War, which is often viewed through the prism of great power rivalry: East versus West, and capitalism versus communism. For many in the developing world, however, the true struggle was not between East and West, but between North and South – a conflict between the exploited, under-developed, and subjugated nations and the yoke of colonialism and imperialism, the metropoles of which had developed at the former's expense.[85] This revolutionary camaraderie between Iranian and Palestinian militants is especially noteworthy in the context of the Shah's ideology, in which the Persian Shah, "the Light of the Aryans,"[86] sat at the apex of the racial hierarchy against the Middle Eastern Other – namely, the Arabs. In other words, revolutionary Iranians were able to make common cause with the Palestinians despite the monarchy's hegemonic, racialized "common sense."

This history demonstrates the deeply organic link between the Palestinian national struggle and Iranian revolutionaries of all political persuasions. Thus, when the Islamic Republic instituted Palestine as a cornerstone of its ideology, it was not seeking to pre-empt allegations that its foreign policy was partial towards Shi'ite Muslims.[87] Rather,

---

[85] For a prime example of the struggle between the North and the South, see Piero Gleijese, *Conflicting Missions: Havana, Washington, and Africa, 1959–1976* (Chapel Hill and London: The University of North Carolina Press, 2002).

[86] Heavily influenced by European fascism and Kemalism, the Pahlavi dynasty expounded an ideology in which "Iranianness" was constructed along an ethnic line, as determined by language and a selective reading of history. Thus, Persian speakers constituted a normative Iranianness in the eyes of the state before the revolution. Afterward, Shi'ite Islamic identity supplanted the Pahlavi dynasty's hierarchy of ethnic supremacy. In other words, Persian speakers, regardless of religion, enjoyed a privileged status during the Pahlavi era; after the revolution, Shi'ite Muslims, irrespective of ethnic identity, became the new standard, as envisioned by the Islamic government, by which to determine a citizen's Iranianness. That Iran's current leader is a Shi'ite Islamic jurist of Azari Turkic origin exemplifies the post-revolutionary hierarchy in which religion and not ethnicity is paramount. That is not to say, however, that racism does not persist on a popular level both inside Iran and certainly within the expatriate community, as well as on a structural level in Iran. For a more thorough reading on the subject, see Alireza Asgharzadeh, *Iran and the Challenge of Diversity: Islamic Fundamentalism, Aryanist Racism, and Democratic Struggles* (New York: Palgrave Macmillan, 2007).

[87] As'ad AbuKhalil wrote in 2014 that tensions between Hamas and Iran over the war in Syria "hurt Iran (and Hezbollah) as that relationship helped dispel the sectarian cast of Iranian policies in the Arab East." "Some determinants of

the Islamic Republic situated the liberation of Palestine (and Quds) as one of its founding pillars because of its profound concern for the Holy Land, which was shared between the Palestinian movement and those who had fought to make the Iranian Revolution a reality. It was believed that victory in Iran would eventually translate into victory in Palestine.

After the revolution, the Islamic Republic institutionalized "Islamic Palestine" by inculcating the next generation of Iranians in the tenets of Palestinian liberation. This potent discourse, however, was to backfire against Khomeini's successors in 2009.

## 4.4 Institutionalizing Palestinian Liberation in Revolutionary Iran

The Iranian government institutionalized Palestinian liberation in a multitude of ways, ranging from textbooks and the country's religio-political calendar to its physical landscape.

Iranian children were exposed early on to emotive stories of oppression and resistance in Palestine. An example of this ideological indoctrination can be found in a second-grade Persian grammar textbook published three years after the revolution. In chapter 15, a Palestinian refugee boy writes a fictional letter to his Iranian peers:

Do you know me? I am your brother. I am Palestinian, we Palestinian children are Muslim.

The name of our country is Palestine and name of your country is Iran. You live in your own country and in your own home. But we are refugees in the desert because the enemy has occupied our home and homeland. We now live in the desert. We spend our days and nights under tents. The tents are our schools. But even here, the enemy won't leave us alone and burns our tents. They show no mercy to our young or old, and they even bomb our hospitals. Do you know why? It's because we want to return to our home and country and expel the enemy from our homeland.

Iranian policy in the Arab East," al-Akhbar English, November 3, 2014. Such a statement seemed to suggest that Iran supported Hamas, a militant Sunni Islamist organization, in order to refute allegations of sectarianism in which Iran only supported Shi'ite groups such as Hizbullah in Lebanon, and SCIRI and others in Iraq. The history outlined above, however, underscores the point that for the Islamic Republic, the issue of Palestine is an Islamic one fully above sectarian considerations.

Ever since your revolution was victorious, our enemy has grown frightened and for this reason harasses us even more.

Our enemy is Israel. Israel is our enemy and is your enemy and the enemy of all free peoples.

We will resist Israel until our very last breath and we know that you will help us. All free peoples will help us. We will resist and with the grace of God we will be victorious and we will return to our dear country where we will live in freedom.

Hoping for victory, God preserve you.[88]

The letter is remarkably close to Khomeini's speeches on Palestine, which were given with more mature audiences in mind:

[Israel] is driving the innocent brothers of our faith out of their homes, destroying their houses and burning their crops, while the Muslim governments remain indifferent to these crimes even occasionally partaking in such crimes or busying themselves with pointless negotiations, leaving the brave Palestinian freedom fighters to courageously resist Israel alone... Our brothers and their defenseless children are burning in the flames while facing many dangers.[89]

In Khomeini's Iran, a new generation were now being drilled in the plight of the Palestinian people through the medium of vivid, emotionally intense stories. Homework questions derived from the letter quoted above asked "Where do the Palestinians live?," "Who has occupied their homeland?," and "Who is their enemy and what does the enemy do to them?"[90] The "Letter from a refugee child" is inset with a drawing of a Palestinian boy and the tents in which he and his dispossessed family live (Figure 4.2).[91] The enlarged eyes are designed to emphasize a sense of innocence in order to invoke deeper sympathy. The letter also highlights that while Iranian children are fortunate enough to have the luxury of proper schools, they should perhaps feel a sense of shame because their "brothers" in Palestine go to school in tents, which to make matters worse are often set ablaze by Israel, "the enemy of all free peoples." They should also feel a sense of obligation

---

[88] *Fārsī: dovvom-i dabestān* (Tehran, S. 1981), pp. 48–51.

[89] Ruhollah Khomeini, "Ḥamleh-ye rezhīm-i ṣahūnīstī be jonūb-i lobnān," March 22, 1978. Najaf. Vol. 3, p. 358. http://farsi.rouhollah.ir/library/sahifeh?volume=3&page=358.

[90] *Fārsī*, pp. 50–51.     [91] Ibid., p. 48.

**Figure 4.2** Image of a Palestinian refugee boy from a textbook

because, as a consequence of Iran's revolution, "the enemy ... harasses" them "even more."

No aspect of the letter is more loaded with Iran's Islamist ideology than the introduction, which treats Palestinians, regardless of sect and the presence of a sizable Christian minority, as Muslims – "brothers" to their Iranian counterparts. Basic language accessible to a child is employed to deliver ideological lessons that emphasize the necessity of returning "Islamic Palestine" to "the Islamic homeland," and Iran's obligation in that just and noble effort.

Just as this state-sanctioned discourse that legitimized resistance to oppression was designed to inculcate a generation in the cause of Palestine, the revolutionary government likewise sought to drill Iran's wider population in the importance of Palestine's liberation. Khomeini's masterstroke, at Ayatollah Montazeri's suggestion,[92] came with his designation of the last Friday of the holy month of Ramadan as Quds Day, a day on which Iran ideologically cemented its status as one

---

[92] It important to note that there is a debate as to who was responsible for recommending the establishment of Quds Day to Khomeini. Some believe that Mustapha Chamran, Mehdi Bazargan, or the Fada'iyan share in the credit. I blame the confusion on the popularity of the issue amongst all factions at the time. See Farahman Alipour, "Felesṭīn dar āyeneh-ye khāṭerāt-i āyatollāh," Rooz Online, December 19, 2010. www.roozonline.com/persian/wijeh/wijehitem/archive/2010/december/19/article/-06dcc80b99.html.

of the most ardent international champions of the Palestinian movement. The day was to unite "hundreds of millions across the Islamic world over the issue of Palestine, with Muslims in each country coming out on a single day..."[93] Khomeini instituted Quds Day hoping that governments would cooperate with popular forces to facilitate a common platform for the liberation of Quds and Palestine, and that the Islamic world's heightened sense of religiosity would "strive to save Quds"[94] from what Khomeini called "the usurper," Israel. In his letter proclaiming the establishment of Quds Day, he underscored the necessity for the day of solidarity, once again employing the imagery of burning houses in Israel's assault on southern Lebanon:

Over the years I have repeatedly reminded Muslims of the usurper Israel's danger, and it is now increasingly launching savage attacks on our Palestinian brothers and sisters in south Lebanon with the aim of destroying Palestinian resistance, continuously bombing homes and dwellings. I call upon Muslims around the world and their governments to unite against Israel and its backers. I invite the Islamic world to commemorate the last Friday of Ramadan, which falls amongst the most blessed days of the month, in order to support the Palestinian people. Such a day will be known as Quds Day, and Muslims around the world must gather in solidarity with Palestinians in their pursuit of their lawful rights.[95]

The historic first Quds Day witnessed "millions of Iranians" demonstrating in solidarity with Palestine "throughout the country," where they wished "Death to Carter, Begin, and Sadat" – the latter being the first Arab head of state to formally recognize Israel.[96] Khomeini marked the occasion with a fiery speech in which he highlighted the universal message of the day: "Quds Day is the day in which the oppressed stand and face their oppressors," and invoked Iran's struggle against the Shah and his foreign backers to inspire Palestinians and fellow Muslims to rise up against their "oppressors": "We, with a smaller number, revolted in the face of numerous enemies and defeated the superpowers... Just as Iran revolted and rubbed the noses of the

[93] Montazeri, *Khāṭerāt*, p. 544.
[94] Ruhollah Khomeini, "Vīzhegīhāye rūz-i qods," August 16, 1979. Qom. Vol. 9, p. 276. http://farsi.rouhollah.ir/library/sahifeh?volume=9&tid=94.
[95] Ruhollah Khomeini, "Entekhāb-i ākharīn jome'h-ye māh-i ramażān be 'onvān-i 'rūz-i qods'," August 7, 1979. Qom. Vol. 9, p. 267. http://farsi.rouhollah.ir/library/sahifeh?volume=9&tid=88.
[96] "Millions mark 'Palestine Day'," *The Washington Post*, August 17, 1979.

oppressors in the dirt, so should the oppressed of other nations. . ."[97] Khomeini used the occasion of the first Quds Day to place the Shah in the same category as Israel, and situated the long-suffering Iranians alongside the oppressed Palestinians. He also ensured that there was no ambiguity about the connection between Quds Day and the state and ideology that established it: "Quds Day is not only a day for Palestinians but is also an Islamic day. It is a day for Islamic government. It is a day in which the flag of the Islamic Republic must be raised in other [Islamic] countries."[98] From the first Quds Day after the revolution until 2009, it had been a day of state-sanctioned mass rallies in which the country's leadership and certain segments of the population walked side by side in solidarity with Palestine and the Iranian government.

Thus, any Iranian who came of age in Iran after the revolution would have been exposed to the issue of Palestine through elementary school textbooks. For those who had already reached adulthood at the time of the revolution, Quds Day provided the opportunity to instill in them the tenets of "Islamic Palestine." Even if they avoided the event, there was still a chance they would learn about the struggle in Palestine through the state media's relentless focus on the issue.

One Tehran Radio communiqué promised that the Iran–Iraq War would "continue until attaining the liberation of Quds (Jerusalem) from the Zionist domination. . ."[99] The decision to continue the war into Iraq after Iran liberated all Iraqi-occupied territory in 1982 was likewise publicized under such slogans as "War, War Until Victory" and "The Road to Jerusalem Goes Through Karbala."[100] The

---

[97] Ruhollah Khomeini, "Vīzhegīhāye rūz-i qods."        [98] Ibid.

[99] David Bernstein, "Iran invades Iraq: 'First stage in liberation of Jerusalem'," *The Jerusalem Post*, July 15, 1982.

[100] Rafiqdoost, *Barāye tārīkh mīgūyam*, p. 218. Abrahamian notes that the slogan actually read: "The Road to Jerusalem Goes Through Baghdad." Perhaps both were used interchangeably as they nearly served the same sentiment. Ervand Abrahamian, *A History of Modern Iran* (Cambridge and New York: Cambridge University Press, 2008), p. 171. Ostovar documents how the IRGC viewed the liberation of Quds as the paramount priority that was "blocked" by the war with Iraq. Thus, successfully defeating Iraq, the "lesser victory," was necessary in order to commence operations to achieve the "greater victory" of freeing Jerusalem. As Ostovar put it, ". . .Iraq became seen as both the literal and figurative gateway to Jerusalem and the first step toward the ultimate emancipation of Muslim societies." Afshon Ostovar, *Vanguard of the Imam: Religion, Politics and Iran's Revolutionary Guards* (New York: Oxford University Press, 2016), p. 110. Interestingly, for the PFLP in the 1970s, "the road to Jerusalem begins in Amman." James L. Gelvin, *The Israel-Palestine*

government resolved to continue the war after one of the most significant military operations, which was named after Quds (*'amalīāt-i bayt al-moqaddas*),[101] led to the liberation of Khorramshahr after two years of Iraqi occupation. In the same vein, the government named the Revolutionary Guards' external operations unit "the Quds Force" to underscore the primacy of the liberation of Palestine. Finally, if all else failed to convince the people to view the issue of Palestine through a state-sanctioned Islamic lens in which sympathy for the former necessitated support for the government that championed the Palestinian cause, the authorities erected statues, named streets and districts, and painted murals in honor of Palestine throughout the country.

Of all the means at its disposal to communicate its worldview, the government preferred the visual medium because it was the easiest way to communicate its religio-political and ideological underpinnings to a national audience in a culturally and symbolically relatable manner.[102] This preference was predicated on the goal of reaching as many people as possible. Whereas written work required literacy and time to read, visuals were quickly accessible to a general audience regardless of education or literacy levels.[103] The visuals were not private property confined to elite "easel paintings"[104] in galleries reserved for privileged audiences, but statues and building-sized murals dotting the entire country's streets, squares, and even highways and observed by millions on a daily basis.[105] The government re-visualized and rebranded Iran's physical and aesthetic landscape in the post-revolutionary period in order to depict, extol, and transmit its ideological universe to the population.

Katherine Verdery notes that

among the most common ways in which political regimes mark space are by placing particular statues in particular places and by renaming landmarks

---

*Conflict: One Hundred Years of War*, 3rd ed. (Cambridge: Cambridge University Press, 2014).

[101] Rafiqdoost, *Barāye tārīkh mīgūyam*, p. 212. Operation Bayt al-Moqaddas came on the heels of similarly named Operation Tariq al-Qods, which led to the liberation of Bostan in December 1981, and Fath al-Mubin, which led to the eviction of Iraqi forces from Shush and Dezful in March 1982. Ostovar, *Vanguard of the Imam*, p. 75.

[102] Ostovar, "Guardians of the Islamic Revolution," p. 106.    [103] Ibid.

[104] Houchang Chehabi and Fotini Christia, "The art of state persuasion: Iran's post-revolutionary murals," *Persica*, 22, 2008, p. 3.

[105] Ibid.

such as streets, public squares, and buildings. These provide contour to landscapes, socializing them and saturating them with specific political values: they signify space in specific ways.[106]

Palace Square is one such square that was infused with "specific political values" when it was renamed and remade into Palestine Square after the revolution. Located where Taleqani Street meets Palestine Street (also given new names after the revolution), the square is situated between Amirkabir University of Technology and the University of Tehran, the bastion of modern Iran's radical politics.

Palestine Square is adorned with two murals and a statue that visualize the Islamic government's legitimating imagery through the sacrality of Palestine and Islamic Iran's role in its liberation. The first mural honors Sheikh ʿAbbas al-Musawi, Hizbullah's Secretary-General who was assassinated by an Israeli helicopter gunship in 1992 (Figure 4.3).[107] Below al-Musawi is the Dome of the Rock mosque in Quds with a Palestinian wearing an "*Allahu akbar*" arm band, both of which remind the passer-by of Palestine's Islamic identity. The shattered Star of David in this context symbolizes the aspirational Islamic victory over Zionism.[108] At the center of the square is a statue displaying the heroic David and Goliath struggle over Palestine, which is represented by a vertical geographical outline encompassing both Israel and the Occupied Territories – the whole of historic Palestine. That a silhouette of the Dome of the Rock is carved out of the

---

[106] Katherine Verdery, *The Political Lives of Dead Bodies: Reburial and Postsocialist Change* (New York: Columbia University Press, 1999), pp. 39–40.
[107] Pouya Alimagham, "Palestine Square–1." 2006. JPEG file.
[108] That Zionism, a modern political movement, has to a certain degree successfully grafted itself onto Jewish symbolism makes it all the more difficult for supporters of Palestinian liberation to demonstrate their opposition to Zionism without likewise using such sensitive and emotive cultural markers. Despite the objections of countless Jews around the world, the Israeli state has time and again presented itself as representing worldwide Jewry. To this effect, Benyamin Netanyahu as recently as 2015, on the eve of his trip to the United States to speak in opposition to the Iran nuclear deal, spoke of all Israelis and the "entire Jewish people" interchangeably and incorrectly as if they were one and the same: "I feel that I am the emissary of all Israelis, even those who disagree with me, of the entire Jewish People… I am deeply and genuinely concerned for the security of all Israelis, for the fate of the nation, and for the fate of our people and I will do my utmost to ensure our future." "Netanyahu calls Congress speech 'fateful, even historic mission'," CBS News, March 1, 2015. Accessed December 6, 2016. www.cbsnews.com/news/netanyahu-leaves-for-fateful-even-historic-speech-to-us-congress/.

**Figure 4.3** Palestine Square: mural of Sheikh ʿAbbas al-Musawi

middle of the statue affirms the significance of Quds to the dispute (Figure 4.4).[109] On one side of the statue a Palestinian is gripping a rock, which highlights the asymmetry of the conflict while also underscoring Palestinian defiance and identity (Figure 4.5).[110] The stone, intrinsic to the iconography of the story of David, is one of the main symbols associated with the Palestinian movement both in Iran and around the world (Figure 4.9).[111]

---

[109] Pouya Alimagham, "Palestine Square–2." 2006. JPEG file.
[110] Pouya Alimagham, "Palestine Square–3." 2006. JPEG file.
[111] Pouya Alimagham, "Raising a rock: 'The uprising of the Muslim people of Palestine'." 2018. JPEG file.

**Figure 4.4** Statue at Palestine Square

Like the *kufiya*, the Palestinian scarf/headdress,[112] the rock is an emblematic symbol organically linked to the Palestinian movement which Green activists utilized to register their protest in 2009. So important is the rock to the Palestinian narrative of resistance that it transcends both space and time, figuring prominently in transnational Palestinian culture.

---

[112] The *kufiya* is often referred to as a Palestinian scarf, even though Arabs and non-Arabs across the region claim it as their own. Kurds often don the head scarf, and Iranians have their own version of it called the *chafiye*, which Khamenei often wears. Additionally, various spellings of the scarf exist, but I have adopted the spelling of the Hebron-based Hirbawi Textile Factory, which specializes in producing *kufiyas*, and spells it as such.

**Figure 4.5** Close-up of the Palestine Square statue

Palestinian brides and grooms are often welcomed to their wedding hall through the *zaffe*, traditional dancing and singing that includes the chorus from the popular song, "Mommy, they demolished our house":

Mother, they demolished our home, and the home of my brother and our neighbor. But don't be upset my precious mother, for they increased our stones. We are Palestinians, we are not terrorists. Ours is a just cause, mother, and we just want to return to our home.[113]

---

[113] Sa'ed Atshan, December 29, 2014, 12:30 p.m. Facebook comment. These lyrics of resistance are such an important and enduring part of Palestinian culture that when Jordanian singer Omar al-Abdallat came to the West Bank, audiences requested the same song three times. When he was asked about his experience performing in Palestine, he responded, "I feel I am in Jordan, because the audiences request the same songs." The majority of Jordan's population, and its queen, are of Palestinian descent. See "'Mommy they demolished our house'

**Figure 4.6** Close-up of the Palestine Square statue (from a different angle)

A second Palestinian in the statue is clutching a Quran, symbolizing the centrality of the religious identity of most Palestinians, and affirming that steadfast belief in the holy book, God, and the Seal of the Prophets, Muhammad, will empower them to overcome the hardship of the Israeli military occupation (Figure 4.6).[114] The other side of the statue recognizes the role of women in the struggle as a Palestinian mother, covered in Islamic headdress, is likewise defiantly gripping a stone while holding her lifeless son (Figure 4.7).[115] The bottom right is

top song at Ramallah performance," Ma'an News Agency, October 4, 2008. www.maannews.com/Content.aspx?id=205420.
[114] Pouya Alimagham, "Palestine Square–4." 2006. JPEG file.
[115] Pouya Alimagham, "Palestine Square–5." 2006. JPEG file.

**Figure 4.7** Close-up of the Palestine Square statue (from a third angle)

a shattered Star of David, underscoring the belief that faith and resistance will triumph over Zionism.

There is a second mural along the sidewalk below the image of Sheikh al-Musawi (Figure 4.8).[116] In contrast to the statue and the first mural, which are both related to Palestine in a manner that does not directly involve Iran, this second mural depicts Iranian soldiers, thus situating Iran in the context of the struggle over Palestine not only as a party to the conflict, but also as its vanguard, affirming the leadership role of the clergy. One of the two clerics in the mural is directing soldiers to a target, which tellingly is a black bird of prey whose claws are insidiously ensnaring three Islamic holy sites.[117] That the Dome of the Rock mosque in Jerusalem is one of them emphasizes not only Israel's "usurpation" of the mosque but also Iran and the clergy's sacred role in returning it to the "Islamic fold."

---

[116] Pouya Alimagham, "Palestine Square–6." 2006. JPEG file.

[117] The bird, which is clutching the Ka'ba in Mecca, Dome of the Rock Mosque in Jerusalem, and Husayn's shrine in Karbala, may very well be a stand-in for the United States for backing what the Iranian government deemed to be illegitimate governments on hallowed ground in Palestine, Iraq, and the Hijaz.

**Figure 4.8** Second mural at Palestine Square

The "specific political values" visualized in Palestine Square show the sacred Muslim identity of Palestine and Quds; that victory will be gained through revolutionary belief in Islam, not in foreign and godless ideologies; and that Iran's Islamic government is endowed with the sacred duty, leadership, and moral clarity to spearhead Palestine's total liberation. This Islamist outlook could be seen in murals across the country (Figure 4.10),[118] as well as in the more mundane context of postage stamps (Figures 4.11 and 4.12)[119] and currency: Khomeini appears on the front of the 1,000-rial banknote with Jerusalem's Dome of the Rock on the reverse (Figure 4.13).[120] In short, Palestinian liberation became part of the country's visual heritage in the post-revolutionary period.

---

[118] Fotini Christia (photographer), July 2006. "Mural located on Dr. Beheshti Street, Yusuf-Abad," part of *Tehran Propaganda Mural Collection* (Cambridge, MA: H.C. Fung Library, Harvard University). Retrieved from http://id.lib.harvard.edu/images/olvgroup11882/urn-3:FHCL:1268241/catalog.

[119] Pouya Alimagham, "Quds belongs to Muslims." 2018. JPEG file; Pouya Alimagham, "Only militant Islam can liberate Quds." 2018. JPEG file.

[120] Pouya Alimagham, "Jerusalem-themed Iranian banknote." 2018. JPEG file.

**Figure 4.9** Raising a rock: "The uprising of the Muslim people of Palestine" To mark the first Palestinian Intifada, the Islamic Republic printed stamps that situated the rock as the symbolic center of Palestinian resistance.

The revolutionary movement in 1978–1979 was emphatically pro-Palestinian, and the Islamists institutionalized Palestine as a symbol for two reasons. First, and most obviously, because both the leadership and those on the ground who voted for the revolution with their feet held pro-Palestinian convictions borne of religious solidarity, humanistic ideals, a sense of being comrades-in-arms fighting for liberation, or a combination thereof. Second, Palestine was and continues to be an issue towards which many in the Islamic world and beyond feel a deeply emotional attachment. Dabashi rightly observes that

The geopolitics of the region cannot, of course, be reduced to the Palestinian predicament; however, nor can it be ever divorced from it. The fundamental historical fact of the last half century is that there is no bleeding wound on

**Figure 4.10** Khomeini's leadership and the liberation of Quds
This four-story mural located on Beheshti Street in Tehran positions Khomeini
beside the Dome of the Rock mosque in Jerusalem and in front of an audience
that is clearly focused on him for the leadership of Palestine's liberation. The
image underscores Khomeini's transnationalism in terms of both his authority
and his goals.

Arab and Muslim consciousness deeper and more hurtful than the plight of
the Palestinians and the barefaced theft of their homeland.[121]

Leaders in much of the Middle East have sought to utilize that
emotive power for their own political purposes.[122] The Islamic

[121] Dabashi, *Iran, the Green Movement, and the USA*, p. 120.
[122] The most obvious and dreadful example can be found in 1991, when Iraqi
president Saddam Hussein fired scud missiles at Israel "in solidarity with
Palestine" during the US-led coalition's bombing of Iraq. At the onset of the
conflict, President George H. W. Bush enlisted the support of Arab states such
as Egypt and Jordan to counter Saddam's claims that the American-led
bombing of Iraq was a war against Arabs and Muslims. Israel was not invited
to join the coalition so as to keep the Jordanians and Egyptians in the coalition.
They did not want to be seen as fighting alongside Israel against a fellow Arab
country. Saddam's missile attacks were designed to provoke an Israeli response

**Figure 4.11** "Quds belongs to Muslims"
This stamp more explicitly emphasizes the Islamic identity of Palestine with both a Persian caption and its English translation but also situates a concerned Khomeini above the Dome of the Mosque to underscore the Islamic Republic's goal of returning Jerusalem to the "Islamic fold."

Republic champions the Palestinian cause out of sincere conviction, while also adding to its legitimacy in the process. The Iranian state affirms its revolutionary stature by supporting the quintessential revolutionary movement of the region with its aura of resistance that had captivated and inspired Iranians across the political spectrum in the 1970s.

so as to prompt the Arab states to withdraw from the coalition. Saddam, a leader who paid much lip-service to the Palestinian cause and erected statues of himself pointing towards Jerusalem, like many of his fellow Arab heads of state, sought to use the issue of Palestine to his benefit. This was especially the case in the first Persian Gulf War. Using loan guarantees, President George H. W. Bush persuaded Israel to not respond for the sake of preserving his coalition.

**Figure 4.12** "Only militant Islam can liberate Quds"
The stamp visualizes the Islamic identity of Palestine through the Dome of the
Rock mosque, showing the struggle in the Holy Land as a central Muslim issue
and underscoring how Islamic militancy can precipitate its return. The vertical
caption on the right reads: "We must use machine guns based on faith and the
power of Islam in order to liberate Jerusalem."

In 2009, two themes dominated the Green Movement's approach to
Palestine: first, the repudiation of Palestine as a way of attacking the
legitimacy of the state; second, the appropriation of the symbolic
legitimacy of Palestine, and its reprogramming into a subversive,
anti-government ideological weapon. The movement's ideological
challenge to the state harnessed the powerful history of Palestine and
its symbolism to attack the state that derived its legitimacy in part
through that very symbolism.

**Figure 4.13** Jerusalem-themed Iranian banknote

## 4.5 Palestine Contested

By September 2009, the government had adapted to the opposition's strategy of co-opting regime holidays to stage anti-government rallies, and canceled two such events, the Night of Power and Taleqani's anniversary, to deprive activists of the opportunity to demonstrate. Quds Day, however, could not be canceled without the government losing "too much face,"[123] so it opted to issue several warnings instead.

[123] Director Alan Eyre, Iran Dubai, to Central Intelligence Agency et al., September 14, 2009, Wikileaks, https://search.wikileaks.org/plusd/cables/09RPODUBAI378_a.html.

No warning was more important than the one delivered by Khamenei a week before the annual Quds Day rallies. Responding to the post-Islamist challenge of the demonstrations, he first defended the Islamic identity of the Islamic Republic:

...if politics are separated from morality, they become devoid of spirituality. Consequently, politics take on a bankrupt nature serving as a means for acquiring power at any cost, obtaining wealth, and advancing one's interests ahead of everything else... This sort of politics becomes a plague onto the people. One of the dangers of separating politics from religion – which some have always promoted in the Islamic world and in our country as well, and today unfortunately some are raising the issue of separating religion and politics – is that when politics are separated from religion then morality and spirituality also become separated.[124]

In a clear warning to the opposition, he went on to promise that although the system tolerated differences of opinion, it would deal harshly with those who challenged the "foundation of the system."[125] In contrast to Khomeini's first Quds Day message calling for solidarity with Palestinians while also declaring that it was "a day for Islamic government,"[126] his successor noted that "Quds Day is devoted to the issue of Quds, in which Iranians show their unity," and that they should "be cautious so that no one could use the occasion of these gatherings to create divisions between us"[127] – a clear attempt to pre-empt anti-government activity. The state also broke with tradition by appointing Ayatollah Ahmad Khatami, a staunch conservative, to give the Quds Day sermon instead of Rafsanjani, whose last sermon on July 17, 2009 had served as an occasion for mass protests.[128] Despite the government's maneuvering and threats, however, the opposition continued to mobilize to make Quds Day a "Green Day."[129]

---

[124] 'Ali Khamenei, "Khoṭbehhāyeh nāmāz jome'h-ye tehrān." September 11, 2009. http://farsi.khamenei.ir/speech-content?id=8033.

[125] Ibid.    [126] Ruhollah Khomeini, "Vīzhegīhāye rūz-i qods."

[127] 'Ali Khamenei, "Khoṭbeh hāyeh nāmāz jome'h-ye tehrān."

[128] Sina Husseini, "Mokhālefat-i rahbarī bā eqāmeh-ye nāmāz jome'h-ye rūz-i quds tavasoṭ-i hāshemī." Rahesabz, September 16, 2009. www.rahesabz.net/story/1613.

[129] Alongside calls from opposition leaders including Mousavi, Karroubi, and Khatami to use Quds Day as a day of action, organizers campaigned online and on the streets to encourage protesters to come out. For instance, nine days before the Quds Day rallies, activists hung a banner on a pedestrian bridge, under which thousands of vehicles pass daily, with an image of Mousavi's face

In keeping with its thirty-year tradition, the Iranian government organized pro-Palestinian protests on the last Friday of the holy month of Ramadan, which in 2009 fell on September 18. Iran, the country in which Quds Day was established with the express purpose of mobilizing Muslims across the world to show their support for Palestine, witnessed not only its usual protests but also extraordinary demonstrations with an unprecedented counter-programmed message. Following a two-month lull on the streets, Green Movement activists took the opportunity to resurface not only to express solidarity with the Palestinians, but also to draw attention to homegrown injustices.

Despite a massive security presence and official warnings to the crowd not to hijack the day by airing "deviant slogans,"[130] "tens of thousands"[131] of people gathered to renew their protests in Mashhad, Rasht, Tabriz, Shiraz, Isfahan, Bushehr, Kerman, Ahvaz, Yazd, and central Tehran, which hosted the largest gatherings.[132] While marchers celebrating Quds Day as the government intended generally outnumbered protesters in Tehran, there were parts of the capital where Green activists constituted the majority.[133] The large crowd in Tehran declared "Death to the dictator, whether the leader [Khamenei] or the doctor [Ahmadinejad]" (*marg bar dīktātor, cheh rahbar cheh doktor*)[134] and warned, "Ahmadi, Ahmadi, this is the last message,

above a caption that read: "Quds Day, Green Day" (*rūz-i qods, rūz-i sabz*). See mirhosseinsabz, "Otūbān-i nīāyesh sho'ār-i rūz-i qods rūz-i sabz." Online video clip, YouTube, September 9, 2009. Accessed March 13, 2015. https://youtu.be/4G9BEt3VLKA.

[130] "Hoshdar-i shadīd-i sepah beh ekhlālgarān dar rahpaymaī-ye rūz-i quds," Alef, September 17, 2009. http://alef.ir/vdcc1mqp.2bq1p8laa2.html?5wml.

[131] "Ḥozūr-i gostardeh-ye moʿtarežān dar rūz-i quds dar īrān," BBC Persian, September 18, 2009. www.bbc.co.uk/persian/iran/2009/09/090918_ba-quds-rally.shtml. To confirm that the opposition's protests were indeed massive, see forougheirani, "Taẓāhorāt-i rūz qods 88." Online video clip, YouTube, September 18, 2009. Accessed March 12, 2015. https://youtu.be/eAEl9bUfPk8.

[132] Timothy Richardson, Dubai, to Central Intelligence Agency et al., September 20, 2009, Wikileaks, https://search.wikileaks.org/plusd/cables/09RPODUBAI386_a.html.

[133] Robert F. Worth, "Despite warning, thousands rally in Iran," *The New York Times*, September 18, 2009. Accessed September 24, 2013. www.nytimes.com/2009/09/19/world/middleeast/19iran.html.

[134] Tazahorat2009, "Iran September 18, 2009. Qods Day anti regime rally part 6." Online video clip, YouTube, September 18, 2009. Accessed August 10, 2010. www.youtube.com/watch?v=pj68-4fEzc0.

the Green Movement of Iran is ready to revolt!" (*aḥmadī, aḥmadī, īn ākharīn payāmeh, jonbesh-i sabz-i īrān āmādeh-ye qīyāmeh*).[135]

## 4.5.1 "No To Gaza, No To Lebanon, I Sacrifice My Life Only For Iran"

The most common slogan of the anti-government Quds Day rallies was "No to Gaza, no to Lebanon, I sacrifice my life only for Iran" (*na ghazzeh, na lobnān, jānam fadā'-ye īrān*).[136] Lebanon was mentioned in the same breath as Palestinian Gaza because much of Iran's foreign policy of supporting armed groups that repeatedly exchange fire with Israel includes not only Hamas, which controls Gaza, but also Lebanon's Hizbullah.[137] The slogan was not necessarily an expression of Iranian isolationism or pro-Israeli sentiment, but a repudiation of a central foreign policy priority of Iran, where the issue of Palestinian liberation had become intertwined with the persona of Ahmadinejad after he gave a series of controversial national and international speeches and interviews.[138]

---

[135] Peive17, "Vesal St. Iran Tehran 18 September 2009 P36." Online video clip, YouTube, September 18, 2009. Accessed August 11, 2010. www.youtube.com/watch?v=9OzK3t58QUY.

[136] 2009IranRevolution, "2009 Iranian Revolution – Nasrolla poster & 'No to Gaza, No to Lebanon…' September 18." Online video clip, YouTube, September 21, 2009. Accessed May 14, 2014.
www.youtube.com/watch?v=JDD-UhSPsvU. Also, see forougheirani, "taẓāhorāt-i rūz qods 88."

[137] Iran's support of Hizbullah has long been a central foreign policy priority. Iran played a critical role in Hizbullah's formation in terms of organization, arms, funds, ideology, and even guidance. Hizbullah was formed with the express purpose of establishing an Iranian-style Islamic Republic in Lebanon and to resist Israel. The former objective has largely been abandoned. It is important to note that Iran had no such role in the origins of Hamas, and Iran's support for Hamas is not on par with its support for Hizbullah. For a selection of the growing literature regarding Hizbullah, see Ahmad Nizar Hamzeh, *In the Path of Hizbullah* (Syracuse: Syracuse University Press, 2004); Hala Jaber, *Hezbullah: Born with a Vengeance* (New York: Columbia University Press, 1997). For a good primer, see Richard August Norton, *Hezbollah: A Short History* (Princeton: Princeton University Press, 2007).

[138] For a collection of excerpts from Ahmadinejad on the issue of Palestine, see Anoushiravan Ehteshami and Mahjoob Zweiri, *Iran and the Rise of Its Neoconservatives: The Politics of Tehran's Silent Revolution* (London and New York: I.B. Tauris, 2007), pp. 107–116. For example: "Our dear Imam [Ayatollah Khomeini] said that the occupying regime [Israel] must be wiped off the map and this was a very wise statement. We cannot compromise over the

While some Green Movement leaders criticized the slogan, one activist using the pen-name Jamal Irani defended it. The writer rejected opposition leaders'[139] recommended changes to the slogan: "Just as Mr. Mousavi and Karroubi repeatedly declared that the leaders of the movement are the people, then whatever slogan stems from the heart of the popular gatherings and is decided upon by the people cannot be changed..."[140] The slogan, claimed the writer, "in no way supports Israel's oppression of the people of Gaza and Palestine," adding a scathing rhetorical question: "How can a people who are themselves suffering from oppression under a tyrannical regime accept the same fate for another defenseless people?"[141]

Jamal argued that the people were simply fed up with the Iranian government taking advantage of the Palestinian issue for its own political objectives:

> The government's exploitation of Palestine and Lebanon for its own propa-gandistic purposes, and its exploitation of its animosity for Israel for its domestic politics has caused the people to hold a negative view in relation to the issue of Palestine and the entirety of the conflict... The government's excessive news coverage of Palestine, Hizbullah, Lebanon, and Israel over the past thirty years has caused people to be entirely agitated with anything related to them. It is likely that 30 percent of the government's media coverage over the past thirty years has been devoted to Palestine alone. This has caused the people to have a negative reaction towards Palestine.[142]

Jamal highlighted two critical points: (1) the Palestinian cause lost credibility among a segment of the opposition because of its thirty-year association with the Iranian government – not just Ahmadinejad – and the fact that the issue had been seemingly forced onto them; and

> issue of Palestine... Our dear Imam targeted the heart of the world oppressor in his struggle, meaning the occupying regime. I have no doubt that the new wave that has started in Palestine, and we witness it in the Islamic world too, will eliminate this disgraceful stain from the Islamic world. But we must be aware of the tricks." Ibid., p. 109.

[139] Mousavi, Karroubi, and Kadivar, the latter of whom is in exile in the United States and was a pupil to dissident cleric and one-time successor to Khomeini, Ayatollah Montazeri, all came out against the slogan and advised demonstrators to foster pro-opposition and pro-Palestine slogans such as "Yes to Gaza, yes to Lebanon, I sacrifice my life for Iran."

[140] Jamal Irani, "Cherā mardom goftand: 'na ghazzeh na lobnān, jānam fadā'ye īrān," Rahesabz, June 23, 2010. Accessed September 24, 2013. www.rahesabz.net/story/18060/.

[141] Ibid.    [142] Ibid.

(2) in the eyes of the movement, the government had exploited Palestine and Lebanon for its own propaganda purposes. The state's implied argument has long been that it warrants not only domestic but also wider Islamic support because it champions the quintessential "Islamic" cause, the liberation of Palestine and Quds, which are dear to millions of Muslims in the transnational "Islamic nation." Jamal and those who shouted "No to Gaza, no to Lebanon...," however, rejected that outlook, labeling the government's strategy as "exploitation," and denying the state the ability to legitimate itself through its solidarity with the Palestinians. The slogan strategically undermined the very basis of the Islamic government by attacking a central issue of its ideology.

Conversations with activists and sympathizers of the movement have yielded another common reason, echoed by Jamal: "The government's one-sided and unjustified support for Hizbullah and Hamas while the people of Iran are in need of that support has consequently intensified the people's hatred for the two."[143] One social media user in Iran added that although he was only seventeen years old, he strongly believed that "If these countries were in a better situation than us they would never help us."[144] There is no way of knowing if this is true, but his frustration shows that a large portion of the population had grown increasingly weary of the Iranian government seemingly prioritizing Palestine at the expense of Iranians. In the same vein, another user commented that her priority was "first Iran and my countrymen and then others."[145] Finally, Hizbullah's Secretary-General, Hassan Nasrallah, garnered antipathy from activists by supporting Khamenei, according to Jamal, "at a time when he is giving a sermon of blood in Iran and killing youths," which "has caused people to hate him [Nasrallah] and take sides against him."[146]

Although expressly a nationalist slogan, "No to Gaza, no to Lebanon, I sacrifice my life only for Iran" condemns the government's "exploitation" of Palestine and Lebanon, and highlights their guilt by association in the eyes of many Green Movement activists and supporters. In their attack on a central foreign policy prerogative and ideological tenet, the slogans were negating the ideological foundations

---

[143] Ibid.    [144] Nima Hatami, May 27, 2013, 12:19 a.m. Facebook comment.
[145] Yalda Ramazani, May 27, 2013, 12:12 a.m. Facebook comment.
[146] Jamal Irani, "Cherā mardom goftand: 'na ghazzeh na lobnān, jānam fadā'-ye īrān."

of support for Palestine, and by default, calling the legitimacy of the state into question.

### 4.5.2 *"Palestine Is Right Here"*

More consequential was a second strand within the movement in which activists did not repudiate Palestine but appropriated it to infuse their protest with a remarkable potency, causing the state's thirty-year emphasis on Palestine to backfire spectacularly. For these radicals, Palestine was a revolutionary symbol of defiance against tyranny that belonged not to the government, but to all peoples suffering under the yolk of oppression. The activists took the political language which the state had drilled into a generation of Iranians, reprogrammed it with a new revolutionary meaning, and leveled it against the regime.

On the eve of the first Quds Day after the election results, Jalal Salehpour underscored the efficacy of this strategy in a piece published on an opposition website:

Putting the Iranian state on par with the Zionist regime, which the Islamic Republic has long condemned as the symbol of usurpation and oppression, is a serious attack on the legitimacy of the Iranian state. In doing so, the Green Movement is placing itself beside the issue of Palestine, appropriating such a state-legitimized symbol in order to de-legitimize the Iranian regime.[147]

Salehpour went on to elaborate the utility of co-opting Palestine and the precise target of their "attack on legitimacy of the state":

Adopting the second trend or position can be a fatal blow to the legitimacy of the regime. The meaning of this blow can be realized when we consider the inner core of the regime's ideology, and that consists of the absolute power of *vilāyat-i faqīh*, anti-imperialism, and anti-Zionism. By claiming the anti-imperialist, anti-Zionist leadership of the Islamic world in the past three decades, the state has been able to mobilize segments of the people in order to legitimize its regime. Now, if the Green Movement could show that its sympathy for the Palestinians is devoid of any personal or political benefit and is genuinely rooted in humanistic ideals and against the racist and oppressive Israeli government, then it can disarm the regime by depriving the state of one its most effective instruments used for acquiring legitimacy.[148]

---

[147] Jalal Salehpour, "Cheh ghazzeh cheh īrān," Rahesabz, September 17, 2009. Accessed March 13, 2015. www.rahesabz.net/story/1653/.
[148] Ibid.

Subverting the regime's meaning and uses of Palestine as a symbol amounted to an attack on the *vilāyat-i faqīh*, the essence and foundation of the Islamic Republic, a strategy Salehpour called "political jiu-jitsu":

> Among the martial arts, jiu-jitsu is a method of fighting in which one fighter neutralizes the opponent by turning the opponent's attack against himself while expending the least amount of energy. Using symbols associated with the Israel-Palestine issue can likewise be an example of this political jiu-jitsu. Green activists can use these legitimated symbols in order to de-legitimize the state.[149]

The following day, Quds Day, tens of thousands of Iranians deployed "political jiu-jitsu" in a multitude of ways. Demonstrators marched through one of Tehran's main thoroughfares, Vali Asr Street, asking the explosive and suggestive question, "Why are you sitting when Iran has become Palestine?" (*mardom cherā neshastīn, īrān shodeh felestīn?*),[150] as well as affirming: "Enough killing – whether in Iran or Gaza" (*che īrān che ghazze, koshtan-i mardom baseh*).[151] One protester hoisted a sign that read: "My Palestinian friend, now I better understand your pain."[152] The power of these slogans and signs lay in the belief that if what was happening in Palestine was unjust, as the Iranian government had stressed for three decades, then how could the injustice transpiring in Iran be acceptable? In an unprecedented challenge to the heart of the government's ruling ideology, the Green activists' discourse equated the Iranian government with Israel, a state that the former had long viewed as an illegitimate usurper oppressing the Palestinians. If Mottahari argued that Iranians wanting to properly mourn Husayn's seventh-century martyrdom should battle the Shimr of today – Israel – then Green activists situated the Iranian

---

[149] Ibid.
[150] Tysfood, "Iran ... Tehran ... Quds protest (13) ... 18.09.09." Online video clip, YouTube, September 18, 2009. Accessed September 24, 2013. www.youtube.com/watch?v=A8R1Z3FEvKc.
[151] Penguinswillfly, "Stop killing people, in Iran and Gaza." Online video clip, YouTube, September 18, 2009. Accessed September 24, 2013. https://youtu.be/CzRCxlKdl6A.
[152] As'ad AbuKhalil, "Protesters' slogans in Iran," The Angry Arab News Service, September 22, 2009. Accessed September 24, 2013. http://angryarab.blogspot.com/2009/09/protesters-slogans-in-iran.html. Through my correspondence with Nafisi, I was able to obtain from her a high-resolution original.

government alongside both Shimr and Israel on the most symbolic of days.

In her work "This land is ours, Tehran – Quds," artist Golrokh Nafisi equated the Palestinian resistance with the protesters' struggle in Iran in 2009 (Figure 4.14).[153] Two activist women, one Palestinian and the other Iranian, are depicted with bands in the color of the Green Movement, emphasizing the humanism and transnational solidarity between the people of Palestine and Iran, as well as the critical role played by women in their respective movements. Their heads are uncovered, illustrating how their shared struggle transcends Islam – unlike government depictions, such as in Palestine Square, where the mother is covered and holding her lifeless son, suggesting women's role in the cause of Palestinian liberation is situated strictly within the confines of religion. The women are encased in barbed wire with their faces covered, symbolizing the necessity of concealing their identities from the repression of their respective rulers, one a seemingly never-ending military occupation and the other a militarized state confronting unarmed demonstrators with paramilitaries, police units resembling infantry battalions, and the IRGC. The white doves and the peace gestures, rather than clenched fists,[154] signify the nonviolence of the two movements.[155] Like the Belfast mural of the IRA and PLO fighters (Figure 4.1), albeit with defiant peace gestures raised instead of an RPG launcher, this illustration visualizes two peoples as constituting "one struggle" for freedom. Most important of all, Nafisi's caption, "This land is ours, Tehran – Quds," highlights that land and sovereignty ultimately belong to the people, not the state, and that solidarity is rooted not in Islamist ideology, as prescribed by the government, but in ideals that transcend religion, ethnicity, and national borders. In other words, Palestinians and Iranians are bound together not by

---

[153] Ibid.

[154] When I asked Nafisi if the two-fingered gesture was a peace sign or if it meant "v" for "victory," she had this to say: "In my opinion, to a certain extent the gesture meant both. In 2009, the issue was more about avoiding the clenched fist in favor of signaling for peace *and* [my emphasis] victory." Golrokh Nafisi, "Re: Salaam Golrokh," Email to Pouya Alimagham, November 19, 2018.

[155] Palestinian resistance against the Israeli occupation, despite media portrayals, is largely nonviolent. The mainstream media, however, typically prefers sensationalist news stories, which predictably have the cumulative effect of depicting Palestinian resistance as exclusively violent.

این خاک مال ماست
تهران - بیت المقدس

**Figure 4.14** "This land is ours, Tehran – Quds"

religion, but by their shared humanity and their common struggle for freedom.

In her correspondence with me, Nafisi explained that for her and her counterparts in Iran, the struggle against state repression transcended *all* national borders: "In my opinion, the Green Movement does not only support the people of Palestine, but all oppressed peoples of the world."[156] The humanism of her work resonated with numerous

---

[156] Golrokh Nafisi, "Re: Palestine-Green Movement artwork," Facebook message to Pouya Alimagham, May 5, 2013.

Iranian bloggers, many of whom subsequently relayed her message by posting her artwork on their blogs.

Another Green Movement visual that warrants special attention is rooted in the work of famed political cartoonist Naji al-'Ali, whose character, Handala, is one of the most emotionally charged and well-known symbols of the global Palestine solidarity movement. Al-'Ali's work was published daily in Cairo, Beirut, Kuwait, Tunis, Abu Dhabi, London, and Paris, and gained widespread popularity, prompting *The Guardian* in 1984 to designate him as "the nearest thing there is to an Arab public opinion."[157] He was the most celebrated cartoonist in the Arab Middle East until his assassination in 1987,[158] and Handala, a barefoot, ragged 10-year-old refugee, was his signature, "an icon of Palestinian defiance."[159] Handala symbolized Palestinian dispossession, poverty, and a refusal to accept their dreadful fate. Al-'Ali specifically chose the age of ten for his character because he was himself forced from his Palestinian homeland at that age, and Handala will "always be ten years old" until he is able to return, "and then he will start growing up."[160]

Handala has become a worldwide symbol of Palestinian liberation, and his image can be found on keyrings, stickers, T-shirts,[161] and other Palestinian memorabilia. The icon can also be seen in politically charged places, such as on the concrete slabs of the "separation wall" that snakes into large swathes of the West Bank, dividing Israel and its major settlement blocs from Palestinians (and often Palestinians from

---

[157] Haifaa Khalafallah, "This pen is mightier...," *The Guardian*, September 21, 1984.

[158] There has been much speculation about al-'Ali's assassination, prompting one writer to say that he is "the Tupac of cartooning." Al-'Ali had many powerful enemies, including Arab heads of state, Yasser Arafat, and the Israelis. That the assassins turned out to be double agents working both for the PLO and the Israeli Mossad when they were arrested by Scotland Yard only made it more difficult to determine who ordered the murder. See Paul Lashmar and Shraga Elam, "MI5 was feuding with Mossad while known terrorists struck in London," *The Independent*, June 19, 1999. www.independent.co.uk/news/world/mi5-was-feuding-with-mossad-while-known-terrorists-struck-in-london-1101024.html.

[159] Ian Black, "Drawing defiance," *The Guardian*, March 10, 2008. Accessed September 25, 2013. www.theguardian.com/world/2008/mar/10/israelandthepalestinians1.

[160] Ibid.

[161] As an undergraduate, I went to the first Palestine Solidarity Conference at UC Berkeley in the spring of 2002 and purchased one such T-shirt.

**Figure 4.15** Handala mural at Palestinian refugee camp in Shatila
Al-ʿAli's Handala inserted in the text of a wall in the Shatila refugee camp in
southern Beirut, Lebanon. The slogan repeatedly states: "All of the soil is the
Palestinian nation."

each other).[162] Handala likewise adorns the walls of Palestinian refugee camps (Figure 4.15).[163]

When Green activists carried Handala's image onto the streets of
Iran on Jerusalem Day, they were wielding all his emotive power and
the history of the Palestinian movement to reaffirm his message of
defiance and to attack the legitimacy of the state. If pro-Palestinian
activists painted images of Handala to show their opposition to the
"separation wall" in the West Bank, then pro-Palestinian Iranian
activists lifted his image above their heads to show their opposition
to the Islamic government on the most meaningful of days. Images
of Handala, wrapped in the color of the protest movement, inscribed
with one brief, hard-hitting sentence: "Palestine is right here"
(Figure 4.16).[164] Alongside the illustration, activists provocatively

---

[162] Ibid.    [163] Pouya Alimagham, "Shatila–1." 2008. JPEG file.
[164] Mojtaba Semienejad, "Palestine is right here." Tehran. twitpic. September 18,
2009. Accessed September 25 2013. http://twitpic.com/i5b4.

**Figure 4.16** "Palestine is right here"

raised green-wrapped rocks, the quintessential David and Goliath symbol of Palestinian resistance (Figure 4.17).[165]

Social media enabled activists to continue their Palestine-themed protest even after they were forced to withdraw from the streets. Digital activists took the same image of Handala wrapped in a green scarf and displayed it as their profile pictures (Figure 4.18),[166] equating the justness of the Palestinian cause with their own protest movement, and the government's treatment of the protesters with Israel's treatment of the Palestinians.

---

[165] Sabzphoto, "Palestine is right here," September 18, 2009. Online image, Flickr, September 25, 2013. Member since 2010. Tellingly, the account holder covered the one noticeable face in the image to protect the identity of the protester.

[166] Hezar Dastan, "@samand352." Twitter. N.d. Accessed September 25, 2013. https://twitter.com/samand352.

**Figure 4.17** The Green Movement's Palestinian symbols of resistance
Activists posted the picture online with the protester's face covered to protect
his identity.

**Figure 4.18** Green Handala as a Twitter profile picture

Just as Jamal Irani explained the rationale behind the slogan "No to
Gaza, no to Lebanon, I sacrifice my life only for Iran," Foad Shams, a
journalist and University of Tehran student, penned a searing piece
leaving little doubt as to the meaning behind the Quds Day message of

"Palestine is right here." The forcefulness of the piece warrants its full quotation:

Handala does not only symbolize Palestinian refugee children. Handala does not just originate in Palestine. Handala has not only turned his back on Israelis and the Arab collaborator regimes. Palestine is not just a sliver along the Mediterranean Sea. Palestine is anywhere where oppression and tyranny exist. Palestine is right here.

Handala represents all peoples who are displaced due to tyranny and oppression and whose eyes can only see the tall cement block wall from the Gaza Strip to [Iran's] Evin Prison.

Handala is born everywhere where people have lost their homes and livelihoods at the hands of history's tyrants. Today, Handala is born on the streets of Tehran. If yesterday Handala was shouting for freedom, prosperity, peace, and equality for all of humanity from Gaza, Bethlehem, and Beirut then today Handala is shouting beside us on the streets and alleys of Tehran.

Handala symbolizes our long-lost idealism and radicalism, which, thankfully, the awakened people of Iran have once again found. Today, Handala is beside us not only turning his back to Israel, imperialism, and the Arab collaborator regimes, but is beside us turning his back against all of history's tyrants under any name or uniform. Today, it is not us staring at the television screens in shock as we watch the crimes taking place in Palestine. Today, it is Handala beside us on the streets of Tehran staring in shock, shedding tears as he understands that he is not alone in his displacement. It is not just him and his Palestinian sisters and brothers who have been served with bullets and tear gas. He sees that his Iranian sisters and brothers are not excluded from the same table of tyranny. Handala knows – as we do – that peace, prosperity, and freedom will prevail in Palestine only when the interference of the Israeli occupation and its imperialist supporters and the Arab collaborationist regimes, and most important of all, the undue and harmful meddling of the Iranian government in Palestine, comes to an end.

Handala is standing beside us and we are beside him shouting together that we only want peace and freedom for all the people of the world and the Middle East, regardless of their race, language, ethnicity, nationality, or religion![167]

---

[167] Foad Shams, "Ḥanẓaleh dar kenār-i māst," *Akhbar-i Rooz*, September 12, 2009. Accessed September 25, 2013. www.akhbar-rooz.com/article.jsp? essayId=23831.

Rather than repudiating Palestine in order to condemn the state as Jamal and many like-minded activists had done, Shams harnessed the legitimacy of Palestine's emotive force to condemn the government. Utilizing "political jiu-jitsu," he argued that Iranians, like their Palestinian counterparts, were "not excluded from the same table of tyranny," placing the Iranian state in the same category as "Israel, imperialism, and the Arab collaborationist regimes." For such internationalists as Nafisi and Shams, their emancipatory ideals were not confined to their own nation. Rather, they saw the plight of others as mirroring their own, and Palestine symbolized that universal struggle against injustice, or as Shams put it: "Palestine is anywhere where oppression and tyranny exists." By universalizing Palestine through its symbol, Handala, Shams was able to decouple Palestine from the Islamic Republic, and instead pair those resisting the government on the streets of Iran with the Palestinians, and the Iranian government with Israel.

Shams' concluding statement echoes Jamal's message but in a different way. While Jamal criticized the Iranian state's support of Palestine because "the people of Iran are in need of that support," Shams called for an end to Iran's backing of armed groups which amounted to "harmful meddling" and was an obstacle to "peace, prosperity, and freedom." While affirming the cause of Palestinian liberation, he attacked the legitimacy of Iran's support of the Palestinians and condemned the government and its interventionist role as counterproductive and destructive. He did not negate the validity of Palestine's struggle, but condemned the state's support of it as "harmful" in order to "disarm the regime by depriving the state of one its most effective instruments used for acquiring legitimacy," the same strategy as Salehpour outlined the day before Quds Day.[168]

A year later, the president of the Palestinian Authority (PA), Mahmoud 'Abbas, relayed Shams' blistering attack on the Iranian state. After Ahmadinejad, whose election "win" sparked the protests, criticized 'Abbas for negotiating with Israel, the PA's spokesman retorted:

He who does not represent the Iranian people, who forged elections and who suppresses the Iranian people and stole the authority, is not entitled to talk about Palestine, or the President of Palestine... We have fought for Palestine

[168] Jalal Salehpour, "Cheh ghazzeh cheh īrān," *Rahesabz*, September 17, 2009. Accessed March 13, 2015. www.rahesabz.net/story/1653/.

and Jerusalem and the Palestinian leadership has provided thousands of martyrs and tens of thousands wounded and prisoners (and) did not repress their people, as did the system of Iran led by Ahmadinejad.[169]

This rejoinder from the PA, which was founded by the same Arafat who had received a hero's welcome when he visited Iran uninvited thirty years before,[170] amplified Shams' accusation that the Iranian state did not have the credibility to talk about justice in Palestine when its conduct mirrored that of the Israeli military occupation.

Foad Shams was arrested nearly three months later on another day of action, Student Day. His file contained around thirty provocative articles, including his piece on Handala.[171] Shams' piece and his subsequent conviction show how, after the government had drilled his generation in political concepts of injustice, usurpation, occupation, and the righteousness of resistance through the tenets of Palestinian liberation, its strategy backfired when the same discourse was employed in the service of a movement that was targeting homegrown injustice in the form of a usurping power that robbed them of their election victory and then brutalized them for objecting. Shams had first heard of Handala through a state-televised documentary dubbed into Persian and broadcast to the entire nation.[172] He used the symbolic power of Handala, knowledge that the state had sanctioned and popularized, to subvert Iran's ideologically laden Palestine rhetoric. How, his piece asked implicitly, can the Iranian state champion justice in Palestine when it has abandoned it at home?

---

[169] The CNN Wire Staff, "Palestinian leader blasts Ahmadinejad over Mideast peace comments," CNN, September 4, 2010. Accessed September 25, 2013. www.cnn.com/2010/WORLD/meast/09/04/west.bank.abbas.ahmadinejad/index.html.

[170] That is not to say that the PA does not face enormous credibility issues inside the Occupied Territories. However corrupt, inefficient, and unpopular the PA may be, it is representative (at least in theory) of the Palestinian people. Many argue that the PA should disband as it is the government of a non-state whose territory is still largely controlled and increasingly encroached upon by Israel and its expanding settlements.

[171] Foad Shams, "Re: 'Ḥanẓaleh dar kenār-i māst'." Facebook message to Pouya Alimagham, September 16, 2013.

[172] Foad Shams, "Re: 'Ḥanẓaleh dar kenār-i māst'." Facebook message to Pouya Alimagham, September 17, 2013.

## 4.6 Conclusion

In the pre-revolutionary period, Iranians from various walks of life, from student and guerrilla groups to the militant clergy and even the bureaucrats in the monarchy's Foreign Ministry, viewed the Palestinian movement with great sympathy. Some guerrillas saw them as a source of inspiration, even going to Lebanon to receive guerrilla training from various Palestinian factions. Thus, it made perfect sense that the PLO leader, Yasser Arafat, came to Iran after the revolution to salute its victors.

After the triumph of the revolution, the state institutionalized the liberation of Palestine as a central ideological pillar in its foreign policy, deriving its legitimacy from an internationally recognized movement cherished by millions in the Islamic world because of the sanctity of Quds. An entire generation was raised on the Islamic tenets of delivering Palestine and Quds from Zionism. But in 2009, these lessons produced unprecedented and unintended consequences. Deconstructing the win–lose and start–finish binaries creates the space to unpack important happenings throughout the uprising, including the Green Movement's ingenuity in harnessing Palestine's emotive power, history, and the Iranian discursive focus on Palestinian liberation to challenge the state on its own terms.

The Green Movement was not united in its demands or objectives. Some wanted the election results to be annulled while others wanted to overthrow Iran's supreme leader, the personification of the Islamic system. There were two distinct strands on Quds Day: one declaring "No to Gaza, no to Lebanon, I sacrifice my life only for Iran"; the other implying: "Yes to Gaza, yes to Lebanon, and yes to the Green Movement; no to Israel, no to the Islamic Republic, and no to oppression." Both took aim at the same central tenet in Iran's state ideology: the emancipation of Palestine and Quds and the Iranian government's vanguard role in that endeavor. One Quds Day slogan negated Palestine in order to refute the state that championed it, and in a wider approach, the other used slogans, artwork, powerful articles, and symbolism to subversively co-opt Palestine and equate the Iranian state with Israel.

The disparity between the two slogans underscores the futility of trying to categorize such a multi-faceted movement. The methods the movement employed to criticize the government and undermine its ideology, however, can be described as revolutionary. Activists took the most prized international symbol of the Iranian state and turned it on its head – a revolutionary act in itself. The Green Movement used new and creative forms of digital media to continue their protests even when the streets became unsafe. Both physically on the streets and digitally on the internet, they contested the meaning and ownership of Palestine as a symbol in order to contest the Islamic Republic – the outcome of the Iranian Revolution.

Despite the IRGC's warnings, Khamenei's cautionary sermon, and the presence of security forces in large numbers, the anti-regime rallies on Quds Day did not result in major clashes like the ones that immediately followed the June 12 election.[173] The crackdown intensified, however, in the months after September 18. Increasing repression on the streets, the arrest of countless activists, forced confessions, publicized trials, reports of rape and torture in Iran's prisons (most notably Kahrizak), and even executions, all resulted in a hardening of views within the movement. By the time of *'Ashura* (December 27), the subject of the next chapter, the severity of the state crackdown had sidelined moderate forces calling for the cancelation of the election in favor of more militant calls for a revolutionary change in the government, specifically the ousting of "Leader of the Islamic Revolution" Ayatollah Khamenei.

---

[173] Timothy Richardson, Dubai, to Central Intelligence Agency et al., September 20, 2009, Wikileaks, https://search.wikileaks.org/plusd/cables/09RPODUBAI386_a.html.

# 5 | Mourning as Protest

Montazeri, Post-Islamism,
and Revolutionary 'Ashura

*Life is to have a belief and to fight for it.*

Khosrow Golsorkhi[1]

## 5.1 Introduction

If the symbolic value of Palestine, central to Iran's foreign policy and Islamic ideology, was appropriated and subversively deployed against the government, it is no surprise that *'Ashura*, the anniversary of Imam Husayn's martyrdom, similarly became an occasion for protest and confrontation. Activists who had made common cause with the occupied Palestinians by depicting their government as an oppressive usurper akin to Israel, also made common cause with the righteousness of Imam Husayn and his band of followers by equating the Islamic Republic with Yazid, the caliph who ordered the massacre at Karbala, by using the sacred and emotive power of the day to imbue their protest with a potent discursive force.

Just as the history of Palestine's ideological institutionalization in revolutionary Iran is important for understanding the gravity of the Jerusalem (Quds) Day protests on September 18, 2009, the history of *'Ashura*, its role in the historic mobilization during the climactic days of the Iranian Revolution, and its post-revolutionary institutionalization are necessary to understanding the fervor of the Green Movement's dramatic protests on December 27, 2009.

The *'Ashura* protests of 2009 are particularly important historically because they coincided with the culmination of the seven-day mourning period for Grand Ayatollah Hussein 'Ali Montazeri.

---

[1] Manjanigh12, "Manjanigh 12 Khorsrow Golesorkhi and Keramat Daneshian's full defense," online video clip, YouTube, February 16, 2013. Accessed August 1, 2014. http://youtu.be/jyvjhUsJyNg?list=PLPyPwMMrlbHNfQbr27Iy6La UNIgdaAefT.

196

Montazeri had become one of the state's most influential critics, employing religious discourse against the government that invoked wider Shi'ite Muslim theology, and using his authority to condemn the Iranian government not only in the eyes of his Iranian followers, but also to Shi'ite Muslims around the world, particularly in Iraq, where Shi'ite Islam's most important shrines are located. Montazeri's transformation from a regime architect to foremost dissident underscores what Asef Bayat calls "the post-Islamist turn."

A non-linear approach to the events of 2009 demonstrates how Green activists harnessed a discourse of resistance in which Islamic symbols were used not to legitimate, but rather to condemn, the Islamic government. By exploiting the occasion of Montazeri's death and 'Ashura seven days later, which coincided with the seventh day of mourning in his honor, the Green Movement again deployed the state's Islamist symbols against the very state that derived its Islamic legitimacy from them. This highlights the central thesis of this work: although the Green Movement failed to cancel the election results or overturn the system that ratified them, protesters nevertheless found success in failure. This chapter also argues that Montazeri is the quintessential post-Islamist, chronicles how his death became another day of protest, and outlines how and why 'Ashura, the annual mourning of Imam Husayn's 680 CE martyrdom, became the most ferocious and violent day of action in the post-election turmoil. Montazeri was a senior Shi'ite religious leader, and the observance of his death was replete with ritual. 'Ashura is likewise a day of mourning rooted in Shi'ism. The two events, only seven days apart, show how religiously imbued occasions were subverted as days of action against a state that is ideologically rooted in religion.

## 5.2 Montazeri as a Post-Islamist

In his seminal work, *Making Islam Democratic: Social Movements and the Post-Islamist Turn*, Asef Bayat argues that post-Islamism marks the stage in which "once ardent supporters" of Islamism undergo a qualitative shift after a period of trial and error. They spend years expending energy and resources establishing a much-theorized Islamic government. Through experience, however, they learn that an actual Islamic government is very different from the blueprint they had envisioned. Popular pressure from below and mistakes from above turn these ardent supporters from architects and proponents of an Islamic system to (often dissident) reformists seeking to merge Islam with individual choice, freedom, democracy and, especially, modernity in the quest for an "alternative modernity."[2] They abandon rigidity, and call into question the "monopoly of religious truth" in favor of "religiosity and rights."[3] Post-Islamists do not shed their personal religious beliefs, but seek to emphasize citizenship, civil rights, and empowerment over the "obligations" of duty-bound "subjects" under an Islamic state that "commands good and forbids wrong."[4] They emphasize "plurality in place of singular authoritative voice, historicity rather than fixed scripture, and the future instead of the past," all of which constitutes a qualitative shift from the state-espoused Islamism.[5] In sum, they want to "rescue Islam and the state by abandoning the idea of an Islamic state."[6]

Mir Hussein Mousavi and Mehdi Karroubi, the two reformist candidates who alleged election fraud in 2009, were not only early proponents of Islamism, but also constituted the Islamic Republic's founding leadership. Ayatollah Montazeri, however, is a better case study than either because he was not only designated Khomeini's heir in 1985 but was also a senior cleric, unlike Mousavi and Karroubi, a layperson and a junior cleric, respectively. Most importantly, Montazeri was a co-founder of the Islamic Republic.

So close was Montazeri to Khomeini and his worldview that the latter mandated him to serve as his deputy in Iran during his fourteen-year exile in neighboring Iraq.[7] Some activist clergymen even believed

---

[2] Asef Bayat, *Making Islam Democratic: Social Movements and the Post-Islamist Turn* (Stanford: Stanford University Press, 2007), p. 10.

[3] Asef Bayat, *Revolution without Revolutionaries: Making Sense of the Arab Spring* (Stanford: Stanford University Press, 2017), p. 149.

[4] Ibid.    [5] Bayat, *Making Islam Democratic*, p. 11.

[6] Bayat, *Revolution without Revolutionaries*, p. 148.

[7] Hussein ʿAli Montazeri, *Khāṭerāt* (Los Angeles: Ketab Corp, 2001), p. 281. It is worth noting that Khomeini spent the first few months of his exile in Turkey, where he saw at first hand the secularism imposed by the Kemalist state. Doubtless, his experience in Turkey helped shape his political worldview. He spent the next fourteen years in Najaf, Iraq, where he formulated his theory of Islamic government, until Saddam Hussein in collaboration with the Shah (with whom Saddam had reconciled by the late 1970s) pressured him to leave so he would not be so close to Iran with such easy access to Iranian visitors and pilgrims. Through aides' contacts, he famously found temporary residence in a Paris suburb in the final months of the revolutionary uprising. Although he was farther from Iran geographically, he nonetheless had better access to world

that should a terrible fate befall Khomeini while in exile, then Montazeri would replace him as the leader of the clerical opposition.[8] Yet, Montazeri's political résumé extended beyond his proximity to Khomeini. The 1970s witnessed the height of repression in Iran under the Shah's rule, and Montazeri, who was on the front line of the struggle against the monarchy, was swept up in the state's dragnet. He was imprisoned four times, and not only tortured but also made to listen to the torture of his son, Muhammad.[9] He was finally amnestied in 1978 in a failed attempt to placate the opposition during the protracted revolutionary uprising.

After the revolution, Khomeini entrusted his most ardent supporter and dedicated Islamist revolutionary with the leadership of the constituent assembly tasked with writing Iran's Islamic constitution. Montazeri dutifully spearheaded efforts to enshrine in the constitution the key principle of the Guardianship of the Jurist (*vilāyat-i faqīh*), a role filled by Khomeini. In the September before the vote, Ayatollah Taleqani died, removing a major obstacle to the ratification of the new constitution. After Taleqani's passing, Montazeri turned down Khomeini's offer of the influential position of Tehran's Friday prayer leader, instead recommending Khamenei for the position and thereby facilitating his meteoric rise. Khomeini, who by 1985 was eighty-three years of age, after much time spent pondering the future of the Islamic Republic, appointed Montazeri his successor.[10] Montazeri was one of

media, which inadvertently provided him with an amplified voice to direct the revolution underway in distant Iran. Incidentally, Bani Sadr notes in his memoirs that it was Sharif-Emami's decision to have Saddam deport Khomeini to Europe so that once there, he could undermine himself by exposing his retrograde views to the liberal opposition based in Europe via Paris. Whatever the reason for Khomeini's arrival in Paris, it proved immensely consequential. See Abolhassan Banisadr, interview recorded by Zia Sedghi, 21–22 May 1984, Paris, France. Iranian Oral History Collection, Harvard University, Transcript 5 (seq. 100). Accessed April 22, 2015.

[8]  Sussan Siavoshi, *Montazeri: The Life and Thought of Iran's Revolutionary Ayatollah* (Cambridge: Cambridge University Press, 2017), p. 93.

[9]  Montazeri, *Khāṭerāt*, p. 333. Montazeri sustained permanent partial hearing loss in his left ear as a result of the abuse (p. 376). The cleric believed that the psychological pressure of being made to listen to the torture of his imprisoned son next door was designed to crush his spirit (p. 340).

[10] Montazeri, *Khāṭerāt*, pp. 441–445. According to Ahmad Khomeini, his father reacted in astonishment when he heard Montazeri admit that Khamenei's sermons were "stronger" than his own, reportedly saying of Montazeri: "This is what is called being simple."

a handful of clerics who enjoyed both the highest religious and revolutionary authority, and perhaps most important of all, he recognized and respected the authenticity and legality of the *vilāyat-i faqīh* as an Islamic institution.

*Vilāyat* (or *wilāya* in Arabic) means "guardianship," or "mandate," and it was commonly employed to denote clerical guardianship over those who were unfit or unable to care for themselves, such as orphans or the insane.[11] Such guardianship could also include the right to manage the estate of a deceased person without an heir, and to grant a divorce to a woman whose husband has disappeared.[12] The term *Vilāyat-i faqīh* (*wilāyat al-faqīh* in Arabic) was first coined by Mullah Ahmad Naraqi (d. 1828) who expanded the purview of the *vilāyat* by arguing "forcefully for the right of the *mujtahid* [an Islamic scholar qualified to interpret Islamic law] to act as a successor to the Imam and vest him with all the power of the Imam."[13] Naraqi intended the position to serve as a counter-balance to treacherous monarchs, not as a substitute.[14] Khomeini, however, radically expanded Naraqi's concept and gave it modern application when he developed *vilāyat-i faqīh* beyond the confines of duty-bound religious law to the political domain of the modern nation-state.[15]

Khomeini's interpretation was premised on the exclusively Shi'ite idea that legitimate authority in the absence of the Hidden Imam – the Prophet Muhammad's twelfth direct descendant, who went into a State of Occultation in the ninth century – can only be vested in the political leader who is most familiar with the Imam's will:

If the sole legitimate successor of the Prophet, if the sole wielder of legitimate authority after him is no longer present on the earthly plane, that means that

---

[11] The justification for *vilāya* was later used by the likes of Mehdi Haeri Yazdi to argue against the Guardianship of the Jurist because it presupposed that citizens needed guardianship as if they were all unfit to care for themselves. Siavoshi, *Montazeri*, p. 209.

[12] Arjomand counts seventeen instances over which *vilāyat* has authority. See S. A. Arjomand, "Ideological Revolution in Shi'ism," in *Authority and Political Culture in Shi'ism* (Albany: State University of New York Press, 1988), pp. 178–209.

[13] Faleh Jabar, *The Shi'ite Movement in Iraq* (London: Saqi Books, 2003), p. 164. Siavoshi (*Montazeri*, p. 196) notes that before the actual conceptualization of the *vilāyat-i faqīh*, the first iteration of the idea that the Islamic jurist should rule emerged at the hands of Mohaqqeq Karaki in the sixteenth century.

[14] Jabar, *The Shi'ite Movement in Iraq*, p. 181.     [15] Ibid.

inherently any worldly power that claims to exercise authority must *ipso facto* be illegitimate unless it can demonstrate in a clear and indisputable fashion that it exercises on behalf of the absent imam.[16]

Accordingly, only the Hidden Imam has the right to rule, and all temporal authority is illegitimate in his absence. A qualified *mujtahid*, a learned Islamic scholar who has the skill to engage in "independent reasoning with respect to legal questions"[17] can, however, exercise the authority "on behalf of the absent imam." Thus, in the age of the Occultation, the just and knowledgeable *faqīh*, according to Khomeini, "has the same authority as the Most Noble Messenger and the Imams ... and it will be the duty of all people to obey him."[18] Khomeini did not suggest that the *faqīh* enjoys the same status and the infallibility of the Prophet and the Imams. Rather, he argued that the *faqīh* serves the same worldly function, especially with regard to implementing the Sacred Law.[19] Arjomand, the foremost scholar on the subject, concludes that Khomeini "extended the arguments of the early *Uṣūlī* jurists, which were designed to establish the *legal* authority of the 'ulamā' on the basis of a number of Traditions from the Prophet and the Imams, to eliminate the duality of religio-legal and temporal authority altogether."[20]

In his early, pre-revolutionary commentaries on the *vilāyat-i faqīh*, Montazeri believed that the *faqīh* should be elected, a belief that eventually gave way to Khomeini's position that it should be a designated role.[21] As head of the body that drafted Iran's Islamic constitution, Montazeri worked with Ayatollah Beheshti to ensure that Khomeini's controversial theory of the *vilāyat-i faqīh*, a concept that did not enjoy the unanimous support of senior clerics[22] in the wider

---

[16] Hamid Algar, *Roots of the Islamic Revolution in Iran* (Oneonta and New York: Islamic Publications International, 2001), p. 15.

[17] Ibid., p. 20.

[18] Ruhollah Khomeini, *Ḥokūmat-i islāmī: vilāyat-i faqīh*. mu'aseseh-ye āmūzeshī-ye pazhoheshī-ye emām khomeinī, 1970, p. 39.

[19] Ibid.　　[20] Arjomand, *Authority and Political Culture in Shi'ism*, p. 194.

[21] Siavoshi, *Montazeri*, p. 199.

[22] Jaber, *The Shi'ite Movement in Iraq*, p. 183. Many of the most senior religious leaders in the Shi'ite world including Ayatollah 'Ali Sistani, who is based in Najaf, Iraq, and is probably the most senior and influential Shi'ite leader, do not accept the legitimacy of the *vilāyat-i faqīh* as an institution in its current form. Sistani's predecessor, Ayatollah Abu al-Qasim al-Kho'i, likewise took issue with the institution as it is implemented in Iran. See also Anoushiravan Ehteshami,

Shi'ite Islamic world, was codified into the constitution.[23] The constitution, especially after the 1989 amendments, endows the Guardian Jurist with vast legislative, executive, and judicial powers. These range from the right to appoint the judiciary chief, who must be a *mujtahid*, and six of the twelve members of the powerful Guardian Council (the other six are appointed by the Supreme Judicial Council, which in 1989 was replaced by a *faqīh*-appointed chief of the judiciary) to endorsing the election of the president or dismissing him from office. He is also empowered to appoint the heads of the country's radio and television networks. Additionally, the office of the *faqīh* is in charge of selecting all the Friday prayer leaders, which ensures that the mosque is not an autonomous institution that can mobilize opposition. Perhaps most important of all, the *faqīh*, not the elected president, is the commander-in-chief of the armed forces, appoints all military commanders, and is the final arbiter of matters related to declaring war and suing for peace.[24]

Despite Montazeri's efforts to create the Islamic framework by which his mentor would rule Iran, he did not always share Khomeini's exact worldview.[25] Although both leaders had spent time as political prisoners, Montazeri had been tortured, and was one of the few leading ayatollahs, including Taleqani,[26] who had spent time in prison

*After Khomeini: The Second Republic* (London and New York: Routledge, 1995), p. 3.

[23] Montazeri, *Khāṭerāt*, pp. 455–458. Montazeri, however, argues in his memoirs that he never envisioned the *faqīh* having such expansive constitutional powers: "Of course, my opinion was that the other clauses of the constitution meant that the jurist had a more supervisory role over legislation and the management of the country in order to ensure that system is Islamic. The limitations on the authority of the jurist were determined in the constitution but they [other members of the Assembly of Experts such as Beheshti] added the word 'absolute' when the constitution was being reviewed" (p. 455).

[24] All such powers are stipulated in one very consequential clause of the constitution, Clause 110. See *Constitution of the Islamic Republic of Iran*, trans. by Hamid Algar (Berkeley: Mizan Press, 1980), pp. 67–68.

[25] Montazeri, until his final years, remained adamant that his intention was always to empower the citizenry to "elect" the *faqīh* and "supervise his work." See Hussein Montazeri, "Payām-i āyatollāh al'oẓmā montaẓerī beh marāje'-i 'eẓām-i taqlīd, 'olāmā' va ḥozeh hayeh 'elmīeh." Personal website, September 13, 2009. Accessed August 15, 2010. http://goo.gl/vbg6jq.

[26] Montazeri notes in his memoirs that Taleqani was famously warm towards other political prisoners, regardless of their beliefs. See Montazeri, *Khāṭerāt*, pp. 381–382.

discussing philosophy, ideology, and armed struggle with other leftist political dissidents.[27] According to one biographer, these discussions equipped him to "acquire a better understanding of their causes."[28]

Montazeri was more sympathetic to the plight of political prisoners in revolutionary Iran, and had a bitter disagreement with Khomeini over their mass execution in 1988, which he vehemently opposed, despite the fact this his son, a veteran of the revolutionary struggle, was killed at the hands of the Mujahedin-i Khalq (MEK), to which most of the executed prisoners belonged.[29]

Historian Ervand Abrahamian opines that the execution of at least 2,800 prisoners[30] was part of Khomeini's strategy to

[l]eave behind disciples baptized in a common bloodbath. The killing would test their mettle, weeding out the halfhearted from the true believers, the weak-willed from the fully committed, and the wishy-washy from the resolute. It would force them to realize that they would stand or fall together.[31]

History attests that Montazeri was not a "true believer," and dissented when thousands of political prisoners were executed without proper

---

[27] Montazeri, *Khāṭerāt*, pp. 381–382.

[28] Baqer Moin, "Grand Ayatollah Hossein Ali Montazeri," *The Guardian*, December 20, 2009. www.theguardian.com/theguardian/2009/dec/20/grand-ayatollah-hossein-ali-montazeri-obituary.

[29] Montazeri even invoked Muhammad's peaceful conquest of Mecca, which the Prophet completed by showing mercy to his long-time enemies, in order to provide the Islamic Republic's leadership with a precedent to stop the massacre. See Montazeri, *Khāṭerāt*, p. 628.

[30] The mass execution could also have been carried out in part to avenge the MEK's Saddam-backed invasion of Iran from Iraqi territory in the final stages of the Iran–Iraq War. Many of the prisoners who were executed had long been imprisoned and had no knowledge or involvement in the MEK's assault, Operation Mersad. Many were not even members of the MEK and were caught in the crossfire of the MEK's invasion and the government's retributive mass execution, estimated by Montazeri at between 2,800 and 3,800 victims. See Montazeri, *Khāṭerāt*, p. 628. Other estimates put the number between 4,000 and 5,000; see "Iran's Intelligence Ministry tries to hide evidence of massacre of thousands of political prisoners in 1988," Center for Human Rights in Iran, August 12, 2016. Accessed May 12, 2018. www.iranhumanrights.org/2016/08/ahmad-montazeri/. At an annual commemoration of the executions held in Berkeley, California, the death toll is estimated at 8,000 political prisoners, more than double Montazeri's estimate. Many participants are former activists or survivors of the revolutionary power struggle now living in exile decades after their struggle helped defeat the monarchy.

[31] Ervand Abrahamian, *A History of Modern Iran* (Cambridge and New York: Cambridge University Press, 2008), p. 182.

trials. He objected in person to the four-man tribunal, describing the
bloodshed as "the greatest crime in the Islamic Republic of Iran."[32] He
also wrote a series of strongly worded letters directly to Khomeini and
the judiciary in which he provocatively asked:

We are upset with the Mujahedin's crimes in the west [of Iran], but we are
bringing their original verdicts and the entire judiciary into question by
exacting vengeance upon the prisoners of old without them having committed any new crimes. Under what criteria is a prisoner who was sentenced to a
lesser punishment now being executed? Now that they have cut off the
prisoners' visits and telephone calls, what will they tell their families tomorrow [after their executions]?[33]

The executions of the late 1980s also claimed the life of Montazeri's
son-in-law's brother, Mehdi Hashemi, for divulging state secrets,[34]
bringing the harsh political reality of post-revolutionary Iran to Montazeri's personal life.

Montazeri's public address on the ten-year anniversary of the revolution was, according to one biographer, a "devastating critique on the
overall performance of the Islamic Republic."[35] Montazeri's criticisms
landed like a bombshell, provoking Khomeini to write a searing

[32] Nearly three decades later, Montazeri's son, Ahmad, posted an audio clip online
that broadcasted his father's contemporaneous opposition to the controversial
mass killings. The Intelligence Ministry promptly had him take down the audio
file, but by then it was too late as it had been downloaded and reposted all over
the internet. "Iran's Intelligence Ministry tries to hide evidence of massacre of
thousands of political prisoners in 1988." The actual audio file can be found
here: Radiozamaneh, "Fāyl-i ṣowtī-ye dīdār-i āyatollāh montaẓerī bā mas'ūlīn-i
eʿdāmhāye tābestān-i 67 [August 15, 1988]." August 10, 2016. Accessed May
12, 2018. https://soundcloud.com/radiozamaneh/yakydru8jded. Ahmad
Montazeri was subsequently arrested for posting the audio clip, sentenced to six
years in prison on the grounds of "endangering national security," and
pardoned shortly after. "Ḥokm-i 6 sāl ḥabs-i aḥmad montaẓerī taʿlīq shod,"
Mehr News Agency, March 4, 2014. Accessed May 13, 2018. goo.gl/LBKbkd.
[33] Montazeri, *Khāṭerāt*, p. 636.
[34] Hashemi was executed for leaking information about Iran buying American
weapons through Israel during the Iran–Iraq War. The leak ultimately led to the
Iran–Contra Affair which almost prompted the impeachment of US president
Ronald Reagan. The Hashemi leak has been attributed to an internal power
struggle in which Hashemi sought to embarrass political rivals such as
Rafsanjani. The objective backfired when Hashemi was executed for leaking
vital state secrets and embarrassing the Islamic Republic, a state that had long
been championing anti-imperialism and anti-Zionism yet was exposed as buying
American weapons through Israel during the war.
[35] Siavoshi, *Montazeri*, p. 135.

response accusing his would-be successor of being "naïve" and believing the "lies of the foreigners."[36] However "broken-hearted" Khomeini claimed to have been as a result of Montazeri's criticism, he threatened him with a dire fate in both the afterlife and in the temporal realm if he did not change his ways:

Since you became a mouthpiece of the hypocrites [Mujahedin[37]] and your speeches have conveyed their wishes to the people via the mass media, you have inflicted heavy blows on Islam and the revolution. This is a great act of treason against the unknown soldiers of the Lord of the Age [the Hidden Imam], may our souls be sacrificed for him, and against the sacrifices made by the illustrious martyrs of Islam and the revolution. If you wish to save yourself from hellfire, you had better confess to all your sins and mistakes and maybe then God will help you... If you continue your deeds, I will definitely be obliged to do something about you. And you know me, I never neglect my obligation.[38]

On March 28, 1989, two months before Khomeini's death, Montazeri was demoted from the position of Khomeini's designated successor to "enemy of the state." Many continued to ask why Montazeri did not keep quiet and bide his time, considering that as Khomeini's successor he could have put an end to this terrible punishment regime. Montazeri's answer was that as a man of religion he had a binding Islamic duty to act then and not later, especially since he felt responsible as a founding member of an Islamic system that was carrying out the executions in the name of his faith: "I was part of this revolution.

---

[36] Khomeini's letter is reprinted in Persian both in Montazeri's memoirs (pp. 673–674) and in the collection of Khomeini's letters and proclamations (pp. 330–331).

[37] "Hypocrites" is a derogatory term that has been part of the state lexicon used to describe the Mujahedin-i Khalq for the past four decades.

[38] Ruhollah Khomeini, "'Adam-i ṣalāḥīat barāye taṣadī-ye rahbarī-ye neẓām-i jomhūrī-ye eslāmī," March 26, 1989. Tehran. Vol. 21, p. 331. http://farsi.rouhollah.ir/library/sahifeh?volume=21&tid=196. Incidentally, pro-government media brazenly re-published Khomeini's letter dismissing Montazeri on the fifth anniversary of his death. See "Beh monāsebat-i sālgard-i fot-i āyatollāh montaẓerī, nāmeh-ye 'azl-i āyatollāh montaẓerī tavasoṭ-i emām khomeinī," Qabas, December 22, 2014. http://tnews.ir/news/E0C434837011 .html#. The historic nature of the letter prompted Princeton University to translate it into English. See Ruhollah Khomeini, "Letter Dismissing Montazeri." Iran Data Portal (Princeton University), March 26, 1989. www.princeton.edu/irandataportal/laws/supreme-leader/khomeini/dismissing-montazeri/.

Thus, I too felt responsible for any innocent person that was executed under the Islamic Republic."[39]

With the ending of Montazeri's official political career his image was removed from all state institutions and political occasions. Before his demotion, his picture was commonly seen beside that of Khomeini, especially in public institutions, preparing the country for the continuity of the revolution and the Islamic Republic in the person of Montazeri.[40] Khomeini also ordered the constitution to be amended to allow junior clerics without the requisite clerical authority but with the necessary political and revolutionary acumen to succeed him and serve as the Guardian Jurist, paving the way for Iran's longest-serving president[41] during the tumultuous 1980s, Hojjat al-Islam ʿAli Khamenei, a low-ranking cleric, to become the next Leader of the Revolution in 1989.

Over the years, Montazeri grew more outspoken about the Islamic republican system, attacking its figurehead, Khamenei, the political role of the clergy, and the authoritarianism of the state. He criticized measures that expanded the powers of the Guardian Council beyond the supervision of elections and ensuring that parliament's legislation was in compliance with Islamic law to vetting candidates for the presidency, which effectively hindered and narrowed the republican aspects of the system.[42] He also opposed state control of radio and television stations, and the government's intolerance of political parties. Montazeri – who was one of the most senior clerics in the Shiʿite Muslim world, a framer of the original Islamic constitution, and a key theoretician of *vilāyat-i faqīh* – also argued that Khamenei did not have the religious authority to rule because the *faqīh* must be a

---

[39] In his memoirs Montazeri goes into considerable detail as to why he wrote such consequential letters. See Montazeri, *Khāṭerāt*, pp. 628–644.

[40] Even soldiers during the Iran–Iraq War prepared for battle by ritually beating their chests to Shiʿite hymns while holding pictures of both Khomeini and Montazeri. See Ipouya, "Shiʿism: From defeat to defiance," online video clip. *YouTube*. January 9, 2009. Accessed June 2, 2015. https://youtu.be/HbHAQwZXPaY.

[41] Iran experienced two short-lived presidencies in the early years of the Islamic Republic. Bani Sadr was chased out of the country, and Muhammad ʿAli Rajai was assassinated while in office on August 20, 1981. Khamenei's presidency became, relatively speaking, the most stable and lasting of the 1980s.

[42] See Montazeri, *Khāṭerāt*, p. 783. The version of the constitution that Montazeri helped formulate did not grant such expansive powers to the Guardian Council. They were added in amendments years later.

Source of Emulation, which according to Montazeri, Khamenei was not.[43] He opined that the clergy should "guide" the people while "allowing them to decide matters that affect them."[44] Such extraordinary criticism garnered the wrath of the state, and he was put under house arrest from 1997 to 2003, a punishment only lifted because of ill health.[45] Montazeri, however, could not be silenced, as his political activism after his incarceration, torture, and internal exile during the Pahlavi era demonstrate. He published tracts in which he returned to his early belief that the *faqīh* must be elected – contradicting Khomeini's position that he must be designated – by arguing that the Guardian Jurist must be infallible and that therefore only the Prophet Muhammad and his twelve direct descendants could be designated as such. Anyone who rules in their name, therefore, is not divinely anointed and must be elected.[46] Experience had taught him that possessing religious knowledge did not necessarily equate to just rule at the hands of clerics, hence his argument for reducing the *faqīh's* power in favor of politically empowering the people to elect the Guardian Jurist. As head of the constituent assembly, he blamed himself for the authoritarian aspects of the first Islamic constitution, and, more importantly, repudiated them.[47]

Montazeri's evolution from co-founder to foremost critic represents the "qualitative shift" that Bayat noted when he described "once ardent supporters" developing into reformists who seek "to marry Islam with individual choice and freedom, with democracy and modernity ... emphasizing rights instead of duties." In Bayat's words, the faithful like Montazeri, as well as secularists, "...felt the deep scars Islamists' disregard for human rights, tolerance, and pluralism had left on the body politic and religious doctrine."[48] They "could no longer

---

[43] Siavoshi, *Montazeri*, p. 173. Also Baqer Moin, "Grand Ayatollah Hossein Ali Montazeri," *The Guardian*, December 20, 2009. www.theguardian.com/theguardian/2009/dec/20/grand-ayatollah-hossein-ali-montazeri-obituary.

[44] Montazeri, *Khāṭerāt*, p. 783.

[45] House arrest commonly puts undue psychological pressure on the sentenced, which, in the case of senior prisoners, often leads to declining health. The state did not want Montazeri to die while under house arrest because then it would have been – or perceived to have been – partially responsible for his death, allowing the opposition to hail Montazeri as a martyr.

[46] Siavoshi, *Montazeri*, p. 203.    [47] Ibid., pp. 218–219.

[48] Bayat, *Revolution without Revolutionaries*, p. 148.

accept Islamists' exploitation of Islam as a tool to procure power and privilege."[49]

Perhaps none of Montazeri's criticisms and stances affirm Bayat's theory more strongly than his views on the Bahá'í faith. Founded in the mid-nineteenth century, and rooted in the millenarian Babi movement, it was a new religion for the new age, or what Bahá'ís call "progressive revelation." Believers posit that God sends a new prophet every one thousand years or so to establish a new Abrahamic religion based on similar tenets, foremost among which is *tawhid* (monotheism), for a new era. The roots of the faith lie in the preceding religion, which in this case is Shi'ite Islam. Muslim clerics in Iran and elsewhere believe that the Prophet Muhammad constitutes the Seal of the Prophets – the final prophet for all mankind – and consider the Bahá'í faith, a religion that supersedes Islam and its predecessors, a heresy. In the eyes of the Iranian Islamist state, belonging to the Bahá'í faith amounts to apostasy, which is a capital offense.[50]

Members of the Bahá'í faith exist in a state of limbo: born in Iran, they speak one or more of the country's various languages, are as familiar with its culture and history as any Iranian, and are not discernible as Bahá'ís through their attire or appearance,[51] yet they suffer from legal restrictions and penalties that uniquely apply to them. The state, for instance, does not recognize Bahá'í marriages.[52] The government accords Iranian Bahá'ís a dubious status below that of full citizens. According to Juan Cole:

Iran's theocracy ... defines members of the nation by their willingness to accept the rule of the supreme jurisprudent and to be subordinate to the apparatus of Islamic law, over which he presides. In a sense, only Shi'ite Muslims are full citizens (only a Shi'ite may be president), with minorities being ranked in the following order: Sunni Muslims, Christians, Jews, and Zoroastrians. Baha'is and secularists have at many points been defined as persons outside the nation altogether because by definition they cannot

---

[49] Ibid.

[50] Human Rights Watch, "World Report 2013: Iran." New York, NY, 2013. www.hrw.org/world-report/2013/country-chapters/iran?page=1.

[51] Bahá'í women, like all other women in Iran, irrespective of faith, are mandated to wear the *hijab*.

[52] Juan R. I. Cole, "The Baha'i minority and nationalism in contemporary Iran," in Maya Shatzmiller (ed.), *Nationalism and Minority Identities in Islamic Societies* (Montreal and London: McGill-Queen's University Press, 2005), p. 142.

sincerely accept the rule of the jurisprudent and because he cannot define a legitimate Islamic niche for them to occupy.[53]

Montazeri believed that even though Bahá'ís may believe in a heretical religion, which clerics pejoratively refer to as a "deviation," they are Iranian citizens deserving equal rights on a par with the "faithful" and must enjoy the same legal protection without prejudice. His position stands in stark contrast to the state narrative, best exemplified by a 2013 *fatwa* issued by Khamenei that called upon the "faithful" – Shi'ite Muslims – "to avoid any sort of interaction with the deviant and misleading cult [the Bahá'í faith]."[54]

On May 24, 2008, Montazeri re-affirmed his belief that the Bahá'í faith, unlike Zoroastrianism, Judaism, Christianity, and Islam, does not have a divinely inspired "heavenly book" and is "not considered one of the religious minorities" recognized by the Islamic constitution, which only affords civil rights and political representation to officially recognized religious minorities. Nevertheless, he stated, "since they [Bahá'ís] are the citizens of this country, they have the right of citizenship and to live in this country. Furthermore, they must benefit from the Islamic compassion, which is stressed in the Qur'an and by the religious authorities."[55] In making this statement, he attempted to alter the basis of Shi'ite jurisprudence, which protected the right of the Shi'ite faithful, in favor of protecting the rights of citizens, irrespective of their faith, thus championing the "individual choice and freedom" of all Iranians as a matter of "rights," "citizenship," and justice.

Montazeri's position illustrates the evolutionary process unfolding in Iran with a new post-Islamist discourse that stresses "rights" over "duties" and "hopes to mix religiosity and rights, faith and freedom (with varied degrees), Islam and democracy; and favors a secular/civil state but a pious society."[56]

---

[53] Ibid., pp. 128–129.
[54] "Tāzehtarīn fatvā-ye rahbarī darbāreh-ye estefādeh az enternet, māhvāreh, mo'āmeleh bā sherkathāye ṣahūnīstī, eżāfeh kārī va...." Tasnim News Agency, July 30, 2013. Accessed May 19, 2015. www.tasnimnews.com/Home/Single/107422.
[55] Hussein 'Ali Montazeri, "Pāsokh beh so'ālāt-i sīāsī." Website for the Office of Grand Ayatollah Montazeri, May 24, 2008. www.amontazeri.com/farsi/pop_printer_friendly.asp?TOPIC_ID=27.
[56] Bayat, *Revolution without Revolutionaries*, p. 149.

Montazeri's continued opposition to the Islamic system in the run-up to the 2009 presidential election and during the post-election turmoil cemented his legacy as an opposition stalwart. He used his standing and eminence in the Shi'ite Muslim world to question the government's religious legitimacy in the eyes of senior clerics outside Iran, especially after the 2009 presidential election, to urge them to vocalize their discontent with the regime. Three months after the election and more than a year after proclaiming his new stance on Iranian Bahá'ís, he wrote a letter addressed to the "Honorable *marja's* and scholars of Qom, Najaf, Holy Mashhad, Tehran, Isfahan, Tabriz, Shiraz and all other corners of the Islamic world," rallying senior Islamic clerics to join the opposition against the Islamic government:

Under these circumstances, the honorable marja's and the Shi'ite clerics have greater responsibilities ... they must see to the added task of defending the dignity of the religion and cleansing from it the illicit acts performed by the government in its name. These illegitimate acts have been done under the banner of religion and Islamic law and are also against the goals of the revolution... The honorable and respected marja's understand the power and influence of their words, and the government needs their approval for the sake of its own legitimacy... The marja's are also aware that the government takes advantage of their silence to its own benefit. Thus, is it advantageous to remain silent on such important issues including dignity and respect for religion, concern for the rights of large groups of people, and the survival of religious beliefs among our youth, especially since the people could consider such silence, God forbid, as amounting to the marja's' approval of the aforementioned acts?[57]

Montazeri's emphatic opposition to the mass executions of the late 1980s prompted Shirin Ebadi, Iran's first Nobel laureate, to refer to Montazeri as "the father of human rights in Iran,"[58] and Green

[57] Hussein Montazeri, "Payām-i āyatollāh al'oẓmā montaẓerī beh marāje'-i 'eẓām-i taqlīd, 'olāmā' va ḥozeh hayeh 'elmīeh," Personal website, September 13, 2009. Accessed August 15, 2010. http://goo.gl/vbg6jq. So important is this letter that Rahesabz, a key opposition website, marked the anniversary of its writing. See M. Maysam, "Nakhostīn sālgard-i nāmeh-ye āyatollāh montaẓerī khaṭāb beh marāje'-i taqlid," Rahesabz, September 13, 2010. Accessed June 3, 2015. www.rahesabz.net/story/23215.
[58] Richard Spencer, "Mourners shout anti-regime slogans as clashes mar Ayatollah Montazeri's funeral," *The Telegraph*, December 21, 2009. www.telegraph.co.uk/news/worldnews/middleeast/iran/6857034/Mourners-shout-anti-regime-slogans-as-clashes-mar-Ayatollah-Montazeris-funeral.html.

activists to exalt him as the "spiritual leader" of their protest move-ment.[59] His political and religious authority made him a thorn in the side of the Islamic Republic, a thorn that was only sharpened by his untimely death.

## 5.3 Mourning Montazeri as Protest

On December 20, 2009, twenty years after the death of Khomeini, Montazeri passed away in his sleep from heart failure aged eighty-seven. While international television coverage of Khomeini's death in 1989 showed millions of the Islamic Republic's supporters chaotic-ally[60] mourning his passing, altogether different emotions came to the fore with the death of Montazeri. Indeed, Montazeri's death could not have been more opportune for an opposition looking for yet another occasion to continue their uprisings, nor, conversely, more ill-timed for a government that was struggling to suppress them.

Although on his death the government recognized Montazeri as a leader of the revolution, official announcements attempted to minimize his role. Some state media omitted his clerical rank and did not acknowledge any of his scholarly or political activities since he was

---

[59] "Yādnāmeh-ye panjomīn sālgard-i dargozasht-i pedar-i mʿanavī-ye jonbesh-i sabz," Rahesabz, October 28, 2014. Accessed June 4, 2015. www.rahesabz.net/story/87270/.

[60] *The New York Times* observed that "So huge and so emotional were the crowds, estimated at three million, that there was doubt whether the authorities would be able to push through them to bury the Shiite Muslim patriarch... As the Ayatollah's body, transferred to an army helicopter when the refrigerated truck carrying it was unable to get through the crowds, first arrived at the burial site at about 11 this morning, a shrieking crowd fell on the coffin ... as the excitement grew, the body of the Ayatollah, wrapped in a white burial shroud, fell out of the flimsy wooden coffin, and in a mad scene people in the crowd reached to touch the shroud. But even as the soldiers pushed the body back into the helicopter, the crowd swarmed over the craft, dragging it back down as it tried to take off." John Kifner, "Amid frenzy, Iranians bury the Ayatollah," *The New York Times*, June 6, 1989, pp. A1, A7. On the twenty-sixth anniversary of the funeral, the BBC reported that several hundred were injured and eight were crushed to death in the flurry of mourners who tried to touch the body of their deceased leader, noting that the funeral grounds hosted several million mourners who constituted a "sea of black." "The death of Ayatollah Khomeini," BBC World Service, June 2, 2015. http://bbc.in/1ANjZYl.

unceremoniously removed as Khomeini's successor in 1989.[61] Fars News, the agency associated with the Revolutionary Guards, described his demotion vaguely as a consequence of him "taking positions against"[62] the Islamic government. Khamenei himself, undoubtedly relieved that Montazeri's scathing criticisms of both the Islamic Republic and his own political and religious authority were over, issued a brief statement begrudgingly recognizing his personal and physical contributions to the revolution as well as his clerical stature, while offering a sanitized summation of his falling out with the state: "Montazeri failed a difficult and dangerous test near the end of Imam Khomeini's life, yet I ask God to show him mercy by accepting his other positive deeds."[63]

Only a month after the presidential election, Montazeri had issued an edict construed by many as an indirect but robust challenge to Khamenei's legitimacy to rule. After concluding that the election was rigged, and witnessing the state's crackdown and the show trials, Montazeri effectively judged that the "unjust" supreme leader was "illegitimate" and, therefore, automatically dismissed from his position.[64]

The notion of the "just ruler" has a long historical tradition in Islam, Shi'ism and Persian kingship. Early Shi'ite jurists considered the first three caliphs after the Prophet Muhammad usurpers, but as early as the eleventh century eminent Shi'ite theologians ruled that the Mongol conqueror, Hulagu, an "infidel" who did not claim the caliphate, was legitimate because he was a just ruler.[65] Despite their

---

[61] Director Alan Eyre, Dubai, to Central Intelligence Agency et al., December 20, 2009, Wikileaks, https://search.wikileaks.org/plusd/cables/09RPODUBAI539_a.html.

[62] Ibid.

[63] 'Ali Khamenei, "Payām-i taslīat-i rahbar-i mo'azam-i enqelāb-i eslāmī dar pay-ye dargozasht-i faqīh-i bozorgvār āyatollāh montazerī," leader.ir, December 20, 2009. www.leader.ir/langs/fa/?p=contentShow&id=6231.

[64] "Āyatollāh montazerī: velāyat-i kesī keh bā shar' va 'aql va mīsāq hāyeh mellī mokhālefat konad jā'erāneh ast," BBC Persian, July 11, 2009. Accessed June 3, 2015. www.bbc.co.uk/persian/iran/2009/07/090710_op_ir88_montazeri_kadivar.shtml. Also see Muhammad Sahimi, "Grand Ayatollah Montazeri's Fatwa," Tehran Bureau, July 12, 2009. Accessed June 3, 2015. www.pbs.org/wgbh/pages/frontline/tehranbureau/2009/07/grand-ayatollah-montazeris-fatwa.html.

[65] S. A. Arjomand, "Introduction: Shi'ism, authority, and political culture," in S. A. Arjomand (ed.), *Authority and Political Culture in Shi'ism* (Albany: State University of New York Press, 1988), p. 4.

obvious connection, a "just ruler," or a ruler who implements "just-ice," have at various times had different meanings. A just ruler has been one who, *inter alia*, fosters order "in harmony with the cosmos," governs in accordance with the Sacred Law, or protects the powerless from the powerful.[66] In a Zoroastrian sense, by contrast, the unjust ruler forfeits his right to rule: "whereas the good king was the symbol of the divine sovereignty (Light) on earth, the wicked king or tyrant was rather that of Ahriman (The Evil Spirit of Darkness)."[67] For Montazeri, justice prioritized safeguarding the rights of the people over the values and ideals of the state.[68] The long history of Persian and Shiʿite traditions of the just ruler lay behind his edict proclaiming Khamenei's authority null and void because his actions rendered his rule unjust.

Khamenei was not his only target. Arguing that the Islamic Republic was "neither a republic nor was it Islamic,"[69] Montazeri, one of the most senior Shiʿite leaders in the world, invalidated not only Khamenei's authority but also that of the entire system of governance in Iran.

Green activists used the occasion of Montazeri's death to honor and defend his legacy, repudiate Khamenei's words, and denounce the state as a whole. Montazeri had been an integral part of the regime's origins, yet his symbolic power was such that his death and burial became integral to the Green Movement's negation of that very state and its ideology.

---

[66] Said Amir Arjomand, *The Shadow of God and the Hidden Imam: Religion, Political Order, and Societal Change in Shiʿite Iran from the Beginning to 1890* (Chicago and London: The University of Chicago Press, 1984), pp. 92–96.

[67] Arjomand quotes Zaehner in *The Shadow of God and the Hidden Imam* (p. 92).

[68] Siavoshi, *Montazeri*, p. 185.

[69] The original article was first published on Montazeri's personal site but is no longer available, probably as a result of government pressure. Western Persian language services, however, ensured that his forceful words remained online. See "Āyatollāh montazerī: masʾūlān cheshm va gūsh va del bar ḥaqāyeq bastehand," Radio Farda, August 27, 2009. www.radiofarda.com/content/o2_montazeri_intellectuals_response/1808375.html. "Āyatollāh montazerī: īn ḥokūmat nah jomhūri ast nah eslāmī," VOA, August 27, 2009. http://ir.voanews.com/content/a-31-2009-08-27-voa8–61545592/567831.html. The full letter can be found on Gooya News. "Pāsokh-i āyatollāh montazerī beh nāmeh-ye 293 nafar az roshanfekrān va nokhbegān: eʿlām konand in ḥokūmat nah jomhūrī ast va nah eslāmī va hīch kas ham ḥaq-i eʿterāż nadarad," Gooya News, August 26, 2009. http://news.gooya.com/politics/archives/2009/08/092747.php.

According to Katherine Verdery,

Dead people come with a curriculum vitae or résumé – several possible
résumés, depending on which aspect of their life is being considered. They
lend themselves to analogy with *other people's* résumés. That is, they encourage identification with their life story, from several possible vantage points.
Their complexity makes it fairly easy to discern different sets of emphasis,
extract different stories, and thus rewrite history.[70]

For the regime, Montazeri's résumé could not have been more problematic as he was one of the Islamic Republic's most important architects, who became its most relentless and authoritative critic. The
opposition mourned him not only as a senior religious scholar who
made significant contributions to Islamic thought and jurisprudence,
but also as a revolutionary who fought both the Shah's regime and the
Islamic Republic, the former imprisoning and torturing him, and the
latter harassing him and placing him under house arrest from 1997 to
2003. His rebellion against the state he co-founded only adds to his
political bona fides in the eyes of a movement that championed him as
one of its own in steadfast opposition to the state he established.

On the night of Montazeri's death, crowds spontaneously came out
onto the streets of Tehran to poignantly celebrate his freedom from the
clutches of the government that had gone to great lengths to silence
him, chanting: "Montazeri the honorable, congratulations on your
freedom" (*montazerī-i bā ghayrat, āzādīet mobārak*). In a prelude of
things to come they declared: "Today is a day of mourning, the green
nation of Iran is mourning" ('*azā 'azāst emrūz, rūz-i 'azāst emrūz,
mellat-i sabz-i īrān ṣāḥib 'azāst emrūz*).[71]

Montazeri's funeral in Qom was attended by tens of thousands
(some accounts put the number at hundreds of thousands[72]) of people.

[70] Katherine Verdery, *The Political Lives of Dead Bodies: Reburial and
Postsocialist Change* (New York: Columbia University Press, 1999), pp. 28–29.
[71] Mehdi Saharkhiz, "Iran 20 December 2009 (29 Azar) Tehran. Mohseni Sq.
protest after death of Ayatollah Montazeri P2," online video clip, YouTube,
December 20, 2009. Accessed August 14, 2010. http://youtu.be/ogadF_IZjTc.
They also chanted, "This is the month of blood, Sayyid Ali will be overthrown"
(*īn māh māh-i khūn ast, sayyid 'alī sarnegūn ast*), variations of which were
common as the holy month of Muharram began and 'Ashura drew near. A more
detailed discussion on the topic and slogan is to follow.
[72] Director Alan Eyre, Dubai, to Central Intelligence Agency et al., December 22,
2009, Wikileaks, https://search.wikileaks.org/plusd/cables/09RPODUBAI543_
a.html. Footage from the event corroborates that there were indeed at least tens

At the shrine of Fatima Maʿsumeh, the sister of the only one of the twelve Imams buried in Iran, Imam Reza,[73] activists held pictures of Montazeri with a black stripe in the corner to symbolize mourning, and a green backdrop to highlight his identification with the post-election protest movement. Drowning out Khamenei's pre-recorded statement of condolence broadcasted on the shrine's loudspeakers, they jumped up and down with hands raised, chanting "Death to the dictator," and echoing in their own words Montazeri's edict: "Khamenei is a murderer, his *vilāyat* [guardianship] is null and void" (*khāmeneī qāteleh, vilāyatash bāṭeleh*).[74] With hands above their heads, they gave voice to Imam Husayn's famous words that became a popular wartime slogan: "We will never accept subjugation" (*heyhāt menna zella*)[75] (Figure 5.1) and condemned the Islamic Republic with slogans from the revolution that brought it to power: "Assistance from God [leads to] imminent victory, death to this deceptive government" (*naṣron min allāh fatḥon qarīb, marg bar īn dowlat-i mardom farīb*).[76] Montazeri's death and funeral took place in the holy month of Muharram, the same month in which the Battle of Karbala occurred in 680 CE. In that fateful year, a massive Umayyad[77] army surrounded the rebellious Imam Husayn, the third Shiʿite Imam and the grandson

of thousands of mourners commemorating Montazeri's death while chanting anti-regime slogans. See Video Blog of the Green Movement, "The funeral of Grand Ayatollah Montazeri – Qum, Iran – Part 1," online video clip, YouTube, December 23, 2009. Accessed August 14, 2010. http://youtu.be/_KwSHb8cwkI.

[73] Director Alan Eyre, Dubai, to Central Intelligence Agency et al., December 22, 2009, Wikileaks, https://search.wikileaks.org/plusd/cables/09RPODUBAI543_a.html.

[74] Mehdi Saharkhiz, "Iran 21 December 2009 (30 Azar) Qom. Funeral of Ayatollah Montazeri p18," online video clip, YouTube, December 21, 2009. Accessed August 14, 2010. http://youtu.be/AUlUZkj8q3Y?list=PLB4DB22F42A4DD1DA.

[75] The Persian pronunciation renders the transliteration as such, but it is an Arabic phrase attributed to Imam Husayn when he rose up in Karbala against the Umayyads. The slogan can also be translated as "We will never bow down" or "How impossible that we be humiliated."

[76] Mehdi Saharkhiz, "Iran 21 December 2009 (30 Azar) Qom. Funeral of Ayatollah Montazeri p19," online video clip, YouTube, December 21, 2009. Accessed August 14, 2010. http://youtu.be/4tWAm4dyrm0?list=PLB4DB22F42A4DD1DA.

[77] After the death of the Prophet, four successors had been chosen through consensus. After the death of ʿAli, the fourth caliph or successor, the Umayyads took control of the caliphate and turned it into a dynasty, ruling between 661–750 CE.

**Figure 5.1** "Martyrdom is the inheritance of the Prophet and His family to their followers"
This three-story-high Tehran mural places a fallen Iranian soldier literally in the hands of the quintessential Shi'ite martyr figure. To the left and right of the Imam Husayn's head at the top reads the Arabic slogan popularized during the Iran–Iraq War: "We will never accept subjugation" (*heyhāt menna zella*).

of the Prophet Muhammad, and his seventy-two companions[78] in the city of Karbala, referred to by one nineteenth-century historian as "The Sepulchre of Hosein."[79] The forces of the Damascus-based caliph, Yazid, offered the Imam two choices: pledge allegiance (*baī'ah*) to his authority or perish. Vowing to never submit to tyranny and unjust rule (*heyhāt menna zella*), Husayn fought and died alongside his companions more than a millennium before the timeless phrase "It is better to

---

[78] Fischer offers a breakdown of the number, noting that thirty of the seventy-two were horsemen and the remaining forty-two were on foot. See Michael Fischer, *Iran: From Religious Dispute to Revolution* (Cambridge, MA: Harvard University Press, 1980), p. 19.

[79] Washington Irving, *Lives of Mahomet and His Successors* (Paris: A. and W. Galignani and Co., 1850), p. 350.

die on one's feet than to live on one's knees" entered the lexicon of resistance.[80] Though defeated, in exposing the illegitimacy and oppression of those who claimed to rule justly in the name of the Prophet, Husayn won a moral victory that has reverberated throughout history.[81]

According to the traditional Shiʿite account, Husayn "refused to acknowledge the sovereignty" of the Umayyads who had usurped the caliphate and turned it into a hierarchal "godless" dynasty.[82] Michael Fischer argues that the Karbala Paradigm of Husayn's death and defiance is "the third part of the origin legend of Muhammad, ʿAli, and Husayn":

...the part that is the most emotionally intense and concentrated, and is the reference point for almost all popular teaching. It is, however, only intelligible as the climax to the story of ʿAli. Its focus is the emotionally potent theme of corrupt and oppressive tyranny repeatedly overcoming (in this world) the steadfast dedication to pure truth; hence its ever-present, latent, political potential to frame or cloth contemporary discontents. The complete origin legend, which might be called the paradigm of the family of the Prophet, focuses rather upon model behavior. Muslims should model themselves on the behavior of Muhammad, ʿAli, Fatima, Husayn, and Zaynab (the Prophet, his cousin and son-in-law, his daughter, his grandson, and his granddaughter).[83]

Husayn exemplified an integral part of that model: "knowing he would die, [he] went to Karbala to witness for the truth, knowing that his death would make him a martyr, an enduring, immortal witness, whose example would be a guide for others."[84] According to Sussan Siavoshi, the traditional interpretation of the Battle of Karbala

---

[80] The quote is attributed to Emiliano Zapata (d. 1919), a leader of the Mexican Revolution. The Zapatista Army of National Liberation, which emerged onto the political landscape of Mexico in the mid-1990s as a resistance force, takes its name from Zapata.

[81] Husayn did not force his family and followers to make the supreme sacrifice for his ideals. On the contrary, when he urged his supporters to flee before the final battle, it is reported that his half-brother, ʿAbbas, responded: "We shall not do that, for how can we live after your death?" See Yitzhak Nakash, *The Shiʿis of Iraq* (Princeton: Princeton University Press, 1994), p. 144.

[82] Mary Heglund, "Two images of Husain: Accommodation and revolution in an Iranian Village," in Nikki R. Keddie and Juan R. I. Cole (eds.), *Religion and Politics in Iran: Shiʿism from Quietism to Revolution* (New Haven and London: Yale University Press, 1983), p. 226.

[83] Fischer, *Iran*, p. 13.    [84] Ibid., p. 25.

highlighted Husayn's foreknowledge of his death, making it a unique historical event that could not be replicated. In 1970, however, Neʿmatollah Salehi Najafabadi produced a modern reinterpretation of Husayn's death. In his controversial *The Eternal Martyr*, Salehi Najafabadi argued that Husayn did not have foreknowledge of his doom, but decided, when all else had failed during the siege of Karbala, that resistance and martyrdom were necessary.[85] This new interpretation poured fuel on the fire of an emerging Islamic revolutionary discourse in which Husayn's legacy called for resistance to injustice and tyranny everywhere and at any time – an inheritance that was drawn upon in 2009.

Green activists invoked the Karbala Paradigm to exalt Montazeri as a fighter for truth and justice like Imam Husayn, and to challenge Khamenei's sovereignty and "corrupt and oppressive tyranny." Equating the Leader of the Revolution with Caliph Yazid, these flag-bearers of Husayn's legacy declared: "This month is the month of blood, Yazid will be toppled" (*īn māh, māh-i khūn ast, yazīd sarnegūn ast*).[86] A variation of the same slogan: "This is the month of blood, Sayyid ʿAli will be overthrown" (*īn māh māh-i khūn ast, sayyid ʿalī sarnegūn ast*)[87] showed that Khamenei, not Ahmadinejad, was their target, and inadvertently rebuked any attempt[88] to categorize the uprising merely as an explosion of reformist energies.

The mourning ceremony concluded with Montazeri's body driven slowly through the streets so the immense crowd could pay its respects. Again invoking Islamic history, the crowd pledged: "We are not from Kufa to stand behind Yazid" (*mā ahl-i kūfeh nīstīm, posht-i yazīd baīstīm*).[89] This powerful slogan referred to the Kufans who had

[85] Siavoshi, *Montazeri*, pp. 69–71.

[86] Mehdi Saharkhiz, "Iran 21 December 2009 (30 Azar) Qom. Funeral of Ayatollah Montazeri p19."

[87] Irandoost09, "27 December 2009 Tehran. Iranians protest against the government of Iran," online video clip, YouTube, December 27, 2009. Accessed June 9, 2018. https://youtu.be/ooEZzuPnloc.

[88] Mousavi, for instance, viewed the uprising strictly through the prism of reform. Mir Hossein Mousavi, "The Green Movement Charter," in Nader Hashemi and Danny Postel (eds.), *The People Reloaded: The Movement and the Struggle for Iran's Future* (New York: Melville House Publishing, 2010), pp. 332–344.

[89] Mehdi Saharkhiz, "Iran 21 December 2009 (30 Azar) Qom. Funeral of Ayatollah Montazeri p15," online video clip, YouTube, December 21, 2009. Accessed August 15, 2010. http://youtu.be/sq-MyQza_Zc?list=PLB4DB22 F42A4DD1DA. "Kufeh" is the Persian rendering of the Iraqi city of Kufa.

invited Imam Husayn to Kufa in 680 CE to receive their pledge of allegiance, but failed to come to his support in his hour of need when he was intercepted *en route* and massacred at Karbala.[90] The slogan echoes a famous moment during the Iranian Revolution when Saddam Hussein, as a favor to the Shah, deported Khomeini from Najaf to Paris where Iranian revolutionaries anticipated his arrival with a banner declaring: "We are not the people of Kufa" (*mā ahl-i kūfeh nīstīm*).[91] In 1978 the movement pledged not to abandon its leader and to continue until the revolutionary overthrow of the monarch, the Yazid of the time. Mourners in 2009 likewise pledged that the movement would not forsake its leaders, and would persevere until the "toppling" of the new Yazid, Khamenei – the Leader of the Revolution and the embodiment of the Islamic Republic. One political analyst inside Iran affirmed the parallel between then and now: "Today we had a very great demonstration in Qom, a small provincial city and the ideological centre of the Islamic regime... The slogans people were chanting were indirectly against the Islamic regime and similar to what was chanted before the revolution against the Shah."[92] Not all the chants were so indirect.

Although there were reports of skirmishes between the crowd and hardline *basij* paramilitaries, security forces were able to take control of the streets only after the mourners had dispersed. In order to prevent further collective action, security forces blocked all the roads around Montazeri's home, and *basij* and IRGC-affiliated personnel took control of the grand mosque in Qom,[93] filling it with hardliners for the traditional prayer ceremony for the departed to prevent activists from

---

[90] The guilt with which these Kufans were afflicted is famous. In subsequent years, many Kufans engaged in a suicidal military campaign against the Umayyads to redeem themselves for abandoning Husayn. See Ostovar, "Guardians of the Islamic Revolution: Ideology, Politics, and the Development of Military Power in Iran (1979–2009)." PhD Thesis, University of Michigan, 2009, p. 24.

[91] Hamid Dabashi, *Shi'ism: A Religion of Protest* (Cambridge, MA: The Belknap Press of Harvard University Press, 2011), pp. 15–16.

[92] Robert Tait, "Funeral of Iranian cleric Montazeri turns into political protest," *The Guardian*, December 21, 2009. www.theguardian.com/world/2009/dec/21/iran-funeral-ayatollah-montazeri-protest.

[93] Robert F. Worth and Nazila Fathi, "Cleric's funeral becomes protest of Iran leaders," *The New York Times*, December 12, 2009. Accessed August 15, 2010. www.nytimes.com/2009/12/22/world/middleeast/22cleric.html?_r=2&hp.

continuing their protests into the night.[94] Regime supporters attacked
the homes of both Ayatollah Sane'i, another high-ranking critic of the
government, and Montazeri, tearing down mourning posters and
smashing windows in retaliation for the fiery anti-regime and anti-
Khamenei slogans voiced during the funeral.[95] The attacks on Montazeri's home and office prompted his son, Ahmad, to cancel the
customary third and seventh day of commemorations.[96] The seventh
day, however, coincided with 'Ashura, creating an explosive day of
passion and spirited defiance. The opportunity to protest provided by
Montazeri's death persisted, therefore, despite the government's best
attempts. As in life, he refused to be silenced.

In Shi'ite Islam, grieving families and friends come together on the
third, seventh, and fortieth days of mourning.[97] Until half a century
ago, these gatherings were often apolitical. As Islamist opposition to
the monarchy grew in the run-up to the Iranian Revolution, elements
within Islamic culture were politicized to create opportunities for
mobilization against the Shah. Charles Kurzman notes that

> the forty-day mourning cycle is a cultural resource that exists in Shi'i Islam
> but does not exist in some other cultures. It is part of the cultural context out
> of which Iranian protest grows. In more strategic terms, it is part of the 'tool
> kit,' 'repertoire,' or 'cultural reservoir' on which Iranian protest can draw.[98]

That it is not to say that Shi'ism is inherently revolutionary. During
Qajar rule, which spanned over a century, Shi'ite clerics often defended
the status quo of the feudal monarchy.[99] There are, however, certain

[94] Director Alan Eyre, Dubai, to Central Intelligence Agency et al., December 22, 2009, Wikileaks, https://search.wikileaks.org/plusd/cables/09RPODUBAI543_a.html.

[95] Fereshteh Ghazi, "Qom dar āstāneh-ye jang-i moqaledān-i āyāt," Rooz Online, December 23, 2009. Accessed June 3, 2015. www.roozonline.com/persian/news/newsitem/archive/2009/december/23/article/-7361f881e6.html. Also see "Rāhpaymāī-ye havādārān-i dowlat dar qom va ḥamleh-ye tāzeh beh daftar āyatollāh yūsef-i ṣāne'ī," Radio Farda, December 23, 2009. Accessed June 3, 2015. www.radiofarda.com/content/o2_hardliners_hit_dissident_ayatollah/1911057.html.

[96] Ghazi, "Qom dar āstāneh-ye jang-i moqaledān-i āyāt."

[97] This ritual is akin to the *shiva* and the *shloshim* mourning periods in Judaism, which last seven and thirty days respectively.

[98] Charles Kurzman, *The Unthinkable Revolution in Iran* (Cambridge, MA: Harvard University Press, 2004), p. 56.

[99] The Tobacco Revolt of 1890–1892 is when many Shi'ite clerics began to challenge the status quo in the modern period, playing a decisive role in the

aspects within Shi'ite history, culture, and discourse that can be organically called upon to inspire political action. During the Constitutional Revolution of 1905–1911, for instance, clerics invoked the seventh-century martyrdom of Husayn to equate the Qajars with Caliph Yazid in order to underscore the tyranny of the court and encourage popular struggle for the cause of constitutionalism.[100] In 1978, the politicization of mourning cycles was instrumental in ensuring that the Iranian Revolution continued to build momentum in the face of severe government repression. These forty-day mourning periods, known in Persian as *chehelom* (or colloquially, *chelleh*), brought more people onto the streets in protest, which ultimately developed into clashes with the Shah's army resulting in the deaths of scores of activists. These martyrs in turn had their fortieth day of mourning which tragically produced more martyrs, whose own fortieth day of mourning would facilitate another day of mass mobilization. Three of these Shi'ite mourning cycles, which the Shah bemoaned as "bereavement tactics,"[101] helped bring the revolution to a crescendo in 1978.

These innovative and strategic revolution-era mourning cycles were appropriated and utilized in 2009 to politicize Montazeri's death and protest the very state that came to power using them. Fatefully, Montazeri's seventh day of mourning fell on *Tasu'a* and *'Ashura*, the two days commemorating Imam Husayn and his half-brother's seventh-century martyrdoms. As with the mourning cycles, *'Ashura* is a part of the Shi'ite Iranian repertoire of action that can be readily activated to mobilize the population.

## 5.4 Revolutionary *'Ashura* in the 1970s

After the revolution's triumph, the state incorporated *'Ashura* and Husayn's legacy as central tenets in Iran's Islamist ideology. It is only in the historical context of the revolution that the potency of the Green

revolt's success. Mansoor Moaddel, however, argues that the merchant class was the main engine of the revolt. Moaddel, "Shi'i political discourse and class mobilization in the Tobacco Protest of 1890–92," in John Foran (ed.), *A Century of Revolution: Social Movements in Iran* (Minneapolis: University of Minnesota Press, 1994), pp. 1–18.

[100] Ervand Abrahamian, "The causes of the constitutional revolution in Iran," *International Journal of Middle East Studies*, 10(3) (August 1979), p. 405.

[101] Mohammad Reza Pahlavi, *Answer to History: By Mohammad Reza Pahlavi The Shah of Iran* (New York: Stein and Day Publishers, 1980), p. 163.

Movement's appropriation of *'Ashura* to renew the uprising can be properly understood. While Shi'ism is not automatically revolutionary, it has a discourse, culture, and history laden with defiant symbolism that can be easily activated for political purposes. No other aspect of Shi'ism is more readily available for activation than *'Ashura*, the annual commemoration of the seventh-century martyrdom of Imam Husayn. Shi'ites believe the Imam to be infallible, just, and the rightful heir (after his father Imam 'Ali and older brother Imam Hassan) to the leadership of the burgeoning Muslim community after the Prophet's passing in 632 CE. In the 1960s and 1970s, Shi'ite leaders across the Muslim world began to use Husayn's martyrdom to inspire their followers to mobilize against the injustice that many of their communities faced in the Middle East, often precisely *because* they were Shi'ites.

The customary mourning of Husayn's martyrdom is usually confined to believers[102] gathering for sermons and eulogies, taking part in rituals of weeping and self-flagellation,[103] and providing food and refreshments in the name of Imam Husayn. There is an important cleansing component to the weeping, as well as a strong machismo aspect to the self-flagellation, as Yitzhak Nakash explained: "A man participating in a procession of flagellation would feel lofty and proud for doing so, knowing that he was being noticed by the crowd."[104] Most importantly, it is believed that such activities place the pious "on good terms with the imams or imamzadehs (the imams' progeny) so as to increase the chances of receiving assistance from them when it is needed."[105] Believers hold that the most critical form of assistance can come on the Day of Resurrection. The closer one is to the Imams, the likelier that they will intercede on one's behalf on the Day of Resurrection.[106] The devout believe Imam 'Ali to be their most effective protector and intercessor.[107] This is the main reason why the Wadi

---

[102] I use the term "believers" reluctantly as even the nominally pious take part in what is often considered a cultural as well as a religious event.

[103] The flagellation ranges from simple chest beating to the striking of foreheads with dulled swords known as the *qamāt* (*qameh* in Persian), which can result in profuse bloodletting. Clerics have prohibited the more severe forms of self-flagellation such as the cutting of the forehead, though it is still practiced in places such as Iraq or rural Lebanon.

[104] Nakash, *The Shi'is of Iraq*, p. 151.

[105] Heglund, "Two Images of Husain," p. 222.

[106] Nakash, *The Shi'is of Iraq*, p. 185.     [107] Ibid., p. 186.

al-Salam cemetery near Imam 'Ali's mausoleum in Najaf, Iraq is one of the largest, if not the largest, cemetery in the world; the closer one is spiritually and physically to Imam 'Ali, the higher the chances of his assistance at such critical junctures.[108]

Millions of Shi'ites across the Muslim world commemorate 'Ashura, with observances varying according to local custom and circumstances. For dispossessed Shi'ite minorities in Lebanon and Iraq, for example, it has been an occasion to express group identity and solidarity throughout much of the modern period. In general, however, marking the tragedy of Karbala, according to Arjomand, "constituted an apolitical theodicy of suffering."[109] In the 1970s, Shi'ite clerical leaders across the Muslim world began imbuing 'Ashura with a modern political meaning: the proper observance of Husayn's martyrdom now warranted steadfast resistance against injustice and oppression. In Fischer's words, "it became practical to stress that the Karbala paradigm is not a passive weeping for Husayn but rather an active fighting for Husayn's ideals, and it is not merely a personal and individual commitment but a social one."[110]

In the religiously diverse Lebanese context,[111] Shi'ite Muslims were the most disenfranchised of all. Iranian-Lebanese cleric Imam Musa al-Sadr launched a movement, *ḥarakat al-muḥrimīn* (Movement of the Downtrodden), to organize Lebanese Shi'ites to have a greater share of political and economic power in a system that deprived them of both. Al-Sadr masterfully reprogrammed and deployed the Shi'ite "cultural reservoir" to inspire his constituents. On the occasion of 'Ashura in 1974, for example, al-Sadr gave Husayn's martyrdom a modern interpretation to foster political consciousness:

A great sacrifice was needed to ... stir feelings. The event of Karbala was that sacrifice. Imam Hussein put his family, his forces, and even his life, in the balance against tyranny and corruption. Then the Islamic world burst forth with this revolution. This revolution did not die in the sands of Karbala; it flowed into the life stream of the Islamic world, and passed from generation

---

[108] Many Afghan Shi'ites believe that Imam 'Ali was ultimately interred in the famous Blue Mosque in the northern Afghan city of Mazar-i Sharif.

[109] Arjomand, *Authority and Political Culture in Shi'ism*, p. 201.

[110] Fischer, p. 213.

[111] Lebanon is one of the most religiously diverse countries in the Middle East, with nearly twenty religious communities registered in a country of about 4.5 million people.

to generation, even to our day. It is a deposit placed in our hands so that we may profit from it, that we draw out of it a new source of reform, a new position, a new movement, a new revolution, to repel the darkness, to stop tyranny and to pulverize evil.[112]

He affirmed that to simply mourn Husayn's martyrdom was to do a disservice to his legacy, proclaiming: "Husayn had many enemies, but those who wish to confine the anniversary of his death simply to mourning and lamentation are the most dangerous for they threaten to erase his legacy and motivation to die fighting tyranny."[113]

These political interpretations laid the foundations amongst many Lebanese Shi'ites to heed Khomeini's call for an Islamic Revolution half a decade later. Although al-Sadr founded the Shi'ite group Amal (meaning "hope" in Arabic), he is considered the father of *all* Lebanese Shi'ites. Sayyid Hassan Nasrallah, the Secretary-General of the Shi'ite militant group Hizbullah[114] (co-founded by militant Lebanese Shi'ites and Iran's Islamic Revolutionary Guards Corps after al-Sadr's disappearance) referred to him as "the imam of the Resistance, the imam of the homeland, the imam of freedom, and the imam of liberation..." and most significantly, as the "founder of the Resistance [Hizbullah] in Lebanon."[115]

Iraqi Shi'ites likewise used the occasion of Husayn's martyrdom to register their protest against a state that marginalized their community both politically and economically. Although they constituted the majority of the population, they were effectively a disadvantaged minority,[116] lacking political power like their counterparts in Lebanon. Iraq's founding monarch, King Faisal, attested to their lack of any real voice in government when he callously said, "taxes and death are for

---

[112] Fouad Ajami, *The Vanished Imam: Musa al Sadr and the Shia of Lebanon* (Ithaca: Cornell University Press, 1986), p. 143.

[113] Ibid., p. 144.

[114] I use the phrase "militant group" because there is no consensus on how to describe Hizbullah. Nasrallah simply calls it "the Resistance" while some call it a party because it is a dominant force in the Lebanese government. Sunni extremists call it the "party of the Devil," and Israel and the United States refer to it as a "terrorist organization."

[115] Hassan Nasrallah, "Prisoner release speech," Now Lebanon, July 18, 2008. Accessed July 30, 2008. www.nowlebanon.com/NewsArticleDetails.aspx?ID=51603&MID=91&PID=3.

[116] Ofra Bengio, "Shi'is and politics in Ba'thi Iraq," *Middle East Studies*, 21(1) (January 1985), p. 2.

the Shi'i and government positions for the Sunnis"[117] – a reality that was intensified with the rise of the Ba'ath Party:

Out of a total of the 53 members of the top command that led the Ba'ath party from November 1963 to 1970, 84.9 percent were Sunni Arabs, 5.7 percent Shi'i Arabs, and 7.5 percent Kurds, whereas the period up to November 1963, the comparable sectarian composition for the population was 38.5; 53.8; and 7.7 percent.[118]

Furthermore, the nominal percentage of Shi'ites in positions of political power fell as the Ba'ath Party tightened its grip on power, with no Shi'ites on its most powerful body, the Revolutionary Command Council, between July 1968 and September 1977.[119]

Thus marginalized, in 1974 Iraqi Shi'ites transformed 'Ashura from a day of mourning to a day of action against the government, leading to several arrests and the execution of five leaders.[120] Upholding 'Ashura's defiant message in 1977, the Islamic Da'wa Party, the main Shi'ite dissident group in Iraq at the time, organized a march of 30,000[121] "mourners" from Najaf to Karbala, the hallowed ground of Husayn's martyrdom. Just as Yazid's forces cut off Husayn *en route* to joining his followers in Kufa in 680 CE, an armored division cut off the marchers *en route* to the holy city in 1977. The "mourners" stormed a police station, shouting: "Saddam clear off! The people of Iraq don't want you," and "The memory of Husayn cannot be obliterated."[122] The demonstration was violently dispersed and several hundred or more people were killed,[123] with even more arrested, prompting two days of rioting that engulfed much of Iraq's southern Shi'ite heartland.

By the late 1970s, when the Baghdad regime banned the annual 'Ashura processions, observing the anniversary of Husayn's

---

[117] Chibli Mallat, "Religious militancy in contemporary Iraq: Muhammad Baqer as-Sadr and the Sunni-Shia paradigm," *Third World Quarterly*, 10(2) (April 1988), p. 723.

[118] Ibid., p. 724.      [119] Ibid., p. 725.      [120] Ibid., p. 724.

[121] T. M. Aziz, "The role of Muhammad Baqir as-Sadr in Shii political activism in Iraq from 1958 to 1980," *International Journal of Middle East Studies*, 25(2) (May 1993), p. 214.

[122] Robert Soeterik, *The Islamic Movement of Iraq (1958–1980)* (Amsterdam: Stichting MERA, 1991), p. 20.

[123] *The Guardian* notes that as many as 2,000 could have been killed. See David Hirst, "Bagdad reaps a religious whirlwind," *The Guardian*, March 1, 1977, p. 2.

martyrdom had become a revolutionary act in Ba'athist Iraq. At the same time, the prohibition attested to the growing potency of a new transnational resistance that had arisen under the flag of Husayn's legacy, even inspiring partisans in Saudi Arabia – the modern-day bastion of anti-Shi'ism.

Shi'ites in Saudi Arabia's eastern oil region have a similar history of political, social, and economic marginalization, with the ruling Saudi royal family discriminating against them as a matter of state policy, and regarding them as heretics even worse than non-Muslims. As the founder of the Saudi state, Ibn Sa'ud, remarked to his British confidant, John Philby: "I should have no objection in taking to wife a Christian or a Jewish woman... The Jews and Christians are both people of the book; but I would not marry a Shi'a ... [who] have been guilty of backsliding and shirk [polytheism]..."[124] Such prejudice was not confined to the state's early years but was echoed in the 1990s by the Grand Mufti of Saudi Arabia, 'Abdul 'Aziz ibn Baz, who issued a "ruling against the Shi'ites, reaffirming that they were infidels..." and "prohibiting Muslims from dealings with them."[125] The ultraconservative clerics in Saudi Arabia are partners in the country's power structure and such an edict is legally binding.[126] One of the consequences of this anti-Shi'ite worldview has been the persecution of Shi'ites and their leaders, such as Ayatollah Nimr Baqir al-Nimr, a leading dissident cleric who has long been at the forefront of Shi'ite protest against discrimination by the Saudi state and religious establishment. In 2012, before being arrested for the last time, he gave a fiery sermon attesting publicly to the harsh reality many Shi'ites have faced in the kingdom over the century:

For the past 100 years, we have been subjected to oppression, injustice, fear, and intimidation. From the moment you are born, you are surrounded by fear, intimidation, persecution, and abuse. We were born into an atmosphere of intimdation. We feared even the walls. Who among us is not familiar with

[124] Yitzak Nakash, *Reaching for Power: The Shi'a in the Modern Arab World* (Princeton and Oxford: Princeton University Press, 2006), p. 44.
[125] Ibid.
[126] Ibid., p. 50. There is a parallel between the status of Shi'ites in Saudi Arabia and Bahá'ís in Iran. Khamenei's 2013 *fatwa* against Bahá'ís quoted earlier sounds too eerily similar to ibn Baz's ruling against Shi'ites. Khamenei called upon the "faithful," – Shi'ite Muslims – "to avoid any sort of interaction with the deviant and misleading cult [the Bahá'í Faith]."

the intimidation and injustice to which we have been subjected in this country? I am 55 years old, more than half a century. From the day I was born and to this day, I've never felt safe or secure in this country. You are always being accused of something. You are always under threat. The head of the State Security Service admitted this to me in prison. He said to me when I was arrested: 'All you Shiites [sic] should be killed.' That is their logic.[127]

Al-Nimr was convicted of dubious charges including taking up arms against the state and serving as a fifth column for a foreign government (meaning Iran, the political center of the Shi'ite world).[128] He was executed on January 2, 2016. The real reason was undoubtedly his activism and inflammatory speeches. Yet, the Saudi authorities have been unable to end Shi'ite protest against the state, or to erase the history of Shi'ism, a history of rebellion rooted in the 1970s as much as in the Battle of Karbala in 680 CE.

Whereas in Iraq, the prohibition against the public commemoration of 'Ashura was designed to prevent the Shi'ite majority from political expression, the ban in Saudi Arabia aimed to preclude the Shi'ite minority from arousing the indignation of the conservative anti-Shi'ite Wahhabi religious establishment.[129] Many therefore went to neighboring Bahrain, one of the few majority Shi'ite countries in the world where the rituals were openly held.[130] Nevertheless, Saudi Shi'ite leaders, like their counterparts across the Muslim world, began utilizing the powerful symbolism of 'Ashura to foster dissent within the kingdom. Flouting the ban on 'Ashura, they held public processions in al-'Awamiya and clashed with security forces as part of an uprising that culminated in the holy month of Muharram in 1979, continuing sporadically until early 1980. Under the banner of Husayn's defiant

---

[127] YaFatimehZahra, "For what sin, Ayatollah Nimr is being sentenced to death? FreeSheikhNimr," online video clip, YouTube, May 12, 2015. Accessed December 4, 2016. https://youtu.be/PEIx-moB_cs.

[128] "Saudi Shia cleric Nimr al-Nimr 'sentenced to death'," BBC News, October 15, 2014. Accessed June 10, 2018. www.bbc.com/news/world-middle-east-29627766.

[129] Toby Matthiesen, *The Other Saudis: Shiism, Dissent and Sectarianism* (Cambridge: Cambridge University Press, 2015), p. 101. Also see Jacob Goldberg, "The Shi'i minority in Saudi Arabia," in Keddie and Cole (eds.), *Religion and Politics in Iran*, p. 239.

[130] Matthiesen, *The Other Saudis*, p. 102.

martyrdom, they raised "pro-Khomeini placards"[131] and demanded "an end to ... discrimination," the release of detained Shiʿite activists, and that the oil from their eastern province remain in the ground since "the revenues are not coming back to those [Shiʿites] who work in the oil fields."[132] Protests in Dhahran province, the nerve center of the peninsula's eastern oil region, ended only after government forces sent in 20,000 troops,[133] killed several protesters, arrested hundreds more, and pledged to improve Shiʿite living conditions.[134]

While Shiʿites in Lebanon, Iraq, and Saudi Arabia rallied under Husayn's flag to defy their marginalization, those in Iran harnessed the discursive power of Imam Husayn not only to resist one of the developing world's most powerful states, but ultimately to bring it down. ʿAli Shariʿati, the foremost ideologue of the revolution, reconceptualized Shiʿism in a manner that resonated with a generation of Iranians that sought change through the prism of their own culture. Shariʿati viewed Shiʿism not as the opium of the masses, but as the key to revolution in Iran. Like Salehi Najafabadi, he believed that Husayn's sacrifice carried meaning and guidance for the modern world. What made Shariati's modern interpretation unique, however, was that he merged Shiʿism with Marxist discourse to foment revolution, and his main ideas went to the very foundations of Islam. Abrahamian summarizes Shariʿati's insurrectionary thought:

> The Prophet's intention was to establish not just a monotheistic religion but a *nezam-e tawhid* (unitary society) that would be bound together by public virtue, by the common struggle for 'justice,' 'equality,' 'human brotherhood' and 'public ownership of the means of production,' and, most significant of all, by the burning desire to create in this world a 'classless society.'[135]

Moreover, the central figures in Shiʿism were at the ideological center of his interpretation: "...the Prophet's rightful heirs, Hussein and the other Shiʿs Imams, had raised the banner of revolt because their

---

[131] John Andrews, "Islamic fact and friction in Saudi Arabia," *The Guardian*, February 4, 1980, p. 7.

[132] James Dorsey, "Saudi minority sect is restive," *The Christian Science Monitor*, February 20, 1980. www.csmonitor.com/1980/0220/022048.html/%28page%29/2.

[133] Goldberg, "The Shiʿi minority in Saudi Arabia," p. 240.

[134] Nakash, *Reaching for Power*, p. 50.

[135] Ervand Abrahamian, "Ali Shariati: Ideologue of the Iranian Revolution," *MERIP Reports*, 102 (January 1982), p. 26.

contemporary rulers, the 'corrupt caliphs' and the 'court elites,' had betrayed the goals of the *umma* and the *nezam-e tawhid.*"[136] Thus, the proper observance of Husayn's martyrdom meant heeding his legacy by resisting the injustices of the day, among which Shariʿati believed "world imperialism, including multinational corporations and cultural imperialism, racism, class exploitation, class oppression, class inequality and *gharbzadegi* (intoxication with the West)"[137] were paramount.

Another example of how revolutionary meaning was derived from a subversive reading of Shiʿism can be found in the works of the Mujahedin-i Khalq. Contemporaries of Shariʿati,[138] they too fostered a militant understanding of Islamic discourse:

...the meaning of *ummat* changed from community of believers to a dynamic society in dialectical motion towards perfection; *tawhid* from monotheism to egalitarianism; *jehad* from crusade to liberation struggle; *shahid* from religious martyr to revolutionary hero; *mojahid* from holy warrior to freedom fighter; *tafsir* from scholastic study of the holy texts to the process of revealing the revolutionary content of the same texts; *ejtehad* from the traditional practice of using reason to deduct specific rules from the religious law, a practice monopolized by the senior clerics, to the radical operation of drawing revolutionary lessons from the same law; *mo'men* from the pious believer to the true fighter for social justice; *kafer* from the unbeliever to the apathetic and the uncaring; *imam* from religious leader to charismatic revolutionary leader; *bot parast* from worshipper of idols to worshipper of private property; and, most noticeable of all, *mostazafin* from the meek to the oppressed masses...[139]

By giving Shiʿism modern-day political application, Shariʿati re-introduced Islam to a generation of Iranians, many of whom had come to believe that religion was irrelevant to a world in which Cold War ideologies predominated.[140] This partly explains why the leaders of

---

[136] Ibid.    [137] Ibid.

[138] There is a commonly held misconception that Shariʿati's thought prompted and informed the Mujahedin's ideology. Abrahamian notes, however, that the Mujahedin's theoretical groundwork was already laid in 1965, long before they discovered Shariʿati. "The guerrilla movement in Iran, 1963–1977," *MERIP Reports*, 86 (March–April 1980), p. 10.

[139] Ervand Abrahamian, *The Iranian Mojahedin* (New Haven and London: Yale University Press, 1989), p. 196.

[140] Ironically, Shariʿati's life's work (and his premature death in 1977) paved the way for the traditional guardians of religion, the clergy, to commandeer the anti-Shah movement that was steeped in Islamic symbolism and revolutionary

the Iranian Revolution were predominantly either men of religion like Khomeini and Taleqani, or believers, such as Mehdi Bazargan and Abolhassan Bani Sadr, Iran's post-revolution interim premier and first president, respectively.

More than any country in the Middle East, Iran in 1978 was the proving ground for the application of Husayn's legacy in the modern context to bring about not just resistance but tectonic shifts. During his exile in Paris, Khomeini had applied this kind of revolutionary discourse to the struggle unfolding in Iran by marking the start of Muharram and the occasion of Husayn's death to sanctify and embolden the uprising a week before 'Ashura:

Our people are the followers of the greatest man in history [Imam Husayn] who with only a few followers launched the great 'Ashura movement and forever buried the Umayyad dynasty in the graveyard of history. God willing ... the dear people [of Iran], the true followers of the Imam [Husayn], will likewise sacrifice their blood and bury the satanic regime of Pahlavi, and raise the flag of Islam throughout this country and elsewhere.[141]

According to Khomeini, the revolting Iranian people, largely unarmed and falling in droves, were like Husayn and his band of rebels, while the Shah and his supporters constituted the modern-day "regime of Yazid."[142] If they believed in Husayn's example of sacrifice to resist Yazid, and their blood was no more precious than that of the "Lord of all Martyrs," then Iranians were similarly duty bound to continue their resistance without compromising.[143] The more the Shah intensified his

interpretations. In other words, he labored to render religion politically relevant, indirectly benefitting the very people whom he believed had subverted Islam's original message of revolution to affirm their status in the hierarchy of power in Iran. See Shari'ati's Tashī'eh 'alavī va tashī'eh ṣafavī ('Alavi Shi'ism vs Safavid Shi'ism, or Red Shi'ism vs Black Shi'ism).

[141] Ruhollah Khomeini, "Koshtār-i mardom-i mosalmān – lozūm-i farār-i sarbāzān az sarbāzkhāneh-hā va edāmeh-ye e'tesābhā," December 11, 1978. Paris. Vol. 5, p. 153. http://farsi.rouhollah.ir/library/sahifeh?volume=5&tid=31.

[142] Ibid., p. 152.

[143] Khomeini specifically concluded: "On seeing that a despotic and cruel tyrant rules the people, the Lord of All Martyrs asserted that the despot must be confronted with whatever number of men available. He resolved to revolt and gave his blood in order to reform society – until Yazid's rule was toppled – and he [Husayn] lived up to his own words. He gave everything, including his blood and that of his children. Is our blood more valuable than that of the Lord of All Martyrs? Why should we fear offering our blood and lives, especially in the

crackdown, the more Iranians exemplified Husayn's legacy through their spirited and revolutionary sacrifice.

Almost two months after the Jaleh Square massacre on Black Friday (September 8, 1978), Muhammad Reza Shah appointed a military government to stem the growing tide of the revolutionary movement. In a show of force, armored vehicles overran the streets of Tehran to deter continued demonstrations around the country.[144] The opposition, however, adjusted to the new security climate and waited for the arrival of Muharram a month later.

Revolutionaries sought to utilize the occasion of the holiest days of Muharram, the ninth and tenth (*Tasu'a* and *'Ashura*), not only to continue the struggle against the Shah, but also to mobilize an immense march that would serve as an unofficial referendum[145] on the monarchy in Iran after nearly a year of the uprising. The street would serve as the ballot and the people would vote with their feet to decide the Shah's fate.

The Khomeini-appointed Revolutionary Council mandated liberal opposition leaders to negotiate with the military government for permission to stage the historic march-turned-referendum. This was granted two days before the arrival of the holiday, and the start of the curfew moved from 9 p.m. to 11 p.m.[146] There was a real fear, however, that the marches were only permitted in order to gather as many of the revolution's supporters as possible in one place and put a violent end to the movement in a massacre analogous to Black Friday two months before but on a much larger and more decisive scale. *The New York Times* captured these anxieties in the run-up to the demonstrations, noting:

path of resisting a cruel monarch who claims to be a Muslim. Yazid was as good a Muslim as the Shah. But, as he treated the Muslims oppressively and cruelly, the Lord of All Martyrs deemed it necessary to resist him even at the cost of his own life." See Ruhollah Khomeini, "Qorbānī dādan dar rāh-i khodā sīreh-ye anbīā ast," October 25, 1978. Paris. Vol. 4., pp. 151–152. http://farsi.rouhollah.ir/library/sahifeh?volume=4&tid=20.

[144] Kurzman, *The Unthinkable Revolution in Iran*, p. 105.
[145] Ruhollah Khomeini, "Rāhpaymāī-ye tāsū'ā va 'āshūrā – referāndom-i ghayr-i rasmī būdan-i ḥokūmat-i shāh," December 14, 1978. Paris, Vol. 5, p. 227. http://farsi.rouhollah.ir/library/sahifeh?volume=5&tid=54.
[146] R. W. Apple, "Iran regime and foes act to avert violence today: Marchers to start at 8 points: Tension mounting in the capital," *The New York Times*, December 10, 1978, p. 3.

There remains the potential for bloodshed... In a show of strength this afternoon, more troops rolled into town and British-built Chieftain tanks and Soviet-built armored personnel carriers took up positions on the airport road. Helicopters buzzed back and forth above downtown routes.[147]

The military regime also informed the opposition that it would station troops nearby in case they "were needed to quell violence,"[148] and demanded that the processions remain "religious and peaceful, not political – a risky proposition considering that the Shah's principal foe is the nation's principal religious leader, Ayatollah Khomeini."[149] Thousands of Iranians left the capital, fearing a military onslaught. The Tehran traffic department recorded that residents had removed 130,000 cars from the capital during the day to avoid their destruction.[150] Rumors spread that thousands of activists were preparing for martyrdom by purchasing their own burial shrouds.[151] In anticipation of a possible bloodbath, the American embassy warned all its citizens in Iran "to stay home during the two-day holiday..."[152] Ayatollah Mahallati in Shiraz likewise cautioned: "Maybe we'll be killed tomorrow. We're facing guns, rifles and tanks. Whoever is afraid shouldn't come."[153] One activist, however, underscored both the enormous cost that might be incurred by attending the march and the potential benefit: "Yes, yes, it may go up in smoke. Liberty does not come at no cost ... and one generation is only a drop in the life of a nation."[154]

Perhaps no quote captured the tension, the real possibility of death, and the militancy of that historic *'Ashura* better than a banner invoking Husayn's defiance that hung in the famed Tehran bazaar: "Every day is *Ashura* and everywhere is Karbala."[155] The banner effectively proclaimed that those who see Husayn's just struggle as an exemplar

---

[147] Ibid.     [148] Ibid.
[149] "Present tense: Teheran braces for still another test of strength," *The New York Times*, December 10, 1978, p. E1.
[150] Apple, "Iran regime and foes act to avert violence today."
[151] Kurzman, *The Unthinkable Revolution in Iran*, p. 120.
[152] Yousef Ibrahim, "While Iranians demonstrate, Americans in Tehran have quiet day: Servants attend protest," *The New York Times*, December 12, 1978, p. A13.
[153] Kurzman, *The Unthinkable Revolution in Iran*, p. 121.
[154] "Million join Iran's peaceful protest," *The Guardian*, December 11, 1979, p. 2.
[155] Youssef Ibrahim, "Teheran is decked with symbols of death," *The New York Times*, December 2, 1978, p. 3. The full version of this memorable slogan is: "Every day is *'Ashura*, every month is Muharram, and everywhere is Karbala."

for action in the face of tyranny must be prepared to make the ultimate sacrifice anywhere and at any time, including Iran in 1978. In other words, the 'Ashura of the Iranian Revolution is especially historic because it marks how Shi'ites transformed what was typically a day of reflection, self-flagellation, and mourning into a day in which the proper observance of Husayn's martyrdom necessitated a revolutionary march. The Karbala Paradigm had developed into a force in which "passive weeping for Husayn" gave way to "active fighting for Husayn's ideals":[156] to live, struggle, and, if necessary, die resisting tyranny. Consequently, the 'Ashura of 1978 – a time of total mobilization – became one for the ages.

On December 10, what may have been the single largest protest event in world history unfolded in Iran to mark the climax of the revolutionary upheaval. According to the opposition, at least seven million people (others estimate as many as seventeen million[157]), or anywhere between a fifth and nearly half the country's population[158] participated in what *The Guardian* called "the Great March."[159] They braved the possibility of bloodshed to vote with their feet in an unofficial referendum on the monarchy, prompting *The New York Times* to note: "...It is widely agreed that the size of the processions, even though they were peaceful, dramatized the lack of support for the monarch..."[160] From eight different starting points the marchers converged on Tehran's Shahyad Square, which symbolized Iran's millennia-old tradition of monarchy,[161] thus negating the legitimacy of the 2,500-year-old institution. The Shah was left with little choice but to prepare to flee the country for a second time. This time the United States and the United Kingdom, however much they had subverted public will with the 1953 coup, would not be able to restore him to his throne.

---

[156] Fischer, p. 213.
[157] Hamid Dabashi, *Iran, the Green Movement and the USA* (London and New York: Zed Books, 2010), p. 207.
[158] Nicholas Gage, "Protesters march for 2D Day in Iran; Violence is limited," *The New York Times*, December 12, 1978, p. A1. Massive protests also occurred in Mashhad, Tabriz, Shiraz, Qom, Abadan, and Sanshan. See "Million join Iran's peaceful protest," *The Guardian*, December 11, 1979, p. 1
[159] "Million join Iran's peaceful protest."
[160] Gage, "Protesters march for 2D Day in Iran; Violence is limited." [161] Ibid.

## 5.5 Shiʿism: A Shared Emotive Universe

Not every revolutionary who took to the streets on ʿAshura to challenge the monarchy believed in Husayn's martyrdom or was pious or
even Muslim. The revolution was triumphant because all the various
classes and factions such as Islamists, liberals, communists, and many
ethnic and religious communities came together in what Mansoor
Moaddel calls "fantastic harmony"[162] for the purpose of the popular
overthrow of the monarchy. Their shared emotive universe included
ʿAshura, night-time chants of "*Allahu akbar*," and even the *hijab*, all
of which in the context of the uprising provided a discourse and
symbolism full of revolutionary meaning. Whether they were Muslim
or Christian, communist or Islamist, Husayn's martyrdom was part of
the social fabric of these revolutionaries' culture – a sacred umbrella
under which they rallied against a relentless and powerful government
that enjoyed the financial, political, and military backing of the leading
superpower of the time, the United States. Communists may not have
believed in Husayn's infallibility, the Imamate, or the existence of God,
but they understood the emotive force of the Imam's sacrifice, especially when it was politicized in order to spearhead the revolution
in 1978.

A Jewish Iranian recalled the days when millions of Tehran's residents, heeding Khomeini's call, shouted the quintessential Islamic
slogan, "*Allahu akbar*" from their rooftops. He and his family "found
themselves up on their rooftop shouting the same words as forcefully
as their Muslim compatriots."[163] "*Allahu akbar*" was especially
powerful in the early days of Islam when the Prophet Muhammad's
message of monotheism (that God is one and the greatest) challenged
the polytheism of his clan and tribe, and the city of his birth, Mecca.[164]
In 1978, many Iranians, irrespective of their faith, found themselves
employing Islamic discourse to express their solidarity with the revolution and negate the ideology of the monarchy.

---

[162] Mansoor Moaddel, *Class, Politics, and Ideology in the Iranian Revolution*
(New York: Columbia University Press, 1993), p. 14.

[163] Hooman Majd, *The Ayatollah Begs to Differ: The Paradox of Modern Iran*
(New York: First Anchor Books (Random House), 2009), pp. 4–5.

[164] "There is no god but God," the other equally important Islamic profession of
faith, complements the phrase "*Allahu akbar*." Together, the two challenged
the pre-Islamic polytheism and status quo of Mecca (and beyond).

In 1973, Khosrow Golsorkhi, a journalist and self-declared Marxist-Leninist, was accused with eleven others of plotting to kidnap the Shah's son. One historian who followed the military trial at the time considered the proceedings a farce:

> Not all the members of the group were in contact with each other, or even knew each other. It seems that the trial of the group was an attempt by the shah's secret police (SAVAK) to exaggerate the danger of the armed opposition and to achieve a perceived success against the guerrilla movement, with accompanying propaganda value.[165]

Under pressure from international human rights groups, the government decided to televise the trial in a semblance of transparency. While many of the other defendants were induced to admit[166] to the charges, plead for their lives, and accept light sentences, five of the defendants – including Golsorkhi – used the platform of the televised trial not only to reject the charges but also to condemn the regime. Employing common Shi'ite symbolism, Golsorkhi condemned the state in a manner relatable to a national audience.

He began his defense with a popular Arabic proverb, "Life is to have a belief and to fight for it."[167] Invoking "Husayn the great martyr of the peoples of the Middle East," he declared that he "first learned about social justice through Islam," which ultimately served as a conduit for him to adopt socialism. He promised to "not beg" for his life and stated that he "hails from a brave and struggling people." He emphasized universal Islamic discourse by noting: "I started my words with Islam" because "true Islam ... is a mandate for the liberation movements in Iran." Invoking Husayn's father, 'Ali, he offered a Marxist critique of Iranian society:

> Marx says that in a class society wealth concentrates on one side and poverty and hunger on the other side ... while those who produce the wealth are the

---

[165] Maziar Behrooz, "A biography of Khosrow Golesorkhi," *The Iranian*, March 20, 2003. http://iranian.com/History/2003/March/Golesorkhi/p.html.

[166] There is little doubt that these defendants were coerced beforehand to "confess" to the allegations.

[167] Various sources attribute the famous phrase to Ahmed Shawqi, the famous Egyptian poet.

deprived class, and Imam ʿAli said, 'No palace is built unless thousands go poor.' Thus, one can cite ʿAli as the world's first Socialist.[168]

Husayn's sacrifice, intertwined by Golsorkhi with his fate, was the overarching message in his defense:

Our lives mirror that of Husayn; he put his life on the line for the deprived ... and our lives are likewise in jeopardy in this court. Husayn was in the minority, and Yazid had palaces, armies, rule and power. Husayn resisted and was martyred. Even though history mentions Yazid but what continues in the dynamics of history is Husayn's path and resistance... The people followed and continue to follow Husayn's path. In a Marxist society, true Islam is compatible. We affirm ʿAli and Husayn's Islam.[169]

Golsorkhi's argument that the lives of all the accused "mirror that of Husayn" situated them alongside Husayn in his struggle against the powerful Yazid. In the context of a military trial in which the head of state also had "palaces, armies, rule, and power," Golsorkhi implied that the Shah was the modern-day Yazid. The Karbala Paradigm thus provided the discourse for even a Marxist-Leninist to condemn the state with a Marxist critique that every spectating Iranian could understand, regardless of their faith, ideology, ethnicity, and educational background.[170]

Five years later, millions of Iranians echoed Golsorkhi's rhetoric and marched on ʿAshura against a monarch whom they identified "with the murderers of Hussein..."[171] While these Iranians harnessed the politicization of ʿAshura to negate the ideological universe of the monarchy, the next generation of activists would do the same, but this time against the very state that had rooted its ideology in Islam and the Imamate.

---

[168] Manjanigh12, "Manjanigh 12 Khorsrow Golesorkhi and Keramat Daneshian's full defense," online video clip, YouTube, February 16, 2013. Accessed August 1, 2014. http://youtu.be/jyvjhUsJyNg?list=PLPyPwMMrlbHNfQ br27Iy6LaUNIgdaAefT.

[169] Ibid.

[170] It is interesting to note that while much has been written about how Khomeini appropriated the discourse of the Left to legitimize his stances, here is a prime example of the two-way street by which Marxists such as Golsorkhi deployed Islamic discourse to similarly legitimate their struggle.

[171] R. W. Apple, "Religious ferment in Iran: A long history: 'A strong mutual attraction'," *The New York Times*, December 12, 1978, p. A12.

## 5.6 The Islamic Republic and Husayn's Martyrdom

Shi'ism's moral authority is based on its posture of resistance, and Husayn's death, according to Hamid Dabashi, solidified defiance and resistance as an integral component of Shi'ism that can be activated at any juncture. Once it achieves power, it ceases to be the defiant Shi'ism of Husayn's martyrdom, assuming instead the mantle of those that slayed Husayn. Shi'ism is "morally triumphant when it is politically defiant, and ... morally fails when it politically succeeds."[172] Simply put, Shi'ism thrives on failure and fails upon success. This partly explains why Shi'ism has a long history of revolt: from Husayn and those who sought to avenge his death to subsequent Shi'ite uprisings like the Nuqtavi, the Hurrifiyya, and the relatively recent Babi revolts, which were rooted in Shi'ite millenarianism. Dabashi affirms that in order for Shi'ism to remain morally potent, it "must always be in a posture of resistance."[173]

Perhaps this perspective offers a partial explanation of the Islamic government's long history of foreign policies that challenged the Israeli occupation and the growing American military presence in the Middle East. The Iranian government's anti-status quo posture is shared between Syria, Hizbullah, and Islamic groups in the Palestinian Territories, constituting what is known as the Resistance Bloc. The leading state in this bloc, however, framed this resistance language long before groups such as Hizbullah came into existence.

During the Iran–Iraq War, for example, world powers, including virtually all the Arab states,[174] supported Iraq's war with Iran. The US navy even intervened on Iraq's behalf in the Tankers War, directly engaging Iran's naval forces in the late 1980s. Far from surrendering, the Iranian government embraced the David and Goliath struggle by naming many of its military operations after Imam Husayn, Karbala, and 'Ashura.[175] Propaganda videos from the war cast the Islamic Republic and the Leader of the Revolution as the flagbearers of

---

[172] Dabashi, *Shi'ism: A Religion of Protest*, p. xvi.     [173] Ibid., p. 313.

[174] Syria and Libya are important exceptions, especially the former as it prevented Iraq from exporting its oil through the pipelines that ran through Syria. In doing so, the Syrian government inhibited to an extent Iraq's ability to finance the war with Iran.

[175] See Efraim Karsh's *The Iran-Iraq War 1980–1988* (Oxford: Oxprey Publishing, 2002).

Husayn's legacy. One such archival video includes footage of Iranian soldiers courageously and selflessly mobilizing for the war effort while an orator hypnotically recites, "Whoever obeys Khomeini's orders is swearing by God to walk the path of Husayn."[176] Iran's Islamic soldiers under the righteous command of Khomeini, it is implied, are carrying on Husayn's struggle against tyranny in the "Holy Defense," the phrase used by Iran to refer to its eight-year military campaign against the "imposed war." Other videos show Iranian soldiers ritually beating their chests to Husayn's name in preparation for combat.[177] Chest-beating, a religious custom typically reserved for the annual commemoration of Husayn's martyrdom, was transformed under the Islamic Republic into a ritual to inspire soldiers to internalize the belief that they were exemplifying Husayn's legacy and continuing the Islamic Revolution by fighting the Yazid of the post-revolution era, Saddam Hussein. During and after the war, the government marshaled support by instituting public commemorations marking the anniversary of Husayn's death,[178] with propaganda murals appearing throughout the country (Figure 5.1).[179] Khomeini often even referred to the Islamic Revolution as the "'Ashura Movement" or "Imam Husayn's Movement."[180]

Soon after the victory of the revolution, and mirroring Shari'ati and al-Sadr's conceptual framework of the timeless applicability of the legacy of Karbala, Khomeini reminded Shi'ites that the struggle against oppression continued even after the Yazid of the day – the Shah – was toppled:

The great phrase 'Every day is 'Ashura, and every land is Karbala,' is often misunderstood. Some incorrectly think it means lamenting every day. What was the role of the land of Karbala on 'Ashura? All lands should serve that role insomuch as the Lord of all Martyrs accompanied by a few men stood

[176] Ipouya, "Shi'ism: From defeat to defiance," online video clip, YouTube, January 9, 2009. Accessed June 2, 2015. https://youtu.be/HbHAQwZXPaY.
[177] Ibid.  [178] Kurzman, *The Unthinkable Revolution in Iran*, p. 55.
[179] Fotini Christia (photographer). July 2006. "Martyrdom Is the Inheritance of the Prophet and His Family to Their Followers," part of *Tehran Propaganda Mural Collection* (Cambridge, MA: H.C. Fung Library, Harvard University). Retrieved from http://id.lib.harvard.edu/images/olvgroup11882/urn-3: FHCL:1268192/catalog.
[180] Ruhollah Khomeini, "Bayān-i 'elal-i mokhāletfat hāyeh doshmanān – pāsokh beh ettehāmāt – falsafeh-ye qīyām-i emām ḥusayn," December 14, 1978. Qom. Vol. 10. p. 315. http://farsi.rouhollah.ir/library/sahifeh?volume=10&tid=84.

against the oppression of Yazid's regime. With only a few, they confronted the emperor of the time, and sacrificed themselves instead of submitting to his oppression. Their refusal was a defeat for the tyrant. The mantra, 'Every day is 'Ashura' means that we must all stand and fight oppression every day, the command is unlimited in terms of time and place. Karbala is right here and we must enliven Karbala's example. The example of the Battle of Karbala is not confined to its actual location or its participants... All lands should perform the role that Karbala served, that is, people must resist oppression whenever and wherever it occurs, and fight it without regard to forces available.[181]

According to Khomeini and his followers, the revolutionary reading of *'Ashura* inspired millions to mobilize for the revolution and brave the Shah's vaunted army in a modern-day triumph of the blood of the martyrs over the sword (Figure 5.2).[182] Yet, many Yazid-like tyrants persist, so Husayn's flag of righteous resistance must be raised to face them down. By voicing such a worldview, Khomeini implicitly cast himself and the government he personified (especially since Shi'ite Islamism is the state ideology) as Husayn's flagbearer. Supporting and fighting alongside Iran under the Islamic Republic is the present-day equivalent of righteous struggle beside Husayn. Conversely, opposing or challenging the Islamic Republic is akin to siding with the oppression of Yazid. Israel, various Middle Eastern governments, the United Kingdom, and above all, the United States are embodiments of modern-day Yazids who oppose the Islamic Republic, and therefore warrant steadfast Husayn-like resistance.

In 2009, the year of the Green Uprising, Iran was encircled by the armed forces of the world's sole remaining superpower, with dozens of American bases in Iraq and Afghanistan as well as in the Persian Gulf[183] region, notably Qatar and Bahrain. For three decades, the Iranian government likened itself to Husayn, portraying Iran, especially to the domestic audience, as the outnumbered righteous defender

---

[181] Ruhollah Khomeini, "Moqāyeseh-ye rezhīm-i pahlavī bā dowlat hāyeh ommavī va 'abbasī – falsafeh-ye 'azādārī-ye emām ḥusayn ('a) – żarūrat-i ḥefz jomhūrī-ye eslāmī bā mohtavā-ye eslāmī," September 26, 1979. Qom, Vol. 10. pp. 122–123. http://farsi.rouhollah.ir/library/sahifeh?volume=10&tid=26.

[182] Pouya Alimagham, "The blood of the martyrs is mightier than the sword." 2018. JPEG file.

[183] Dabashi is right to ridicule the debate between Arabs and Iranians about the historical name of the Persian Gulf. In reality, he argues, it is the "American Gulf."

**Figure 5.2** "The blood of the martyrs is mightier than the sword"
On the first anniversary of the Islamic Revolution, the state issued stamps that
cast the victory of the revolution as the blood of thousands of selfless martyrs
ultimately prevailing over the military might of the Shah's US-backed regime.

of truth in the face of a superior and "arrogant"[184] global enemy, the
United States and its "local agents." Three months after ordering a
crackdown on the nonviolent uprising, Khamenei continued to present
the Islamic Republic as the manifestation of resistance to oppression,
not its perpetuator:

[184] Government officials often refer to the United States as the embodiment of
"global arrogance." See Khamenei's speech marking the anniversary of the US
embassy seizure: Ayatullah Khamenei Speeches English. "[English Sub]
National Day against global arrogance – Ayatullah Ali Khamanei speech
2013," online video clip, YouTube, November 16, 2013. Accessed August 6,
2014. http://youtu.be/8VYEsbv-U2s.

All the governments in the world have enemies and they have friends. This has been true throughout history. Everyone has some friends and some enemies, both domestic and abroad... The Prophet's government and 'Ali's government both had friends and enemies... The Islamic system also has some friends and some enemies. But the issue is who are the enemies and the friends. If the government is such that all those cruel and unjust governments and the Zionists are enemies of it, then this is something to be proud of... All the Shimrs of the world oppose the Islamic Republic, and all the oppressed support it. There are indeed enemies like America, Britain, which has a 200-year history of animosity against Iran, and the Zionists. Let these enemies be the enemies.[185]

This worldview was epitomized by a Tehran mural that appeared before 'Ashura in 2013, portraying US president Barack Obama as Shimr, who is infamous for decapitating Husayn (Figure 5.3).[186]

Domestically, however, the government has much more difficulty in deploying Husayn's symbolism to legitimate itself. The inherent calculus between the ruler and the ruled places the government, despite being a Shi'ite theocracy, in a position of power, which is diametrically opposed to Husayn's legacy of resistance and martyrdom in opposition to power – especially unjust power. In other words, while the Islamic government in Iran is doctrinally rooted in Shi'ism via the *vilāyat-i faqīh*, it is paradoxically and counterintuitively assuming the mantle of those who murdered the Prophet's grandson, the cornerstone of Shi'ism's martyrology. In sum, the Iranian government is in a "posture of resistance" internationally but loses that posture domestically because it is the ultimate arbiter of power. This domestic paradox becomes especially pronounced when it faces homegrown resistance that appeals to that same Husayn-centered Islamic discourse.

The slogans espoused by the Green Movement during Montazeri's funeral invoked the holy month of Muharram, underscoring the doctrinal contradiction inherent in the system of governance that is rooted in Shi'ism. "We are not from Kufa to stand behind Yazid" and "This is the month of blood, Yazid [Khamenei] will be overthrown" are obvious examples, but none is more scathing than the one that highlights

---

[185] "Khoṭbeh-ye namāz jome'h-ye tehrān." Khamenei.ir, September 11, 2009. http://farsi.khamenei.ir/speech-content?id=8033. Also see Director Alan Eyre, Dubai, to Central Intelligence Agency et al., September 14, 2009, Wikileaks, https://search.wikileaks.org/plusd/cables/09RPODUBAI379_a.html.
[186] "Naṣb-i tāblo-ye bozorg-i "bārāk obāmā" dar maydān-i vali'asr-i tehrān (+ 'aks)," 'Asr-i Iran, January 2013. http://goo.gl/Aqwjb5.

**Figure 5.3** President Barack Obama alongside Shimr
The Tehran mural was located on one of the capital's main thoroughfares, Vali
Asr Street. The caption reads "Be with us, be safe," implying that American
policy vis-à-vis the Islamic Republic of Iran was as unjust and treacherous as
Shimr's beheading of the Prophet's grandson. In other words, to look to
President Obama for leadership, security, and mercy was self-defeating and
analogous to siding with Shimr against Husayn.

the paradox of a government that represses in Husayn's name:
"'Husayn, Husayn' is their slogan, Kahrizak is their pride" (*ḥusayn,
ḥusayn,' sho ʿāreshūn, kahrīzak eftekhāreshūn*).[187]

Kahrizak is the detention center that became a lightning rod for
criticism after reports emerged that several activists had died in custody, probably under torture. The abuse became increasingly undeniable for the government when the son of Abdolhussein Rouhalamini, a
prominent conservative advisor to presidential candidate Mohsen
Rezai, died in prison.[188] The reality of prisoner abuse in post-election

[187] Mehdi Saharkhiz, "Iran 21 December 2009 (30 Azar) Qom. Funeral of
Ayatollah Montazeri p55," online video clip, YouTube, December 21, 2009.
Accessed August 14, 2010. http://youtu.be/v3pOiaRU-mM.
[188] Initially, the government stated that Mohsen Rouhalamini died in custody after
contracting meningitis in Kahrizak. That he was the son of a well-connected

Iran caused activists to give voice to a slogan that contrasted the source of the state's legitimacy, which is theoretically rooted in the justice of the twelve Imams, with the injustice delivered by the same state via Kahrizak – a symbol of how far the government has deviated from the self-professed "'Ashura Movement" of resistance to oppression.

While the dynamism of the Green Movement cannot be simply categorized as "Islamic," it rose to challenge the Islamic Republic "in precisely Islamic terms"[189] utilizing the emotive power of Shi'ism to legitimate its defiance and discredit the totality of the state. The uprising in 2009 is consistent with a long history stretching as far back as the Umayyads (r. 661–750) in which avowed Islamic states breed opposition movements in exactly the same Islamic terms.[190] Strategically appropriating and subverting the core Islamic symbols of the state such as 'Ashura, the uprising in 2009 leveled an ideological attack on the state more powerful than any armed assault. The potency of the Green Movement's nonviolent challenge, especially on 'Ashura, is precisely why the government dealt more harshly with protesters arrested on that day than on any other day of action. The state accused captured demonstrators of "waging war on God"[191] and "desecrating"[192] the anniversary of Husayn's seventh-century martyrdom simply because they used Husayn's Islamic legacy of steadfast and exemplary resistance against unjust power to condemn a government that laid claim to his mantle.

regime insider who protested the official narrative prompted an investigation, after which a team of doctors categorically rejected the official reasons for his death. Instead, they noted, Rouhalamini died after sustaining multiple beatings. "'Elat-i marg-i rūḥalamīnī bīmārī va menenzhīt nabūd / joz'īāt-i naẓarīeh-ye pezeshk-i qānūnī," Mehr News Agency, August 31, 2009. Accessed May 23, 2018. goo.gl/dkDrR1. See also Timothy Richardson, Dubai, to Central Intelligence Agency et al., July 27, 2009, Wikileaks, https://search.wikileaks.org/plusd/cables/09RPODUBAI301_a.html. For the results of the commission tasked with investigating prisoner abuse, see Director Alan Eyre, Dubai, to Central Intelligence Agency et al., January 12, 2010, Wikileaks, https://search.wikileaks.org/plusd/cables/10RPODUBAI11_a.html.

[189] Ibid.
[190] Dabashi, *Iran: A People Interrupted* (New York and London: The New Press, 2007), p. 218.
[191] "Ezheī az e'dām-i 3 nafar az dastgīrshodegān-i 'āshūrā khabar dād," Rahesabz, January 1, 2009. www.rahesabz.net/story/6865/.
[192] "Rāhpaymāī-ye mardom sarāsar-i keshvar 'alayh-i bīḥormatī be 'āshūrā," Khabar Online, December 30, 2009. www.khabaronline.ir/detail/33396/.

## 5.7 Revolutionary '*Ashura* in 2009

The protests in the first week after the election prompted international news agencies to refer to the uprising as "the largest and most widespread demonstrations since the 1979 Islamic revolution..."[193] There were relatively few clashes during that first week. Only after Khamenei's Friday sermon (referred to by activists as "The Sermon of Blood") did the state launch a systematic and comprehensive crackdown. The following day, mobile-phone camera footage captured the dramatic death of Neda Agha Soltan, a 27-year-old woman. The footage was subsequently uploaded onto YouTube and spread like wildfire across the world, prompting one journalist to opine that her death was "probably the most widely witnessed death in human history."[194]

The footage capturing Soltan lying on her back, with activists screaming her name and trying helplessly to stop the bleeding, brought international condemnation of the state's brutality. She became the subject of countless documentaries and articles, and a rallying point for people the world over identifying with the uprising. That a woman became an icon of the revolt should come as no surprise since Iranian women were a force in politics long before the election, but especially during the campaign rallies and the tumultuous aftermath. At the same time, her death symbolized the severity of the government crackdown, striking fear into the hearts of Iranians, particularly parents who did not want their sons and especially their daughters to suffer a similar fate, and causing many young people to demobilize of their own accord.[195] Many parents were sympathetic to the cause of their activist children, not only because they agreed with them that the government was unjust, repressive, and had stolen the election, but also because in their youth they themselves had participated in a historic revolutionary uprising that claimed the lives of thousands of their compatriots. One organizer who was expelled from the University of Tehran for her

---

[193] Parisa Hafezi, "Thousands mourn Iranians killed in protests," Reuters, June 19, 2009. http://in.mobile.reuters.com/article/worldNews/idINIndia-40437520090618.

[194] Krista Mahr, "Top 10 Heroes: 2. Neda Agha-Soltan," *Time*, December 8, 2009. http://content.time.com/time/specials/packages/article/0,28804,1945379_1944701_1944705,00.html.

[195] Jason Rezaian, telephone interview, July 26, 2010.

activism aptly captured what these parents saw as the continuity of the process when she summarized what her mother told her: "I don't want you to go but I'm not going to stop you because you're standing up for what you believe in and I'm not going to stop you for doing that because I would've and did the same thing."[196]

Under the weight of government repression, the protests evolved from daily events to ones staged under the cover of political holidays spread out over the next six months; one continuous revolt became several Green uprisings spread out on Iran's religio-political calendar. Scores of people were arrested during this period, and the repression had a deleterious effect on the continuity and vitality of the movement. Misagh Parsa, in his *Social Origins of the Iranian Revolution*, notes:

Repression is a key factor affecting opportunities for action. In general, reduced repression increases the likelihood of insurgency, while an upsurge in repression reduces the likelihood of protest by raising the cost of mobilization and collective action. Under repressive situations, victims of social processes find themselves incapable of overcoming their adversaries, not because they cannot conceive of alternative possibilities, but because they are unable to maintain their resources, networks, and solidarity structures in the face of repression.[197]

Perhaps no quote captures the severity of the government repression better than the words uttered by Ayatollah Ahmad Jannati, a conservative stalwart and head of the powerful Guardian Council: "If you show weakness now, the future will be worse. There is no room for Islamic mercy."[198]

By the time of the *'Ashura* protests in December 2009, which coincided with the end of the seven-day mourning period for the passing of Ayatollah Montazeri,[199] the repression had significantly reduced the number of participants ready to brave the government's threats and come onto the streets. According to one activist, many stayed home

---

[196] G.T., personal interview, October 22, 2013.

[197] Misagh Parsa, *Social Origins of the Iranian Revolution* (New Brunswick and London: Rutgers University Press, 1989), p. 24.

[198] "Aḥmad jannatī: do nafar rā e'dām kardīd, dastetān dard nakonad," Radio Farda, January 29, 2010. www.radiofarda.com/content/F11_Iran_postelection_Janati_Executions_Dissidents/1943483.html.

[199] "Nakhostīn vākonesh-i rahbar īrān beh ḥavādes-i rūz 'āshūrā," BBC News, December 30, 2009. www.bbc.com/persian/iran/2009/12/091230_ap_iran_khamanei_alamolhoda.shtml.

because the state had warned protesters that any demonstration on 'Ashura amounted to "waging war against God,"[200] a crime that could carry the death sentence.[201] Those who did come out, however, were so radical and committed that family objections were not enough to stop them.[202]

While the pro-government forces were able to disrupt Khatami's speaking engagement on *Tas'ua*, the state was unable to cancel 'Ashura commemorations. *Tas'ua* is typically a day of private mourning in which Iranians stay indoors. Khatami, a reformist former president who emphatically supported the uprising, was scheduled to give a Muharram speech at Jamaran Mosque, which famously served as Khomeini's residence in the 1980s. The sanctity of the event and the location did not stop Khatami's opponents from shouting down the speaker, causing the event to be canceled.[203] 'Ashura, however, was a major public event steeped in Shi'ite and Iranian culture that could not be canceled.

On December 27, 2009, the emotive universe of Shi'ite Islam was brought to the fore in a common language that equated the activists with Husayn, and the government with his murderers. The chant "O'Husayn, Mir Hussein," the mantra of Mousavi's candidacy that was transformed into a resistance slogan in the post-election uprising,[204] was especially meaningful during Muharram, the month of Husayn's

[200] S. V., personal interview, April 15, 2014.

[201] *Moḥārebeh* is an Islamic concept rooted in the Quran in which verses call for death for those who wage war on God, his final Prophet, or sow corruption in society. Many Islamic scholars believe that the intention of such verses was to protect civilians and property in times of war. The Iranian government has deployed the charge against anyone who threatens the Islamic Republic.

[202] 'Alireza Doostdar, email interview, August 2, 2010. This very important point is echoed in the leaked US diplomatic cables: "...ongoing regime violence against protesters has decreased GPO [Green Party Opposition] turnout, from the millions of June 15 to a smaller committed core of (at most) hundreds of thousands... Although the number of GPO'ers willing to take to the streets has decreased from the days immediately following the June election, those remaining on the streets seem to have radicalized..." See Director Alan Eyre, Dubai, to Central Intelligence Agency et al., January 12, 2010, Wikileaks, https://search.wikileaks.org/plusd/cables/10RPODUBAI13_a.html.

[203] Director Alan Eyre, Dubai, to Central Intelligence Agency et al., December 28, 2009, Wikileaks, https://search.wikileaks.org/plusd/cables/09RPODUBAI547_a.html.

[204] GREENUNITY4IRAN, "Iran 27 December 2009 Tehran. Hafez Talaghani protest," online video clip, YouTube, December 27, 2009. Accessed August 15, 2010. http://youtu.be/RDfEXvDuaSU.

martyrdom, because it directly equated Mousavi and the movement's struggle against the government with Husayn's battle against tyranny fourteen centuries earlier. Shouting Husayn's name in confrontation not only imbued the protest with a powerful meaning, but emboldened activists with an emotional edge to face the wrath of the security forces awaiting them. Emerging on a day enshrined in the legacy of spirited resistance and martyrdom with a slogan that had turned into a battle cry on *'Ashura*, they were in no mood to absorb the government's attacks.

They set up barricades – the quintessential symbol of urban insurrection – in preparation for the anticipated street skirmishes.[205] In one battle, an angry crowd pinned down a sizable contingent of riot police against shuttered stores and pelted them with stones and bottles. When one of the policemen fired a shot that struck a protester, the crowd descended on him in a rage. With their backs against the wall, the security forces swung their batons as the crowd threw projectiles at close range. Outnumbered and overwhelmed, the riot police took a defensive posture and refrained from using their batons as the crowd torched all their motorcycles. With car alarms wailing, the demonstrator's blood on the ground, and the flame from the motorcycles spreading to nearby stores, they chanted a slogan that captured the militancy of the day: "I will kill the one that killed my brother" (*mīkosham, mīkosham, ānkeh barādaram kosht*)[206] – another slogan appropriated from the revolution – and engaged the policemen in fist fights.[207] One policeman was separated from the group and beaten badly while other

---

[205] GREENUNITY4IRAN, "Iran 27 December 2009 Tehran. Making barricade," online video clip, YouTube, December 27, 2009. Accessed June 9, 2018. https://youtu.be/QlYYoXwUIRY. See also this view of a barricade from a pedestrian bridge, GREENPOWER0, "Sangar sāzī va bastan-i khīābān/'āshūrā-27 December – Must see," online video clip, YouTube, December 27, 2009. Accessed June 9, 2018. https://youtu.be/MdJPDX_sHeU.

[206] One interview subject opined that of all the slogans from the movement, this one resonated with her the most: "In that moment the thing I wanted to do most, and it's interesting because I'm extremely opposed to killing, violence, and even capital punishment, but this particular slogan really resonated with me… At that moment I felt like, not kill them, but I felt like I could do something to them [security forces] because I had seen so much death in front of my eyes and felt that I could use my hands to transmit the pain that they have given me right back to them." G.T., personal interview, October 22, 2013.

[207] Sohrab1901, "Nabard-i tan beh tan va nafas gīr-i mardom bā gārd-i vīzheh - 'āshūrā," online video clip, YouTube, December 27, 2009. Accessed August 15, 2010. http://youtu.be/JZ2urTPUGf0.

demonstrators tried to stave off the crowd to save his life in a scene that was replicated elsewhere when another policeman was captured, beaten, and then rescued from the rest of the crowd.[208]

In another skirmish, an angry crowd chased down a group of riot police on motorcycles, knocking two of them to the ground. Before they could flee, the crowd quickly set their motorcycles alight and pummeled the policemen. In another incident, the crowd attacked a police van, shattering the windshield, kicking and rocking the van as they pulled the driver out of the vehicle to beat him.[209] In yet another clash, men and women throwing stones were put to flight by the riot police, but one man urged the crowd not to flee and they halted. One protester emerged at the front of the crowd waving a green Husayn flag, with another urging them to "come forward" (*bīyān jolo*). Many heeded his call with chants of "Death to the dictator." Emboldened, they rushed towards the riot police, invoking Imam Husayn as they shouted "O'Husayn" while protesters at the back of the large crowd began chanting "Death to Khamenei." Once the chants reached the front of the crowd who were squaring off against the riot police, the chanting became unanimous, as if a wave had moved through the ocean until it reached the shore.[210] 'Ashura was indeed the day in which the oppressed faced their enemy.

Had the riot police not antagonized the protesters and had the motorcyclists not tried to break up the demonstrations, 'Ashura 2009 may not have been as violent. Montazeri's son affirmed that much of the violence on 'Ashura was responsive: "Ordinary people have no interest in setting property on fire. They wanted to demonstrate for their legitimate interests. They were provoked by the state."[211] Unable to prevent the protests, security forces ensured they

[208] GREENPOWER0, "Ātash zadan-i lebās-i nīrū-ye enteẓāmī – Tehran December 27," online video clip, YouTube, December 27, 2009. Accessed August 15, 2010. https://youtu.be/kN1FDnz3P_0.
[209] Ibid.
[210] Irandoost09, "27 December 2009 Tehran. Clashes between protesters and security forces in Iran," online video clip, YouTube, December 27, 2009. Accessed August 15, 2010. http://youtu.be/Y68hw0a6CDA.
[211] "Saeed Montazeri on protests in Iran," *Spiegel Online International*, January 5, 2010. Accessed August 16, 2010. www.spiegel.de/international/world/0,1518,670071,00.html. Also, see Director Alan Eyre, Dubai, to Central Intelligence Agency et al., January 3, 2010, Wikileaks, https://search.wikileaks.org/plusd/cables/10RPODUBAI1_a.html.

would come at a high physical cost to the protesters, often attacking demonstrators without being provoked. Footage from one procession clearly shows thousands of revolutionary mourners marching through the street with their hands up in the peace sign, only to reach a blockade of security personnel who quickly assaulted them with batons and tear gas.[212] Opposition websites reported that the wailing of ambulance sirens could be heard in central Tehran, with flames and columns of billowing smoke changing the skyline.[213]

Not all events, however, were overtaken by violence. In one Tehran street march where no security personnel were present to incite them, several protesters carried Husayn flags as they chanted, "We love Husayn, we are supporters of Mir Hussein" (*mā āsheq-i ḥusaynīm, yāvar-i mīr ḥusseinīm*), and again invoked Kahrizak to chastise the state that rules in the name of Islam yet commits such atrocities: "Rape in prison, was this also in the Quran?" (*tajāvoz tūye zendān, īnam būd tūye qu'rān?*).[214] As they marched near Amirkabir University of Technology, they reminded the government of the legitimacy it had lost after its dramatic murder of Neda Agha Soltan: "Coup government, you're Neda's murderer" (*dowlet-i kūdetaī, to qātel-i nedaī*).[215] Political grievances at times also encompassed economic issues. In another march, a large crowd walking past the Petroleum Ministry called out: "What happened to the oil money? It was spent on the *basij*" (*pūl-i naft chī shodeh, kharj-i basījī shodeh*),[216] implying that oil wealth was being corruptly funneled to regime loyalists to repress the very population that should have benefited from the "black gold."[217]

The slogans that invoked Husayn's martyrdom, however, were the most poignant, concise, and befitting of his annual commemoration.

---

[212] Sherlock72, "Police attack peaceful procession of mourners – Iran 27 December 2009 Ashura," online video clip, YouTube, January 2, 2010. Accessed August 15, 2010. http://youtu.be/xwv6VtHtoSI.

[213] "Sotūn hāyeh dūd va ātash bar farāz-i khīābān hāyeh markazī-ye tehrān," Rahesabz, December 27, 2009. www.rahesabz.net/story/6364/.

[214] Millioniollim, "27–12–2009–Iran–Tehran–650," online video clip, YouTube, December 27, 2009. Accessed August 15, 2010. http://youtu.be/Djo7QRALhqc.

[215] Ibid.

[216] GREENUNITY4IRAN,"Iran 27 December 2009 Tehran Hafez Talaghani Protest."

[217] In his last will and testament, Khomeini, like so many before and after him, referred to oil as the "black gold." "Matn-i kāmel-i vaṣīat nāmeh-ye emām khomeinī (rah)," 'Asr-i Iran, October 6, 2009. Accessed September 27, 2018. goo.gl/3nkNpE.

One group of activists gathering under a bridge chanted: "Today is a day of mourning, the green nation of Iran is mourning" (ʿazā ʿazāst emrūz, rūz-i ʿazāst emrūz, mellat-i sabz-i īrān sāḥib ʿazāst emrūz).[218] In a more hard-hitting slogan, a crowd marching on Revolution Street declared that "This month is the month of blood, the regime will be toppled" (īn māh, māh-i khūneh, rezhīm sarnegūneh),[219] and on Azadi (Freedom) Street, crowds chanted: "This army of Husayn supports Mir Hussein" (īn lashkar ḥusayneh, yāvar-i mīr ḥusseineh).[220] Crowds trampling a banner-sized picture of Khamenei proclaimed "Death to the dictator,"[221] and destroyed a street sign named in honor of the Leader of the Revolution.[222] These acts and slogans intertwined with the symbolism of the day to ensure that there was no doubt about the subject of their wrath: a man of power cast as the symbolic manifestation of Yazid facing "Husayn's army" of unarmed marchers in 2009's ʿAshura.

In another scene, crowds observing the importance of the day coinciding with the seventh day of mourning for Montazeri declared, "Montazeri is alive, long live the Source of Emulation" (montaẓerī zendeh ast, marjaʿ pāyandeh ast), appropriating one of the most famous slogans from the revolution to denounce Ahmadinejad: "Mahmoud the traitor, may you be turned out of the country, you've ruined our land, you've killed the nation's youth, God is greatest, you've put thousands in burial shrouds, God is greatest, death to you, death to you, death to you, DEATH TO YOU!" (maḥmūd-i khā'en, āvāreh gardī, khāk-i vaṭan rā, vīrāneh kardī, koshtī javānān-i vaṭan, allāhu akbar, kardī hezārān tan kafan, allāhu akbar, marg bar to, marg bar to, marg bar to, MARG BAR TO!).[223]

[218] GREENUNITY4IRAN, "Tehran. Hafez Talaghani protest."
[219] GREENUNITY4IRAN, "Iran 27 December 2009 Tehran. Enghelab St.," online video clip, YouTube, December 27, 2009. Accessed August 15, 2010. http://youtu.be/PKJtj61F5FA.
[220] UNITY4IRAN, "Iran 27 December 2009 Tehran. Azadi St. protest," online video clip, YouTube, December 27, 2009. Accessed July 5, 2015. https://youtu.be/dKbDojqsl4c.
[221] GREENUNITY4IRAN, "Tehran. Hafez Talaghani protest."
[222] Esteqlāl, āzādī, jomhūrī īrānī, "27–12–2009–Iran–Tehran–310," online video clip, YouTube, December 27, 2009. Accessed July 5, 2015. https://youtu.be/V7nLezMYAT4.
[223] Millionoillim, "27–12–2009–Iran–Tehran–270," online video clip, YouTube, December 27, 2009. Accessed August 16, 2010. http://youtu.be/XbUTK6oNp7M.

Demonstrations and slogans were not confined to Tehran, with protests reported in Tabriz, Shiraz, Arak, Mashhad, Ardebil, and Montazeri's home town of Najafabad.[224] The protests continued into the night, with night-time chants of "*Allahu akbar*" sounding from the rooftops just as in the first post-election weeks when the thirty-year pro-government political ritual was subverted. The rooftop chants on 'Ashura were markedly louder and more pervasive than on other recent days of action;[225] they were also more provocative given the highly emotive and religious nature of the day. The anonymity of the night-time chants enabled the Green Movement's countless sympathizers to participate in the 'Ashura uprising without fear of the retribution that was fully underway almost immediately after the historic day of action.

The spontaneity of the 'Ashura protests cannot be overstated. Not only did the authorities fail to anticipate it, but the *de facto* leader of the opposition, Mir Hussein Mousavi, was likewise surprised:

For the commemoration of 'Ashura, despite several requests, neither Karroubi, Khatami, myself nor any other friend issued any statement. Yet, people spontaneously came to the scene and showed that the extensive social networks formed spontaneously during and after the election, would not wait for statements and announcements.[226]

'Ashura proved that although Mousavi had used previous holidays on Iran's political calendar to call for protests, they would have happened without his direction. Activists were their own organizers and they did not rely on any one leader to coordinate events.

After the dust settled, state media tallied the torching of nine residential buildings, nine vehicles, seven shops, two banks and three power stations as well as eighteen garbage bins.[227] Eight protesters were killed including Mousavi's 42-year-old nephew, Sayyid 'Ali

---

[224] Director Alan Eyre, Dubai, to Central Intelligence Agency et al., December 28, 2009, Wikileaks, https://search.wikileaks.org/plusd/cables/09RPODUBAI549_a.html.

[225] Ibid.

[226] Mir Hussein Mousavi, "Bayāneh-ye shomāreh-ye 17 mīr ḥussein mūsavī va rāh-i ḥal hāyeh bīrun raft az boḥrān," Kaleme, January 1, 2010. Accessed August 16, 2010. www.kaleme.org/1388/10/11/klm-7047.

[227] "In Iran, extent of unrest damage determined," PressTV, December 28, 2009. Accessed August 16, 2010. www.presstv.ir/detail.aspx?id=114838&sectionid=351020101.

Mousavi. Some even believed that the state intentionally killed him to increase pressure on the candidate-turned-dissident.[228] The government, however, was unapologetic. On the contrary, the state considered the events of 'Ashura a desecration on a par with the greatest of sins. The conservative Guardian Council released a statement condemning the turmoil, arguing that it "showed that the rioters are against the religious beliefs of the nation."[229] The IRGC-affiliated Fars News quoted a senior official who accused protesters of being "seditionists,"[230] while another affirmed that "our revolution has its roots in 'Ashura and Imam Husayn…" and 'Ashura's "desecration" was the outcome of a foreign plot, the masterminds of which were the United States, United Kingdom, Zionists, and Bahá'ís.[231] The authorities threatened a "crushing response" for "those who show no respect to religious sanctities," while other conservative bodies accused those who "resorted to insults on 'Ashura" as "not [being] Muslim or Shia because they would respect 'Ashura rituals even if they had objections."[232] The state arrested scores of political opposition leaders – to say nothing of the activists – in what amounted to the largest wave of arrests since the uprising's early days.[233]

The government's fierce reaction was a result of two factors: the state was increasingly frustrated that the movement endured despite

---

[228] Director Alan Eyre, Dubai, to Central Intelligence Agency et al., December 28, 2009, Wikileaks, https://search.wikileaks.org/plusd/cables/09RPODUBAI549_a.html.

[229] "Widespread condemnation of 'Ashura protests," *Tehran Times*, December 29, 2009. Accessed August 16, 2010. www.tehrantimes.com/Index_view.asp?code=210803.

[230] "Shekastan-i ḥormat-i 'ashūrā chehreh-ye aṣlī-ye jāhelān va fetnehgarān rā āshkār kard," Fars News Agency, December 29, 2009. Accessed November 5, 2018. https://goo.gl/nivGxK. Also see Director Alan Eyre, Dubai, to Central Intelligence Agency et al., December 28, 2009, Wikileaks, https://search.wikileaks.org/plusd/cables/09RPODUBAI549_a.html.

[231] "Ahamīat-i rāhpaymāī-ye emrūz labbayk be rahbarī ast," Fars News Agency, December 30, 2009. www.farsnews.com/newstext.php?nn=8810081569.

[232] "Widespread condemnation of Ashura protests."

[233] Farahmand Alipour, "Sedāye pāye kūdetā dar tehrān; mowj-i jadīd va gostardeh-ye dastgīrī-ye fa'ālān-i sīāsī āghāz shod," Rahesabz, December 28, 2009. www.rahesabz.net/story/6517/. The BBC noted that Iran's police chief, Ismail Ahmadi Moghaddam, claimed that over 500 people were arrested in the three days after 'Ashura. See "Supporters of Iran's government stage big rallies," BBC News, December 30, 2009. http://news.bbc.co.uk/2/hi/middle_east/8435007.stm.

the government's best efforts to suppress it; and the Islamic Republic, which rode to power atop the massive *Ashura* protests of 1978, was now being equated with Yazid on the most meaningful of days. In the words of one prominent reformist, "'Ashura is never a good day to be seen as an oppressor."[234]

## 5.8 Conclusion

The history of *Ashura's* politicization during the 1970s, and especially during the Iranian Revolution, is especially instructive. Shi'ite Muslims in Lebanon, Iraq, Saudi Arabia, and pre-revolutionary Iran harnessed the defiant message inherent in *Ashura* by invoking Husayn's legacy of resistance and martyrdom to confront the homegrown tyranny of the day; therefore, the demonstrations in 2009 were in keeping with *Ashura's* recent history of political mobilization. The authorities could not forgive the demonstrators' appropriation of *Ashura* to condemn the Islamic Republic, and alleged blasphemy. Green activists, however, were abiding by *Ashura's* political message of resistance in the face of unjust power, equating the Islamic Republic with the Ba'ath Party in Iraq, the virulently anti-Shi'ite Saudi regime, the Lebanese government in its marginalization of its Shi'ite community, the Israeli state in its occupation of Quds and the Palestinians,[235] the US-backed monarchy in pre-revolutionary Iran, and, most importantly, Caliph Yazid and

---

[234] Ibid.

[235] Mottahari's famous speech forcefully argued: "What would the Prophet of Islam do if he was still alive today? What issue would occupy the Prophet's thoughts? By God we are responsible regarding this crisis. By God we have responsibility. By God we are being ignorant. By God this very issue would break the heart of the Prophet today. The problem that would fill Husayn ibn 'Ali's heart with sorrow today is this issue. If Husayn ibn 'Ali was here today, he would say 'if you want to mourn for me today, if you want to lament over me, your slogan today must be "Palestine."' The Shimr of 1300 years ago is dead and gone. Get to know the Shimr of today. Today the walls of this city should tremble to the slogan of Palestine. And what efforts have we Muslims exerted for Palestine? By God it's a shame for us to call ourselves Muslims. It's a shame to call ourselves Shi'ites of 'Ali ibn Abi Talib. The enemy has ravaged our fellow Muslim's land, murdered and imprisoned their men, violated their women and took their jewelry from their ears and hands... Are they not Muslims?" The full text of his speech is posted online and the actual audio clip can be found on YouTube, see Ruh, "Shahīd morteżā moṭaharī va felesṭīn," Doshmantarin, November 15, 2010. Accessed September 24, 2013. http://doshmantarin.blogsky.com/1389/08/24/post-10/, and 'Alireza Bahmanpour,

Shimr. This was an insult of the highest order for a government that came to power through the historic and revolutionary 'Ashura of 1978 and which professed to rule in accordance with the justness of the Imamate and Husayn's righteous example.

On December 27, 2009, the 'Ashura protests created an entirely new discourse in Iran, asserting that although the Iranian government, specifically the institution of the *vilāyat-i faqīh*, derives its legitimacy from Shi'ism and the twelve Imams, it does not have a monopoly on their uses and meanings. Iran and Shi'ite Islam's emotive universe is a shared discourse, and the activists effectively appropriated the state's language and its revolutionary credentials, both of which have roots in that same emotive universe, to castigate that very state on its own terms. This is most apparent in an online discussion about the meaning of 'Ashura in the modern context. Detailing the contemporary relevance of 'Ashura, one user rather affectingly opined: "Oppression, oppressor, Zeinab's patience, the children's thirst, freedom, chivalry, courage, morning prayers, and ... O'Husayn, Mir Hussein."[236] This social media user placed Mir Hussein Mousavi's struggle against the Iranian government in the same breath as Husayn's rebellion, with vivid references to iconic moments of the Battle of Karbala in which Yazid's forces surrounded Husayn and his followers in the arid desert and prevented them from accessing the wells – an inexcusable breach of long established customs. The parched lips of the children symbolized Yazid's "oppression." 'Abbas's willingness to fight and die a brutal death while attempting to obtain water for his dying family, along with Imam Husayn's sacrifice in his resolute refusal to accept the sovereignty of the "oppressor," exemplified their "chivalry" and steadfast "courage." Zeinab's endurance in surviving the battle and traversing Islamic lands to share the story of her brother's martyrdom ensured that Husayn's legacy did not perish with him in the land of Karbala, but transcended time and place, so much so that activists in Iran invoked Husayn in their uprising against "oppression" both in 1978 and again in 2009.

Unlike their 1978 predecessors, Green activists did not use 'Ashura to negate the ideological universe of the state in the way revolutionaries

"Ayatullah's historical speech about Palestine," online video clip, YouTube, June 18, 2010. Accessed September 24, 2013. http://youtu.be/-SxOUMLfX7c.
[236] Mohammad I., November 15, 2013, 10:12 a.m., Google+ comment.

did three decades before. Rather, they used the state's own discourse to legitimate their struggle and condemn the government that ruled in the name of Islam and Husayn's legacy. This was a reminder to the Islamic Republic that Husayn, the quintessential Muslim rebel, never held power but died fighting it to become Shiʿite Islam's martyr *par excellence*.[237]

The death of Montazeri on the twentieth along with Student Day on the seventh and ʿAshura ensured that December was the most explosive month of protest after June when the election results marked the launch of the uprising. Even in death, Montazeri challenged the legitimacy of the Islamic government when his funeral became an occasion for continued protests. More to the point, his transition from regime architect to foremost dissident exemplifies a trend in Iran that constitutes an even bigger threat to the state. In what Asef Bayat calls the "post-Islamist turn," many leaders and supporters of the Islamic Republic have shed their once ardently held ideological beliefs in favor of a system that focuses on civil rights rather than doctrinal rigidity and obligations. Montazeri's death coalesced with the Green Uprising and its potent use of Islamic symbolism to illustrate that although Islam can be exploited to serve power, it can also be harnessed, through Husayn's transnational and undying legacy, to produce a powerful discourse of popular resistance. In doing so, Montazeri and the Green Movement rescued Islam from the banditry of the republic that rules in its name.

---

[237] This phrase is borrowed from Fischer, who wrote: "The theme of martyrdom was of course central to the revolution. Husayn is the martyr par excellence." Fischer, p. 214.

# 6 | Conclusion
## History as Prologue

## 6.1 Introduction

Iran has a long history of resistance against both the autocratic state and imperialism, and in the intersection of the two the latter has often enabled and sustained the former. Mossadeq's oil nationalization campaign (1951–1953) epitomizes the mobilization against imperialism, while the Tobacco Revolt (1890–1892), the Constitutional Revolution (1905–1911), and the Iranian Revolution (1978–1979) exemplify popular revolts against a combination of colonial control and its local agents – monarchs beholden to imperial powers – that facilitated both foreign and domestic political subjugation and economic exploitation. The Green Uprisings, however, centered exclusively on defying the repressive indigenous state. The movement's multi-faceted energy was entirely focused on a devastating attack on the state's ideology that undermined the legitimacy not only of Mahmoud Ahmadinejad, but also of the entire political system governing Iran.

This work has argued against the narrow win–lose binary by demonstrating that although the Green Movement failed to cancel Ahmadinejad's election "victory" or to overthrow the state, both of which at certain junctures were expressly the aims of activists in the movement, it nonetheless succeeded in that "failure." Indeed, the Green Uprisings found success in challenging the Islamic Republic in a manner unprecedented in its thirty-year history. The government's power lies in its highly organized and efficient security apparatus as well as its potent ideological foundations, which are rooted in a combination of Islam and the Iranian Revolution. While the Green Movement did not contest the government in military terms, it did challenge it on an ideological and discursive level, bringing to the fore a large segment of Iranian society's post-Islamist turn. Green activists appropriated and subverted the state's entire ideological symbolism and used it against that very state on its own terms. Even the Islamic Revolutionary

**Figure 6.1** Banners of resistance
Emblems of the (from left) Badr Brigade, Hizbullah, and the IRGC. The far right is a Green Movement appropriation of the IRGC banner.

Guards Corps (IRGC), the regime's most loyal, ideological, and powerful line of military defense, did not evade the movement's non-violent ideological assault.

Among the Green Movement's many attacks on the state's Islamist ideology, students sang revolutionary songs on Student Day (December 7) to an image of the Iranian flag that was purposefully devoid of the Islamic Republic's emblem (see Chapter 3). Just as Iran's flag was contested, so was the banner of its main ideological military force, the IRGC. On October 14, 2009, Mousavi's Facebook page, an organizing tool for those who could access the social media website, published a forceful image in which the IRGC's iconic logo had been subverted with a new message (Figure 6.1).[1]

The focal point of the original IRGC emblem (second from the right) is a rebellious fist clutching a rifle, above which is a Quranic verse in Arabic that reads: "Prepare against them whatever arms and cavalry you can muster..." – a sacred call to arms in the path of righteousness.[2] The fist is emerging from the Arabic word for "no," *lā*, which underscores both the revolution's defiance and Islam's central belief:

[1] Mir Hossein Mousavi Facebook Page, "Qalam," October 14, 2009, 12:30 p.m. Facebook post. www.facebook.com/mousavi/photos/a.82250529453.75658 .45061919453/154196369453/?type=1&theater. Only the subverted banner of the IRGC was posted on Mousavi's Facebook page. I took the liberty of situating it alongside the other banners in order to highlight the similarities and differences.

[2] Afshon Ostovar, "Guardians of the Islamic Revolution: Ideology, Politics, and the Development of Military Power in Iran (1979–2009)." PhD Thesis, University of Michigan, 2009, p. 112.

there is no god but God (*lā ilaha illa allāh*). Underneath the rifle is a representation of the Quran from which an olive branch extends, signifying both the longing for peace and "...the paradise promised to those who are conscious of God."[3] The globe, likewise a feature of various Iranian guerrilla groups' banners, symbolizes the fact that neither the IRGC nor the Islamic Revolution is confined to Iran's borders – as Khomeini put it: "Just as the Prophet was from Arabia but his Islamic message was not only for his land, Iran's Islamic Revolution belongs to all lands."[4] Rather, the revolution and the IRGC's outlook transcend what Khomeini in 1970 castigated as the colonial borders that "separated various segments of the Islamic nation from each other and artificially created separate nations ... about ten to fifteen petty states."[5] The year of the military force's establishment, 1979, is noted at the bottom, and its full name is inscribed in Persian on the right. The IRGC's role in the founding of Lebanon's Hizbullah and the Islamic Supreme Council of Iraq[6] and its armed wing, the Badr Brigade, is evident in the configurations of their respective banners (the left two), which are modeled on the IRGC logo.

The Green Movement's appropriation of the IRGC banner (far right) includes an equally defiant hand clenching a pen instead of a rifle and is the only banner of the four devoid of a weapon, highlighting both the movement's peaceful nature and its discursive assault on the state's ideology. In other words, if the state championed the notion that the blood of the revolution's martyrs is mightier than the sword (Figure 5.2), then the Green Uprising's robust ideological challenge enlivened the old adage: "the pen is mightier than the sword." This preference for righteous words over a sacred call to arms is affirmed by the Quranic verse enshrined above the pen: "By the pen, and what they inscribe."[7] The verse begins with *nūn*, a unique letter in Quranic

---

[3] Quran 13: 35. This point was also partly derived from Ostovar, "Guardians of the Islamic Revolution," p. 112.

[4] Ruhollah Khomeini. "Sokhrānī dar jam'-i dāneshjūyan-i 'arabestanī-ye moqīm-i īrān." November 2, 1979. Qom. Vol. 10, pp. 446–9. https://farsi.rouhollah.ir/library/sahifeh-imam-khomeini/vol/10/title/115.

[5] Ruhollah Khomeini, *Ḥokūmat-i islāmī: vilāyat-i faqīh*. mu'aseseh-ye āmūzeshī-ye pazhoheshī-ye emām khomeinī, 1970, p. 30.

[6] The Islamic Supreme Council of Iraq was originally known as the Supreme Council for the Islamic Revolution in Iraq until it changed its name in 2007 to reflect Iraq's new post-Ba'ath reality.

[7] This is the opening verse to chapter 68 (The Pen) of the Quran.

exegesis,[8] placed above the unofficial name of the digital force rebelling against the state on the internet – The Online Resistance Unit of the Mobilized Green Pen Corps. The use of "the Mobilized" constitutes an appropriation *within* the appropriation: the name of the government's hardline paramilitary force, The Mobilization Resistance Force ("the Mobilized" for short[9]), is subverted at the same time that the IRGC is being undermined. The year of the movement's historic uprising, 2009, is noted at the bottom, and green, the color of the movement, predominates. The verse, the letter *nūn* above the name, and the fact that the same *lā* from *lā ilaha illa allāh* and the Quran remain in this new oppositional banner together refute claims that the movement is anti-religion or "waging war on God,"[10] demonstrating that resistance to an unjust government that rules in the name of Islam is not un-Islamic. The entire logo is superimposed on a globe, underscoring the movement's transnational and diverse support base, including the international Iranian community, its worldwide audience via increased global connectivity, and its humanism that transcends religion, race, and nationality – as artist Golrokh Nafisi put it, it is connected to and supports "all oppressed peoples of the world."[11]

The co-option of the IRGC's banner highlights the common theme outlined throughout this book: how the uprising ingeniously used the government's own discourse and symbolism against itself. After the climactic month of December, the Green Movement looked ahead to the state's most prized political holiday, the anniversary of the Iranian Revolution's victory. This time, however, the goal was not only to subvert the day as before but to deliver a final ideological blow to the state. This concluding chapter will show that although the government defeated the uprising's street presence on February 11, 2010, the Green

---

[8] There has been much speculation throughout the centuries as to why this chapter begins with a sole, unconnected letter, though it is not the only chapter in the Quran to begin with letters with unknown or uncertain meanings. In terms of the subverted IRGC banner, the fact that the meaning is unknown can allude to the hidden identity of the image's creator, or the anonymous, countless millions that support the Green Movement.

[9] The full name in English is The Organization for Mobilization of the Oppressed. Its full name in Persian is *sāzemān-i mostaż'afīn-i basīj*, or in short, the *basīj*.

[10] "Ezheī az e'dām-i 3 nafar az dastgīrshodegān-i 'āshūrā khabar dād," Rahesabz, January 1, 2009. www.rahesabz.net/story/6865/.

[11] Golrokh Nafisi, "Re: Palestine-Green Movement artwork," message to Pouya Alimagham, May 5, 2013. Facebook message.

Movement endured despite the state preventing it from co-opting yet
another state-sanctioned political holiday. The chapter asks and pro-
poses an answer to the overarching question: What does it mean for
the Green Uprising to be "over"?

## 6.2 Repression and the Crowd's Failure to Appropriate Revolution Day

The *ʿAshura* protests on December 27 represented a hardening of both
the movement and the state's resolve to crush it. Eight died on
Husayn's commemoration, amounting to one of the bloodiest days in
the course of the uprising. In the aftermath the state intensified its
crackdown to discourage continued protests, especially in view of the
upcoming Revolution Day holiday (22 Bahman), an annual political
event in which supporters march in step with the government.

To dissuade activists from likewise hijacking 22 Bahman (February
11), the regime began trying detained protesters. Those arrested on
*ʿAshura* were dealt with especially harshly; nearly a dozen were sentenced to death for "waging war on God."[12] The state also started
executing prisoners, including Arash Rahmanipour and Muhammad
Reza Alizamani, both of whom were convicted of political crimes that
probably took place before the uprising. Many believed, however, that
their executions were hastened to terrorize a mobilized population.[13]
Televised forced confessions – a mainstay of modern Iran both before
and after the revolution which had reached unprecedented levels in the
early post-revolutionary period – were revived to humiliate victimized
activists and sow fear among the fence-sitters, participants, and supporters of the uprising.[14]

[12] "Ārash raḥmānīpūr va moḥammad reżā ʿalīzamānī, eʿdām shodand,"
Rahesabz, January 28, 2010. Accessed July 10, 2015. http://rahesabz.net/story/
8919/.
[13] Director Alan Eyre, Dubai, to Central Intelligence Agency et al., February 2,
2010, Wikileaks, https://search.wikileaks.org/plusd/cables/10RPODUBAI27_
a.html.
[14] One such victim of these forced confessions speaks about it in length in his
memoirs, noting that as an international journalist of dual Iranian and Canadian
citizenship, he was forced to admit to the falsehood that he was part of an
international conspiracy whereby the foreign media worked in tandem with
foreign governments to pave the way for a velvet revolution in Iran much like the
ones that swept through Georgia in 2003 or Ukraine in 2004. See Maziar
Bahari, *Then They Came for Me: A Family's Story of Love, Captivity, and*

Furthermore, just as the internet was a weapon in the hands of activists who used it either to coordinate action through social media or to broadcast raw footage of events to a global audience via YouTube, the medium was also a weapon in the hands of the state,

*Survival* (New York: Random House, 2011), pp. 162–173. Although he was never tried, Bahari (p. 225) had this to say about the show trials he observed: "A number of sources told me that the trials were produced on Khamenei's direct orders, meant to show the strength of the regime and disgrace the reformist leaders who were paraded in front of the press in their prison uniforms." Mehdi Saharkhiz, the point man for activists' footage from the uprising, responded to the forced confession of his father, a journalist imprisoned before the election after publishing letters critical of Khamenei, by co-opting and subverting the state's tactic of televising such confessions with his own YouTube "confession" in which he stated: "I confess. I confess that I am the son of a prisoner, my father is a prisoner. I confess that I am not ashamed that my father is in prison and I am proud of him. I confess that my father is not a thief, he is not a murderer, he is not a looter nor a rioter. He is one of the 'Dirt and Dust' and a friend of the 'Dirt and Dust.' I confess that my father disrupted the comfortable sleep of some people, and gave them nightmares. Those same people who filled their own pockets by stealing the nation's wealth and left people in nightmares. I confess that my father is famous for his honesty. And I confess his bravery had made life harder for the cowards in power in our time. I confess that they kidnapped my father and broke his ribs. I confess that they did not even take him to a hospital, and instead took him to solitary confinement. I confess that my father was denied the right to an attorney. He was not even allowed to phone his daughter on Father's Day. I confess that for weeks we had no word from him, and even on my mother's birthday we did not receive any news. I confess that my mother spent her wedding anniversary in loneliness. And I confess that this year, my father could not visit my martyred uncle's grave because he was in jail. I confess that Isa Saharkhiz is a soldier of war and a brother of a martyr. I confess that he did not use his positions to gain money or power in this regime. I confess that he has worked for years either when he was an official in the Ministry of Culture or when he was the head of the news department in the Islamic Republic News Agency or even when he was working for the IRNA office in the United Nations. I confess that my father works in a country where the representative of the judiciary system bit him. I confess that in my country the person who bites gets a promotion and later becomes a minister. I confess that the wolves that are running the country now don't even think the savage who bites should be fired. I confess that my dad's greatest sin is being innocent. I confess he is guilty of speaking justly. I confess that he has already expressed his views and beliefs before he was kidnapped and whatever they have him confess is a pure lie and not his opinion. I confess that I am proud of having a father like him. I confess that I wish maybe someday I can be just a little like him. That would be the greatest achievement of my life. I confess that my father and his friends were not only detained but tortured. We confess that we voted and they stole our votes. We confess that this one was not an election but a coup d'etat. We confess that no court was assembled and what was shown on state TV was nothing but a movie of big lies. We confess that our brothers and sisters were not only tortured

which published photos of protesters and invited fellow citizens to identify them so they could be arrested. As early as June, Gerdab, a news outlet tied to the IRGC, published twenty-eight photos with protesters' faces circled, inviting government supporters to identify the "rioters" who served the agenda of "the hypocrites, monarchists, terrorist groups, and counter-revolutionaries."[15] The state's tactic of encouraging citizens to reveal the identities of their neighbors continued throughout the uprising and came to a head in the post-ʿAshura crackdown when the commander of the security forces announced that 70 percent of ʿAshura "rioters" had been identified and arrested after the publication of the photos.[16] Although the percentage is almost certainly an exaggeration designed to intimidate activists, there is no doubt that many were in fact identified and detained through this harrowing approach.

The government's use of the internet to suffocate the movement was an ominous sign of things to come. Iran in 2009 is an early example of how governments around the world are using the internet and mobile phones to monitor their own citizens. This is not a phenomenon unique to "those people over there," but also a growing reality in the United States, the "beacon of the free world." Edward Snowden, the analyst who defected from the National Security Agency (NSA) and leaked a mass of classified information about the government's covert techniques for intruding into the lives of its citizens, showed that government surveillance is certainly a reality not just "over there." According to Snowden, the ever-expanding surveillance state in the United States

but were raped in the most savage way possible. We confess that Kahrizak was not a jail but a place for torture and rape. We confess that those who are running the country are far from being human. We confess that we are fighting together for our rights and will not back down. We confess that it is you [the government] that is scared of us as we are not scared because we are standing together. We confess that we will fight until the very last drop of our blood for our absolute right to a free Iran. We confess that we have faith in victory and getting our rights." Mehdi Saharkhiz, "I Mehdi Saharkhiz confess for Isa Saharkhiz (please make your own)," online video clip, YouTube, August 15, 2009. Accessed May 17, 2015. https://youtu.be/AZjdLq3H1S8. For a detailed history of forced confessions in modern Iran, see Ervand Abrahamian, *Tortured Confessions: Prisons and Public Recantations in Modern Iran* (Berkeley: University of California Press, 1999).

[15] "Eghteshāshgarān rā shenāsāī konīd (līst-i avval)," Gerdab, June 21, 2009. Accessed July 9, 2015. http://gerdab.ir/fa/pages/?cid=407.

[16] "70 darṣad-i eghteshāshgarān bā moʿarefī-ye mardom dastgīr shodand," Mehr News Agency, February 11, 2010. Accessed July 9, 2015. http://goo.gl/JCvmsn.

has the authority and capability to activate the microphones on Americans' mobile phones, listen to personal conversations, and monitor online and phone activity, including text messages typed in real time:

As you write a message, you know, an analyst at the NSA or any other service out there that's using this kind of attack against people can actually see you write sentences and then backspace over your mistakes and then change the words and then kind of pause and – and – and think about what you wanted to say and then change it. And it's this extraordinary intrusion not just into your communications, your finished messages but your actual drafting process, into the way you think.[17]

As early as 2011, in an unnerving *Guardian* article, Ana Marie Cox noted that governments and companies collect our online activity in the form of "data" so they can predict and possibly influence our behavior:

The masters of modern spycraft have learned from the masters of marketing the science of predicting human behavior. One of the main reasons for 'bulk' collection, one that seems less alarming on its surface, is to watch for patterns of behavior that indicate possible terrorist activity. But when an organization is sufficiently skilled at predicting human behavior, the next phase, almost inevitably, is to try to influence it.[18]

Subsequent history, in the form of the 2016 US presidential election, proved that Cox's assessment of the utility of the internet in the hands of governments was prophetic. The intervention of foreign governments in the 2016 American election by way of affecting voting patterns through Facebook is part of a wider trend that finds commonality in Iran in 2009 when the Iranian government harnessed the internet for its own insidious purposes. In sum, one of the legacies of the Green Uprising is to demonstrate how effective the internet is both in terms of

---

[17] Edward Snowden, interview by Brian Williams, May 28, 2014, Moscow, Russia, NBC News. Accessed July 9, 2015. www.nbcnews.com/feature/edward-snowden-interview/edward-snowdens-motive-revealed-he-can-sleep-night-n116851. Also, see Glenn Greenwald, *No Place to Hide: Edward Snowden, the NSA, and the U.S. Surveillance State* (New York: Metropolitan Books, 2014); and Evgeny Morozov, *The Net Delusion: The Dark Side of Internet Freedom* (New York: Perseus Books Group, 2011).

[18] Ana Marie Cox, "Who should we fear more with our data: The government or companies?" *The Guardian*, January 20, 2014. Accessed September 6, 2011. www.theguardian.com/commentisfree/2014/jan/20/obama-nsa-reform-companies-spying-data.

protest activity and its suppression, the latter constituting an early warning of things to come both in Iran and elsewhere.

In addition to the ever-widening security net that by February was ensnaring opposition members of all strata, the state also implemented measures designed to neutralize Green activists on Revolution Day. It disrupted the internet, SMS and telephone services in order to prevent coordination, lined the main street of the pro-government march with thousands of security personnel, and, for the first time, installed loud-speakers along the 6-mile march route to drown out potential anti-government slogans.[19] The government even took advantage of Revolution Day falling on a Thursday, the day before Iran's day of rest, and a religious holiday afterward to announce a long holiday to encourage would-be protesters to go on vacation.[20]

The state's systematic measures were not the only way it tried to ensure that the Green Movement would not be able to co-opt Revolution Day. The authorities coupled their crackdown and attempts to control the day's message with a relentless effort to encourage their own supporters to flood the streets, specifically in Tehran where the day's events were planned to culminate at Azadi Square, the scene of the unofficial referendum on 'Ashura in 1978 and the Green Movement's most impressive gathering on June 15, 2009. The state-led coordination aimed to produce a colossal show of force in support of the government and the Leader of the Revolution, and to take a physical stand by hammering "the last nail in the seditionists' coffin."[21] The opportunity to co-opt another political holiday in order to rally against the regime – a tactic the opposition had employed to great effect on previous holidays to circumvent state repression and renew its protest – was no longer available.

While the government was preparing the death knell for the uprising's street presence, Green activists still hoped that they would evade the state's efforts to stop them from hijacking the government's most politically potent holiday, Revolution Day – the day on which a protracted popular revolution had brought the Shah's seemingly all-powerful state to a definitive end and precipitated the rise of the Islamic Republic. Many hoped the appropriation of such an important day

---

[19] Director Alan Eyre, Dubai, to Central Intelligence Agency et al., February 10, 2010, Wikileaks, https://search.wikileaks.org/plusd/cables/10RPODUBAI33_a.html.
[20] Ibid.    [21] Ibid.

would amount to the beginning of the end of the government, an anticipation best visualized by an image posted on Mousavi's Facebook page (Figure 6.2).[22]

The hourglass image noted all the uprising's main days of action: June 15, Quds Day (September 18), National Struggle Against Global Arrogance Day (November 4), Student Day (December 7), *Tasu'a* and *'Ashura* (December 26 and 27), and the last, which was to be Revolution Day (February 11). All but June 15 (the single largest day of protest in the history of the uprising) were state-sanctioned holidays, which the Green Movement appropriated and subverted. The hourglass ended with Revolution Day, symbolizing the forthcoming victory of the uprising, or as one observer noted, the Green Movement's "D-Day."[23]

If the struggle between the Green Movement and the government was a poker game, then both sides went "all in," leaving one winner, which was undoubtedly the government. The state's repressive measures coalesced with its efforts to amass its supporters to ensure that the day went off as the government planned. State media boasted that fifty million people across the country, five million of whom were in Tehran, marched to "burst" the "bubble of America's seditious plot."[24] While these estimates from the state's most conservative daily newspaper, *Kayhan*, the editor of which is personally chosen by Khamenei, are highly exaggerated, helicopter footage confirms an undeniably massive and unprecedented show of force for the government.[25] More symbolically important, *Kayhan* proclaimed that the "epic march" demonstrated the people's affirmation of Khomeini's ideals through the renewal of their oath of allegiance (*bai'ah*) to Khamenei's authority (*vilāyat*).[26]

*Bai'ah* is an Islamic concept that goes back to the time of the Prophet Muhammad who, along with his successors, secured loyalty not

---

[22] Mir Hossein Mousavi Facebook page, "Green hourglass," November 26, 2009. Facebook post. www.facebook.com/mousavi/photos/a.172726419453 .118347.45061919453/186592339453/?type=3&theater.

[23] Win Dayton, Istanbul, to Secretary of State Hillary Clinton, January 29, 2010, Wikileaks, https://search.wikileaks.org/plusd/cables/10ISTANBUL40_a.html.

[24] "Ḥobāb-i fetneh-ye āmrīkā tarakīd ḥamāseh-ye bi sābeqeh-ye mellat dar 22 bahman," *Kayhan*, February 16, 2009. Accessed July 11, 2015. http://kayhanarch.kayhan.ir/881127/14.htm#other1401.

[25] Zelzalosolh, "[Must see | Part 1 | Bahman 22 2010] Helicopter over Tehran five million dawn," online video clip, YouTube, February 12, 2010. Accessed May 15, 2015. https://youtu.be/HbYqckFvUJI.

[26] "Ḥobāb-i fetneh-ye āmrīkā tarakīd ḥamāseh-ye bī sābeqeh-ye mellat dar 22 bahman."

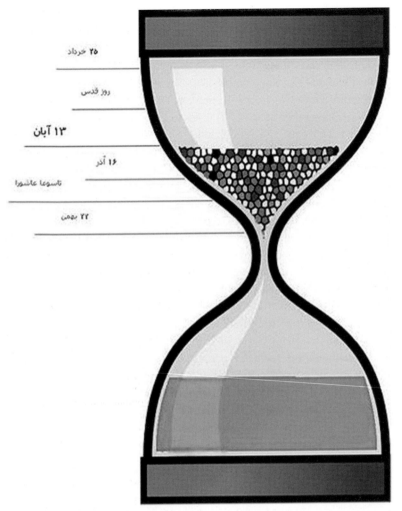

**Figure 6.2** Nearing the end: the hourglass of the Movement's major days of action

through written agreements but via powerful and binding oaths. So important were these pledges that to violate them amounted to perjuring oneself before God.[27] That state media framed its victory on February 11 using this terminology only demonstrates its self-

---

[27] Roy Mottahedeh, *Loyalty and Leadership in an Early Islamic Society* (Princeton: Princeton University Press, 1980), p. 42.

legitimating reliance on Islamic symbolism, history, and discourse, all of which the Green Movement co-opted and subverted to legitimate itself and condemn the Islamic Republic using its very own language.

After Revolution Day, the opposition was shocked and demoralized to see the footage, which the state repeatedly broadcast to the nation. Many simply could not fathom that the government enjoyed such support. Others argued that the attendees either did not know any better, were lured with the promise of a free lunch, or were simply coerced into participating. The truth is, however, that the government endured a storm that inundated many of its counterparts in neighboring Arab countries two years later in the Arab Uprisings *because* of such support, which cannot so easily be brushed aside by denying government supporters their agency.[28]

In comparison, the Shah's government lacked such organic roots when the revolutionary upheaval began to shatter his authority in 1978–1979. The Shah's few supporters simply transferred their wealth abroad, packed their suitcases, and left the country when it became apparent that the revolution would triumph. Indeed, historians often

---

[28] Iranians have long denied the agency of their fellow countrymen and women in order to explain events in a manner that suits their own biases, as if Iranians in 1978–1979 and 2009 were mindless robots easily duped by an all-powerful foreign entity to risk life and limb for delusional goals. Countless members of the Iranian expatriate community blame the Iranian Revolution on the West, arguing that the Americans, British, French or a combination thereof "tricked" the Iranians to come out in support of the revolution. In 2009, the government similarly blamed the uprising on a foreign conspiracy. In fact, Iranians in both historic uprisings were fully aware of the dangers of protesting, and their own cost–benefit calculation took into consideration their very real grievances. The opposition in 2009 likewise failed (and continues to fail) to respect the agency of those millions who came out in support of the government on February 11, 2010. There are many reasons why so many Iranians publicly backed Ahmadinejad in particular and the system in general, including, importantly, his spearheading of the change in privatization laws to the benefit of the poor. The new law (see Chapter 2) "set aside 40 percent of the shares of privatized firms for distribution among low-income households at highly discounted prices. These shares were labeled 'justice shares.' As many as two thousand public enterprises were targeted for privatization under this plan, their value estimated at between 100 and 140 billion dollars. The distribution of justice shares also served as an indirect mechanism by which to reward the low-income supports of the regime, particularly the Basij mlitia for their loyalty and support... In the first phase of this process, justice shares were distributed to 4.6 million eligible voters; the value of these shares were assessed at $2.3 billion." Nader Habibi, "The economic legacy of Mahmoud Ahmadinejad," *Middle East Brief*, 74 (June 2013), p. 3. www.brandeis.edu/crown/publications/meb/MEB74.pdf.

remark that the Shah's dictatorship was a problem for a "one-bullet
solution," in which a lone assassin could potentially cause the destruction of the state since so much power and decision-making was vested
in one man. Once decapitated by the death of the monarch, the state
would crumble. The Islamic Republic, on the other hand, has been
building institutions throughout the country since its inception and,
consequently, the enormously entrenched state reaches deep into society. A prime example can be found in the IRGC, which was established
to protect the leadership of the revolution and now controls a large
percentage of the Iranian economy through, *inter alia*, its Khatam al-
Anbia engineering firm and its connections to powerful foundations –
investments that amount to "a multi-billion-dollar industrial
empire."[29] These business ventures, coupled with its ideological zeal
and multi-layered institutional capacity for violence, guarantee it has a
vested and unshakable interest in maintaining the status quo. In contrast, the Shah's conscripted army continuously unraveled in the face
of the revolutionary uprising in 1978, barely maintaining a semblance
of cohesion by early 1979 – until various guerrilla groups in tandem
with revolutionary volunteers delivered the *coup de grace* on February
11, 1979 (Revolution Day).[30]

The Islamic government was thus able to harness that institutional
power, along with its corresponding support base, to shut down the
opposition's plans to co-opt the state's most important political holiday. The mere fact that it was also able to commandeer such a massive
display of support prompted many Green activists to believe that

[29] Afshon Ostovar, *Vanguard of the Imam: Religion, Politics, and Iran's
Revolutionary Guards* (New York: Oxford University Press, 2016),
pp. 146–147.
[30] Kurzman notes: "Each military operation exposed the troops to fraternization
and further appeals from protesters. Dissident officers therefore encouraged
more deployment of soldiers in the streets, while loyalists such as the head of the
ground forces proposed keeping the soldiers away from nefarious influences:
'We should round up the units and send them someplace where [the
demonstrators] won't have any contact with the soldiers. Because yesterday they
came and put a flower in the end of a riffle barrel, and another on the [military]
car... The soldiers' morale just disappears.' On several occasions, eyewitnesses
reported that large throngs of protesters had persuaded soldiers to give up their
arms, throw off their uniforms, and join the demonstrations." Kurzman, *The
Unthinkable Revolution in Iran* (Cambridge, MA: Harvard University Press,
2004), p. 115.

changing the status quo through street action was becoming a hopeless cause.

In his analysis of the causes of the Iranian Revolution, Charles Kurzman circumvents complex theories in favor of a real-time decision in which "fence-sitters," those sympathetic to the cause but not yet participating, decide at a critical juncture that revolution is possible – an epiphany that finally prompts their participation. Until the moment when those fence-sitters – the bulk of the people who ultimately made the Iranian Revolution – crossed that mental threshold, only die-hard revolutionaries were on the streets. Kurzman's explanation, or what he calls the "anti-explanation . . . runs counter to the project of retroactive prediction. . . Instead of seeking recurrent patterns in social life, anti-explanation explores the unforeseen moments when patterns are twisted or broken off."[31]

A number of factors came together to cause many sympathizers to cross that mental threshold in the early winter of 1978, believing that the victory of the revolution was a very real possibility and that their personal participation made it all the more likely. Consequently, the 'Ashura protests of December 10, 1978, were undoubtedly the largest protest event in modern Iranian history. In contrast, severe government repression in February 2010 coupled with an immense public outpouring of support for the state provoked the opposite sentiment: that the Green Uprising may not win and that one's personal participation not only may not make a difference, but could actually come at great personal cost.

## 6.3 The Uprising Endures: Complicating the Claim of Its Finality

What does it mean to say that the Green Uprising is "over"? What does it mean when Western media, and even some esteemed experts on Iran, echo the sentiment of Iran's leaders by referring to the revolt as a "failed" revolution?[32] It is certainly true that the movement failed to

---

[31] Ibid., p. 138.

[32] A sample of Western media news outlets, encompassing NBC News, Fox News, *The Guardian*, and *Der Spiegel*, all refer to the Green Uprising as a "failed" revolution. See Robert Windrem, "Who to follow on Twitter? Iranian President Hassan Rouhani," NBC News, November 2, 2015. Accessed May 26, 2018. www.nbcnews.com/news/world/who-follow-twitter-iranian-president-hassan-

abrogate Ahmadinejad's election "win." It is also certainly true that it
did not succeed in overthrowing the state. The win–lose and start–
finish binaries, however, are simply too narrow an analytical lens.
Indeed, it is this work's contention that the uprising is far from over
in many ways.

In his seminal book, *The Other Cold War*, Heonik Kwon supplants
the dominant Cold War paradigm that focuses on the two superpowers
of the day in favor of examining how the global struggle impacted
people at grassroots level. He argues that the Cold War did not end for
many of its victims with the fall of the Berlin Wall or the implosion of
the Soviet Union. There was no sense of closure, for instance, for
families whose sons and daughters fought and died for both sides of
the American war in Vietnam until the communist state finally allowed
those families to administer proper burial rights, which were previously banned as feudal superstitions. It was only several years after the
formal end of the Cold War when the revolutionary state relented and
allowed these families to formally acknowledge their dead that they
had a sense that the war was finally over.[33]

Iran after Revolution Day likewise continued to grapple with the
ramifications of the events of 2009. Three of the uprising's leading
personalities, Mir Hussein Mousavi, Zahra Rahnavard, and Mehdi
Karroubi, have been under house arrest since early 2011. The state also
implemented a media ban on Khatami, the popular reformist former
president who publicly backed the movement.[34] Many activists

rouhani-flna4B11205274. Perry Chiaramonte, "Hell on earth: Inside Iran's
brutal Evin prison," Fox News, January 28, 2013. Accessed May 26, 2018.
www.foxnews.com/world/2013/01/28/inside-evin-look-at-world-most-
notorious-political-prison.html. Geoffrey Macnab, "Iran's green revolution in
animation," *The Guardian*, January 20, 2011. Accessed May 26, 2018. www
.theguardian.com/film/2011/jan/20/iran-animation-the-green-wave. "Germany
grants asylum to fifty Iranian dissidents," *Der Spiegel*, January 26, 2010.
Accessed May 26, 2018. www.spiegel.de/international/world/long-wait-ends-
germany-grants-asylum-to-50-iranian-dissidents-a-708537.html. Even the
renowned sociologist, Misagh Parsa, considered the uprising a failure. Misagh
Parsa, "What happened to Iran's Green Movement?" *The Arab Weekly*, June 8,
2017. Accessed October 13, 2018. https://thearabweekly.com/what-happened-
irans-green-movement.

[33] Heonik Kwon, *The Other Cold War* (New York: Columbia University
Press, 2010).

[34] Fereshteh Qazi, "Jaʿfarī-dowlatābādī modīrān-i nashrīāt rā tahdīd kard," Rooz
Online, February 10, 2015. Accessed July 13, 2015. www.roozonline.com/
persian/news/newsitem2/article/-cc06e1f063.html.

withered away in Iran's political prisons, and more continued to reel from the physical and psychological trauma of those tumultuous days. Futures were ruined as many students were expelled from universities or prohibited from continuing their education either in prison or after their release. The uprising is a daily lived experience full of grief for the families of the 112 people killed either on crowded streets or alone in captivity – families of such departed as Sohrab A'rabi, Mina Ehterami, Amir Ashraf Tajmir, Somayyeh Ja'farqoli, Salar Tahmasebi, Parisa Kolli, Reza Fattahi, Taraneh Mousavi, Mohsen Entezami and over a hundred others.[35] The anguish is especially pronounced for those families that never obtained a sense of closure because the state prevented them from having a proper burial for fear that it would serve as a rallying cry for the opposition.[36]

A closer look at modern Iranian history is instructive in analyzing the supposed finality of the Green Uprisings. It is often said that

---

[35] Rahesabz published profiles of all the deceased on the third anniversary of the election, though the list cannot encompass the entire death toll as some names have yet to be released. A breakdown of the age and gender of the departed offers a window into the demographics of the uprising. Of the 112 who died in the uprising, twelve were female and one hundred male, the youngest of whom was aged twelve. Fourteen were teenagers, thirty-three were between twenty-one and twenty-five years of age, twenty-two between twenty-six and thirty, eleven between twenty-one and forty, and seven were forty-one or older. The breakdown does not reflect the percentage of women's involvement in the revolt, especially since they were far less aggressive in engaging security forces, therefore, they suffered fewer casualties. The percentage of youth dead, however, does affirm that young people comprised the bulk of the protesters. The number of the deceased aged over forty illustrates that it was not exclusively a youth movement but a multi-generational one. See "Enteshār-i asāmī-ye 112 tan az jānbākhtegān-i ḥavādes̲-i b'ad az entekhābāt," Rahesabz, June 12, 2012. Accessed July 11, 2015. www.rahesabz.net/story/54490/.

[36] Makhmalbaf accused the government of seizing the dead body of Mousavi's nephew in order to prevent "both an impartial examination of the corpse and a burial." See Director Alan Eyre, Dubai, to Central Intelligence Agency et al., December 28, 2009, Wikileaks, https://search.wikileaks.org/plusd/cables/09RPODUBAI549_a.html. Other instances abound, such as when the families of Mostafa Kashani Rasa and Fatemeh Semsarpor were disallowed from observing customary mourning practices. "Enteshār-i asāmī-ye 112 tan az jānbākhtegān-i ḥavādes̲-i b'ad az entekhābāt," Rahesabz, June 12, 2012. Accessed July 11, 2015. www.rahesabz.net/story/54490/. There is also much information about how the state tried to or succeeded in suppressing Neda Agha Soltan's burial. I am reluctant to include a citation because most of the sources rely on the testimony of her fiancé, Caspian Makan, whose credibility has been undermined. There should not be any doubt, however, that the state succeeded to a certain extent in controlling the funeral of the uprising's most iconic martyr.

repressive governments get the enemies that they deserve. When the
Shah's military violently crushed the June 1963 Uprising, many young
activist members of such opposition groups as the Liberation Movement were radicalized, and broke with the peaceful approach of their
organizations. They came to believe that the crackdown proved that
nonviolent struggle against the Shah's regime was futile, and that
armed struggle was the only path to liberation. One exiled student
newspaper effectively captured the transition that many young people
underwent in the aftermath of the bloodshed:

> The Uprising of 5 June (15 Khordad) is one of the most important events in
> all Iranian history and the most bloody event in contemporary Iranian
> history. It has forced us to draw the following ... conclusions: ... that the
> unarmed struggle – however popular and widespread – cannot possibly
> succeed against such a bloodthirsty regime. The only way to bring down
> this detestable regime is through a concerted armed struggle.[37]

Spirited activists such as these were baptized in the blood of the 1963
Uprising, and went on to establish underground armed groups that
fought a guerrilla war with the Shah in the 1970s. Their resistance
demonstrated that however powerful the Shah's US-made military and
US–Israel-trained SAVAK may have been, the regime was not invin-
cible,[38] helping to foster the belief that revolution was possible, and
even going so far as to lead the insurrection that precipitated the state's
final collapse on Revolution Day (February 11, 1979).

   This is not to say that a guerrilla uprising is on Iran's political horizon
in the aftermath of 2009. On the contrary, the circumstances that gave

---

[37] Ervand Abrahamian, *The Iranian Mojahedin* (New Haven and London: Yale
   University Press, 1989), p. 85.
[38] Fada'iyan theorist Amir Parviz Pooyan outlined the guerrilla strategy of
   shattering through armed struggle the proletariat's sense of the state's absolute
   power, fostering their belief that revolution was possible: "The enemy's absolute
   domination, which is reflected in the minds of the workers as their absolute
   inability to change the established order, has the indirect effect of fostering
   submission to the enemy's culture. Thus, terror and suppression, which
   represents the power of the enemy, causes the worker's submission to the
   dominant culture... Therefore, in order to liberate the proletariat from the
   dominant culture, cleanse their minds and lives of poisonous, petty bourgeois
   thoughts, end its alienation from its distinct class outlook, and equip it with
   ideological ammunition, it is necessary to shatter the illusion that it is absolutely
   powerless to destroy the enemy. Revolutionary power serves this purpose."
   Amir Parviz Pooyan, "Żarūrat-i mobārezeh-ye mosalaḥāneh va rad-i te'orī-ye
   baqa," Siahkal.org, 1970. www.siahkal.com/publication/pooyan.htm.

rise to the militant groups of the 1970s are wholly absent today. Rather, the point is that the end of the uprising in 1963 constituted the beginning of a new kind of struggle for many. For Khomeini, the leader of the 1963 Uprising, it was only the opening salvo in a protracted struggle that culminated more than fifteen years later in the revolutionary overthrow of the monarchy. History can indeed be non-linear, with the conclusion of one event lighting a new, different path ahead.

Future historians may well look at the defeat that the Green Movement sustained on Revolution Day in 2010 as a prelude to an entirely new phase in Iran's modern history, one that may be, but is not limited to, a cyber war – quite possibly the future (if not the present) of nonviolent underground resistance as well as intrastate warfare.[39]

Numerous occurrences after Revolution Day refute the claim that it is "over." First, many in the Arab world looked to Iran in 2009 as an exemplar for action, as articulated by an Egyptian activist:

During the Iranian elections, we Egyptians were surprised to find out that Iranian women, who we've heard of as being oppressed and covered from top to bottom, have gone to streets demonstrating against the elections, asking for their political rights. Young university students, who we are told are marginalized and oppressed by the Islamic government, are also demonstrating against the system and the Mullah. And so, we were all, without exception, fascinated by the situation in Iran and wanted to support this call for change. At the same time, there was a recurring thought in the media and in people's minds that, I remember, was clearly articulated by an Iranian activist, living and studying in the USA on CNN. He said: 'If it happened in Iran, it would happen in Egypt.' That is exactly what was on our minds, if Iranians could stand up to its extremely oppressive and theocratic government, then we Egyptians can easily break the vicious cycle of our autocratic government. We can do the same. In helping Iranians, we were helping our dream for a democratic nation to come true, we were helping ourselves. We thought that this was the time to garner the attention of the international community to the Middle East to Iran first then to the rest of the countries there that still suffer from oppressive governments.[40]

[39] For a quick introduction to how cyber warfare is emerging as a new means of intrastate violence, which is best exemplified in the US-Israeli Stuxnet cyber attack on Iran's nuclear facilities in 2010, see the harrowing documentary from Oscar-winning filmmaker Alex Gibney on Stuxnet, *Zero Days* (Magnolia Pictures, 2016).

[40] Dalia Ziada (Egyptian blogger and human rights activist), interview by Sherine El-Taraboulsi, April 18, 2010. Accessed July 14, 2015, transcript.

This activist and many of her revolutionary counterparts had a vested interest in seeing the Green Uprising succeed and, consequently, used Google Translate to relay information in Persian, posting alerts on Twitter as to which embassies in Tehran were offering first aid to injured demonstrators.[41] After the Iranian government succeeded in crushing the uprising, Egyptians found their inspiration in the inferno of revolution that was sparked in Tunisia two years later and spread like wildfire across the region.

While Iranian activists were unable to annul the election results or uproot the system that ratified them, their uprising nonetheless served as a precedent that informed the nonviolent and digital tactics of their counterparts elsewhere in the Arab world. Wael Ghonim, who was catapulted into the global limelight after setting up a Facebook page to call for the first protests in Egypt after Tunisia's strongman Zine El 'Abidine Ben 'Ali fled to Saudi Arabia, gave voice to the cross-pollination of transnational protest on the eve of Mubarak's downfall: "I would tell Iranians to learn from the Egyptians, as we have learned from you guys..."[42] Iranians did not inspire the Arab Spring, but Egyptians still gleaned much from their successes and failures.

This give and take affirms that the world is not easily categorized into neat geographical or linguistic boundaries, just as it was not during the Cold War. In the 1970s, Iranian guerrillas defied the East–West global division in favor of a North–South paradigm, and made common cause with their Arab neighbors against imperialism and oppression. In the post-Cold War order, the struggle against authoritarianism (and neoliberalism) forges commonalities between peoples even if they do not share a common language and their governments have done their best to keep them apart.

As such, the Arab Uprisings were not confined to the Arab world and eventually reached Iran. After Ben 'Ali's toppling on January 14, 2011, Egyptians and Yemenis quickly mobilized, and on February 11, 2011, thirty-two years to the day after the triumph of Iran's revolution, Egypt's dictator was ousted. Three days later, the flames of protest were ignited in Libya, Bahrain, and Iran, the first non-Arab country to be inspired by the Arab Uprisings. A full year after the Green

---

[41] Ibid.

[42] "Egyptian activist's message to Iranians: Learn from Egyptians, and we learned from you," Center for Human Rights in Iran, February 10, 2011. Accessed May 10, 2018. www.iranhumanrights.org/2011/02/wael-ghonim-on-iran/.

Movement's so-called failure, Mousavi and Karroubi called for demonstrations in solidarity with Tunisians and Egyptians against "tyranny."[43] Iranian activists answered the call by harnessing the energy
and momentum of their neighbors to resurface and declare:
"Mubarak, Ben ʿAli, now the turn of Sayyid ʿAli [Khamenei]"
(*mubārak, ben ʿalī, nowbat-i sayyid ʿalī*),[44] prompting the state to
place Mousavi, Rahnavard, and Karroubi under indefinite house
arrest.

The Green Movement, along with its counterparts in the Arab
Spring uprisings, shared a common problem that was simultaneously
their main source of strength. Neither revolt posited a systematic
alternative to the status quo. The revolutions of the past unfolded at
a time when the ideological climate of anti-capitalism, social justice,
and anti-imperialism informed their worldview, with even Cold
War-era Muslim intellectuals like Shariʿati, Mottahari, and Taleqani
fostering doctrines versed in discourses that necessitated revolution,
not reform. Since the 1980s, however, neoliberalism has not only
reshaped economies and their political and economic elites, but has
also transformed the opposition by "deradicalizing dissent." In Bayat's
formulation:

The political clout of neoliberalism lies in its ability to serve as a form of
governmentality, in its ability to structure people's thinking to internalize the
methods of the market society, considering them to be a commonsense way
of being and doing things, against which no concrete alternative is imagined
or needed. Treating it as 'natural' is a key power of neoliberalism; when it is
not talked about as a problem or as an ideology such as, say, communism, it
becomes the natural way of life.[45]

The youth-led Green and Arab uprisings operated within the normative framework of neoliberalism and did not have a radical vision of
an alternative. Instead, they focused on their respective figureheads as
well as human rights, women's rights, or personal rights, without
giving any consideration to how such rights are affected and affirmed

[43] "Dar khāst-i mojavez-i rāhpaymāī beh samt-i maydān-i āzādī, dar ḥemāyat az
ḥarakat-i żedd-i estebdādī-ye mardom-i mantaqeh," Kalame, February 6, 2011.
Accessed May 25, 2018. www.kaleme.com/1389/11/17/klm-46546/.
[44] Mardomak News. "Mubārak, ben ʿalī, nowbat-i seyyed ʿalī." Online video clip,
YouTube, February 14, 2011. Accessed July 14, 2015. https://youtu.be/
QqmkvTsH1FY.
[45] Bayat, *Revolution without Revolutionaries*, p. 23.

by class, position, and power.[46] The uprisings, a contradictory combination of revolution and reform, were mass-based popular revolts that emerged from below to induce the state above to reform itself on behalf of the movements.[47] In Egypt, the power structure largely resisted these demands, though it did facilitate cosmetic change at the top by ousting Mubarak to achieve a modicum of appeasement, then maneuvered for counter-revolution.

In Iran in 2009–2010, where the uprising's challenge to the system was far more comprehensive than that in Egypt, no such change occurred. The government interpreted the pre-election campaign and the post-election uprising as part of a single Western-orchestrated velvet revolution, and resisted any and all demands. The state deployed its multi-layered security apparatus to put down the revolt, mobilizing its support base to show its strength at critical junctures, and Khamenei and the power structure affirmed Ahmadinejad's election "win." In response, the crowd's slogans gradually transitioned from attacking Ahmadinejad and calling for a re-run of the election to targeting Khamenei and the entire Islamic system that ratified the election's outcome. Yet, the power structure did not oust Khamenei as it had Mubarak, since doing so would have undermined the Islamic polity, with the Guardian Jurist as its cornerstone. In other words, the Egyptian state could continue without Mubarak, but Iran's Islamic system would negate itself ideologically and foundationally if it ousted Khamenei.

Moreover, while the Arab and Iranian revolts of the twenty-first century operated within the discursive framework of neoliberalism, the Green Uprising went further by leveling a total attack on Iran's Islamic government, and not just its figurehead. From upending its symbols of legitimation to situating the government alongside Israel and Caliph Yazid, Green activists likened themselves to oppressed Palestinians and Husayn's righteous band of rebels as part of a devastating assault on the entirety of Iran's governing ideology.

Comparing the Green Uprising to the Iranian Revolution is also instructive. In the Iranian Revolution of 1979, all factions united behind the undisputed leadership of Khomeini although they lacking a consensus on what a post-Shah system should look like. Khomeini,

[46] Ibid., p. 25.      [47] Ibid., p. 18.

on the other hand, not only rejected the monarchy but also unfurled a blueprint for an anti-monarchical Islamic government, and dutifully maneuvered to that end as soon as he returned from his long exile on February 1, 1979. By contrast, Mousavi, the main figurehead of the Green Movement, was not a revolutionary figure who formulated an ideology that negated the system the way Khomeini did, but a reformist who wanted to change the Islamic Republic from within in order to save it.

At the same time, the fact that the Green Movement did not advance a specific ideological alternative is its greatest strength. Although it lacked organizational structure, it was nonetheless open, inclusive, and horizontal, and harnessed the emotive universe common to all Iranians, allowing a wide array of aggrieved women and men to mobilize under what Rahnavard referred to as the "umbrella" of the Green Movement.[48] Issues related to gender equality, civil rights (such as freedom of speech, conscience, and assembly), social freedoms, government transparency and accountability, the separation of mosque and state, free and fair elections, corruption, inflation, social justice, unemployment and under-employment, and adventurism abroad, precipitated mass participation in the post-election uprising.[49] These issues persisted after 2009 and intertwined with moments when activists emerged to air slogans that invoked the Green Movement, dispelling allegations that the uprising was finished.

Another example of the movement belying claims that it is "over" can be found in the election of centrist candidate, Hassan Rouhani. Worried about disillusionment with the political process after the 2009 post-election turmoil, Khamenei beseeched citizens to vote in the 2013 election even if they did not agree with the Islamic Republic as a polity:

---

[48] Zahra Rahnavard, "'If a nation wants to change its destiny...' Zahra Rahnavard on women's rights and the Green Movement *Kalame*," in Nader Hashemi and Danny Postel (eds.), *The People Reloaded: The Movement and the Struggle for Iran's Future* (New York: Melville House Publishing, 2010), p. 265.

[49] On the first anniversary of the uprising, Mousavi published "The Green Movement Charter," which enumerated many such points as the general expression of the movement's broad support base. Mir Hossein Mousavi, "The Green Movement Charter," in Hashemi and Postel (eds.), *The People Reloaded*, pp. 332–344.

My first and most important recommendation is participation in the election as the most crucial thing for the country. It is possible that some – for whatever reason – will not support the Islamic Republic but should still want to support their country. Thus, they should go and cast their vote.[50]

That he talked about the Islamic Republic in such unprecedented terms attests to the system's crisis of legitimacy – one of the important victories of the uprising that problematizes claims of its "failure." More to the point, partisans gathered in Tehran at night to mark Rouhani's election win in 2013, declaring: "The Green Movement isn't dead, it has brought Rouhani to power" (*jonbesh-i sabz namordeh, rohānī ro āvordeh*); "Long live the Green Movement, long live Mousavi" (*jonbesh-i sabz zendeh bād, mūsavī pāyāndeh bād*);[51] "Mousavi, Mousavi, we have retrieved your vote" (*mūsavī, mūsavī, rayeto pas gereftīm*);[52] and "Martyred brother, we have retrieved your vote" (*barādar shahīdam, rayeto pas gereftam*).[53] This last slogan was the fulfillment of a promise pledged on the streets four years before.[54] They demanded the release of political prisoners[55] and an end to the

[50] 'Ali Khamenei, "2 rūz māndeh beh entekhābāt – nokāt-i entekhābātī-ye rahbar-i enqelāb," leader.ir., June 12, 2013. http://farsi.khamenei.ir/package?id= 22298&news_id=22904. Furthermore, it can be argued that the state permitted Rouhani to run in an attempt to make amends to the opposition. It is also worth noting that the government learned from the experience of the 2009 election when it loosened restrictions on the internet to facilitate interest in the election but then had to also contend with activists using online media for coordination. In 2013, however, the authorities encouraged voter participation but "throttled" the internet to "preserve calm" – a euphemism meaning to prevent another uprising. See "Vazīr-i ertebāṭāt: dalīl-i oft-i sor'at-i internet dar ayyām-i entekhābāt amnīatī būd," Tasnim News Agency, June 25, 2013. Accessed July 14, 2015. www.tasnimnews.com/Home/Single/85703.

[51] Kaleme.com official YouTube channel, "Barādar shahīdam rayeto pas gereftam," online video clip, YouTube, June 15, 2013. Accessed July 14, 2015. https://youtu.be/fGwga1VErN4.

[52] Salehi Erfan, "Mūsavī, mūsavī, rayeto pas gereftīm," online video clip, YouTube, June 15, 2013. Accessed July 14, 2015. https://youtu.be/ZGZPqASKxDw.

[53] Kaleme.com official YouTube channel, "barādar shahīdam rayeto pas gereftam."

[54] Ninashnash864, "Barādar shahīdam rayeto pas mīgīram," online video clip, YouTube, July 17, 2009. Accessed July 14, 2015. https://youtu.be/O-ha8NrexQA.

[55] Ali Adabi, "Jashn-i mardom shab-i 25 khordād dar mohavateh-ye farhangestān-i honar," online video clip, YouTube, June 17, 2013. Accessed July 14, 2015. https://youtu.be/8zsi8YJzdXU.

house arrest of the movement's leaders.[56] Amidst the jubilation, they also remembered the anniversary of the poster girl of the movement, Neda Agha Soltan, by marking the anniversary of her dramatic death: "It is grand, it is grand, yet her absence is at hand" (*'ālīeh, 'ālīeh, jā-ye nedā khālīeh*).[57]

Likewise, citizens welcomed the triumphant return of Rouhani's foreign minister, Muhammad Javad Zarif, from negotiations with world powers over Iran's nuclear program. Zarif secured a preliminary deal and was welcomed at the airport with slogans defying Israel and *Kayhan*, the agreement's opponents, and invoking the Green Uprising: "O'Husayn, Mir Hussein."[58] Similarly, nearly a decade after massive crowds had gathered to protest under the cover of Rafsanjani's post-election Friday sermon, activists-turned-mourners observed his passing in January 2017 by offering condolences to Mousavi and Karroubi (*mūsavī, karūbī, taslīat, taslīat*),[59] a poignant gesture since Rafsanjani had broken with the state in support of the two leaders. During Rouhani's re-election bid in the same year, supporters added Mousavi's campaign color, green, alongside Rouhani's purple,[60] to underscore the connection between the two, and invoked Mousavi's name outright at every juncture, such as at campaign rallies in Tehran[61] and Hamadan.[62] To clarify that the differing colors represent

---

[56] Sabzjamehgan, "Mūsavī,mūsavī,parcham-i īrānamo pas gereftam/dar jashn-i pīruzī-ye rohānī rouhani tehran election june 2013," online video clip, YouTube, June 16, 2013. Accessed July 14, 2015. https://youtu.be/O7HI_5CrKQs.

[57] Green Protestor, "Tazāhorāt-i mardom dar khīābān-i valī'asr-i tehrān dar pay-ye pīruzī-ye rohānī dar entekhābāt-i 92," online video clip, YouTube, June 15, 2013. Accessed August 21, 2018. https://youtu.be/NCT81F9mwVo.

[58] "Esteqbāl az zarīf dar forudgāh bā sho'ār-i 'ya husayn mīr hussein'," Kaleme, April 3, 2015. Accessed July 14, 2015. www.kaleme.com/1394/01/14/klm-212990/.

[59] Radio Rap, "Vīdīo-ye kāmel az marāsem-i tashī' jenāzeh-ye hāshemi rafsanjānī va she'r [sic] mīr hussein va karūbī," online video clip, YouTube, January 9, 2017. Accessed May 22, 2018. https://youtu.be/wcTtScr6jjU.

[60] "Hemāyat-i javānān az rohānī bā dastbandhāyeh sabz va banafsh / esteqbāl az 'amalkard-i jahāngīrī dar avvalīn monāzereh," ILNA News, April 29, 2017. Accessed May 22, 2018. goo.gl/CGHSNY.

[61] Reza Safari, "Hamāyesh-i entekhābātī-ye rohānī va sho'ār-i yā husayn mīr hussein dar varzeshgāh-i āzādī," online video clip, YouTube, May 13, 2017. Accessed May 22, 2018. https://youtu.be/kKG4WhTKLIE.

[62] Reza Safari, "Sho'ār-i ya husayn, mīr hussein dar hamāyesh-i entekhābātī-ye hassan rohānī dar hamadān," online video clip, YouTube, May 8, 2017. Accessed May 22, 2018. https://youtu.be/Q5qnAa53nck.

the same movement, at Rouhani's second election win activists proclaimed: "There is no green or purple, the movement continues" (*sabz o banafsh nadāreh, jonbesh edāmeh dāreh*).[63]

The Joint Comprehensive Plan of Action (commonly known as the Iran nuclear deal) was finalized in Vienna on July 14, 2015. On the streets of Iran activists chanted: "The next deal will be about our civil rights" (*tavāfoq-i ba'dī-ye mā ḥoqūq-i shahrvandī-ye mā*).[64] As we have seen, each of the political movements in modern Iranian history has constituted a renewed struggle in which the next generation of Iranians rose up to secure their freedom through the rule of law against those that either refused to establish it, or operated as if they were above it. Mousavi marked the first anniversary of the uprising by affirming the Green Movement's place in Iran's genealogy of struggle:

The Green Movement is an extension of the Iranian people's quest for freedom, social justice and national sovereignty, which had been previously manifested in the [1906] Constitutional Revolution, the 1951 Oil Nationalization Movement, and the [1979] Islamic Revolution.[65]

## 6.4 Conclusion

The grassroots history point of view from which the Green Uprising is chronicled in this book intentionally de-centers the movement's leadership in favor of the women and men on the ground who fearlessly made history in 2009 and beyond. The bottom-up lens empowers the reader to see beyond the win–lose binary and to discern other important and consequential developments, such as the uprising's post-Islamist challenge and its unprecedented discursive attack on the Islamic Republic's symbols and ideology. This reading shows,

---

[63] Freedom Messenger, "Sabz o banafsh nadāreh jonbesh edāmeh dāreh 30/2/1396," online video clip, YouTube, May 20, 2017. Accessed August 21, 2018. https://youtu.be/X6-BVG59Wis.

[64] Khabarnet info, "Tavāfoq-i ba'dī-ye mā hoqūq-i shahrvandi-ye ma," online video clip, YouTube, July 14, 2015. Accessed July 14, 2015. https://youtu.be/iDnoGcMTe04. Although American politicians credit the debilitating sanctions with prompting Iran's participation in the negotiation process, it should also be mentioned that the government, which has a long history of dealing with sanctions, was undoubtedly more willing to negotiate because it feared that the economic situation would so deteriorate as to re-ignite the uprising. Thus, the Green Uprising can also be credited with indirectly facilitating a compromise.

[65] Mousavi, "The Green Movement Charter," p. 336.

moreover, that the revolt is not over, especially in terms of its reper-
cussions and impact on Islamism in the Islamic Republic of Iran and
possibly elsewhere. Indeed, how can the state persist in its current form
and argue that it leads by raising Husayn's banner of resistance to
unjust power when it killed over 112 unarmed activists throughout the
uprising, eight of whom died on 'Ashura in 2009? How can the
authorities continue to distract their citizenry from internal issues by
invoking the specter of external enemies such as Israel, when it was
accused on Quds Day in 2009 of being as oppressive as Israel's military
occupation of the Palestinians?[66]

The events that took place between June 2009 and February 2010
(and sporadically afterward) mean that there is no going back to the
relative innocence of pre-election Iran. The memory of those momentous occasions remains in the hearts and minds of those activists. The
taste of victory that they enjoyed on the days of mass action when they
felt that anything was possible changed them, as did the sacrifice of so
many of their fellow citizens and the bitter aftertaste of the defeat of
Revolution Day. Memories endure, hopes persevere, grievances persist,
and anger festers – often quietly, but not always.

The nationwide uprising in Iran in late 2017 and early 2018, though
it had more to do with corruption, unemployment, inflation, and the
stratification of wealth than any direct lineage to its predecessor in
2009, is not completely disconnected from that history. In 2009, it
took months for the protesters to transition from "Where is my vote?"
in June to "This month is the month of blood, Sayyid 'Ali will be
toppled" (*īn māh, māh-i khūn ast, sayyid 'alī sarnegūn ast*)[67] in
December. The state's crackdown hardened demonstrators, who in
turn cascaded one ideological attack after another on the system by
subverting its symbols of legitimation. So hard-hitting were these nonviolent attacks that the government never fully recovered from them. It
is no wonder that in the nationwide protests nearly a decade later,
demonstrators not only recycled Green Movement slogans that challenged the Islamic Republic's ideological foundations, such as "No to

---

[66] Iran is just one example of governments using external threats, however real, to
distract from internal issues and justify the state's encroachment on civil
liberties.
[67] Mehdi Saharkhiz, "Iran 20 December 2009 (29 Azar) Tehran. Mohseni Sq.
protest after death of Ayatollah Montazeri P2," online video clip, YouTube,
December 20, 2009. Accessed May 22, 2018. https://youtu.be/ogadF_IZjTc.

Gaza, no to Lebanon, I sacrifice my life only for Iran,"[68] but also took far less time transitioning from the economic grievances that started the tumult[69] to attacking the system as a whole. In fact, the slogans against Khamenei, the ideological center of the Islamic Republic, began almost from the beginning by picking up at the point where the Green Uprising left off, such as when protesters in Tehran chanted, "Khamenei should know, he will soon be overthrown" (*khāmeneī bedūneh, beh zūdi sarnegūneh*).[70] Among the legacies that colored later protests, not only was the political taboo of openly criticizing Khamenei shattered in 2009, but so was his legitimacy and that of his institution, the *vilāyat-i faqīh*.

This study began by noting the slogan preferred by the Islamic Republic to summarize its reading of the Iranian Revolution, "Independence, freedom, Islamic Republic," which signified the onward march of the revolution to wrest its independence from the United States and its freedom from the tyranny of a US-installed monarch, together with the Islamic Republic as guarantor of both prized ideals. This powerful mantra was given mundane normality when the state emblazoned it on the country's early 5,000- and 10,000-rial banknotes, which depict Islamic revolutionaries marching under this banner (Figure 6.3).[71]

Fittingly, this work now concludes with the most potent battle cry of the next chapter in Iran's storied history of resistance. "Independence, freedom, Iranian Republic" (*esteqlāl, āzādī, jomhūrī-ye īrānī*) was voiced by Green activists on a number of occasions throughout the

---

[68] Masoud Dalvand, "Tehrān na ghazzeh na lobnān, jānam fadā'-ye īrān 9 day 96," online video clip, YouTube, December 30, 2017. Accessed May 22, 2018. https://youtu.be/HLAG0I6YJO4.

[69] See, for instance, Kaveh Ehsani and Arang Keshavarzian's thoughtful piece, "The moral economy of the Iranian protests," *Jacobin*, January 11, 2018. Accessed May 22, 2018. www.jacobinmag.com/2018/01/iranian-protests-revolution-rouhani-ahmadinejad. See also Asef Bayat's article, "The fire that fueled the Iran protests," *The Atlantic*, January 27, 2018. Accessed May 22, 2018. www.theatlantic.com/international/archive/2018/01/iran-protest-mashaad-green-class-labor-economy/551690/.

[70] Man Iranam, "Khāmeneī bedūneh, beh zūdi sarnegūneh – 9 dey tehrān," online video clip, YouTube, December 30, 2017. Accessed September 30, 2018. https://youtu.be/h73jmA0bLkM.

[71] Pouya Alimagham, "Iranian banknote: 'Independence, Freedom, Islamic Republic'." 2018. JPEG file.

**Figure 6.3** Iranian banknote: "Independence, freedom, Islamic Republic"

uprising,[72] and a form of it was relayed on the country's banknotes (Figure 6.4).[73] It is indeed true that "money talks."

Just as the state's favored slogan encapsulated its understanding of the Iranian Revolution, this motto epitomizes the Green Movement's

[72] See, for instance, the footage from the protests on November 4, the anniversary of the US embassy seizure, GREENPOWER000, "Esteqlāl āzādī jomhūrī-ye īrānī 13 ābān-i sabz," online video clip, YouTube, November 4, 2009. Accessed July 13, 2015. https://youtu.be/FLvFaCPYyrM; or this clip from *Ashura*: GREENPOWER0, "Tehran December 27 – esteqlāl āzādī jomhūrī-ye īrānī =6dey," online video clip, YouTube, December 27, 2009. Accessed July 13, 2015. https://youtu.be/tGWrjbQHVtI.

[73] This image along with thirteen others was posted on Payvand. See "Exhibit: Iranian banknotes uprising," Payvand, November 16, 2009. Accessed July 13, 2015. http://payvand.com/blog/blog/2009/11/16/exhibit-iranian-banknotes-uprising/. Rahesabz enumerated the reasons why people were writing slogans on Iran's currency: the fourth point is especially telling as the author argues that it is a form of "popular media" in which the anonymity of the citizen journalist is guaranteed thereby securing their protection from the state's ubiquitous crackdown. N. Nowruzi, "9 dalīl barāye eskenās nevīsī," Rahesabz, January 21, 2010. Accessed July 13, 2015. www.rahesabz.net/story/7005/. That the government even managed to stamp out this innovate tactic illustrates the severity of the crackdown. The central bank announced that it would no longer accept currency with such writing on it thereby preventing such "popular media" from circulating. See "Neveshteh hāyeh eskenās-hā pāk mīshāvānd," Tabnak, July 7, 2009. Accessed July 13, 2015. www.tabnak.ir/fa/pages/?cid= 79871. The government's measures are probably in response to a public recommendation made by Morteza Talaei in October 2009. See "Vākonesh-i ṭalāī beh shoʿārnevīsī ru-ye eskenās va dīvār," Aftab News, October 11, 2009. Accessed July 13, 2015. http://aftabnews.ir/vdcbszb9.rhb59piuur.html.

**Figure 6.4** "Money talks"
The back of this banknote tellingly has a question mark above the "Islamic" in "Islamic Republic of Iran." "Republic" is crossed out to emphasize the anti-democratic nature of the system, especially regarding the outcome of the presidential election – a point affirmed in the other banknote where "Republic" is crossed out and "dictatorship" handwritten above. To the left is a quote attributed to the anti-clerical Islamist ideologue, ʿAli Shariʿati (d. 1977): "Don't believe what a government says if that government is the only entity that has the right of expression."

post-Islamist challenge, stipulating that independence and freedom are not synonymous with an Islamic Republic. Rather, Iran enjoys "independence without freedom"[74] *because* it is governed by an Islamic Republic, and a post-Islamist republic, as the uprising forcefully argues, aspires to succeed where Iran's experiment with Islamism has so woefully failed.

---

[74] To quote the title of R. K. Ramazani's *Independence without Freedom: Iran's Foreign Policy* (Charlottesville: University of Virginia Press, 2013).

# References

1388sabz, "Shoʿārhāye mardomī ʿalayh-i istebdād dar sālrūz 13 ābān." Online video clip. YouTube. November 4, 2009. Accessed August 11, 2010. https://youtu.be/8vuAuz6J520.

2009IranRevolution, "2009 Iranian Revolution – Nasrolla poster & 'No to Gaza, No to Lebanon...' September 18." Online video clip. YouTube. September 21, 2009. Accessed May 14, 2014. www.YouTube.com/watch?v=JDD-UhSPsvU.

AFP, "Youth rallies for Mir Hossein Mousavi." Online video clip. YouTube. June 10, 2009. Accessed July 3, 2010. https://youtu.be/G-Pl7Gtliog.

Al Jazeera English, "Presidential candidates court Iran youth." Online video clip. YouTube. June 10, 2009. Accessed July 4, 2010. https://youtu.be/381DirqYxoE.

Ali Adabi, "Jashn-i mardom shab-i 25 khordād dar moḥavateh-ye farhangestān-i honar." Online video clip. YouTube. June 17, 2013. Accessed July 14, 2015. https://youtu.be/8zsi8YJzDXU.

Amirpix, "Clash between election protestors and police in Tehran." Online video clip. YouTube. June 14, 2009. Accessed August 7, 2010. https://youtu.be/Lp0KRMF78IY.

"Clash between election protestors and police in Tehran." Online video clip. YouTube. June 14, 2009. Accessed August 7, 2010. https://youtu.be/CCwrqBpbqjA.

Ayatullah Khamenei Speeches English, "[English Sub] National day against global arrogance – Ayatullah Ali Khamanei speech 2013." Online video clip. YouTube. November 16, 2013. Accessed August 6, 2014. http://youtu.be/8VYEsbv-U2s.

Bahmanpour, Alireza, "Ayatullah's historical speech about Palestine." Online video clip. YouTube. June 18, 2010. Accessed September 24, 2013. http://youtu.be/-SxOUMLfX7c.

DamnFool2k, "ʿArafāt dar īrān – sāl-i 1357." Online video clip. YouTube. September 14, 2013. Accessed February 18, 2015. http://youtu.be/EPXWG_ZDWxY.

Erfan Salehi, "Mūsavī, mūsavī, rayeto pas gereftīm." Online video clip. YouTube. June 15, 2013. Accessed July 14, 2015. https://youtu.be/ZGZPqASKxDw.

Esteqlāl, āzādī, jomhūrī īrānī, "27–12–2009–Iran–Tehran–310." Online video clip. YouTube. December 27, 2009. Accessed July 5, 2015. https://youtu.be/V7nLezMYAT4.

Farhad50626, "Taẓāhorāt-i dāneshjūyān-i dāneshgāh-i shahīd beheshtī dar rūz-i 16 āẕar." Online video clip. YouTube. December 7, 2009. Accessed August 12, 2010. https://youtu.be/_IuUoFzD7bw.

FEELTHELIGHT, "Iran, Tehran: Wounded girl dying in front of camera, Her name was Neda." YouTube. June 20, 2009. Accessed August 11, 2010. http://youtu.be/bbdEf0QRsLM.

Forougheirani, "Taẓāhorāt-i rūz qods 88." Online video clip. YouTube. September 18, 2009. Accessed March 12, 2015. https://youtu.be/ eAEl9bUfPk8.

Freedom Messenger, "Dāneshgāh-i būʿali-i hamadān 16 aẕar." Online video clip. YouTube. December 14, 2009. Accessed April 24, 2014. https:// www.YouTube.com/watch?v=4R4PCwFiQAc.

"Pāreh kardan-i plākārd-i bozorg-i khāmeneī." Online video clip. You-Tube. November 4, 2009. Accessed August 11, 2010. https://youtu.be/ nVjqewNANCY.

"Sabz o banafsh nadāreh jonbesh edāmeh dāreh 30/2/1396." Online video clip. YouTube. May 20, 2017. Accessed August 21, 2018. https://youtu .be/X6-BVG59Wis.

"Taẓāhorāt-i dānesh āmūzān-i yek dabīrestān-i dokhtāraneh." Online video clip. YouTube. December 7, 2009. Accessed February 2, 2015. http://youtu.be/Ee60WyR3YZg.

FreeIran4life, "Front of Ghoba mosque in Tehran." Online video clip. YouTube. June 28, 2009. Accessed August 10, 2010. www.YouTube .com/watch?v=7njmARTzzKU.

Ghovaza, "VIDE0524." Online video clip. YouTube. December 7, 2009. Accessed August 12, 2010. https://youtu.be/qG5xM8YTRng.

Goodzila82, "20-km human chain in Tehran – June 8th." Online video clip. YouTube. June 8, 2009. Accessed August 3, 2010. www.YouTube.com/ watch?v=PP-iji4VTQQ.

Green Protestor, "Taẓāhorāt-i mardom dar khīābān-i valīʿasr-i tehrān dar pay-ye pīruzī-ye rohānī dar entekhābāt-i 92." Online video clip. You-Tube. June 15, 2013. Accessed August 21, 2018. https://youtu.be/ NCT81F9mwVo.

GREENPOWER0, "Ātash zadan-i lebās-i nīrū-ye enteẓāmī – Tehran December 27." Online video clip. YouTube. December 27, 2009. Accessed August 15, 2010. https://youtu.be/kN1FDnz3P_0.

"Rahbar-i mā olāgheh, ye dastesham cholāqeh / 13 ābān." Online video clip. YouTube. November 4, 2009. Accessed May 15, 2015. https:// youtu.be/X1huhn49Zcc.

"Sangar sāzī va bastan-i khīābān/'āshūrā – December 27 – must see."
Online video clip. YouTube. December 27, 2009. Accessed June 9,
2018. https://youtu.be/MdJPDX_sHeU.

"Taẓāhorāt-i dāneshjūyān-i dāneshgāh-i najafābād 16 aẓar." Online video
clip. YouTube. December 7, 2009. Accessed August 12, 2010. https://
youtu.be/7Kr1BPVWlnI.

"Tehran December 27. Esteqlāl āzādī jomhūrī-ye īrānī =6dey." Online
video clip. YouTube. December 27, 2009. Accessed July 13, 2015.
https://youtu.be/tGWrjbQHVtI.

"Tehran uni protest 7dec/sorūd-i yār-i dabestānī dāneshgāh-i
tehrān16aẓar." Online video clip. YouTube. December 7, 2009.
Accessed August 12, 2010. https://youtu.be/Myn_Cm6bgZI.

GREENPOWER000, "Esteqlāl āzādī jomhūrī-ye īrānī 13 ābān-i sabz."
Online video clip. YouTube. November 4, 2009. Accessed July 13,
2015. https://youtu.be/FLvFaCPYyrM.

GREENUNITY4IRAN, "Iran 27 December 2009 Tehran. Making barricade." Online video clip. YouTube. December 27, 2009. Accessed June
9, 2018. https://youtu.be/QlYYoXwUIRY.

"Iran 27 December 2009 Tehran. Enghelab St." Online video clip. You-
Tube. December 27, 2009. Accessed August 15, 2010. http://youtu.be/
PKJtj61F5FA.

"Iran 27 December 2009 Tehran. Hafez Talaghani protest." Online video
clip. YouTube. December 27, 2009. Accessed August 15, 2010. http://
youtu.be/RDfEXvDuaSU.

Ipouya, "Shi'ism: From defeat to defiance." Online video clip. YouTube. January 9, 2009. Accessed June 2, 2015. https://youtu.be/HbHAQwZXPaY.

Irandoost09, "27 December 2009 Tehran. Clashes between protesters and
security forces in Iran." Online video clip. YouTube. December 27,
2009. Accessed August 15, 2010. http://youtu.be/Y68hw0a6CDA.

"27 December 2009 Tehran. Iranians protest against the government of
Iran." Online video clip. YouTube. December 27, 2009. Accessed June
9, 2018. https://youtu.be/ooEZzuPnloc.

"27 December 2009 Tehran. People stop a police car and free protesters
from inside it." Online video clip. YouTube. December 27, 2009.
Accessed August 15, 2010. http://youtu.be/-ihMFrNcUkM.

IranFree88, "Dāneshgāh-i 'elm o san'at 16 aẓar." Online video clip. You-
Tube. December 7, 2010. Accessed August 12, 2010. https://youtu.be/
u54Hva9a_eI.

"Dāneshgāh-i qazvīn 16 āẓar." Online video clip. YouTube. December 7,
2009. Accessed August 13, 2010. https://youtu.be/2kUOh1fzWWI.

Iranriggedelect, "Massive mourning rally." Online video clip. YouTube. June
18, 2009. Accessed August 7, 2010. https://youtu.be/M091xSOCNL8.

Irsngreen1, "Namāz jome῾h-ye tehrān dāneshgāh-i tehrān." Online video clip. YouTube. July 17, 2009. Accessed August 11, 2010. www.You Tube.com/watch?v=FRQQydgYBLU.

"Namāz jome῾h-ye tehrān dāneshgāh-i tehrān." Online video clip. You-Tube. July 17, 2009. Accessed January 11, 2014. http://youtu.be/ IkgW44w9tuI.

Īstāde bā mosht, "Mā hameh majīd tavakolī hastīm." Online video clip. YouTube. December 10, 2009. Accessed February 2, 2015. http:// youtu.be/xNgN1rbXjLc.

Kaleme.com Official YouTube Channel, "Barādar shahīdam rayeto pas gereftam." Online video clip. YouTube. June 15, 2013. Accessed July 14, 2015. https://youtu.be/fGwga1VErN4.

khabarnet info, "Tavāfoq-i ba῾dī-ye mā ḥoqūq-i shahrvandī-ye mā." Online video clip. YouTube. July 14, 2015. Accessed July 14, 2015. https:// youtu.be/iDnoGcMTe04.

Khajesharif, "Marg bar setamgar, cheh shāh bāsheh, cheh rahbar / dāneshgāh-i sharīf 16 āẕar." Online video clip. YouTube. December 7, 2009. Accessed August 12, 2010. https://youtu.be/zVfGynPs07Q.

Man Iranam, "Khāmeneī bedūneh, beh zūdi sarnegūneh – 9 dey tehrān." Online video clip. YouTube. December 30, 2017. Accessed September 30, 2018. https://youtu.be/h73jmA0bLkM.

"Yā hussein, mīr hussain – tajamo῾-i e῾terāzāmīż-i mardom – masjīd-i qobā." Online video clip. YouTube. June 28, 2009. Accessed August 10, 2010. https://youtu.be/oney1QF03iM.

Manjanigh12, "Manjanigh 12 Khorsrow Golesorkhi and Keramat Dane-shian's full defense." Online video clip. YouTube. February 16, 2013. Accessed August 1, 2014. http://youtu.be/jyvjhUsJyNg?list=PLPyPwM MrlbHNfQbr27Iy6LaUNIgdaAefT.

Mardomak News, "Mubārak, ben ῾alī, nowbat-i seyyed ῾alī." Online video clip. YouTube. February 14, 2011. Accessed July 14, 2015. https:// youtu.be/QqmkvTsH1FY.

Masoud Dalvand, "Tehrān na ghazzeh na lobnān, jānam fadā'-ye īrān 9 day 96." Online video clip. YouTube. December 30, 2017. Accessed May 22, 2018. https://youtu.be/HLAG0I6YJO4.

Mehdi Saharkhiz, "I Mehdi Saharkhiz Confess for Isa Saharkhiz (please make your own)." Online video clip. YouTube. August 15, 2009. Accessed May 17, 2015. https://youtu.be/AZjdLq3H1S8.

"Iran 20 December 2009 (29 Azar) Tehran. Mohseni Sq. protest after death of Ayatollah Montazeri P2." Online video clip. YouTube. December 20, 2009. Accessed August 14, 2010. http://youtu.be/ogadF_ IZjTc.

"Iran 21 December 2009 (30 Azar) Qom. Funeral of Ayatollah Montazeri p15." Online video clip. YouTube. December 21, 2009. Accessed August 15, 2010. http://youtu.be/sq-MyQza_Zc?list=PLB4DB22F42A4DD1DA.

"Iran 21 December 2009 (30 Azar) Qom. Funeral of Ayatollah Montazeri p18." Online video clip. YouTube. December 21, 2009. Accessed August 14, 2010. http://youtu.be/AUlUZkj8q3Y?list=PLB4DB22F42A4 DD1DA.

"Iran 21 December 2009 (30 Azar) Qom. Funeral of Ayatollah Montazeri p19." Online video clip. YouTube. December 21, 2009. Accessed August 14, 2010. http://youtu.be/4tWAm4dyrm0?list=PLB4DB22F 42A4DD1DA.

"Iran 21 December 2009 (30 Azar) Qom. Funeral of Ayatollah Montazeri p55." Online video clip. YouTube. December 21, 2009. Accessed August 14, 2010. http://youtu.be/v3pOiaRU-mM.

"Majid Tavakoli's speech December 7th 09 16." Online video clip. You-Tube. December 7, 2009. Accessed August 13, 2010. https://youtu.be/ Lin9PWr55RU.

"My YouTube story: Mehdi Saharkhiz." Online video clip. YouTube. May 12, 2010. Accessed October 2, 2014. http://youtu.be/ AbKqXt8F8fo.

Mightierthan, "Poem for the rooftops of Iran: Defenseless people." Online video clip. YouTube. June 16, 2009. Accessed August 9, 2010. www.YouTube.com/watch?v=p6bbEMxo2Xo.

"Poem for the rooftops: Let us not forget." Online video clip. YouTube. June 21, 2009. Accessed August 9, 2010. www.YouTube.com/watch? v=QocvegFNuzc.

Millionoillim, "27–12–2009–Iran–Tehran–270." Online video clip. You-Tube. December 27, 2009. Accessed August 16, 2010. http://youtu.be/ XbUTK6oNp7M.

"27–12–2009–Iran–Tehran–650." Online video clip. YouTube. December 27, 2009. Accessed August 15, 2010. http://youtu.be/ Djo7QRALhqc.

Mirhosseinsabz, "Otūbān-i nīāyesh sho'ār-i rūz-i qods rūz-i sabz." Online video clip. YouTube. September 9, 2009. Accessed March 13, 2015. https://youtu.be/4G9BEt3VLKA.

Mousavi1388, "Riot police caught by crowd – Protests in Tehran after election." Online video clip. YouTube. June 14, 2009. Accessed August 7, 2010. https://youtu.be/dSECAvBTanQ.

Mowjcamp, "16 Azar, Azad University Tehran Shomal." Online video clip. YouTube. December 7, 2009. Accessed August 12, 2010. http://youtu .be/ZdIVmrKEZGI.

MrDemocrature, "15th June 2009. Millions protest in Iran against election fraud in Iran." Online video clip. YouTube. June 16, 2009. Accessed April 24, 2014. www.YouTube.com/watch?v=FjQLC4w1XMY.

Ninashnash864, "Barādar shahīdam rayeto pas mīgīram." Online video clip. YouTube. July 17, 2009. Accessed July 14, 2015. https://youtu.be/O-ha8NrexQA.

Oldouz84, "ALLAHO AKBAR ARSHE ELAHI RA BE LARZE DAR KHAHAD AVARD 26 KHORDAD." Online video clip. YouTube. June 16, 2009. Accessed August 9, 2010. https://youtu.be/ztE-z0ooXd4.

Peive17, "Vesal St. Iran Tehran 18 sep 2009 P36." Online video clip. YouTube. September 18, 2009. Accessed August 11, 2010. www.YouTube.com/watch?v=9OzK3t58QUY.

Penguinswillfly, "Stop killing people, in Iran and Gaza." Online video clip. YouTube. September 18, 2009. Accessed September 24, 2013. https://youtu.be/CzRCxlKdl6A.

Radio Rap, "Vīdīo-ye kāmel az marāsem-i tashīʿ jenāzeh-ye hāshemī rafsanjānī va sheʿr [sic] mīr hussein va karūbī." Online video clip. YouTube. January 9, 2015. Accessed May 22, 2018. https://youtu.be/wcTtScr6jjU.

Reza Safari, "Hamāyesh-i entekhābātī-ye rohānī va shoʿār-i yā ḥusayn mīr ḥussein dar varzeshgāh-i āzādī." Online video clip. YouTube. May 13, 2017. Accessed May 22, 2018. https://youtu.be/kKG4WhTKLIE.

"Shoʿār-i ya ḥusayn, mīr ḥussein dar hamāyesh-i entekhābātī-ye ḥassan rohānī dar hamadān." Online video clip. YouTube. May 8, 2017. Accessed May 22, 2018. https://youtu.be/Q5qnAa53nck.

Sabzjamehgan, "Mūsavī,mūsavī,parcham-i īrānamo pas gereftam/dar jashn-i pīruzī-ye rohānī rouhani tehran election june 2013." Online video clip. YouTube. June 16, 2013. Accessed July 14, 2015. https://youtu.be/O7HI_5CrKQs.

Saeidkermanshah, "Protest continued – Protestors are going to Freedom (Azadi) Square." Online video clip. YouTube. June 15, 2009. Accessed August 7, 2010. https://youtu.be/9_hr7G4At84.

SamaniAli, "Tehran. Shariaty St. 28 June 2009." Online video clip. YouTube. June 28, 2009. Accessed August 11, 2010. https://youtu.be/B2vjeXJk6Jc.

Shabakeh-ye khabarī-ye tebiān-i īrān, "Fīlm-i kāmel-i namāz jomeʿh-ye 26 tīr 1388." Online video clip. YouTube. July 17, 2009. Accessed August 20, 2014. www.YouTube.com/watch?v=N1OlYlESRDU.

Sherlock72, "Police attack peaceful procession of mourners – Iran 27 December 2009 Ashura." Online video clip. YouTube. January 2, 2010. Accessed August 15, 2010. http://youtu.be/xwv6VtHtoSI.

Sohrab1901, "Nabard-i tan beh tan va nafas gīr-i mardom bā gārd-i vīzheh -ʿāshūrā." Online video clip. YouTube. December 27, 2009. Accessed August 15, 2010. http://youtu.be/JZ2urTPUGf0.

Steve W., "Tehrān – 6 dey 1388 – 'āshūrā – dastgīrī-ye 3 basījī." Online video clip. YouTube. December 27, 2009. Accessed June 9, 2018. https://youtu.be/IEi-YprarhA.

Sullivansilver, "Tajamoʻ-i dāneshjūyān dāneshgah-i tehrān dar moqābel-i vezārat-i keshvar." Online video clip. YouTube. June 7, 2009. Accessed August 3, 2010. www.YouTube.com/watch?v=46P9VHgnpeg.

Tazahorat2009, "Iran September 18, 2009. Qods Day anti regime rally part 6." Online video clip. YouTube. September 18, 2009. Accessed August 10, 2010. www.YouTube.com/watch?v=pj68-4fEzc0.

TheElection88, "Karoobi among the people in Ghoba street." Online video clip. YouTube. June 28, 2009. Accessed August 10, 2010. https://youtu .be/TZupydS90jY.

Thenima1, "Iran silent protest ... Valiasr Street ... 16 June 2009." Online video clip. YouTube. June 16, 2009. Accessed April 25, 2014. www .YouTube.com/watch?v=GVBZQCsqdjo.

Tysfood, "Iran ... Tehran ... Quds Protest (13) ... 18.09.09." Online video clip. YouTube. September 18, 2009. Accessed September 24, 2013. www.YouTube.com/watch?v=A8R1Z3FEvKc.

UNITY4IRAN, "Iran 27 December 2009 Tehran. Azadi St protest." Online video clip. YouTube. December 27, 2009. Accessed July 5, 2015. https://youtu.be/dKbDojqsl4c.

"Iran Tehran 4 November 2009. Shariati St Seyed Khandan protest P37." Online video clip. YouTube. November 4, 2009. Accessed August 11, 2010. https://youtu.be/WGqGiXi0Ct8.

Video Blog of the Green Movement, "The funeral of Grand Ayatollah Montazeri – Qum, Iran – Part 1." Online video clip. YouTube. December 23, 2009. Accessed August 14, 2010. http://youtu.be/_KwSHb8cwkI.

YaFatimehZahra, "For what sin, Ayatollah Nimr is being sentenced to death? FreeSheikhNimr." Online video clip. YouTube. May 12, 2015. Accessed December 4, 2016. https://youtu.be/PEIx-moB_cs.

Zelzalosolh, "[Must see | Part 1 | Bahman 22 2010] Helicopter over Tehran five million dawn." Online video clip. YouTube. February 12, 2010. Accessed May 15, 2015. https://youtu.be/HbYqckFvUJI.

## Digital Sources (Social Media)

Atshan, Sa'ed, December 29, 2014, 12.30 p.m. Facebook comment.

"Fāyl-i ṣowtī-ye dīdār-i āyatollāh montaẓerī bā mas'ūlīn-i eʻdāmhāye tābestān-i 67 [August 15, 1988]." August 10, 2016. Accessed May 12, 2018. https://soundcloud.com/radiozamaneh/yakydru8jded.

Hatami, Nima, May 27, 2013, 12.19 a.m. Facebook comment.

Iranpour, Mohammad, November 15, 2013, 10.12 a.m. Google+ comment.

Mir Hossein Mousavi Facebook page, "E'teṣāb, rāhpaymāī va tajamoʻ-i fardā, farmān-i allāh akbar-i emshab." June 14, 2009. Accessed January 22, 2014. http://goo.gl/kHZwzk.

"13 ābān." October 14, 2009. Accessed January 22, 2014. www.facebook.com/photo.php?pid=2494413&id=45061919453.

"Qalam." October 14, 2009, 12.30 p.m. www.facebook.com/mousavi/photos/a.82250529453.75658.45061919453/154196369453/?type=1 &theater.

"16 āẓar." November 8, 2009. Accessed January 29, 2009. http://goo.gl/dlLHcO.

"16 āẓar: rūz dāneshjū-ye sabz." November 26, 2009. Accessed January 29, 2009. http://goo.gl/Pi45VM.

Nafisi, Golrokh, "Re: Palestine-Green Movement artwork." Message to Pouya Alimagham, May 5, 2013. Facebook message.

Rajavi, Maryam, "On 4 March, 100th anniversary of Father Taleghani's birth, true spirit of Iran's anti-monarchical revolution, we honor his memory #iranelection." March 4, 2010, 8.45 a.m. Tweet.

Ramazani, Yalda, May 27, 2013, 12.12 a.m. Facebook comment.

Sabz, Mani, "Emshab alaho akbar saat 22 faramosh nashe baraye to dahani zadan be in akhound harom zade.V." Facebook comment. December 30, 2009.

Shams, Foad, "Re: 'Ḥanẓaleh dar kenār-i māst'." Message to Pouya Alimagham. September 16, 2013. Facebook message.

## Diplomatic and Government Sources

Ambassador Anne E. Derse, Baku, to Secretary of State Hillary Clinton, June 12, 2009, Wikileaks, https://search.wikileaks.org/plusd/cables/09BAKU474_a.html.

Chargé d'Affaires Don Lu, Baku, to Central Intelligence Agency et al., July 21, 2009, Wikileaks, https://search.wikileaks.org/plusd/cables/09BAKU575_a.html.

Chargé d'Affaires Doug Silliman, Ankara, to Secretary of State Hillary Clinton, August 13, 2009, Wikileaks, https://search.wikileaks.org/plusd/cables/09ANKARA1185_a.html.

Ankara, to Secretary of State Hillary Clinton, December 8, 2009, Wikileaks, https://search.wikileaks.org/plusd/cables/09ANKARA1744_a.html.

Ankara, to Secretary of State Hillary Clinton, January 8, 2010, Wikileaks, https://search.wikileaks.org/plusd/cables/09ANKARA1185_a.html.

Chargé d'Affaires Richard LeBaron, London, to Secretary of State Hillary Clinton, June 18, 2009, Wikileaks, https://search.wikileaks.org/plusd/cables/09LONDON1442_a.html.

Deputy Principal Officer Sandra Oudkirk, Istanbul, to Secretary of State Hillary Clinton, June 17, 2009, Wikileaks, https://search.wikileaks .org/plusd/cables/09ISTANBUL220_a.html.

Director Alan Eyre, Dubai, to Central Intelligence Agency et al., September 8 2009, Wikileaks, https://search.wikileaks.org/plusd/cables/09RPODU BAI373_a.html.

Dubai, to Central Intelligence Agency et al., September 14, 2009, Wikileaks, https://search.wikileaks.org/plusd/cables/09RPODUBAI378_a.html.

Dubai, to Central Intelligence Agency et al., September 14, 2009, Wikileaks, https://search.wikileaks.org/plusd/cables/09RPODUBAI379_a.html.

Dubai, to Central Intelligence Agency et al., November 2, 2009, Wikileaks, https://search.wikileaks.org/plusd/cables/09RPODUBAI469_a.html.

Dubai, to Central Intelligence Agency et al., November 4, 2009, Wikileaks, https://search.wikileaks.org/plusd/cables/09RPODUBAI474_a.html.

Dubai, to Central Intelligence Agency et al., November 5, 2009, Wikileaks, https://search.wikileaks.org/plusd/cables/09RPODUBAI479_a.html.

Dubai, to Central Intelligence Agency et al., December 7, 2009, Wikileaks, https://search.wikileaks.org/plusd/cables/09RPODUBAI521_a.html.

Dubai, to Central Intelligence Agency et al., December 8, 2009, Wikileaks, https://search.wikileaks.org/plusd/cables/09RPODUBAI525_a.html.

Dubai, to Central Intelligence Agency et al., December 10, 2009, Wikileaks, https://search.wikileaks.org/plusd/cables/09RPODUBAI532_a.html.

Dubai, to Central Intelligence Agency et al., December 20, 2009, Wikileaks, https://search.wikileaks.org/plusd/cables/09RPODUBAI539_a.html.

Dubai, to Central Intelligence Agency et al., December 22, 2009, Wikileaks, https://search.wikileaks.org/plusd/cables/09RPODUBAI543_a.html.

Dubai, to Central Intelligence Agency et al., December 23, 2009, Wikileaks, https://search.wikileaks.org/plusd/cables/09RPODUBAI545_a.html.

Dubai, to Central Intelligence Agency et al., December 28, 2009, Wikileaks, https://search.wikileaks.org/plusd/cables/09RPODUBAI547_a.html.

Dubai, to Central Intelligence Agency et al., December 28, 2009, Wikileaks, https://search.wikileaks.org/plusd/cables/09RPODUBAI549_a.html.

Dubai, to Central Intelligence Agency et al., Janurary 3, 2010, Wikileaks, https://search.wikileaks.org/plusd/cables/10RPODUBAI1_a.html.

Dubai, to Central Intelligence Agency et al., January 12, 2010, Wikileaks, https://search.wikileaks.org/plusd/cables/10RPODUBAI11_a.html.

Dubai, to Central Intelligence Agency et al., January 12, 2010, Wikileaks, https://search.wikileaks.org/plusd/cables/10RPODUBAI13_a.html.

Dubai, to Central Intelligence Agency et al., February 2, 2010, Wikileaks, https://search.wikileaks.org/plusd/cables/10RPODUBAI27_a.html.

Dubai, to Central Intelligence Agency et al., February 10, 2010, Wikileaks, https://search.wikileaks.org/plusd/cables/10RPODUBAI33_a.html.

Dubai, to Central Intelligence Agency et al., February 24, 2010, Wikileaks, https://search.wikileaks.org/plusd/cables/10RPODUBAI47_a.html.

Director Ramin Asgard, Dubai, to Central Intelligence Agency et al., June 3, 2009, Wikileaks, https://search.wikileaks.org/plusd/cables/09RPODU BAI232_a.html.

Dubai, to Central Intelligence Agency et al., June 4, 2009, Wikileaks, https://search.wikileaks.org/plusd/cables/09RPODUBAI233_a.html.

Dubai, to Central Intelligence Agency et al., June 11, 2009, Wikileaks, https://search.wikileaks.org/plusd/cables/09RPODUBAI245_a.html.

Dubai, to Central Intelligence Agency et al., June 13, 2009, Wikileaks, https://search.wikileaks.org/plusd/cables/09RPODUBAI247_a.html.

Dubai, to Central Intelligence Agency et al., June 15, 2009, Wikileaks, https://search.wikileaks.org/plusd/cables/09RPODUBAI249_a.html.

Farland, Tehran, to Secretary of State, August 10, 1972, Wikileaks, https://search.wikileaks.org/plusd/cables/72TEHRAN4789_a.html.

Kay McGowan, Dubai, to Central Intelligence Agency et al., June 18, 2009, Wikileaks, https://search.wikileaks.org/plusd/cables/09RPODUBAI255_a.html.

Dubai, to Central Intelligence Agency et al., June 23, 2009, Wikileaks, https://search.wikileaks.org/plusd/cables/09RPODUBAI258_a.html.

Dubai, to Central Intelligence Agency et al., July 29, 2009, Wikileaks, https://search.wikileaks.org/plusd/cables/09RPODUBAI306_a.html.

Kirk, Mark, "Press Release of Senator Kirk: Senatork Kirk Statement on Muslim Brotherhood." Personal website. February 2, 2011. Accessed March 25, 2011. http://kirk.senate.gov/record.cfm?id=330818.

Lowrie, Cairo, to Department of State, November 7, 1973, Wikileaks, https://search.wikileaks.org/plusd/cables/1973STATE219402_b.html.

Margaret P. Grafeld, Iran Tehran, to Secretary of State, April 4, 1977, Wikileaks, https://search.wikileaks.org/plusd/cables/1977TEHRAN028 73_c.html.

Principal Deputy Assistant Secretary Patrick Moon, Kathmandu, to Secretary of State Hillary Clinton, June 18, 2009, Wikileaks, https://search.wikileaks.org/plusd/cables/09KATHMANDU520_a.html.

Sheryl P. Walter, Iran Tehran, to Department of Defense et al., October 16, 1979, Wikileaks, https://search.wikileaks.org/plusd/cables/1979TEHR AN11002_e.html.

Lebanon Beirut, to Department of State, February 19, 1979, Wikileaks, https://search.wikileaks.org/plusd/cables/1979BEIRUT00977_e.html.

Timothy Richardson, Dubai, to Central Intelligence Agency et al, July 1, 2009, Wikileaks, https://search.wikileaks.org/plusd/cables/09RPODU BAI269_a.html.

Dubai, to Central Intelligence Agency et al., July 20, 2009, Wikileaks, https://search.wikileaks.org/plusd/cables/09RPODUBAI293_a.html.

Dubai, to Central Intelligence Agency et al., July 27, 2009, Wikileaks, https://search.wikileaks.org/plusd/cables/09RPODUBAI301_a.html

Dubai, to Central Intelligence Agency et al., September 20, 2009, Wikileaks https://search.wikileaks.org/plusd/cables/09RPODUBAI386_a.html.

Win Dayton, Istanbul, to Secretary of State Hillary Clinton, January 29, 2010, Wikileaks, https://search.wikileaks.org/plusd/cables/10ISTAN BUL40_a.html.

## Visual Sources

AbuKhalil, As'ad, "Protesters' slogans in Iran." The Angry Arab News Service. September 22, 2009. Accessed September 24, 2013. http://angryarab.blogspot.com/2009/09/protesters-slogans-in-iran.html.

Alimagham, Pouya, "The 13th anniversary of the Islamic Republic of Iran's establishment." 2018. JPEG file.

"Assistance from God leads to victory." 2018. JPEG file.

"The blood of the martyrs is mightier than the sword." 2018. JPEG file.

"Iranian banknote: 'Independence, Freedom, Islamic Republic." 2018. JPEG file.

"Jerusalem-themed Iranian banknote." 2018. JPEG file.

"A new beginning: the seizure of the US embassy." 2018. JPEG file.

"Only militant Islam can liberate Quds." 2018. JPEG file.

"Palestine Square–1." 2006. JPEG file.

"Palestine Square–2." 2006. JPEG file.

"Palestine Square–3." 2006. JPEG file.

"Palestine Square–4." 2006. JPEG file.

"Palestine Square–5." 2006. JPEG file.

"Palestine Square–6." 2006. JPEG file.

"Quds belongs to Muslims." 2018. JPEG file.

"Raising a rock: 'The uprising of the Muslim people of Palestine'." 2018. JPEG ffle.

"Shatila–1." 2008. JPEG file.

"YouTube deleted files screenshot." 2018. JPEG file.

Christia, Fotini (Photographer). July 2006. "*Martyrdom Is the Inheritance of the Prophet and His Family to Their Followers,*" [photograph] part of *Tehran Propaganda Mural Collection* (Cambridge, MA: H.C. Fung Library, Harvard University). Retrieved from http://id.lib.harvard.edu/images/olvgroup11882/urn-3:FHCL:1268192/catalog.

July 2006. "*Mural Located on Dr. Beheshti Street, Yusuf-Abad,*" [photograph] part of *Tehran Propaganda Mural Collection* (Cambridge, MA: H.C. Fung Library, Harvard University). Retrieved from http://id.lib.harvard.edu/images/olvgroup11882/urn-3:FHCL:1268241/catalog.

July 2006. "*We Will Continue on the Path of the Imam and the Martyrs of the Revolution,*" [photograph] part of *Tehran Propaganda Mural Collection* (Cambridge, MA: H.C. Fung Library, Harvard University). Retrieved from http://id.lib.harvard.edu/images/olvgroup11882/urn-3:FHCL:1268189/catalog.

Curtis, Liz (Photographer). 1982. "PLO-IRA," part of *Peter Moloney Collection*. Peter Moloney. Retrieved from https://petermoloneycollection.wordpress.com/1982/02/16/plo-ira/.

Dastan, Hezar. "@samand352." Twitter. N.d. Accessed September 25, 2013. https://twitter.com/samand352.

"Exhibit: Iranian banknotes uprising." Payvand. November 16, 2009. Accessed July 13, 2015. http://payvand.com/blog/blog/2009/11/16/exhibit-iranian-banknotes-uprising/.

*Fārsī: dovvom-i dabestān* (Tehran, S. 1981), p. 48.

"Israel is continually delegitimized and demonized in Republican demonstrations and publications." *The Jerusalem Post.* April 7, 2009. www.jpost.com/Opinion/Op-Ed-Contributors/IRA-PLO-cooperation-A-long-cozy-relationship.

Mir Hossein Mousavi Facebook page, "Green hourglass." November 26, 2009. Facebook post. www.facebook.com/mousavi/photos/a.17272641 9453.118347.45061919453/186592339453/?type=3&theater.

"Like clockwork - Co-opting political holidays." November 26, 2009. Facebook post. www.facebook.com/mousavi/photos/a.172726419453 .118347.45061919453/186592639453/?type=3&theater.

"Naṣb-i tāblo-ye bozorg-i "bārāk obāmā" dar maydān-i vali ʿasr-i tehrān (+ ʿaks)." ʿAsr-i Iran. January 15, 2013. http://goo.gl/Aqwjb5.

Sabzphoto, "Palestine is right here." September 18, 2009. Online image. Flickr. Accessed September 25, 2013. ,www.flickr.com/photos/sabz photo/4916927633/.

Semienejad, Mojtaba, "Palestine is right here." Tehran. twitpic. September 18, 2009. Accessed September 25, 2013. http://twitpic.com/i5b41.

## Interviews

Abolhassan Banisadr, Interview recorded by Zia Sedghi, May 21, 22, 1984, Paris, France. Iranian Oral History Collection, Harvard University, Transcript 4 (seq. 84). Accessed April 22, 2015.

Interview recorded by Zia Sedghi, May 21, 22, 1984, Paris, France. Iranian Oral History Collection, Harvard University, Transcript 4 (seq. 86). Accessed April 22, 2015.

Interview recorded by Zia Sedghi, May 21, 22, 1984, Paris, France. Iranian Oral History Collection, Harvard University, Transcript 5 (seq. 100). Accessed April 22, 2015.

Interview recorded by Zia Sedghi, May 21, 22, 1984, Paris, France. Iranian Oral History Collection, Harvard University, Transcript 5 (seq. 101). Accessed April 22, 2015.

Alimagham, Shahram, Personal interview, June 26, 2018.

ʿAlireza Mahfoozi, Interview recorded by Zia Sedghi, April 7, 1984, Paris, France. Iranian Oral History Collection, Harvard University, Transcript 1 (seq. 5). Accessed April 25, 2015.

Interview recorded by Zia Sedghi, April 7, 1984, Paris, France. Iranian Oral History Collection, Harvard University, Transcript 1 (seq. 7–8). Accessed April 24, 2015.

Interview recorded by Zia Sedghi, April 7, 1984, Paris, France. Iranian Oral History Collection, Harvard University, Transcript 1 (seq. 20–22). Accessed April 28, 2015.

Anonymous, Email interview. June 20, 2009.

Personal interview. June 25, 2011.

Payman. Personal interview. August 6, 2010.

Dalia Ziada (Egyptian blogger and human rights activist), Interview by Sherine El-Taraboulsi. April 18, 2010. Accessed July 14, 2015. transcript.

Doostdar, ʿAlireza. Email interview. August 2, 2010.

Edward Snowden, Interview by Brian Williams. May 28, 2014. Moscow, Russia. NBC News. Accessed July 9, 2015. www.nbcnews.com/feature/ edward-snowden-interview/edward-snowdens-motive-revealed-he-can-sleep-night-n116851.

Massoud Rajavi, Interview recorded by Zia Sedghi, May 29, 1984, Paris, France. Iranian Oral History Collection, Harvard University, Transcript 1 (seq. 20). Accessed April 23, 2015.

Interview recorded by Zia Sedghi, May 29, 1984, Paris, France. Iranian Oral History Collection, Harvard University, Transcript 1 (seq. 20–21). Accessed April 23, 2015.

Interview recorded by Zia Sedghi, May 29, 1984, Paris, France. Iranian Oral History Collection, Harvard University, Transcript 2 (seq. 21). Accessed April 24, 2015.

Mohammad Shanehchi, Interview recorded by Habib Ladjevardi, March 4, 1983, Paris, France. Iranian Oral History Collection, Harvard University, Transcript 1 (seq. 22). Accessed April 30, 2015.

Interview recorded Habib Ladjevardi, March 4, 1983, Paris, France. Iranian Oral History Collection, Harvard University, Transcript 2 (seq. 35, 48). Accessed April 30, 2015.

Interview recorded by Habib Ladjevardi, March 4, 1983, Paris, France. Iranian Oral History Collection, Harvard University, Transcript 2 (seq. 48). Accessed April 30, 2015.

Interview recorded by Habib Ladjevardi, March 4, 1983, Paris, France. Iranian Oral History Collection, Harvard University, Transcript 2–3 (seq. 53–62). Accessed April 30, 2015.

Interview recorded by Habib Ladjevardi, March 4, 1983, Paris, Frace. Iranian Oral History Collection, Harvard University, Transcript 4 (seq. 66–67). Accessed May 2, 2015.

Interview recorded Habib Ladjevardi, March 4, 1983, Paris, France. Iranian Oral History Collection, Harvard University, Transcript 4 (seq. 93). Accessed May 2, 2015.

Nafisi, Golrokh, "Re: Palestine-Green Movement artwork." Facebook message to Pouya Alimagham. May 5, 2013.

"Re: Salaam Golrokh." November 19, 2014. Email to Pouya Alimagham.

Rezaian, Jason, Telephone interview. July 26, 2010.

S., B., Personal interview. June 30, 2012.

Saharkhiz, Mehdi, Personal interview. May 19, 2013.

"The role of social media in the Iranian people's struggle." Interview by Behnood Mokri. Voice of America. Washington DC, February 28, 2011. Television.

T., G., Personal interview. October 22, 2013.

V., S., Personal interview. April 14, 2014.

## Persian News Sources and Periodicals

Aftab News
Akhbar-i Rooz
Alef
Amontazeri.com
'Asr-i Iran
BBC Persian
Deutsche Welle (Persian)
Doshmantarin
Fars News Agency
Gerdab
Ghalam News
*Ghanoon Daily*
Gooya News

Iranian Labour News Agency (ILNA)
Iranian Students News Agency (ISNA)
Kalame
*Kayhan*
Khabar Online
Khamenei.ir
Mehr News Agency
Ministry of the Interior
Qabas
Radio Farda
Rahesabz
Rooz Online
Tabnak
Tasnim


## Foreign Sources in Persian

BBC Persian
Deutsche Welle


## English Sources and Periodicals

*ahramonline*
Al Jazeera
al-Akhbar English
The Angry Arab News Service
*The Arab Weekly*
The Associated Foreign Press
Associated Press
*The Atlantic*
BBC News
boston.com
*The Boston Globe*
CBS News
Center for Human Rights in Iran
CNN
*The Christian Science Monitor*
*The Daily Beast*
The Dawn Blog
*Foreign Policy*
Freedom House

*The Guardian*
Human Rights Watch
*The Independent*
Informed Comment
*The Iranian*
*Jacobin*
*The Jerusalem Post*
*The Los Angeles Times*
Ma'an News Agency
Medium
*The Nation*
*The New York Times*
*The New Yorker*
*Newsweek*
Now Lebanon
*The Observer*
Persian2English
Iran Data Portal (Princeton)
PressTV
Reuters
Spiegel Online International
Slate
Tehran Bureau
*Tehran Times*
*The Telegraph*
*Time*
*The Times*
*The Washington Post*
Wired

## Persian Books and Documents

Ahmadzadeh, Massoud. "Mobārezeh-ye mosalaḥāneh ham estrātezhī, ham tāktīk." Siahkal.org, 1971. www.siahkal.com/publication/RMassoud-All-chapters.pdf.

Bani Sadr, Abolhassan. Dar sar-i tajrobeh: khāṭerāt-i abolḥassan-i banī ṣadr, avvalīn ra'is jomhūr-i īrān (Frankfurt, Islamic Revolution Publishing, 2013).

Dehghani, Ashraf. *Hemaseyeh moqavemat*. Siahkal.com. 1971. Accessed April 25, 2015. www.siahkal.com/english/part1.htm#Chambers.

*Fārsī: dovvom-i dabestān* (Tehran, S. 1981).

*Khāṭerāt-i shāpūr bakhtīār: nakhost vazīr-i īrān (1979).* Iranian Oral History Project (Center for Middle Eastern Studies Harvard University), (Bethesda: IranBooks, Inc., 1996).

Khomeini, Ruhollah. "ʿAdam-i ṣalāḥiat barāye taṣadī-ye rahbarī-ye neẓām-i jomhūrī-ye eslāmī." March 26, 1989. Tehran. Vol. 21, p. 331. http://farsi.rouhollah.ir/library/sahifeh?volume=21&tid=196.

"Ahamīat-i ḥefẓ-i jomhūrī-ye islāmī – naqsh-i roḥānīat dar ṭūl-i tārīkh – ṭarḥ-i khīānatbār-i sāzesh bā isrāʾīl." November 16, 1981. Tehran. Vol. 15, pp. 369–370. http://farsi.rouhollah.ir/library/sahifeh?volume=15&tid=176.

"Bayān-i dīdgāh-i islām dar mored-i masāʾel-i mokhtalef." Interview. December 28, 1978, Neauphle-le-Château, Paris. Vol. 5, p. 295. http://farsi.rouhollah.ir/library/sahifeh?volume=5&tid=70.

"Bayān-i ʿelal-i mokhāletfat hāyeh doshmanān – pāsokh beh ettehāmāt – falsafeh-ye gīyām-i emām ḥusayn." December 14, 1978. *Qom* 10, 315. http://farsi.rouhollah.ir/library/sahifeh?volume=10&tid=84.

"Entekhāb-i ākharīn jomeʿh-ye māh-i ramażān be ʿonvān-i 'rūz-i qods'." August 7, 1979. *Qom* 9, p. 267. http://farsi.rouhollah.ir/library/sahifeh?volume=9&tid=88.

"Ettehād shūm qodrathā dar moqābel-i islām." February 28, 1988. Tehran. Vol. 20, p. 486. http://farsi.rouhollah.ir/library/sahifeh?volume=20&tid=257.

"Ghalabeh-ye īmān bar qodrathāye shayṭānī." February 17, 1979. Tehran. Vol. 6, p. 179. http://farsi.rouhollah.ir/library/sahifeh?volume=6&tid=72.

"Ghayreqānūnī būdan-i majles va dowlat-i manṣūb-i shāh va mafāsed-i rezhīm." February 1, 1979. Tehran. Vol. 6, p. 16. http://farsi.rouhollah.ir/library/sahifeh?volume=6&tid=7.

"Ḥamleye rezhīm-i ṣahūnīstī be jonūb-i lobnān." March 22, 1978. Najaf. Vol. 3, p. 358. http://farsi.rouhollah.ir/library/sahifeh?volume=3&page=358.

*Ḥokūmat-i islāmī: vilāyat-i faqīh.* muʾaseseh-ye āmūzeshī-ye pazhoheshī-ye emām khomeinī, 1970.

"Hoshdār be moslemīn-i jahān dar mored-i felestīn va efshā-ye jenāyathāye rezhīm-i shah." February 1979. Najaf, Iraq. Vol. 2, p. 322. http://farsi.rouhollah.ir/library/sahifeh?volume=2&tid=269.

*Kashf alasrār.* 1942.

"Koshtār-i mardom-i mosalmān – lozūm-i farār-i sarbāzān az sarbāzkhāneh-hā va edāmeh-ye eʿtesābhā." December 11, 1978. Paris. Vol. 5, p. 153. http://farsi.rouhollah.ir/library/sahifeh?volume=5&tid=31.

"Moqāyeseh-ye rezhīm-i pahlavī bā dowlat hāyeh ommavī va 'abbasī – falsafeh-ye 'azādārī-ye emām ḥusayn ('a) – żarūrat-i ḥefz jomhūrī-ye eslāmī bā mohtavā-ye eslāmī." September 26, 1979. Qom, Vol. 10. pp. 122–123. http://farsi.rouhollah.ir/library/sahifeh?volume=10&tid=26.

"Rāhpaymāī-ye tāsū'ā va 'āshūrā – referāndom-i ghayr-i rasmī būdan-i ḥokūmat-i shah." December 14, 1978. Paris, Vol. 5. p. 227. http://farsi.rouhollah.ir/library/sahifeh?volume=5&tid=54.

"Qorbānī dādan dar rāh-i khodā sīreh-ye anbīā ast." October 25, 1978. Paris. Vol. 4., pp. 151–152. http://farsi.rouhollah.ir/library/sahifeh?volume=4&tid=20.

"Ṣolḥ-i meṣr va isrāīl (kamp dayvīd)." March 25, 1979. Qom. Vol. 6, p. 410. http://farsi.rouhollah.ir/library/sahifeh?volume=6&tid=164.

"Taẓāhorāt-i tāsū'a va 'āshūrā sīāsat-i jomhūrī-ye islāmī." December 11, 1978. Paris. Vol. 5, p. 207. http://farsi.rouhollah.ir/library/sahifeh?volume=5&tid=46.

"Tashakor az 'elām-i hemāyat – poshtībānī az felesṭīn." September 19, 1957. Najaf. Vol. 3, p. 476. http://farsi.rouhollah.ir/library/sahifeh?volume=3&tid=289.

"Vīzhegīhāye rūz-i qods." August 16, 1979. Qom. Vol. 9, p. 276. http://farsi.rouhollah.ir/library/sahifeh?volume=9&tid=94.

Montazeri, Hussein 'Ali. *Khāterāt-i āyatollāh ḥusseīn 'alī montaẓerī* (Los Angeles: Ketab Corp, 2001).

Pooya, Amir Parviz. "Żarūrat-i mobārezeh-ye mosalaḥāneh va rad-i te'orī-ye baqa'." Siahkal.org, 1970. www.siahkal.com/publication/pouyan.htm.

Rafiqdoost, Mohsen. *Barāye tārīkh mīgūyam: khāṭerāt-i mohsen-i rafīqdūst (1978–1989)* (Tehran: Andisheh Press, 2013).

Shari'ati, 'Ali. *Tashī'eh 'alavī va tashī'eh ṣafavī*.

"Matn-i kāmel-i vaṣīat nāmeh-ye emām khomeīnī (rah). 'Asr-i Iran. October 6, 2009. Accessed September 27, 2018. goo.gl/3nkNpE.

## English Books, Articles, and Pamphlets

Abbasgholizadeh, Mahboubeh. "'To do something we are unable to do in Iran': Cyberspace, the public sphere, and the Iranian women's movement," *Signs* 39(4) (2014), 831–840.

Abrahamian, Ervand, "Ali Shariati: Ideologue of the Iranian Revolution," *MERIP Reports*, 102 (January 1982), 24–28.

"The causes of the constitutional revolution in Iran," *International Journal of Middle East Studies*, 10 (3) (August 1979), 381–414.

*The Coup: 1953, the CIA, and the Roots of Modern U.S.-Iranian Relations* (New York and London: The New Press, 2013).

"The crowd in Iranian politics, 1905–53," *Past & Present* 41 (December 1968) (Oxford University Press), 184–210.

"The crowd in the Persian Revolution," *Iranian Studies*, 2 (4) (Autumn 1969), 128–150.

"The guerrilla movement in Iran, 1963–1977," *MERIP Reports*, 86 (March–April 1980), 3–15.

*A History of Modern Iran* (Cambridge and New York: Cambridge University Press, 2008).

*Iran Between Two Revolutions* (Princeton: Princeton University Press, 1982).

*The Iranian Mojahedin* (New Haven, Yale University Press, 1989).

*Tortured Confessions: Prisons and Public Recantations in Modern Iran* (Berkeley: University of California Press, 1999).

Afary, Janet, *The Iranian Constitutional Revolution, 1906–1911: Grassroots Democracy, Social Democracy, and the Origins of Feminism* (New York: Columbia University Press, 1996).

Ajami, Fouad, *The Vanished Imam: Musa al Sadr and the Shia of Lebanon* (Ithaca: Cornell University Press, 1986).

Algar, Hamid, *Roots of the Islamic Revolution in Iran* (Oneonta and New York: Islamic Publications International, 2001).

Alimagham, Pouya, "The Iranian legacy in the 2011 Egyptian Revolution: Military endurance and U.S. foreign policy priorities," *UCLA Historical Journal*, 24 (I) (2013), 45–59.

Alpher, Yossi, *Periphery: Israel's Search for Middle East Allies* (Lanham: Rowman & Littlefield, 2015).

Ansari, Ali, *Confronting Iran: The Failure of American Foreign Policy and the Next Great Conflict in the Middle East* (New York: Basic Books, 2006).

Arjomand, Said A. (ed.), *Authority and Political Culture in Shi'ism* (Albany: State University of New York Press, 1988).

*The Shadow of God and the Hidden Imam: Religion, Political Order, and Societal Change in Shi'ite Iran from the Beginning to 1890* (Chicago and London: The University of Chicago Press, 1984).

*The Turban for the Crown: The Islamic Revolution in Iran* )Oxford: Oxford University Press, 1988).

Aryan, Khadijeh, "The boom in women's education," in Tara Povey and Elaheh Rostami-Povey (eds.), *Women, Power and Politics in 21st Century Iran* (New York: Routledge, 2016), pp. 35–52.

Asgharzadeh, Alireza *Iran and the Challenge of Diversity: Islamic Fundamentalism, Aryanist Racism, and Democratic Struggles* (New York: Palgrave Macmillan, 2007).

Ashraf, Ahmad, "Theocracy and charisma: New men of power in Iran," *International Journal of Politics, Culture, and Society*, 4 (1) (Autumn 1990), 113–152.

Aziz, T. M., "The role of Muhammad Baqir as-Sadr in Shii political activism in Iraq from 1958 to 1980," *International Journal of Middle East Studies*, 25 (2) (May 1993), 207–222.

Bahari, Maziar, *Then They Came for Me: A Family's Story of Love, Captivity, and Survival* (New York: Random House, 2011).

Batutu, Hanna, *The Old Social Classes and the Revolutionary Movements of Iraq: A Study of Iraq's Old Landed and Commercial Classes and of Its Communists, B'athists, and Free Officers* (London: Saqi Books, 2000).

Bayat, Asef, *Life as Politics: How Ordinary People Change the Middle East* (Stanford: Stanford University Press, 2010).

*Making Islam Democratic: Social Movements and the Post-Islamist Turn* (Stanford: Stanford University Press, 2007).

*Revolution without Revolutionaries: Making Sense of the Arab Spring* (Stanford: Stanford University Press, 2017).

Bengio, Ofra, "Shi'is and politics in Ba'thi Iraq," *Middle East Studies* (Taylor and Francis Group), 21 (1) (January 1985), 1–14.

Bowden, Mark, *The Guests of the Ayatollah The Iran Hostage Crisis: The First Battle in America's War with Militant Islam* (New York: Grove Press, 2006).

Briggs, Laura, *Reproducing Empire: Race, Sex, and U.S. Imperialism in Puerto Rico* (Berkeley and Los Angeles: University of California Press, 2002).

Butko, Thomas J., "Revelation or revolution: A Gramscian approach to the rise of political Islam," *British Journal of Middle Eastern Studies*, 31 (1) (May 2004), 41–62.

Chehabi, Houchang and Fotini Christia, "The art of state persuasion: Iran's post-revolutionary murals," *Persica* 22 (2008), 1–13.

Cole, Juan R. I., "The Baha'i minority and nationalism in contemporary Iran," in Maya Shatzmiller (ed.), *Nationalism and Minority Identities in Islamic Societies* (Montreal and London: McGill-Queen's University Press, 2005).

*Constitution of the Islamic Republic of Iran*. Trans. by Hamid Algar (Berkeley: Mizan Press, 1980).

Cook, David, *Martyrdom in Islam* (Cambridge and New York: Cambridge University Press, 2007).

Cronin, Stephanie, "Popular protest, disorder, and riot in Iran: The Tehran crowd and the rise of Riza Khan, 1921–1925," *International Review of Social History*, 50 (2) (2005), 167–201.

Dabashi, Hamid, *Iran: A People Interrupted* (New York and London: The New Press, 2007).

*Iran, the Green Movement and the USA* (London and New York: Zed Books, 2010).

"Review of *Social Origins of the Iranian Revolution*, by Misagh Parsa," *Contemporary Sociology*, 20 (2) (March 1991), 211–212.

*Shi'ism: A Religion of Protest* (Cambridge and London: The Belknap Press of Harvard University Press, 2011).

*Theology of Discontent: The Ideological Foundation of the Islamic Revolution in Iran* (London and New Brunswick: Transaction Publishers, 2008).

Ebadi, Shirin, *Iran Awakening: A Memoir of Revolution and Hope* (New York: Random House, 2006).

Ehteshami, Anoushiravan, *After Khomeini: The Second Republic* (London and New York: Routledge, 1995).

Ehteshami, Anoushiravan and Mahjoob Zweiri, *Iran and the Rise of Its Neoconservatives: The Politics of Tehran's Silent Revolution* (London and New York: I.B. Tauris, 2007).

Esposito, John, *The Iranian Revolution: Its Global Impact* (Miami: Florida International University Press, 1990).

Falk, Richard, "The Iran hostage crisis: Easy answers and hard questions," *The American Journal of International Law*, 74 (2) (April 1980), 411–417.

Farber, David, *Taken Hostage: The Iran Hostage Crisis and America's First Encounter with Radical Islam* (Princeton: Princeton University Press, 2005).

Foran, John (ed.), *A Century of Revolution: Social Movements in Iran* (Minneapolis: University of Minnesota Press, 1994).

Gasiorowski, Mark J., "The 1953 coup d'etat in Iran," *International Journal of Middle East Studies*, 19 (3) (August 1987), 261–286.

"The CIA looks back at the 1953 coup in Iran," *Middle East Report*, 216 (Autumn 2000), 4–5.

Gelvin, James L., *The Arab Uprisings: What Everyone Needs to Know* (Oxford: Oxford University Press, 2012).

*The Israel-Palestine Conflict: One Hundred Years of War.* 3rd ed. (Cambridge: Cambridge University Press, 2014).

Gleijese, Piero, *Conflicting Missions: Havana, Washington, and Africa, 1959–1976* (Chapel Hill and London: The University of North Carolina Press, 2002).

Greenwald, Glenn, *No Place to Hide: Edward Snowden, the NSA, and the U.S. Surveillance State* (New York: Metropolitan Books, 2014).

Habibi, Nader, "The economic legacy of Mahmoud Ahmadinejad," *Middle East Brief*, 74 (June 2013). www.brandeis.edu/crown/publications/meb/ MEB74.pdf.

Hafez, Sherine, "The revolution shall not pass through women's bodies: Egypt, uprising and gender politics," *The Journal of North African Studies*, 19 (2) (2014).

Hamzeh, Ahmad Nizar, *In the Path of Hizbullah* (Syracuse: Syracuse University Press, 2004).

Hashas, Mohammed, "Abdolkarim Soroush: The neo-Mu'tazilite that buries classical Islamic political theology in defence of religious democracy and pluralism," *Studia Islamic*, 1 (1) (2014), 147–173.

Hashemi, Nader and Danny Postel (eds.), *The People Reloaded: The Green Movement and the Struggle for Iran's Future* (New York: Melville House Publishing, 2010).

Hobsbawm, Eric, *On History* (New York: The New Press, 1997).

Hoodfar, Homa and Samad Assadpour, "The politics of population policy in the Islamic Republic of Iran," *Studies in Family Planning*, 31 (1) (March 2000), 19–34.

Hoodfar, Homa and Shadi Sadr, "Islamic politics and women's quest for gender equality in Iran," *Third World Quarterly*, 31 (6) (2010), 895–903.

Irving, Washington, *Lives of Mahomet and His Successors* (Paris, A. and W. Galignani and Co., 1850).

Jaber, Hala, *Hezbollah: Born with a Vengeance* (New York: Columbia University Press, 1997).

Jaberi, Faleh A., *The Shi'ite Movement in Iraq* (London: Saqi Books, 2003).

Karabell, Zachary, *Architects of Intervention: The United States, the Third World, and the Cold War, 1946–1962* (Baton Rouge: Louisiana State University Press, 1999).

Karsh, Efraim, *The Iran–Iraq War 1980–1988* (Oxford: Oxprey Publishing, 2002).

Kashani-Sabet, Firoozeh, "Who is Fatima? Gender, culture, and representation in Islam," *Journal of Middle East Women's Studies*, 1 (2) (2005), 1–24.

Keddie, Nikki, *Roots of Revolution: An Interpretive History of Modern Iran* (New Haven and London: Yale University Press, 1981).

Keddie, Nikki, and Juan R. I. Cole (eds.), *Religion and Politics in Iran: Shi'ism from Quietism to Revolution* (New Haven and London: Yale University Press, 1983).

Khalidi, Rashid, *Palestinian Identity: The Construction of Modern National Consciousness* (New York: Columbia University Press, 1997).

Kinzer, Stephen, *All the Shah's Men: American Coup and the Roots of Middle East Terror* (Hoboken: John Wiley & Sons, Inc., 2003).

Korman, Sharon, *The Right of Conquest: The Acquisition of Territory by Force in International Law and Practice* (Oxford: Oxford University Press, 1996).

Kurzman, Charles, *The Unthinkable Revolution in Iran* (Cambridge, MA: Harvard University Press, 2004).

Kwon, Heonik, *The Other Cold War* (New York: Columbia University Press, 2010).

McFarland, L. Stephen, "Anatomy of an Iranian political crowd: The Tehran bread riot of December 1942," *International Journal of Middle East Studies*, 17 (1) (February 1985), 51–65.

Mahdi, Ali Akbar, "The Iranian women's movement: A century long struggle," *The Muslim World*, 94 (October 2004), 427–448.

Majd, Hooman, *The Ayatollah Begs to Differ: The Paradox of Modern Iran* (New York: First Anchor Books (Random House), 2009).

Mallat, Chibli, "Religious militancy in contemporary Iraq: Muhammad Baqer as-Sadr and the Sunni-Shia paradigm," *Third World Quaterly* (Taylor and Francis Group), 10 (2) (April 1988), 699–729.

Matthiesen, Toby, *The Other Saudis: Shiism, Dissent and Sectarianism* (Cambridge: Cambridge University Press, 2015).

Mehran, Golnar, "Doing and undoing gender: Female higher education in the Islamic Republic of Iran," *International Review of Education*, 55 (5/6) (November 2009), 541–559.

"The paradox of tradition and modernity in female education in the Islamic Republic of Iran," *Comparative Education Review*, 47 (3) (2003), 269–286.

"Social implications of literacy in Iran," *Comparative Education Review*, 36 (2) (May 1992), 194–211.

Milani, Abbas, *The Shah* (New York: Palgrave Macmillan, 2012).

Mirsepassi, Ali, *Democracy in Modern Iran: Islam, Culture, and Political Change* (New York and London: New York University Press, 2010).

*Transnationalism in Iranian Political Thought: The Life and Times of Ahmad Fardid, The Global Middle East* (Cambridge: Cambridge University Press, 2017).

Moaddel, Mansoor, *Class, Politics, and Ideology in the Iranian Revolution* (New York and Oxford: Columbia University Press, 1993).

Moghissi, Haideh, "Islamic cultural nationalism and gender politics in Iran," *Third World Quarterly*, 29 (3) (2008), 541–554.

*Populism and Feminism in Iran: Women's Struggle in a Male-Defined Revolutionary Movement* (New York: St. Martin's Press, 1994).

Morozov, Evgeny, *The Net Delusion: The Dark Side of Internet Freedom* (New York: Perseus Books Group, 2011).

Mottahedeh, Roy, *Loyalty and Leadership in an Early Islamic Society* (Princeton: Princeton University Press, 1980).

Nabavi, Negin (ed.), *From Theocracy to the Green Movement* (New York: Palgrave Macmillan, 2012).

Nakash, Yitzak, *Reaching for Power: The Shi'a in the Modern Arab World* (Princeton and Oxford: Princeton University Press, 2006).

*The Shi'is of Iraq* (Princeton: Princeton University Press, 1994).

Nashat, Guity, "Women in the Islamic Republic of Iran," *Iranian Studies*, 13 (1–4) (1980) 165–194.

Norton, Richard August, *Hezbollah: A Short History* (Princeton: Princeton University Press, 2007).

Ostovar, Afshon, "Guardians of the Islamic Revolution: Ideology, Politics, and the Development of Military Power in Iran (1979–2009)." PhD Thesis, University of Michigan, 2009.

*Vanguard of the Imam: Religion, Politics, and Iran's Revolutionary Guards* (New York: Oxford University Press, 2016).

Owen, Roger, *The Rise and Fall of Arab Presidents for Life* (Cambridge: Harvard University Press, 2012).

Pahlavi, Mohammad Reza, *Answer to History: By Mohammad Reza Pahlavi The Shah of Iran* (New York: Stein and Day Publishers, 1980).

Parsa, Misagh, *Social Origins of the Iranian Revolution* (New Brunswick and London: Rutgers University Press, 1989).

Parsi, Trita, *Treacherous Alliance: The Secret Dealings of Israel, Iran, and the U.S.* (New Haven and London: Yale University Press, 2007).

Peters, Kathrin, "Images of protest: On the 'woman in the blue bra' and relational testimony," in Martin Butler, Paul Mecheril, and Lea Brenningmeyer (eds.), *Subjects, Representations, Contexts* (Bielefeld: Transcript Verlag, 2017).

Rahnema, Ali, *An Islamic Utopian: A Political Biography of Ali Shari'ati* (New York: I.B. Tauris, 2000).

Ramazani, R. K., *Independence without Freedom: Iran's Foreign Policy* (Charlottesville: University of Virginia Press, 2013).

*Revolutionary Iran: Challenge and Response in the Middle East* (Baltimore and London: The John Hopkins University Press, 1986).

Rolston, Bill, "'The brothers on the walls': International solidarity and Irish political murals," *Journal of Black Studies*, 3 (3) (January 2009), 446–470.

Roy, Sara, *Failing Peace: Gaza and the Palestinian-Israeli Conflict* (London and Ann Arbor: Pluto Press, 2007).

Rudé, George, *The Crowd in History: A Study of Popular Disturbances in France and England 1730–1848* (New York and London: John Wiley & Sons, Inc., 1964).

Sameh, Catherine, "From Tehran to Los Angeles to Tehran: Transnational solidarity politics in the One Million Signatures Campaign to end discriminatory law," *Women's Studies Quarterly*, 42 (3/4) (Fall/Winter 2014), 166–188.

Shaery-Eisenlohr, Roschanack, *Shi'ite Lebanon: Transnational Religion and the Making of National Identities* (New York: Columbia University Press, 2008).

Shams, Alex, "Revolutionary religiosity and women's access to higher education in the Islamic Republic of Iran," *Journal of Middle East Women's Studies*, 12 (1)(March 2016), 126–138.

Shatzmiller, Maya (ed.), *Nationalism and Minority Identities in Islamic Societies* (Montreal and London: McGill-Queen's University Press, 2005).

Siddiqi, Ahmad, "Khatami and the search for reform in Iran," *Stanford Journal of International Relations*, 6 (1) (Winter 2005).

Siavoshi, Sussan, *Montazeri: The Life and Thought of Iran's Revolutionary Ayatollah* (Cambridge: Cambridge University Press, 2017).

Soeterik, Robert, *The Islamic Movement of Iraq (1958–1980)* (Amsterdam: Stichting MERA, 1991).

Tarock, Adam, *Iran's Foreign Policy Since 1990: Pragmatism Supersedes Islamic Ideology* (Hauppauge: Nova Science Publishers, 1999).

Tilly, Charles, *The Politics of Collective Violence* (Cambridge: Cambridge University Press, 2003).

Tilly, Charles, and Lesley J. Wood, *Social Movements 1768–2008* (Boulder: Paradigm Publishers, 2009).

Verdery, Katherine *The Political Lives of Dead Bodies: Reburial and Post-socialist Change* (New York: Columbia University Press, 1999).

## English Pamphlets and Reports

Ennals, Martin, Amnesty International Annual Report 1974/75 (1975).

"Shah's U.S. visit: Newest plot against Iranian people." *Resistance* (A Publication of I.S.A.U.S., Member of Confederation of Iranian Students). (Vol. 4, No. 8). (September 1977).

# Index

را خبا

صاح

نسطان تیر احمد مرداد

ساعی اللہ